I0754888

Some books teach us truth, others motivate us, and some show us how to apply what we know. Rarely does a book do all three, but *Discipology* does. You'll understand disciple-making at a new level by reading this important book.

Ed Stetzer, dean, Talbot School of Theology

Peyton's best book yet. Starting with a groundbreaking premise, this christological work offers a practical framework for moving from talking about discipleship to actual disciple-making.

Brian Sanders, founder and executive director, Underground Network

Peyton Jones beautifully weds orthodoxy with orthopraxy. He applies first-century principles to a twenty-first-century context with clarity and conviction. This book will reorient your ministry around Jesus's rhythms and cultivate real disciple-making movement.

Dhati Lewis, president, MyBLVD; visionary pastor, Blueprint Church

If you want to do discipleship the Jesus way and see spectators become "sent ones," *Discipology* is the clearest and most compelling road map I've seen. A must-read for every leader.

Dr. Larry Walkemeyer, global pastor, Light & Life Church

Discipology is field-tested, grounded in Scripture, and refreshingly practical.

Dave Ferguson, CEO, Exponential

Peyton reframes disciple-making as the missing engine of genuine movement: mobilization before multiplication. This field-tested guide calls leaders to move from managing churches to activating people into Jesus's mission.

Brad Brisco, author, *Missional Essentials*

In *Discipology*, Peyton Jones unpacks scriptural principles in ways you can't unsee. The discipleship patterns he uncovers from Jesus and Paul are theologically rich and practical. I'll revisit these principles again and again.

Karl Vaters, contributor at Helping Small Churches Thrive

Peyton Jones brings us back to the compelling genius of Jesus's disciple-making strategy—biblical, practical, and urgently needed for leaders shaping a culture of multiplication today.

Dr. Ed Love, executive director of church multiplication and discipleship, The Wesleyan Church

Jesus gave the church one commission: to make disciples. Too many Christians don't know what this means. *Discipology* challenges and encourages us to rediscover the lost art of disciple-making for the twenty-first century.

Dr. Winfield Bevins, founder, Creo Arts; author, *How Beauty Will Save the World*

This brilliant, accessible work dives into the source code of discipleship: the person and ministry of Jesus. Jones lays out a simple, reproducible process that revolutionized Palestine and sets the foundation for us to follow.

Mike Chong Perkinson, PCJC Network Lead

Finally, a practical, theologically grounded field guide for disciple-making. Peyton breaks down Jesus's methods so everyone can get off the pew and on mission.

Rev. Dr. Deb Walkemeyer, strategic catalyst for multiplication, Free Methodist Church USA

Over decades, the church has morphed discipleship into programs. Peyton dismantles myths and restores Jesus's timeless, joyful model of discipleship. *Discipology* revitalizes and excites believers to reengage in disciple-making.

Andy Froiland, pastor

Warning: If you're content with your current view of discipleship, don't read this book! Peyton Jones disruptively reveals the revolutionary nature of the early church and shows how to step into Jesus's rhythms of disciple-making.

Steve Pike, founder, Next Wave Community

Jesus's parting words matter: "Go and make disciples!" Most of us have grown up in a church-growth world, so making churches seemed like a good idea. But what about the 60 to 70 percent of people who will never enter a church? Read this book. Then go!

Greg Wigfield, lead pastor, Destiny Church

In church planting, we often get the cart before the horse: Plant a church, then make disciples. *Discipology* reminds us that everything in ministry starts with making disciples.

Frank Wooden, executive director, Plant SoCal

Discipology bridges the gap between learning about discipleship and making disciples in everyday life. Peyton offers clear, engaging insights that reflect how Jesus trained his disciples.

Cathy Tastad, superintendent, The Pacific Northwest Conference of the Free Methodist Church

Most discipleship ends with the last page of a book or sermon. In *Discipology*, Peyton Jones reveals what's been hiding in plain sight: Mobilization precedes movement. He provides a clear, Jesus-inspired pathway to mobilize believers into disciple-makers.

David Sunde, pastor; author, *Homegrown Disciples*

Jones is both prophetic and pragmatic, inspiring and instructional. *Discipology* is a clarion call back to Jesus's original blueprint for making and mobilizing disciples, equipping the church to reimagine its future.

Rich Robinson, founder and director, 5Q Collective

In a world where discipleship programs abound but impact little, Peyton Jones offers a practical methodology that mobilizes. *Discipology* combines Jesus's practices with generations of wisdom in a framework that feels both time-tested and fresh.

Jessie Cruickshank, author, *Ordinary Discipleship*

DISCIPOLOGY

DISCIPOLOGY

THE ART AND SCIENCE OF MAKING DISCIPLES

ZONDERVAN REFLECTIVE

Discipology

Published by Zondervan, 3950 Sparks Drive SE, Suite 101, Grand Rapids, MI 49546, USA. Zondervan is a registered trademark of The Zondervan Corporation, L.L.C., a wholly owned subsidiary of HarperCollins Christian Publishing, Inc.

Requests for information should be addressed to customercare@harpercollins.com.

Zondervan titles may be purchased in bulk for educational, business, fundraising, or sales promotional use. For information, please email SpecialMarkets@Zondervan.com.

ISBN 978-0-310-18033-3 (hardcover)
ISBN 978-0-310-18035-7 (audio)
ISBN 978-0-310-18034-0 (ebook)

Author represented by The Steve Laube Agency.

HarperCollins Publishers, Macken House, 39/40 Mayor Street Upper, Dublin 1, D01 C9W8, Ireland (https://www.harpercollins.com)

Cover design: Jonlin Creative
Cover art: © ArtBalitskiy, Primiaou, Mariia Levchenko, Viktoriia Ablohina, Ulimi / Getty Images
Interior design: Denise Froehlich
Interior images: © stock.adobe.com

Printed in the United States of America

26 27 28 29 30 31 32 33 / TRM / 10 9 8 7 6 5 4 3 2

Contents

Foreword

Every so often a book comes along that doesn't simply contribute to the conversation but clarifies it. *Discipology* is that book. Peyton Jones has written a work that brings us back to the original genius of Jesus's method and the simplicity of his mission. If you long for a church that looks more like the Gospels and less like our Western defaults, this book is a gift.

I've said again and again that movements rise when everyday people are mobilized. Peyton carries that same conviction, but he grounds it deeply in what Jesus actually did. As you open these pages, let me give you four compelling reasons you should read this book and share it with others:

1. Jesus is the model, and his process still works.

Before Jesus ever launched a movement, he trained twelve disciples through a simple, brilliant, and deeply relational process. Peyton calls it what it is: Time, Teaching, and Tactics—three rhythms anyone can understand and reproduce.

This book pulls back the curtain on the way Jesus formed disciple-makers and shows how his process can be practiced today with just as much power and clarity.

Read this book if you want to follow Jesus's actual method, not just admire his mission.

2. Mobilization precedes multiplication.

Once you see Jesus's process, this truth becomes impossible to ignore: Mobilization always comes before multiplication. The Western church has tried to reverse the order for decades, planting more churches and launching more initiatives without first forming mobilized disciples. Peyton explains why that approach stalls and why the book of Acts is simply the natural result of the Gospels lived out.

Read this book if you want multiplication that is organic, sustainable, and Spirit-driven, not forced.

3. We need to move from addition to activation.

Our default scorecard focuses on addition: more people, more programs, more activity. But Peyton reframes success the way Jesus did by concentrating on how many disciples are activated, not just how many attend. He shows how gatherings can grow while the mission stalls and how churches can measure the wrong things without knowing it. This book shifts your imagination from accumulating attendees to releasing disciple-makers.

Read this book if you want a new scorecard—one that reflects the actual priorities of Jesus.

4. Movements are built on mobilized people.

This is where *Discipology* aligns naturally with the heartbeat of Exponential. Movements are not led by celebrities; they're sparked by mobilizers. People who invest in others. People who train others. People who release others.Peyton helps you see how every movement in history—ancient or modern—has grown through ordinary people mobilized into mission. And he gives leaders practical tools to do the same.

Read this book if you want to become a catalyst for a movement that will outlast you.

Discipology is field-tested, grounded in Scripture, and refreshingly practical. It will challenge the way you pray, disciple, and lead. More importantly, it will help you return to Jesus's original strategy—one that still changes lives, neighborhoods, and whole cities when it's practiced.

My prayer is that you won't just read this book. I pray you practice it. I pray you begin meeting with a handful of people the way Jesus met with the Twelve. I pray you model what you want multiplied. And I pray that years from now, the legacy of your ministry won't be measured in buildings or budgets but in the lives of ordinary people mobilized for the mission of Jesus.

That's how movements start.

That's how movements spread.

That's how movements last.

And that's why I'm proud to commend *Discipology* to you.

DAVE FERGUSON
Exponential CEO and author of *Hero Maker*,
B.L.E.S.S., and *Multiplier*

Preface

It is impossible to teach a man what he thinks he already knows.

—EPICTETUS

We've been trying to solve the wrong problem. Or, rather, we've been trying to solve a secondary problem first. For the past fifteen years, we've placed the proverbial cart before the horse, focusing on multiplication ahead of mobilization.

As important as multiplication is, *mobilization* has always been what causes movement. Multiplication is merely the effect. The failure to multiply, therefore, is caused by a bottleneck in mobilization. Ergo, mobilization must precede multiplication. The evidence of this claim is that the narrative of the Gospels chronologically precedes the book of Acts. Let me explain. The Gospels chronicle three years of Jesus kick-starting the engine of mobilization into twelve people through disciple-making, resulting in the multiplication we read about in Acts. If mobilization is the cause, multiplication is the effect, leading to movement. The early church multiplied only because it was mobilized.

Failing to understand this has led to many within the multiplication movement to attempt to multiply churches that aren't mobilized. It's been twenty years since the multiplication movement kicked off, and although the church has been greatly helped by understanding the importance of multiplication, it still struggles to mobilize people in the pews. At the heart of our struggle is a prevailing ignorance of Jesus's mobilization strategy, which is why I've written this book. *Discipology* is the study of mobilization in the way of Jesus.

As an author, I too got it twisted by writing *Church Plantology* first, as if multiplication were the primary concern. Yet, when we lift the hood on multiplication movements, both throughout church history and across the globe, at the core of all of them is an engine of mobilized people. This might help to explain the lack of traction in movement dynamics in the Western Hemisphere compared to what is experienced exclusively in the Southern Hemisphere. There, they are focused on what causes movements: disciple-making itself.

So why is disciple-making our Achilles' heel in the West—the vulnerable spot in our multiplication practices? This book would point to one root cause: ignoring Jesus as the master disciple-maker and ignoring his strategy. Jesus commanded his church to make disciples above all else for a reason—mobilization. *Discipology* seeks to reclaim the art and science of making disciples the way Jesus patterned it for us, to mobilize the kingdom, so that our multiplication efforts aren't wasted.

Discipology is a hybrid between a foundation of theological recovery and a practical pathway for disciple-making. It's a pathway based on what Jesus practiced. My aim is to provide the church with more than a practitioner guide or handbook for disciple-making—not just another book to add to the scores of books on discipleship or disciple-making. It's a pathway based on what Jesus practiced. For this reason, *Discipology* is a hybrid of a foundation of theological recovery and a practical pathway for disciple-making. I write to you, the leader, first. Jesus had to convince only a small number of people, and the catalytic process turned the world upside down. Without your modeling disciple-making outside the pulpit, there will never be change in the pews. It starts with you as a leader, but it can't end with you. Therefore, this book is a part of a larger ecosystem of tools, including the *Disciple Maker's Journey: A Discipology Journal*, for those who will follow your lead and embark on their own disciple-making journey.

The church is stuck. We are immobilized. I have poured my blood, sweat, and tears into these resources to mobilize a church that is stuck. It is a daunting task, and I've shared Paul's sentiments multiple times on this journey: "Who is sufficient for these things?" (2 Cor. 2:16 ESV). In a letter to his friend and editor Pascal Covici, Steinbeck wrote, "The writer must believe that what he is doing is the most important thing in the world. And he must hold to this illusion even when he knows it is not true."[1] I believe that if *Discipology* reveals the secret of mobilization through the disciple-making practices of Jesus, then there is nothing more important in all the world. It would be an illusion, however—no, a delusion—if I thought *I* could come up with it. I couldn't. The true value of *Discipology*, therefore, must be that it recovers something lost instead of inventing something new. If there is any glory due from the writing of this book, it is Christ's, for, as Kepler confessed, "I was merely thinking God's thoughts after him."[2] It is my hope that this book will reveal the strategic brilliance of Jesus and set it on full display for his church to accomplish its mission. Any praise for what's within these pages is a crown to be laid at his feet, for it is his disciple-making practices that are being uncovered, not mine.

Whereas *Church Plantology* traced the accumulated brilliance of Paul's planting practices through Acts and the Epistles, this book will trace Jesus's disciple-making mastery. In training the Twelve, Jesus incorporated three rhythms into his disciple-making strategy: *time, teaching*, and *tactics*. Together, these three rhythms produce mobilization. These three basic elements will serve as the simple framework of this book to assist you in mobilizing your church, small group, or youth group. That said, no one book or system can ever be the answer. The only solution for the church's immobility is people who actively practice disciple-making. This is the precise reason that Jesus spent three years mobilizing missionaries. My prayer is that the labor, time, and testing that brought this book to print may do the same and continue what Jesus started.

Until he comes,
PEYTON JONES

---

1. Henry Raymont, "Steinbecks' Letters Will Be a Book," *New York Times*, June 2, 1969.
2. This is a popular paraphrase of the general sentiment of Johannes Kepler in *Harmonices Mundi* (1619). The exact quote is even more beautiful: "I give thanks to Thee, Lord God our Creator, that Thou hast allowed me to see the beauty in Thy work of creation, and to take delight in the works of Thy hands. Behold, I have now completed the work to which I was called. I have used the talents Thou hast lent me. I have disclosed the glory of Thy works to the people to the extent that my finite mind was able to comprehend Thy infinite perfection. If I have said anything unworthy of Thee, or aspired to my own glory, graciously forgive it."

Introduction

> The illiterate of the 21st Century will not be those who cannot read and write but those who cannot learn, unlearn, and relearn.
>
> —ALVIN TOFFLER

Amid the waste of desert sands, a toppled and crumbling fifty-nine-foot statue slants as it sinks, its stone foundations giving way to the devouring elements that surround it. Percy Bysshe Shelley's immortalization of the inscribed hieroglyphs scrawled on its surface reads,

> My name is Ozymandias, King of Kings
> Look on my Works, ye Mighty, and despair!
> Nothing beside remains.[1]

The half-buried statue of Ozymandias, the mighty Ramses II, pharaoh during the exodus and self-proclaimed "King of Kings," was meant to intimidate future generations. Having built more structures than any pharaoh before him, Ramses's monolith boasted that all he built would outlast him and his successors: "Look on my Works, ye Mighty, and despair!" As the sands of time inevitably swallowed his empire, his final boast morphed into a cautionary tale

---

1. Percy Bysshe Shelley, "Ozymandias," Poetry Foundation, accessed September 20, 2025, https://www.poetryfoundation.org/poems/46565/ozymandias.

for today's leaders—a warning to any who are tempted to fool themselves into thinking the hallowed monuments and ecclesiastical structures they've built are immune.

That Which Is Eternal

Despite his boastful inscription, Ozymandias was *not* the King of kings. For the true bearer of that title wisely left his stamp on people rather than buildings. His command to "go and make disciples of all nations, until the end of the age" outlined a kingdom without end. Not only did his kingdom subvert the powerful Roman Empire (yet another vain contender bent on Babel's mission to make a name for itself that reached to the heavens), but it alone has managed to upend the world and outlast all other contenders by millenia.

For the rightful King of kings had a boast of his own: "On this rock I will build my church, and the gates of hell shall not prevail against it" (Matt. 16:18 ESV). In this phrase, Jesus used the familiar words *pulai hadou*, a Jewish expression for the "realm of the dead." Jesus was not smack-talking Satan and the minions of hell but challenging *death* itself. The thrust of Jesus's statement boasts that even the relentless tides of death would not stop his church from advancing after him, continuing "to the end of the age" (Matt. 28:20 ESV). This would be accomplished through the very practice Jesus primarily invested in for three years: disciple-making.[2] The ability of Jesus's kingdom to blow the gates of death off its hinges established the enduring power of the Great Commission, a mandate to make disciples who make disciples in perpetuity. No man-made empire could ever outlast a movement that could outlast death itself. Only his kingdom could outlast anything man-made—monolith or monument.

Therefore, when the church wrings its hands about ecclesiastical states of decline, it merely decries the decaying of aging wineskins: ecclesiastical traditions, fads, styles, preferences, and practices. As C. S. Lewis has observed, "Everything that is not eternal is eternally out of date."[3] Yet Christ continues to brew the new

2. Kevin DeYoung, "The Gates of Hell," Ligonier Ministries, November 19, 2011, https://learn.ligonier.org/devotionals/gates-of-hell.
3. C. S. Lewis, *The Four Loves* (Harcourt Brace, 1960), 188.

wine of multiplying disciples, constantly fermenting in each successive generation. Throughout church history, movements such as the Celtic missionaries, the Wesleyan Methodists, and the Jesus movement have witnessed the church's revitalization in dark times, as Jesus promised. Where there is success, a recovery of Jesus's disciple-making strategy has caused a partial recapturing of first-century mobilization. Mobilization is defined as the Spirit-empowered process of activating ordinary believers into their God-given mission. Whenever mobilization happens, multiplication is the effect.

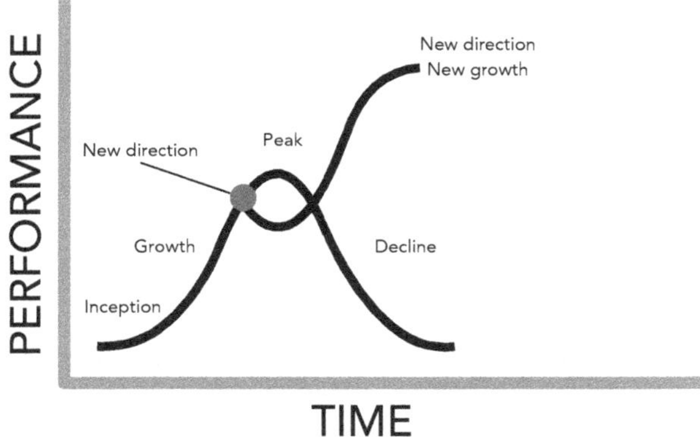

The Rise and Fall of All Things

If mobilization were graphed on the timeline of church history, it would reveal a successive number of rises and falls throughout the ages. Sociologists identify these shifts of roller-coaster up-and-down movements within organizations as a phenomenon of recurring surges illustrated by the sigmoid curve. Just as God hardwired physical phenomena into the cosmos, or the way things work, like the law of gravity, he also hardwired predictable social phenomena in our human makeup, as with the sigmoid curve.

Sigmoid curves follow a predictable pattern: a beginning, an upward climb, a peak, and an eventual decline.[4] From businesses to institutions—including churches and denominations—the timelines of all institutions follow this pattern. As the decline begins, the only way for an organization to

4. Rosemary Hipkins and Bronwen Cowie, "The Sigmoid Curve as a Metaphor for Growth and Change," *Teachers and Curriculum* 16, no. 2 (2016): 3.

prevent its own extinction is by taking innovative steps to start a new venture. If those steps are taken, however, a new incline begins, repeating the sigmoid curve and marking a new movement of growth. This pattern of growth is the same rhythm that keeps the church advancing. As movements rise and fall, it's their willingness to adapt, renew, and press forward that ensures the mission continues.[5] However, through disciple-making Jesus hardwired the church for an endless series of new ventures on the sigmoid curve—experiencing both the ecstasy of momentum through Spirit-led movements and the agony of decline when it loses focus on the Great Commission.

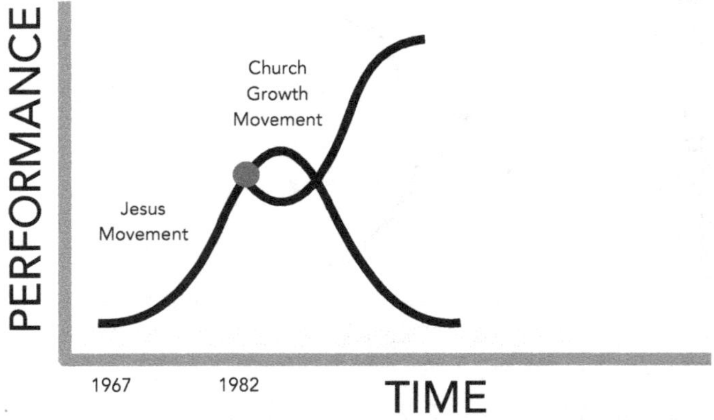

For example, in the tumultuous 1960s, the Jesus movement sprang up, sparking renewal across the West. Teacher Chuck Smith and hippy-turned-modern-missionary Lonnie Frisbee tag-teamed the challenge of reaching a generation of young people who seemed all but lost. Like all movements, it eventually peaked and declined, starting in the 1970s. Yet along its trajectory on the sigmoid curve it birthed the church growth movement of the '80s and '90s. While it's popular to criticize the weaknesses of past movements, each one brought timely and unique advancements to the American church. The Jesus movement, for instance, helped the Western church regain a relevant foothold during the 1960s by missionally engaging the culture that nearly swallowed it whole. Not only did

5. Paul spoke to this in Ephesians 4:12, describing the church growing to fill the Jesus-shaped hole he left in the world: "Until we all attain to the unity of the faith and of the knowledge of the Son of God, to mature manhood, to the measure of the stature of the fullness of Christ" (ESV). This reminds us that God is still shaping his church—stretching it, growing it, molding it—until it fully reflects the stature and fullness of Christ himself.

the Jesus movement help the church resist the culture, it harnessed and revolutionized it, embodying what Jay Kim has said: "The church was never meant to be a derivative of the cultural moment but, rather, a disruption of it."[6]

Out of the decline of the Jesus movement, the church growth movement emerged—driven largely by evangelists—and helped reverse the shrinking of the American church. True to the pattern of the sigmoid curve, the twilight of the church growth movement gave rise to the dawn of yet another movement: the church multiplication movement. And like all other movements before it, the multiplication movement wrestled with the limitations of its predecessors.

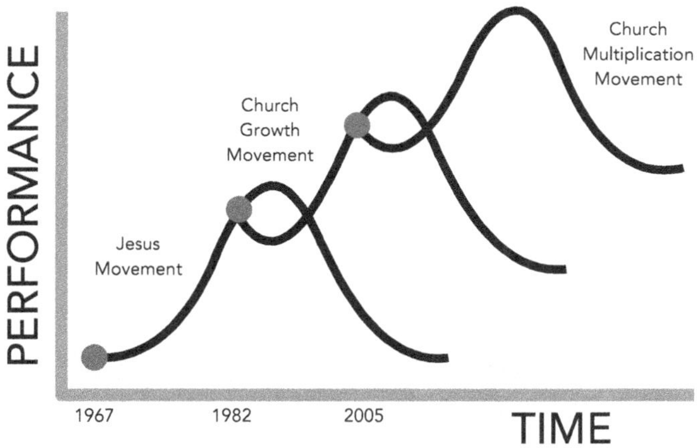

How We Got Here

As the church growth movement waned, this new catalytic movement waxed strong—igniting kingdom expansion through a surge of new church plants and multisite campuses.[7] The Exponential organization—founded by Todd Wilson and Dave Ferguson—emerged as the rallying point for the movement,

---

6. Jay Y. Kim, *Analog Church: Why We Need Real People, Places, and Things in the Digital Age* (Downers Grove, IL: IVP, 2020), chap. 1, Kindle.
7. Bob Buford, a kingdom-minded entrepreneur and philanthropist, was a key yet behind-the-scenes figure in the church growth movement. After the tragic loss of his son, he reassessed his priorities, shifting from church growth to church multiplication, a transformation he described in *Halftime: Moving from Success to Significance* (1994). His influence, including the mentoring of leaders such as Rick Warren and Bill Hybels, culminated in the 2005 Burning Bush conference, which sparked networks such as Exponential, NewThing, Acts29, and many more.

gathering leaders like an ecclesiastical Lollapalooza. Their goal was to shift the percentage of churches multiplying from a mere 4 percent to Malcom Gladwell's 16 percent tipping point. Church planting became the new frontier, and the conferences that championed multiplication quickly became the places where the cool kids hung out.

As the sigmoid curve predicted, a new trajectory was already forming even before the multiplication movement peaked: the missional movement. While the multiplication movement emphasized the multiplication of larger churches and multisite expansions, the missional movement stirred quietly beneath the surface—a subcurrent reshaping the conversation. It never captured the mainstream spotlight, perhaps because it called the church back to a grassroots, countercultural model of decentralized house churches, missional communities, and microchurches. In truth, there wasn't much return on investment for denominations or networks when small gatherings stayed small, simple, and scattered in a nation with a "bigger is better" mentality. Yet what the missional movement lacked in size and funding it made up for in prophetic insight. New voices emerged, calling the church to return to the New Testament model of everyday mission. Their writings became a rallying cry for the church to live on mission in the streets, neighborhoods, and homes. The problem is, although many agreed in theory, they struggled to turn conviction into practice—further revealing the importance of what Jesus did, not preaching from platforms, but training in the trenches.

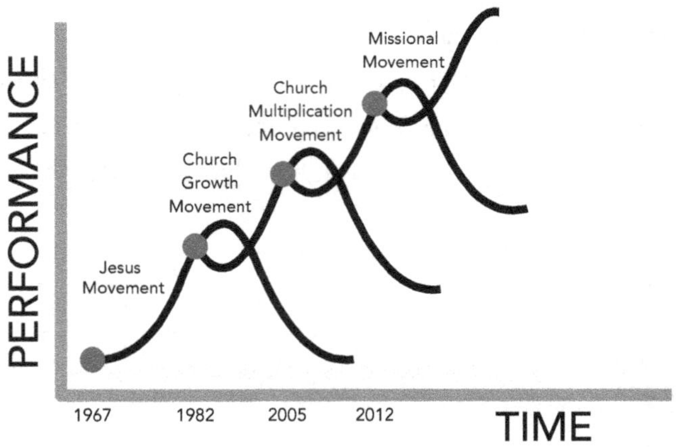

That said, the missional movement was prophetic in both senses: foretelling and forthtelling. In forthtelling, it admonished that the church was never meant to be confined within church walls. In foretelling, it spoke a timely word exposing the fragility of our ecclesiastical structures—fragility that the COVID-19 pandemic would soon confirm. When the doors of buildings shut, something deeper opened: a collective realization that without weekend services, programs, or performance-based gatherings, believers had to rediscover what it meant to follow Jesus in their homes, neighborhoods, and new digital communities. In that disruption, the missional movement found a fresh hearing, because suddenly the old models were no longer options. In their place, a new openness emerged: a hunger to reclaim the decentralized, disciple-making mission that Jesus himself modeled.

During the lockdowns, when there was no building to gather in, the broader church became a receptive—if captive—audience to the missional message. The crisis sparked new questions: "What is church if we can't gather?" and "How do I reach others if I can't bring them to a building?" These questions exposed the cracks in systems that had relied too heavily on large physical gatherings and centralized programming.

Despite its name, the missional movement still focused on new forms of gathering as the silver bullet instead of scattering empowered disciples. Everything still revolved around gathering—only now redesigned to happen in living rooms, coffee shops, and public spaces. The missional movement asked the right questions but never fully delivered the necessary answers—at least not ones that were missional enough to get the church unstuck.

All of these movements—the church growth movement, the multiplication movement, and the missional movement—signaled the beginning of something vital: a necessary, though incomplete, step toward mobilization. In telling the church what it could do "better," they remained focused on what the church did inside the walls instead of mobilizing disciple-makers outside them. Shaped by leaders and built for leaders, these movements never quite ignited the grassroots awakening they longed for. Despite catching glimpses of mobilization, they missed the framework Jesus himself modeled—not systems to expand, but people to send. These Spirit-led movements played a vital role in the church's progression along the sigmoid curve—each one used by God to advance the mission in its time. But even in their fruitfulness they shared a common flaw: Their focus remained on the institutional church—how to grow it, systematize it, and multiply it.

What the church has been waiting for is not a new way to gather. It's been waiting for a movement that will *mobilize* it.

The Dawn of the Mobilization Movement

And, as the sigmoid curve predicts, another movement was already developing below the surface of the missional movement—one that emerged in full during the pandemic. When the church couldn't gather, it learned to scatter—or, rather, its people did. Whether through a renewed passion for disciple-making or a growing fascination with microchurches, the rumblings of mobilization have begun to ripple through the pews, even if not yet proclaimed from the pulpits. Have you heard their whispers? It's the sound of an incline on the sigmoid curve—just beneath the surface of what church historians may one day call the mobilization movement. And, in many ways, it's what all the previous movements have been building toward—the tipping point—not for new churches, but for established churches ready to mobilize everyday believers to reach their surrounding communities. Whereas previous movements often required churches to restructure or reinvent themselves, the mobilization movement affirms that mobilizing disciples doesn't require changing your church's model—it starts with changing your mindset. You don't have to tear it down and start over. You can begin right where you are, with what you have. Mobilization doesn't replace your model; it releases your people.

Mobilization isn't just the next step—it's the key to everything that follows.

Without mobilization everything else grinds to a halt—even multiplication. At its core, a failure to multiply is really a failure to mobilize. And, honestly, why would we want to multiply churches that *weren't* mobilized

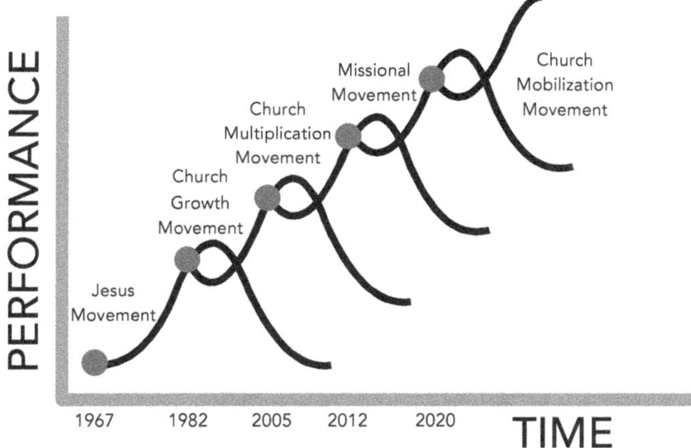

anyway? This is why Jesus's mission strategy prioritized mobilization over multiplication. He knew that mobilization must precede multiplication—just as the Gospels come before the book of Acts. The Gospels chronicle how Jesus mobilized people through disciple-making, showing it as the cause, with the multiplication in Acts as the effect. Mobilization is the engine that unleashes the combustion of movement. That's why *Discipology* focuses on Jesus's timeless disciple-making practices chronicled in the Gospels. Jesus mobilized the Twelve for three years before ever commanding them to mobilize others. Jesus knew that if they took care of mobilization, the multiplication would take care of itself.

A Sneak Peek

In the next chapter, we'll unpack the *what*, *why*, and *how* of Discipology. But for now here's a quick preview to give you a sense of where this book is headed. *Discipology* is built on the overlap of three key rhythms in Jesus's disciple-making strategy: *time*, *teaching*, and *tactics*. When these three are practiced together, they produce mobilization—represented by the atomic symbol at the center where all three circles converge. Together, they form a strategic three-stage framework:

1. Time: Forming disciples
2. Teaching: Training disciples
3. Tactics: Sending disciples

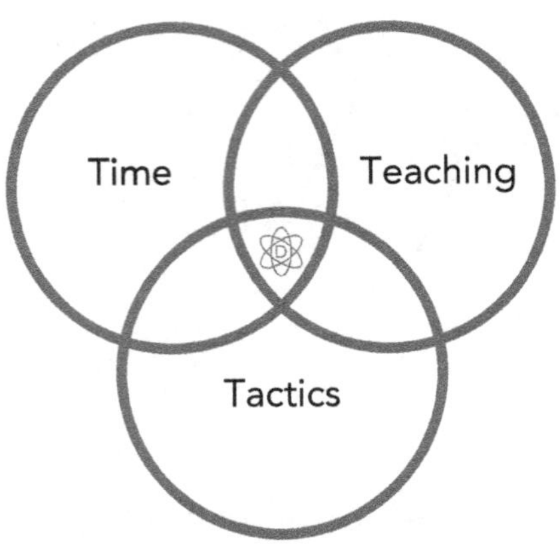

Jesus spent three years training the Twelve, and each year had a specific focus to achieve one of these three outcomes:

TIMELINE	RHYTHM	ACTION	OUTCOMES
Year 1	Time	Forming disciples	Development in disciples
Year 2	Teaching	Training disciples	Demonstration to disciples
Year 3	Tactics	Sending disciples	Deployment of disciples

Don't worry. Discipology does not demand a rigid, one-size-fits-all three-year program. The goal is simply to help you trace how intentionally Jesus trained his disciples over the three years of his ministry. Once you see it, you can't unsee it.

For the spreadsheet lovers, accountants, and those with mild OCD tendencies among you—*Discipology* is structured around an introduction and three main sections, each focused on one of the core rhythms of disciple-making: time, teaching, and tactics.[8] Each section explores the specific

8. Math people (shudder) walk among us . . . but God can use anyone. He chose Matthew the tax collector to eliminate any doubt.

outcome produced by that rhythm and is further divided into three chapters. These chapters follow the same rhythm, examining the Time patterns Jesus modeled, his Teaching principles he trained, and finally the Tactics you can apply on your own journey of making disciples. This layered framework reflects the disciple-making journey itself: simple at the start, but increasingly rich, integrated, and transformative as you go.

The patterns are what Jesus modeled for disciples in the Time rhythm.

The principles are what Jesus taught disciples in the Teaching rhythm.

The practices are what Jesus deployed disciples to do in the Tactics rhythm.

Here's how the structure of the book breaks down across each rhythm:

Part I: Understanding Discipology
- The Disciple-Making Dilemma
- The Discipology of Jesus

Part II: Time—Where Disciples Are Formed
- Jesus's First-Year Pattern of Time
- Principles of Time
- Practices for Time

Part III: Teaching—Where Disciples Are Trained
- Jesus's Second-Year Pattern of Teaching
- Principles of Teaching
- Practices for Teaching

Part IV: Tactics—Where Disciples Are Sent
- Jesus's Third-Year Pattern of Tactics
- Principles of Tactics
- Practices for Tactics

Conclusion

If the structure didn't give it away already, let me be clear: I don't want you sitting on the sidelines. Disciple-making was never meant to be a spectator sport—it's a participatory sport. As a trainer by trade, I know how difficult it is to move people from knowledge to action. And the problem we leaders have is that we talk for a living. When we talk about things we don't do, we still get an endorphin release, meaning we often get the same feelings from talking about things that we would doing them. But we don't get the experiences—and definitely not the results. And here we are, feeling good about talking about things we should do, but don't.

But our Master trainer modeled patterns, revealed principles, and left practices for us to follow. The patterns we observe in his three years of public ministry will reframe how we understand disciple-making. The principles will reorient how we think. And the practices will reshape our praxis. As a former RN, firefighter, and paramedic, I learned that rigid adherence to methods fails in the field. Principles are all one can fall back on. That's why Jesus gave us all three: ever shifting patterns, timeless principles, and variable practices. Jesus knew that you can't just read a book and copy someone else's story, but once you understand the principles, you'll understand how to apply them. To paraphrase American business theorist Harrington Emerson, the methods are many, the principles few; the methods are always changing, the principles never do. Our goal is to rediscover the patterns, principles, and practices of Jesus—and to embody them.

Your journey to becoming a practitioner is key to the transformation of the people around you. If you want people to quote you, say great things. If you want people to follow you, as they did Jesus, and Paul, do great things. Jesus was a doer, and he said that when a disciple is fully trained, they will become like their Master—a doer also. Therefore, this is *not* just another book on discipleship to add weight to shelves already sagging under the weight of theory. The world doesn't need another book about discipleship—it needs individuals and churches ready to recover the disciple-making rhythms of Jesus.

Jesus intended his disciple-makers to be both informed and transformed—people who understand the principles and practice the way. Too often, we approach this journey like Princeton professor Dr. Jones, lecturing about discipleship as an academic exercise. And while theorists tell other people's stories, practitioners write them. If you're willing to don the disciple-making fedora, crack a whip, and raid temples for lost people, you won't just study someone else's adventure—you'll choose your own. And you might earn a new nickname, like "Indiana" in the process. My hope is that you'll be unrecognizable when you finish this journey. Perhaps that's why Jesus was fond of handing out new monickers to his disciples at the start of their journey into disciple-making. Jesus intended us to be both informed and transformed—people who understand the principles and practice the way. The book you're holding is a catalytic guide to help spark a disciple-making movement in your neighborhood, city, or church—but it's only one part of a greater ecosystem.

The Discipology Ecosystem

You see, no matter where you are today, your story isn't over. It could be the greatest turnaround in history. So how do we step into the story Jesus is still writing through you? It starts by recognizing your role in it. Just as Jesus built an immersive disciple-making environment with a cast of characters, your journey will unfold within a similar ecosystem with the people God has surrounded you with.

One look at the Gospels, and it becomes obvious: Jesus's training was immersive. While we may not have the luxury of three years on mission together, I can offer you tools to re-create a similar disciple-making ecosystem necessary for disciple-making wherever you are.

Just as in the Gospels, your disciple-making journey includes a cast of key characters:

- **The catalyst (you)**
- **The disciple-makers (the people in your group, small group, or microchurch)**
- **The disciples (those you're helping to follow Jesus)**

The Catalyst

If you're holding this book, you're likely a catalyst.[9] It's designed for disciple-making leaders—pastors, youth pastors, discipleship directors, and small-group leaders—who want to mobilize others. But it's equally useful for everyday disciple-makers seeking to deepen their understanding. Give this book enough time, and those who were disciple-makers will become catalysts. At least, that's how Jesus designed it to work.

Everything starts with you as the catalyst. In *What Actually Starts Movements*, Emanuel Prinz synthesizes data from 147 movements and concludes that, among twenty-one shared qualities, the most crucial is the presence of a catalyst—someone who leads the charge. The research also shows that catalytic leaders aren't simply born; they are made. "He or she can grow into these traits and competencies."[10]

My hope is that as you read, you'll follow Jesus's catalytic example—not just making disciples but also multiplying disciple-makers.

If you're a pastor, you'll mobilize your church.

If you're a small-group leader, you'll mobilize your small group.

If you're a youth pastor, you'll mobilize your youth group.

Make no mistake: You must lead from the front as Jesus did, or no one will follow. Disciple-making can't be delegated—it must be demonstrated. Your disciple-makers will be mobilized in teams of two.

Disciple-Makers

Next are those you will mobilize to become disciple-makers—ideally, everyone you lead. I've partnered with Through the Word to create a tactical Bible plan for Discipology. The Gospels don't just tell the story of Jesus; they trace the transformation of ordinary people into world-changing disciple-makers. This journal invites would-be disciple-makers to take that same

9. You are either a catalyst or a disciple-maker who has decided to go deep. My hope is that all disciple-makers eventually gain a hunger for this book and explore Discipology in-depth. If we're correctly following Jesus's pattern of Discipology, eventually all disciple-makers become catalysts.

10. Emanuel Prinz, *What Actually Starts Movements: Partnering with God for Kingdom Multiplication* (100 Movements Publishing, 2025), 9.

journey of transformation. Designed for everyday Christians—not just church leaders—it walks them step-by-step from their earliest attempts to confidently sharing Jesus and inviting others to follow him. Each day includes simple prompts to help them listen to Jesus and take practical action. They don't need to have it all figured out—just a willingness to follow, like the Twelve. The journal helps them track their successes, challenges, experiences, and growth.

When you come together during the week—at a small group, youth group, or elsewhere—you can reflect on your experiences with Jesus, compare battle scars, and encourage one another to take practical next steps. For that, there are additional tools to download at Discipology.com.

The Disciples

Making disciples doesn't have to be complicated—and neither does starting the journey. God has placed people around each of us who don't know Jesus. Disciple-making is simply walking alongside others to help them follow him.

Through the Word has partnered with Discipology to create a tool called Walk—a free plug-and-play path for discipling anyone. No prep. No pressure. Just open the Discipology plan on the Through the Word app and begin walking alongside someone through the gospel of John to help that person follow Jesus. With low barriers to entry and a clean, intuitive design, the Discipology plan is built for real conversations, real relationships, and real growth. It removes the guesswork out of disciple-making and makes the journey accessible to everyone.

Those are the basic components of the ecosystem and all anyone needs for training wheels to start riding the disciple-making bike. If, however, you would like to find out more or go even deeper, visit www.Discipology.com or scan the QR code:

The Lasting Monument

What follows in this book is a blueprint for disciple-making as modeled by the Master disciple-maker himself. But it's not just for leaders. It's for everyone. If you'll heed the call first given on the shores of Galilee—"Follow me"—he will make you fishers of people, just as he did his first disciples. It was the promise to make them something that they were not . . . yet. And he'll do it for the people in your church or group. Why else would he have picked such down-to-earth, nonreligious types?

Speaking leader to leader, I've had the privilege of occupying pulpits once filled by my heroes, such as D. Martyn Lloyd-Jones. And while preaching is powerful, disciple-making runs deeper. Jesus did both, and Scripture calls us to do the same. It's not either-or—it's both-and. But any leader willing to follow Jesus and brave the unfamiliar venture of disciple-making will discover a new capacity rising within—the boldness of Peter, the love of John, the strategy of Paul—not just to preach sermons but to spark movements that multiply.

Such a leader will eventually stub a toe on buried treasure—like the unsuspecting farmer in Jesus's parable who sold everything to buy the field. Despite my rich preaching experience, I would gladly trade every pulpit I've ever stood in to sit at the feet of Jesus and learn disciple-making from him—to become a fisher of people, like he was. Thankfully, I learned to make disciples outside of Sundays, on the streets of South Wales, inside factories or fire stations, and over cups of coffee at Starbucks.

As you begin to uncover the art and science of disciple-making, you'll find yourself walking the dusty roads with the Twelve, learning the same tough lessons through trial and error. Sometimes you'll feel as if you're huddling around the campfire at night as Jesus debriefs that day's experiences. And when you wake the next morning, you'll know that another adventure will unfold before you as you complete your experiential training under his careful eyes.

To paraphrase A. W. Tozer, "People are always looking for methods, but God is looking for people."[11] That's all Jesus looked for when he called his first disciples—ordinary people like you and me—and it's all he's looking for now. If we can return to Jesus's timeless rhythms of Discipology, we will unleash the

11. Tozer wrote "men" instead of people. It rolls off the tongue better, yet Peter said the Spirit would be poured out on all flesh in the last days—not just men.

mobilization witnessed in the early church. And when that happens, methods, multiplication, and movements will outlast us.

Let Ozymandias keep his broken statue, buried beneath the sands of forgotten kingdoms. By embracing the Discipology strategy of Jesus, we won't be building stagnant stone structures that crumble or monuments to ministries that die with us. In their place we'll be shaping transformed lives, mobilized to make disciples who make disciples. Disciples of a kingdom that never crumbles. Because Christ's legacy isn't carved in granite; it's etched in people through the making of disciples—generation after generation—where the Spirit whispers the echo of the "King of Kings": *Look upon my works, ye mighty, and despair* . . .

PART I

UNDERSTANDING DISCIPOLOGY

Before we can talk about the *how* of mobilization through disciple-making, we need to understand *what* it is—and *why* it mattered so deeply to Jesus. Our definitions of discipleship and disciple-making are crucial for understanding where we are now and where God is still calling us to go. Learn how recovering the practices of first-century disciple-making will shake us free from the ruts we're stuck in and catalyze a fresh movement of mobilization.

The next two chapters will focus on what Discipology is, how Jesus applied it, and why.

CHAPTER 1

The Disciple-Making Dilemma

> So the problem is not so much to see what nobody has yet seen, as to think what nobody has yet thought concerning that which everybody sees.
>
> **—ARTHUR SCHOPENHAUER**

Thomas Edison didn't invent the light bulb.

That usually surprises people. After all, the dream of electric light was nothing new, and other inventors had gotten close. Before Edison came along, there were over twenty clunky prototypes burning out too fast or too dim to be useful. But, in 1879, Edison, who had been chasing it for years, changed the game by creating something that *lasted*.

The pieces were all there—filaments, glass, current—but nothing *worked*. Not for long, anyway. The light couldn't handle the current. Edison and his team tested more than six thousand different materials for filaments, yet failed repeatedly . . . until one day his team discovered a carbonized bamboo filament. History was made when they flipped the switch and *the light stayed on*!

It wasn't a lightning-bolt-from-heaven kind of moment but the result of the grit and sweat of thousands of failures leading to one flash of brilliance.

From the moment they saw that steady glow, it was *Eureka!* A breakthrough that created a new era.

What came next was more than just a brighter room. It was a brighter *world*. Where the world had once turned dark after sunset, lit only by candles, gas lamps, and flickering lanterns, cities now glowed after dark.

And here's the thing: *The power had always been there.*

Edison didn't invent electricity; he discovered how to conduct it. He had discovered the means of harnessing one spark that could light up thousands. Disciple-making is supposed to work like that: one person's life carrying the light of Jesus to another until whole communities begin to glow. As with the light bulb, it's not about the flashy brilliance of a single leader, here and gone in an instant, but about the sustainable and transferable power. A simple, Spirit-empowered process that changes everything, one life at a time.

The problem?

We've done to disciple-making what others did with the light bulb—we've built models that flicker and fade. Programs that burn bright for a moment, then burn out. Somewhere along the way, we forgot what disciple-making really *is*. Like Edison, we don't need to invent something new—we need to rediscover what made it so transferable. The eureka moment won't come from a flashy new curriculum or trend. It will only come from going back to Jesus. His filament was the design that conducted the power from Jerusalem to the ends of the earth. Jesus already invented the longer lasting light bulb, the only model bright enough to light the world "until the end of the age." It's time we used it.

The *What, Why,* and *How* of Disciple-Making

The word *disciple* occurs 269 times in the New Testament, while *Christian* shows up only 3.[1] If you're a leader, you likely already know that disciple-making is important—that's the "why." If someone asked "*Why* should we

1. Daniel Im, *No Silver Bullets: Five Small Shifts That Will Transform Your Ministry* (B&H, 2017), chap. 2, Kindle.

make disciples?" most of us would answer, "Because Jesus commanded us to." Simple enough.

And if someone asked us to define *what* a disciple is, we could probably manage. "A disciple is somebody who follows Jesus to become like him." So far, so good.

But if someone asked us to explain *how* to make a disciple—step-by-step—we might come up short. We may have sat through (or even preached) sermons on discipleship that got us amped. We walked out of the church like we'd just watched a *Rocky* film—pumped up and ready to punch someone in the face with our newfound disciple-making fervor. But somewhere between the church parking lot and real life, a giant question mark hit us.

How?

And that leads us to the real issue: Why don't we know how to make disciples in the first place?

The first bottleneck to disciple-making is simple: Most of us don't know how because it was never done to us. The truth is most Christians have never been personally discipled. According to a 2015 Barna study, only 23 percent of Christians are discipled one-on-one.[2] That's a bad track record when Jesus commissioned us to go and make disciples. Jesus could point to those instructions and say, "I gave you one job."

Most of us fall into the 77 percent who never had someone walk alongside us show us what following Jesus looks like in real life—let alone how to

2. "New Research on the State of Discipleship," Barna, December 1, 2015, www.barna.com/research/new-research-on-the-state-of-discipleship; "Two in Five Christians Are Not Engaged in Discipleship," Barna, January 26, 2022, www.barna.com/research/christians-discipleship-community.

practically pass it on to others. Still, that same study found that 28 percent of Christians were actively involved in some kind of discipleship community, like a small group or home study. That's a start. It shows the hunger is still there.

Without that "how" part, we are pretty lost.

Maybe that's why so few Christians actually make disciples . . .

But I think I have an explanation:

We tend to make disciples in the same way we ourselves were discipled.

And if that's true, the flipside is also true.

We tend to *not* make disciples how we were *not* discipled.

But what's missing in most churches is a clear, practical disciple-making pathway.

That's why most sermons on the Great Commission take a lick at the hard pop of the *what* and the *why* of disciple-making but rarely get to the chewy center of the *how*.[3]

I'm guessing that for the 77 percent of Christians who were never discipled, the following thirty-second elevator speech was the closest thing they got—a nice stranger at the front of the church smiled and said,

> You're saved! Welcome to the family of God. Your entire life is about to change. There's a couple of things you need to know. First, you need to read the Bible. I've got one for you here. [We are handed a thousand-page intimidating book with black leather, gold letters, and no instructions.] Next, you need to pray. Don't worry if you don't know how to do that, silly. It's easy! Just talk to God like you'd talk to a friend. Oh, you'll also want to tell other people about Jesus, because there are other people out there like you who need to know. And church . . . that's important! You need to come back to get "fed," and the Bible tells us "not to forsake the assembly of the saints." [You didn't get that last part, but the person said *fed*, and you

3. I'm talking about Tootsie Pops—you gotta teach the next generation or how else will they know?

don't remember seeing any food.] Well, that's it! I'll see you next . . . wait . . . I almost forgot. There's a devil. He *hates* your guts! Wants to steal, kill, and destroy you! He's going to make your life miserable now. So watch out! Okay, bye! See you next Sunday!

Sound familiar?

It feels like jumping out of—no, scratch that—like being kicked out of an airplane for the first time with no preparation. Someone thrusts a parachute pack into your arms, smiles, and says, "Good luck out there, but don't forget to pull the rip cord!" as their foot lands squarely in your gut, kicking you out of the hatch. And as you plummet to earth, you wonder what a rip cord even is . . . and how to use it. But now gravity is your new instructor.

That's not making disciples. It's what happens when we don't make time for people.

Truth be told, we weren't informed at the beginning of our journey that making disciples was supposed to be our bag. In *The Master Plan of Evangelism*, Robert Coleman put it this way: "We must know how a course of action fits into the overall plan God has for our lives if it is to thrill our souls with a sense of destiny."[4] Yet everyone has a unique part to play in making disciples. Jesus said he'd be with us in disciple-making until the end of the age, and last time I checked, that task isn't complete. But if we're unclear on what, why, and how, how can we expect the church to make disciples with confidence? Most Christians who don't make disciples aren't being *disobedient*; they're just *disoriented*. The majority of Christians *want* to make disciples—but first they need to be *made into disciples themselves*. They need to see how it's done.

Nobody modeled disciple-making for us. Yet the label on the Great Commission, to "make disciples," has been posted for two thousand years, so we'd be forgiven for collectively assuming that somebody knew how to "do the thing" printed on the box. At church, everyone talks like they get it, so we smile and nod along, and pretend we do too. But inwardly, we feel ashamed, like we *should* know it already yet are too shy to raise our hands to

4. Robert E. Coleman, *The Master Plan of Evangelism* (Revell, 1993), 21.

ask the "stupid question" of *how*. After two thousand years, admitting we're still unclear about disciple making feels akin to asking for help with our times tables in a calculus class! So as leaders, we run programs, teach studies, and preach topical sermons *about* disciple-making without ever really doing it. But that quiet discomfort—that we never feel brave enough to vocalize—reveals a much deeper problem. And what's modeled in the pulpit is lived in the pews.

Despite all the easy pat answers on the *what* and *why* of disciple-making, many of us are still confused—and we've turned Jesus's clear command into a vague suggestion, reduced discipleship to a buzzword, and continued to kick people out of the hatch clutching a parachute.

It may not be our generation's fault.

But it is this generation's opportunity to fix it.

Max Planck, a pioneer of quantum physics, noted that "a new scientific truth does not triumph by convincing its opponents and making them see the light, but rather because its opponents eventually die, and a new generation grows up that is familiar with it."[5] When my generation dies, my prayer is that the next will not only grasp what disciple-making really is and why it matters but will also know how to do it.

For that dream to become a reality, like Princess Leia, we must turn to our "only hope." We must return to the source—to Jesus himself—and the model that he left us. By reclaiming Jesus's original Discipology framework—the three simple rhythms of time, teaching, and tactics—we can stop guessing and start mobilizing.

This doesn't mean, however, that we don't already have some experience with the three rhythms of Jesus's Discipology. Since the majority of us are most familiar with the *Teaching* rhythm, let's start there.

The Teaching Rhythm

Many of us came through churches shaped by the church growth movement, where *teaching* was seen as the primary engine of spiritual formation—even *as*

5. Max Planck, *Scientific Autobiography and Other Papers* (Philosophical Library, 1950), 33.

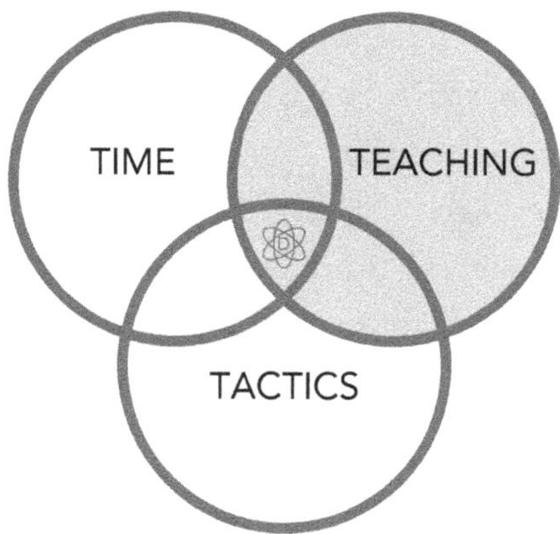

discipleship itself. In the universe of most Word-based churches, the pulpit is the center of gravity. People gather in crowds, and pastors preach their hearts out believing that good biblical teaching alone will produce disciples.

But what if I told you that Jesus didn't think that—teaching was only one-third of his process?

According to Acts 5:42, teaching was a daily foundational practice of the early church: "Every day, in the temple and from house to house, they did not cease *teaching* and preaching that the Christ is Jesus" (ESV, emphasis mine). Yet Jesus taught us that although Teaching conveys information, it doesn't necessarily produce transformation. Just ask him about the Pharisees. The teaching circle was everything to them.

= INFORMATION

If a church focuses only on the Teaching rhythm, it risks valuing right doctrine as the highest aim of a gathering—at the cost of everything else. That kind of thinking produces a smugness from what the great Bible teacher

Dr. Martyn Lloyd-Jones called "dead orthodoxy."[6] I'm not talking about those who hold firmly to the essentials of the faith, but those who split hairs over the finer points of nonessential doctrine.

When I was the evangelist at Dr. Lloyd-Jones's Sandfields church in Wales, it wasn't uncommon at pastors' conferences to hear someone whisper about being visited on a Sunday by some "Westminster Orphans"—Christians who had sat under "the Doctor" (Lloyd-Jones) and, as a result, could never sit under anyone else. After you'd preached, they would march up to you with a notebook full of doctrinal nitpicks and put you on full blast. Ironically, they were great proponents of grace—yet seemed to possess so little of it themselves. They talked like they'd charge the gates of hell for the gospel, but after meeting them, it was easy to see why nobody wanted to follow them. To be fair, the Westminster Orphans should not reflect upon the Doctor himself, one of my heroes who mentored my mentors,[7] but they do serve as a cautionary tale. Lloyd-Jones was one of the greatest teachers in church history. Yet the best teaching in the world doesn't automatically produce transformation—because it wasn't designed to.

Not on its own, anyway.

True discipleship needs more than the absorption of information—it needs transformation. And that requires another rhythm: *Time.*

The Time Rhythm

Megachurch pastor Rick Warren scanned the heaving Sunday-morning crowds over the crest of his pulpit and was convicted by something few leaders were willing to admit in the 1990s. Despite the numbers and hype, Warren was convinced that something was missing.

Instead of being satisfied with packed pews and multiple services, he

---

6. Martyn Lloyd-Jones, "Dead Orthodoxy," chap. 6 in *Revival* (Crossway, 1987).
7. The laptop this book was written on rests on Lloyd-Jones's pulpit Bible if that tells you anything of my great respect for preaching. And his protégé, and my mentor Peter Jeffery, was the finest preacher I've ever heard in my life. He would have agreed with and embodied the principles in this book. His own story of activation is found in the book *Chains of Grace: Peter Jeffery's Story*, in the *Life Stories* series (Leominster: Day One Publications, 2008).

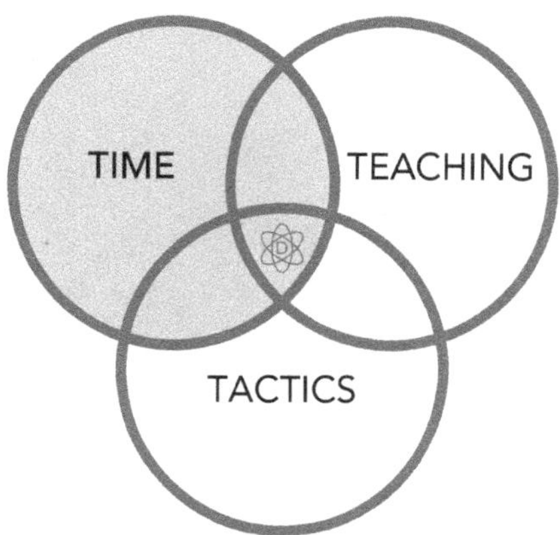

correctly diagnosed what many were feeling about the church growth movement: Teaching crowds wasn't enough to sustain spiritual growth. People were showing up but not growing up.

Warren recognized what J. I. Packer wrote about the effects of the church growth movement in America, that it was "3,000 miles wide and half an inch deep."[8] He knew the answer wasn't less growth—but deeper connection.[9]

The solution? Warren designed the *Purpose Driven* system to help move people from crowd to commitment—from passive pew sitters to active participants in the church. His *Purpose Driven* framework was based upon a baseball diamond as it guides someone from the starting point of conversion (first base) to small-group involvement (second base) to the discovery of their spiritual gifts and service in the church (third base) and ultimately to mission (home plate). When his manifesto of the model, *The Purpose Driven Church*, hit the shelves in 1995, it broadsided the evangelical world like a Mack truck.

Typical of the church growth movement's strengths, bigger crowds meant preaching the gospel to more people. But crowds are like consumers: They crave more teaching, like the crowds following Jesus in search of bread.

---

8. J. I. Packer, *A Quest for Godliness: The Puritan Vision of the Christian Life* (Crossway, 1990), 22.
9. Many who criticize the church growth movement ignore the fact that the early church exploded at Pentecost. Size has never been the enemy of spirituality. Size does, however, produce problems—problems that the early church had to grapple with. None of the disciples ever stated that the church was sick or wrong because it was large. Rather, they went wide and deep simultaneously. Rather than an either-or mentality regarding size and depth, the apostles adopted a both-and stance.

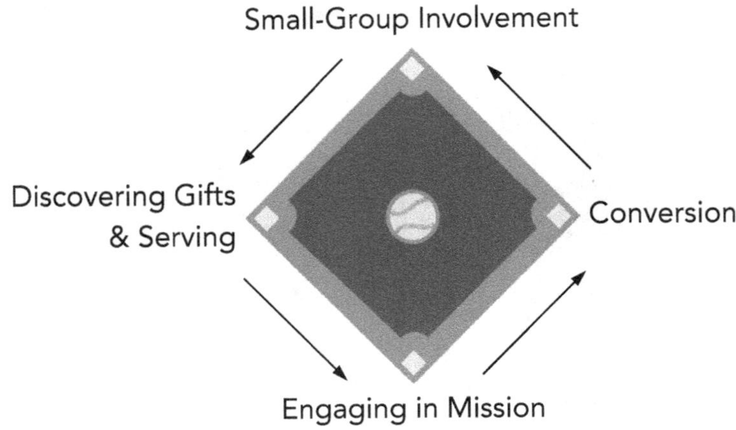

Warren's first goal therefore, was to get them to first base: conversion. But how to make them disciples? To address the deficiency of a teaching-only system, Warren added the rhythm of *Time* to move people to second base: or community groups.

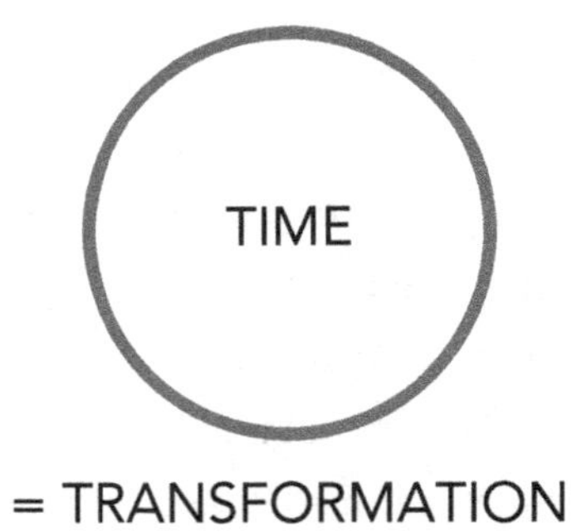

If the *Teaching* rhythm conveys information, *Time* facilitates transformation. But it happens through community. Transferring information from a pulpit swallows a mere thirty minutes on a Sunday—but community is costly. It requires time—an investment fewer people are willing to make. But Warren recognized that when people enter the rhythm of *Time*, they go from staring at the back of other people's heads in rows and start looking into each other's faces in circles during the week—and that's where *transformation* happens.

The Time rhythm takes us out of the crowd and places us into community—where community creates circles, and circles foster interaction. discussion. Community also forces us to rub up against one another's weaknesses and rough edges—and in that friction transformation takes place.

So when Warren's small groups outnumbered his Sunday attendance two to one, that wasn't just a stat—it was a *statement*. Not surprisingly, Warren's decentralized community groups weathered the storm of the COVID-19 lockdowns and multiplied from six thousand to nine thousand!

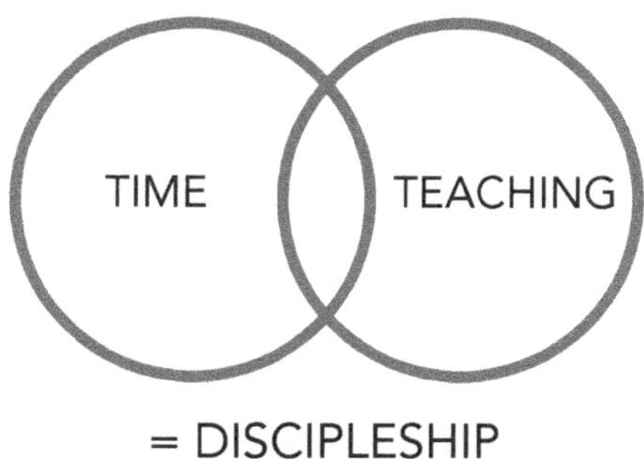

= DISCIPLESHIP

Warren cracked the *discipleship* code. But as helpful as the *Purpose Driven* model was to the church growth movement, it still didn't crack the code on *disciple-making*. Perhaps that's because the baseball diamond designated home plate as mission—and stopped there, just short of actually *making disciples*.[10] But mission often meant serving inside the church walls rather than outside them. Warren's system did a fantastic job of getting people into discipleship environments where they could learn and connect, but churches were still not being mobilized outside the church walls en masse. For mobilization to happen, the last rhythm of Jesus's Discipology process is needed to make the shift from discipleship to disciple-making.

---

10. This should not in any way be viewed as a criticism. The church is deeply indebted to Rick Warren, and I never allow someone to criticize him in my presence—not because he is perfect, but because I read in *Decision* magazine that after *The Purpose Driven Life* was so successful, Warren paid back his salary of decades to Saddleback Church and also started to reverse tithe (to tithe 90 percent rather than 10 percent). Anyone who does that has my respect. I always ask the critics to reverse tithe before they continue any personal criticism.

Disciple-Making Defined

There is a tension here: We should celebrate discipleship wins—people growing in groups, discovering their gifts, even stepping into service—yet our churches are quietly falling short of *making disciples*. The discipleship model brought us to the edge of the mission field—but not into it.

People were moved from the crowd into community, and from community to contribution. *Discipleship* was happening within the building. But outside the building, *disciple-making* was not.

The reason? Somewhere along the way, we confused the terms *disciple-making* and *discipleship* as if they are interchangeable. But they're two different things. We swapped Jesus's command to *make disciples* with the safer, more familiar substitute of *discipleship*, and that has confused everything since. To (mis)quote Inigo Montoya, "You keep using that word *discipleship*, but I don't think it means what you think it means." We thought *discipleship* was what Jesus commanded in the Great Commission, but what he actually said was "Go. *Make disciples.*"

In confusing the terms, we erroneously thought that we were already doing it.

To help us spot the difference, some definitions are helpful.

Discipleship: The ongoing process of developing as a Jesus follower. Discipleship happens after conversion and is the process of maturing spiritually in the faith—learning to become more like Christ through practices like prayer, Bible study, and fellowship with other believers. It is spiritual growth.

Disciple-making: The intentional process of helping others become followers of Jesus. Making disciples involves evangelistically guiding others to follow Jesus in a proactive mobilization effort that multiplies disciples.

Until we stop conflating the two, we'll keep discipling believers within the church without ever reproducing new ones.

Think of the two terms *discipleship* and *disciple-making* like two different types of tires: a street tire and an off-road tire. In the Great Commission, Jesus called his disciples to make disciples (a) *to the ends of the earth* and (b) *until the end of the age*. To cover *that* kind of distance requires serious mud-slinging, off-roading, deep-tread, reinforced all-terrain monster tires. But when we approach the vehicle to navigate the rugged off-road disciple-making mission before us, we make a critical mistake: We slap the wrong tires onto it.

Discipleship, as we've come to practice it, is like a spare tire—what earlier generations called a doughnut tire. These emergency spares were designed to get you to safety after a blowout but came with limits: no faster than fifty miles per hour, and no farther than thirty-miles. In other words, doughnut tires will get you nowhere fast—a pretty accurate summary of our Great Commission progress. So when the church hears Jesus say, "Go make disciples," we reach for the doughnut of discipleship—when we should be slapping on all-terrain monster disciple-making tires kitted out for the journey. Like Keith Green sang, "It's no wonder we're moving so slow."[11]

It's hard to read the Great Commission and apply the doughnut of discipleship to its disciple-making mandate:

11. Keith Green, "Jesus Commands Us to Go!," track 7 on *Jesus Commands Us to Go!*, performed by Keith Green, Pretty Good Records, July 20, 1984, compact disc.

> Jesus came to them and said, "All authority in heaven and on earth has been given to me. Therefore go and make disciples of all nations, baptizing them in the name of the Father and of the Son and of the Holy Spirit, and teaching them to obey everything I have commanded you. And surely I am with you always, to the very end of the age." (Matt. 28:18–20)

Let's break down the imperatives of making disciples:

1. Go to all nations.
2. Baptize them.
3. Teach them to obey all Christ commanded.
4. Rely on the presence and power of Christ.

Is it just me, or does Jesus's disciple-making list sound a lot more like a mission to people who *don't yet* believe rather than instructions for Christians already in the club? Going to all nations. Making disciples because they don't yet exist. Baptizing them. Teaching them to obey Christ's commands for life transformation. Relying on the power and presence of God as you go.

Mission work is worlds away (sometimes literally) from sitting in a spiritual support group, sipping Christian crack, and discussing books while pounding coffee cake. No matter how you slice it, disciple-making *is* mission.

Now consider the steps to discipleship:

1. Gather fellow Christians who want to grow in their faith.
2. Pick a book of the Bible, a Christian-living book, or a small-group curriculum.
3. Discuss what you read during the week.
4. Eat copious amounts of cookies, coffee cake, or—ironically—doughnuts.[12]
5. Drink mugs of Christian crack (also known as coffee).

---

12. Nobody speaks against doughnuts. "Doughnuts. Is there anything they can't do?"—Homer Simpson, philosopher of the modern age. A man who clearly missed his calling.

6. Pray for a few minutes at the end.
7. Rinse and repeat for an average of six to eight weeks.

Once you lay those two lists side by side, it becomes painfully clear: We've swapped the tires of disciple-making with discipleship, and *accidentally turned the Great Commission inward*, stripping it of its missional edge. And, sadly, many Christians believe they're fulfilling the Great Commission—because they no longer recognize the difference between the two.

DISCIPLESHIP	DISCIPLE-MAKING
Happens after conversion	Leads to conversion
Self-focused	Others-focused
With Christians	With non-Christians
A weekly event	A lifestyle
Centered on a topic	Centered on Jesus
Investment in self	Investment in others
Ends with you	Ends with others

If Jesus had commanded us to focus on discipleship instead of disciple-making, the Great Commission might have sounded like this:

Instead of **"Go"**

> Stay where you are. Build community and gather regularly. Keep things steady and consistent.

Instead of **"to all nations"**

> Stick with your own kind—people who are like you; your small group, your church family, familiar faces, and shared experiences.

Instead of **"baptizing them"**

Invite them to a group, class, or gathering. Offer a safe place to learn. Let growth happen slowly over time.

Instead of **"teaching them to obey"**

Encourage personal growth. Focus on becoming more Christlike, developing character, and growing in faith; learn truth from Scripture, deepen understanding, and build spiritual habits.

If that was the destination, we'd have arrived long ago. But despite our slow progress in accomplishing the Great Commission, nobody's going to force us to pull over the car and change the tire. We can keep riding on the doughnut—hoping the current system will carry us a little farther without popping. Or we can stop and put the rugged, all-terrain disciple-making tires back on the church—the ones Jesus designed to get us the traction necessary for mobilization.

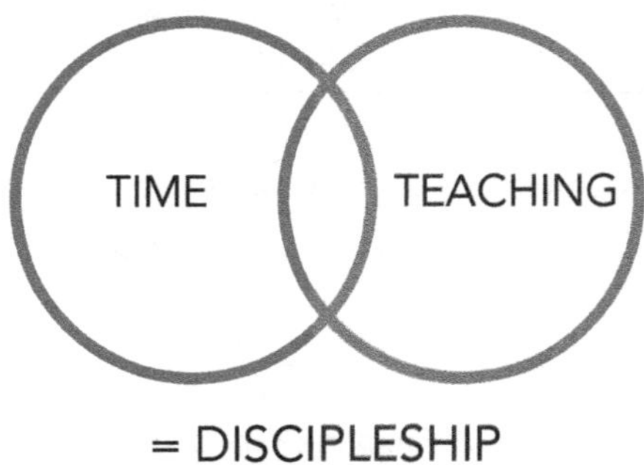

= DISCIPLESHIP

None of this should be taken as a detraction or criticism of discipleship. Discipleship is necessary and worth spending our time on, but it's also *incomplete.* Although discipleship combines time and teaching, it's missing the Tactics rhythm. But we must be patient with people as they discover each rhythm. It's been popular for years to critique those who know only the *Teaching* rhythm, punching down at leaders with large crowds, labeling them as "peddling to consumers" as we pat ourselves on the back. As Jonathan Edwards once mused about human nature, "If one worm be a little exalted above another, by having more dust, or a bigger dunghill, how much does he make of himself!"[13] But there are far worse things than being stuck in the Teaching rhythm—like *not* being in the Teaching rhythm, and not hearing the gospel at all. That first step on our journey of entering the Teaching rhythm, should be celebrated. And while it was *great* to experience teaching and gain information, we discovered something *greater* when we discovered the second rhythm—time—and made the seismic leap from crowd to community, where relational community brought transformation. That is also cause for celebration. But the goal of the Great Commission is mobilization—and that only happens when we overlap the last and final rhythm of Discipology. One rhythm is great; two rhythms are greater. But it's not until we step into the third and final rhythm—the Tactics rhythm—that we discover the greatest. In fact, the Teaching rhythm can dominate Sundays, while the teaching and time combo rocks discipleship groups during the week. But when all three rhythms work together to produce disciple-making outside of our meetings, that's when mobilization happens.

The Tactics Rhythm

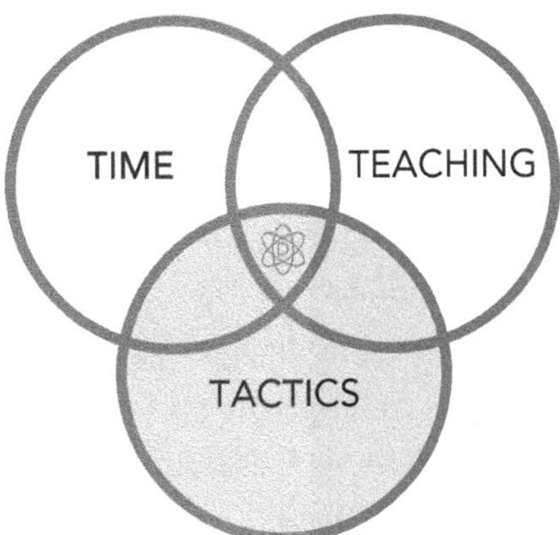

To sum up: The church is great when it *teaches* truth. It's greater when it invests the *time* to see people transformed. And the church is greatest when

13. Jonathan Edwards, "The Excellency of Christ," in *The Works of Jonathan Edwards*, vol. 1 (Banner of Truth, 1974), 680.

it's doing all three by entering into the *tactical*—because that third rhythm *activates* you on mission.

Think of the three rhythms as a progression toward disciple-making:

- Teaching produces information.
- Time produces transformation.
- Tactics produce activation.

According to a shocking Barna study, only 5 percent of believers ever reach this Tactics rhythm and actively start reproducing themselves through disciple-making.[14] And that's where the church is stuck: activation. When I was a young youth pastor, I used to bang my head against the wall trying to activate students to do all the "Christian" things they were supposed to do.

- Read your Bible.
- Pray.
- Share your faith.
- Serve.
- Come to church.

I tried everything to motivate them—guilt, hype, even bribery (don't judge me). But it always felt as though I were dragging them uphill in a shopping cart with square wheels. Then one day we took them on a mission trip to Eastern Europe—and everything changed. I remember walking through a series of train cars on a bullet train speeding the European interior. Car after car, I saw those same "unmotivated" kids laying hands on strangers, praying with them, and leading them to Christ. I could barely believe my eyes. Their gifts—hidden before—were *coming alive* right before my eyes.

Now that they'd been activated in their unique calling through exercising their giftings, something had clicked into place:

14. "Two in Five Christians Are Not Engaged in Discipleship," Barna, January 26, 2022, www.barna.com/research/christians-discipleship-community.

- They *wanted* to read the Bible—because they needed answers.
- They *wanted* to pray—because they needed power.
- They *wanted* to share their faith—because real people were desperate for hope.
- They *wanted* to gather—because the mission was bigger than themselves.

And when they returned home, they were never the same. Only the Tactics rhythm brought everything else into clear focus for the youth. They had been firmly embedded in the Time and Teaching rhythms of my youth group, but the second their boots hit the mission field, *bam*! It was as if the missing puzzle piece clicked into place. Turns out a mission trip was more effective than a guilt trip . . . who knew?

From then on, pushing youth out of their comfort zones onto tactical short-term church-planting missions to New Zealand, Hungary, and Mexico provided the turning point in following Jesus. It's why Jesus deployed the disciples on tactical mission in the third year. Short-term trips are often criticized by those who say they do more for those who go than those they go to. Fair enough. But it was certainly beneficial for the Twelve. That's why Jesus sent them *out* on *two* short-term mission trips that year—and received them back all fired up with the spark of mission now lit. Every time my own youth came back, mission was no longer a once-a-year event but a way of life. The trick was knowing what to do with them after they returned.

The Discipology Flywheel

No matter how we attempt to solve the problem of disciple-making, we can't unlock the problem without the right keys. Think of mobilization as a door with a triple lock. Unlocking two of the locks with Time and Teaching still leaves us with a locked door. The problem is everyone wants you to use *their* keys. *Their* products. *Their* programs. But I want you to grab the keys that Jesus left under the mat. Here's the catch: We don't need to unlock them all at once. If the three rhythms are a progression, then everybody has to start somewhere.

DISCIPLE-MAKING

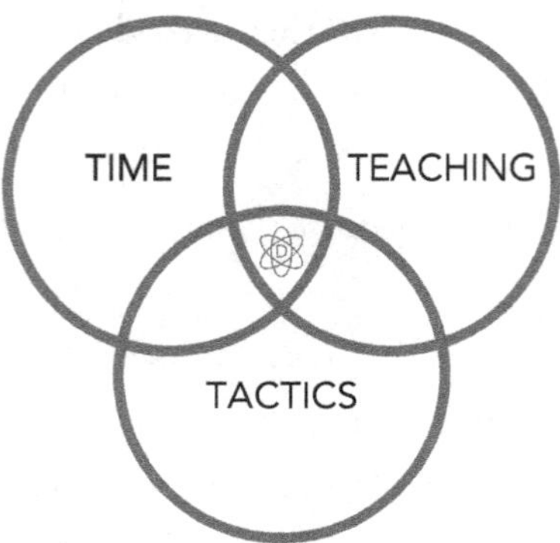

Jesus moved through the rhythms with the Twelve, adding the next rhythm only when they were ready—not just as steps to complete or progress but as a system that sustained a movement. And that's what Discipology will do for your friends, small group, youth group, or church. And you can't skip any of the rhythms, or you'll end up with something less than mobilization:

- Without *time*, you'll lack relationship but get a program that doesn't transform.
- Without *teaching*, you'll lack depth but get a social group who don't know what they believe.
- Without tactics, it lacks impact.

This was the Achilles' heel of the missional movement. (Remember that from the introduction? Wait . . . you didn't read the introduction? You need to back up and read it, partner. How will we change the world together if you're skipping introductions? I'll see you right back here when you're done.)

Ahem.

As I was saying: The Achilles' heel of the missional movement was that it reacted too negatively to the church growth movement, where teaching was everything. In response, the pendulum swung to the Time rhythm. The missional movement championed presence, relationships, and incarnational ministry—but in the process they treated teaching altogether like the kid who smelled at school. Despite being a daily activity of the early church, preaching and teaching were left on the sidelines, waiting last to be picked for the team. Both movements grasped a different Discipology rhythm, but neither accomplished mobilization.

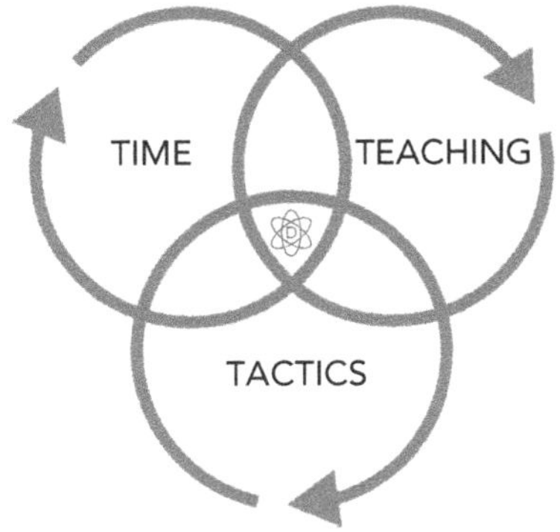

The three rhythms of Discipology produce a *mobilization flywheel.* A flywheel is a machine designed to maximize the release of energy through the momentum of perpetual motion. Jim Collins used the flywheel in his book *Good to Great* as a metaphor for the combination of the three essential components an organization needs to get traction; in this case, time, teaching, and tactics generate a powerful disciple-making momentum. The challenging thing about flywheels is that they don't spin from one big push. The unstoppable momentum builds through steady combined effort from multiple points working in sync to overcome the force of inertia—and in the church that force can be strong. But once the flywheel is rolling, it's hard to stop. In the book *The Mobilization Flywheel* by Todd Wilson and Larry Walkemeyer, the authors note, "Leaders want a magic wand, not a flywheel."[15] Yet if you dissect any world-changing movement in church history, you'll find a Discipology flywheel at the core. It started in Acts. And it's been present in every mobilization movement since.

---

15. Larry Walkemeyer and Todd Wilson, *The Mobilization Flywheel: The Key to Releasing Everyday Christians into a Lifestyle of Multiplying Mission* (Exponential, 2022), 22.

The Discipology Flywheel in Church History

But the Discipology flywheel has turned throughout church history whenever someone returns to intentional disciple-making. In a similarly dark hour, John Wesley rediscovered how to operate the Discipology flywheel to mobilize the church outside the four walls, turning Britain upside down. Wesley mobilized circuit riders like Francis Asbury, and that momentum spread to America. During Wesley's lifetime (1703–1791), Methodism grew from a few students at Oxford into a movement of around 132,000 members—about 72,000 in Britain and 60,000 in America.[16] By 1850 there were 1.46 million in Britain, and Methodists made up 34 percent of all religious adherents in the States.[17]

What was Wesley's secret?

At the laying of the foundation for the New Chapel—where he trained his circuit riders—Wesley preached: "What is Methodism? . . . Is it not a new religion? . . . Methodism, so called, is the *old* religion, the religion of the Bible, the religion of the primitive Church."[18]

"Primitive church" was Wesley's term for the early church of the first century. He wasn't trying to invent something new—he was recovering something ancient—something from Acts. "In religion, I am for as few innovations as possible," Wesley once said. "I love the old wine best."[19]

Wesley's innovation wasn't invention but implementation. He simply rediscovered and reactivated Jesus's model by scouring the pages of the New Testament. Here are the ways that Wesley modeled all three circles of Discipology.

---

16. David Bebbington, *Evangelicalism in Modern Britain: A History from the 1730s to the 1980s* (Routledge, 1989), 52.
17. Kevin M. Watson, "The Explosive Growth of Methodism from 1776 to 1850," *Kevin M. Watson (blog)*, June 17, 2009, https://kevinmwatson.com/2009/06/17/the-explosive-growth-of-methodism-from-1776-to-1850/.
18. John Wesley, *"On Laying the Foundation of the New Chapel, Near the City Road, London"* (Sermon 132), preached April 21, 1777; in "Sermon 132," *John Wesley Sermons*, ResourceUMC, accessed September 20, 2025, https://www.resourceumc.org/en/content/sermon-132-on-laying-the-foundation-of-the-new-chapel-near-the-city-road-london.
19. John Wesley, *The Letters of the Rev. John Wesley*, vol. 8, ed. John Telford (Epworth Press, 1931), 150.

Time

Wesley spent significant time with people, refusing to rely on pulpiteering alone. He harnessed the Time rhythm through bands (groups of three to five people), classes (ten to twelve people), and societies (fifty to seventy-five people), he created relational environments for confession, accountability, prayer, and encouragement. Wesley understood that transformation happens in community—through the rhythm of Time.

In contrast, George Whitefield, who drew larger crowds and focused on the Teaching rhythm alone, later lamented the lack of cohesion among his own followers:

> My brother Wesley acted wisely—the souls that were awakened under his ministry he joined in societies, and so preserved the fruits of his labour. This I neglected, and my people are a rope of sand.[20]

Whitefield's movement lacked mobilization, and when he died, the momentum died with him after his movement disbanded. Whereas Whitefield's focus was crowds gathering to him, Wesley's was regular, relational rhythms of people gathering without him. After Wesley died, the mobilization flywheel of the Methodist movement continued to turn and gain speed. The movement exploded—to 1.46 million by the 1851 census in Britain,[21] and over 1.66 million in the States by 1860, nearly a thirtyfold increase in the seventy years after his death.[22]

Teaching

Make no mistake—Wesley was a teacher at heart. His preaching was robustly biblical and theological. But his real genius was in bringing *Teaching* to the people. He wrote and distributed simple explanatory notes on the New

20. George Whitefield, quoted in Tony Cooke, "Encouraging Lessons from John Wesley," Tony Cooke Ministries, accessed August 20, 2025, https://tonycooke.org/articles-by-tony-cooke/lessons-john-wesley.
21. Bebbington, *Evangelicalism*, 52.
22. Nathan O. Hatch, *The Democratization of American Christianity* (Yale University Press, 1989), 122–25.

Testament, catechisms, and sermon outlines. He founded schools to teach literacy and established printing presses to distribute material. But, most importantly, Wesley empowered ordinary people *to teach* others. Leaders were raised up from within the movement—not imported from seminaries. His teaching was reproducible and practical, and, as was said of Jesus, "the common people heard him gladly" (Mark 12:37 KJV). Without a strong emphasis on Scripture, there would have been no Methodist movement.

Tactics

Wesley, like his Master, was a master *tactician*, unparalleled in the West since the apostle Paul. He mobilized his followers on mission, challenging them to serve the poor and modeling evangelistic mission by training circuit riders. The circuit-rider system was based on Jesus's itinerant ministry in the Gospels: move around, then send others to build on that work. Except Wesley never stopped sending himself, clocking over 250,000 miles on horseback (enough to circle the globe ten times!). Wesley personally discipled an army of lay preachers who rode hundreds of miles across the British countryside preaching the gospel and establishing faith communities. By the time of Wesley's death in 1791, there were 115 circuits and 300 preachers carrying out his work. By 1840, fifty years after his death, the circuits numbered 399, and the number of preachers was 492 in the UK and 2,000 in America.[23] Today, over 20 million Methodists trace their spiritual heritage back to Wesley's ministry. All because he tapped into Jesus's Discipology flywheel.

Now, before you start picturing Wesley as some rogue reformer thumbing his nose at the institutional church, you need to understand something crucial. Wesley *loved* the church. As an ordained Anglican till he died, he saw himself not as a rebel but as an ally and servant of the established church. He defended it fiercely and remained loyal to it his entire life, refusing to form a new denomination. Why? Because he believed the church excelled at *centralization*—gathering, organizing, and holding ground. But Wesley also

---

23. John Hucks, "John Wesley and the Eighteenth Century Methodist Movement: A Model for Effective Leadership" (PhD diss., Regent University, 2003).

saw its weakness: the church of his day struggled with the *decentralization* necessary for *mobilization*. So he filled the gap.

The primitive Methodist movement echoed the early church in Jerusalem—centralized in the temple courts but scattered *from house to house*: "And the Lord added to their number daily . . ." (Acts 2:47). In short, Wesley didn't *abandon* the church but *activated* it.

Discipology teaches us not to replace or abandon existing or established churches but to empower them where they are. Discipology does not present a new model of church. It's model neutral. Jesus's Discipology rhythms are intended to activate believers *beyond the walls*, regardless of what happens *within* them. Here's the good news: If how the church gathers doesn't matter, then mobilization can happen in any church, regardless of the model or liturgy. That's what sets the mobilization model apart—it focuses not on how the church gathers but on how it scatters. A high liturgical Anglican parish can scatter just as effectively as a house church. A megachurch with LED walls can scatter using the same principles. Discipology doesn't focus on the centralization of the church, but the practice of decentralization that any church can engage in without ever changing its model. While the church gathers on Sunday with smells and bells, the people can be mobilizing in the community according to their unique gifts and passions. The church gathers like inhaling and scatters like exhaling. Both are necessary to breathing, and the bride that Christ breathed his last for comes in many shapes and sizes—reflecting Christ in a unique way. Discipology can be implemented in every church, network, or denomination because what matters most isn't the *form* the church takes when we gather but the *force* it becomes when we scatter.

This book centers on the exhale—our scattering—as a supplementary field guide to the mobilization movement; the New Testament itself being the primary handbook.

Mobilization Before Multiplication

Ignoring the Discipology flywheel hardwired into the Great Commission will derail mobilization before it ever gets moving. That's why we can't put the cart of multiplication before the mobilization horse. Multiplication won't produce mobilization any more than two eggs will mate to produce a chicken. Dave Ferguson, champion of both mobilization and multiplication publicly recognized this priority at Exponential 2024, when recounting a conversation with an investor who supported his vision of church multiplication. The investor's simple question: "Exponential is multiplying churches, Dave—but what kind of churches are they multiplying?" Ferguson reminded the multiplication community that multiplication alone, without an emphasis on the disciple-making DNA, runs the risk of multiplying nonmobilized churches, replicating inefficiency at scale. To back this, Exponential's latest research study points back to the priority of mobilization after twenty years of stellar multiplication work:

- Nineteen percent of churches are now shrinking.
- Forty-three percent of churches have plateaued.
- While seven percent are multiplying at level 4, zero percent are multiplying at level 5.[24]

The need for prioritizing mobilization is now more obvious than ever.

The definition of a level 5 church is one that has multiplied churches to the fourth generation, but it can't happen without mobilization as the driving force. In 2015, Exponential searched for level 5 multiplying leaders in America. After an extensive search, they could locate only one: Ralph Moore, founder of the Hope Chapel movement. After making disciples—three people at a time—for over fifty years, Moore's quiet mobilization sparked a movement that has now planted over 2,639 churches and counting, as a living proof of concept. Unlike Moore, few leaders are willing to slow down and invest precious time in a strategic few, like Wesley and Paul, but Moore proves it still works. To an age where ministry is presented as a marathon—with leaders trying to stay in the pulpit as long as possible, Moore ran a relay race, handing it off to the next generation as Jesus modeled. The difference is trying to be the hero versus what Dave Ferguson called the *hero maker*.[25]

---

24. *2025 Becoming Five Multiplication Study: Research Report* (Lifeway Research, 2025), 6–10.
25. Dave Ferguson and Warren Bird, *Hero Maker: Five Essential Practices for Leaders to Multiply Leaders* (Zondervan, 2018), 29.

Moore concludes that "You can plant a church and disciple-making doesn't necessarily happen. But when you make disciples, church planting always happens."[26] Let's reframe that: If church planting = multiplication, and disciple-making = mobilization, then Moore is saying this:

1. Multiplication doesn't produce mobilization.
2. But mobilization always leads to multiplication.
3. Therefore, *mobilization must come first.*

Aim at multiplication and you likely get neither. But aim at mobilization and you get both. If you focus on the result (multiplication), you'll ignore the cause (mobilization). Over his fifty years of ministry, Moore didn't focus on church planting to get 2,639 congregations planted—he focused on disciple-making. Ironically, the two movements that Moore has been influential in measured success by conversions (church growth movement), and by churches planted (multiplication movement), but rarely by mobilization.

Mobilization does not merely require a shift in strategy. This is a complete shift of paradigm.

But Jesus has a way of breaking paradigms and flipping our script. Counting churches without activating people will lead to spinning our wheels in the mud without ever gaining traction. If disciple-making was the very thing that gained the early church, then we have to make a choice. Alistair Begg once quipped to a room full of us pastors that "my fear is not that I'd fail, but that I'd succeed in the wrong things." We need to choose how we fail: by doing the right things clumsily as we chart a new course—or succeeding at the wrong things, while avoiding the Great Commission altogether. The statistics twenty years from now will tell one of two stories. The question is, What story will the mobilization movement tell?

To glimpse what our future could be, we look back to Acts for how the early church succeeded.

26. I heard Moore say this at a training event.

The First-Century Flywheel in Action

The early church went far and fast on the all-terrain, deep-tread tires of disciple-making. Paul gave us a glimpse of his mobilization strategy in 2 Timothy 2:2: "And the things you have heard me say in the presence of many witnesses entrust to reliable people who will also be qualified to teach others." Did you catch it? That's not just one generation of disciples—it's four. If level 5 multiplication spans four generations, it only happens with a disciple-making flywheel mobilizing people in a multigenerational strategy for movement. Let's break that verse apart to demonstrate:

Generation 1: Paul
Generation 2: Timothy
Generation 3: Reliable people
Generation 4: Others

Paul to Timothy. Timothy to reliable people. And those people to others. This level 5 mobilization led to explosive growth in the early church. Michael Cooper observes that the church was catalyzed "from a small band of 120 disciples between AD 27 and 29 to a movement of an estimated 95,000 by AD 67"—an eight-hundred-fold increase.[27]

This kind of fourth-generation disciple-making looks ahead to the next generation. It's always tempting to think that ministry is all about our giftings rather than the giftings of others. The problem is we die pretty quickly—blink and we miss it.

FOURTH GENERATION MOBILIZATION

2 TIMOTHY 2:2

PAUL → TIMOTHY → RELIABLE PEOPLE → OTHERS

27. Michael T. Cooper, *Ephesiology: A Study of the Ephesian Movement* (William Carey, 2020), chap. 2, Kindle.

I was barely older than Marty McFly when I started ministry at nineteen—but these days it's Doc Brown staring back at me in the mirror. And, like him, I keep thinking, "We've got to save the kids!" One of the clearest signs that we've failed at disciple-making is that we're losing the next generation fast. If we had been making disciples as Jesus intended, the youth wouldn't be slipping through our fingers but activated and engaged on mission. I don't have a time-traveling DeLorean, but it's not too late to train the next generation to make disciples with the generation after them. Generational transfer—the perpetual nature of disciple-making—is woven into the fabric of the New Testament itself, having been written largely by second-generation disciples.

Noodle on this: Two of the four gospels were written by members of the original Twelve, but Mark was a disciple of Barnabas. Luke was a third-generation disciple of Paul, who was discipled by Barnabas. That's half of the Gospels. Paul wrote more New Testament books than anyone, and Luke has the highest word count between Luke and Acts. Paul, who launched his mission at forty-five, handed the baton to the next generation—young leaders such as Luke, Timothy, Titus, and Epaphroditus, because the future depends on those who come after us. He understood that *mobilization is intrinsically about the next generation*. In fact, every epic story tells the same tale:

Without Neo, the Matrix controls humanity—but Neo needed mentoring from Morpheus.
Without Frodo, the Shire was lost—but Frodo required the guidance of Gandalf.
Without Luke, the Empire wins—but Luke was introduced to the Force by Obi-Wan.

Luke was the "new hope" the movie title refers to. And Obi-Wan, Gandalf, and Morpheus realized they weren't the answer themselves, but the next generation was. That's why Jesus mobilized young people. Churches in the West aren't shrinking simply because people are leaving—but because we've failed to mobilize the next wave to carry it forward. Without first-century practices, we fail to see first-century results.

But it's not too late.

If we learn disciple-making in the way of Jesus, mobilization will take place. He didn't require his church to invent something new but to implement something timeless. This chapter has answered the *what* and *why* of disciple-making, but to answer the *how*, there's only one place left to turn—to Jesus himself, the Master disciple-maker.

CHAPTER 2

The Discipology of Jesus

When you change the way you look at things, the things you look at change.

—MAX PLANCK

What exactly is Discipology? If you've never heard the term before, you're not alone. The necessity for words to be invented arises when something is missing in the conversations about a topic—when the existing words we're using to discuss it have been hijacked or lost their meaning. When using the same glossary but different dictionaries, that word is broken. Because we've strayed so far from Jesus's framework of disciple-making, a new word is needed. That word is *Discipology*.

The suffix *-ology*, meaning "study" or "science," comes from the Greek word *logos*, which has a wide range of meanings such as "word" or "reason." It can also mean "rationale," "principle," or "structure." We apply it to everything from biology (the study of life) to psychology (the study of the mind). Discipology, then, is the art and science of making disciples. The science of disciple-making is drawn from the specific principles Jesus consistently followed as he made disciples. As I stated in *Church Plantology*,

> Inventors take credit for what they've created. Scientists make discoveries. The pioneers of the scientific method didn't see themselves as inventing

> anything. Johannes Kepler is credited with saying, "Science is the process of thinking God's thoughts after him." Isaac Newton echoed Kepler, saying, "This most beautiful system of the sun, planets, and comets, could only proceed from the counsel and dominion of an intelligent and powerful Being." Rather than their science positioning them to invent new theories, their belief that everything had an intelligent design positioned them to "rediscover" what God had hidden. Thus, properly understood, a discovery is uncovering something that was already there.[1]

In disciple-making, our "scientific" discoveries are just the principles of God's original design.

Thankfully, making disciples isn't all science—it's also a lived experience, and that's where the art of it comes into play. Science gives you the rules, but art gives you the freedom. While the principles of disciple-making are fixed—rooted in Jesus's method—the expression is fluid, shaped by culture, context, and creativity. Jesus didn't expect us to reinvent the mission, yet he provided margin for reimagining mobilization on the ground. That's just time-tested missionary thinking. Faithfulness to the scientific principles of Time, Teaching, and Tactics should not feel like rigid repetition but artistic application. Therefore:

Science = The Principles

Art = The Application

In this way, disciple-making is both the process of scientific rediscovery and artistic innovation. Innovation in any field is a blend of mastery and creativity—first we learn the principles, then we find fresh ways to apply them. A chef respects what ingredients do (science) but experiments with the combinations (art) to draw out new flavors. As Mike Peters of The Alarm once said, "The exciting thing about writing any song is that there is a finite set of

1. Peyton Jones, *Church Plantology: The Art and Science of Planting Churches* (Zondervan, 2021), chap. 1, Kindle.

notes, but an infinite set of possibilities in how you arrange them."[2] God may have prepared good works for us to walk in before the foundation of the world (Eph. 2:10), but as we step into them, the unique expression of our calling becomes poetry in motion.

The Genius of Discipology

Jesus was a genius in disciple-making, and the brilliance of his Discipology was that he didn't lay down the three rhythms just for the Twelve—he modeled them for us through the Gospels. We can observe his patterns of *time*. We can assimilate his principles of *teaching*. We can apply his *tactics* of a lived-out blueprint. If Discipology is the art and science of disciple-making, then Jesus was both scientist and artist. He modeled the Discipology framework as a rhythm—flexible and relational—something that can be adapted by real people in real time today.

Without that to guide us, the alternative is what C. S. Lewis has observed—our tendency to make things up: "We have all departed from that total plan [of Christianity] in different ways, and each of us wants to make out that his own modification of the original plan is the plan itself."[3] This results when theorists attempt to write books about practitioner subjects like disciple-making, making you book smart but sidewalk stupid. Learn from a theorist and you'll think great thoughts. Learn from a practitioner and you'll do great things. Rediscovering Jesus's framework will replace our own ideas of what we think he did.

Rediscovering the Principles of Discipology

If Discipology is the science of uncovering what was already there, it's no surprise others have rediscovered it too. If I'd made up the rhythms of time, teaching, and tactics, nobody else would've seen them—but others have. I've

2. "Mike Peters of the Alarm Talks Cancer Battle and New Album 'Forwards,'" posted June 14, 2023, by Yahoo Entertainment, YouTube, https://www.youtube.com/watch?v=6QYFT9IX3Pc.
3. C. S. Lewis, *Mere Christianity* (HarperOne, 2001), 218.

long held the conviction that if God is speaking to one knucklehead, he's probably speaking to several. For example, John Mark Comer's work *Practicing the Way* reduces the disciple-making process to three outcomes: (1) become like him, (2) think like him, and (3) act like him. Todd Wilson, in his book *More: Find Your Personal Calling and Live Life to the Fullest Measure*, identifies three elements as well: be, do, and go.[4]

There are obvious parallels of their frameworks with Discipology:

DISCIPOLOGY	PRACTICING THE WAY	MORE
Time	Become Like Him	Be
Teaching	Think Like Him	Do
Tactics	Act Like Him	Go

John Blanchard's *Lead Like Jesus* uses the tags *heart*, *head*, and *hands* to describe holistic discipleship. Hugh Halter echoes the same model: "There are three areas we can focus on: The Head (mind) of Jesus: having the same focus as Christ and viewing the world as he does. The Heart of Jesus: allowing our hearts to break over the things that break Jesus's heart. The Hands (mission) of Jesus: embodying the good news of Jesus and doing the work of God on earth."[5] Practitioners across the globe recognize the three essential elements for making disciples and mobilizing the body of Christ. Though the art of disciple-making may vary in expression, the science remains constant. After all, scientific laws are grounded in repeatable observations—reality that plays out in front of our eyes. We can depend upon the law of gravity. We count on the laws of thermodynamics because they've been observed so consistently that we can base our actions upon their reliability.

Disciple-making has the same relationship with reality. Just as the Creator established the laws that govern the universe, Jesus embedded a design into disciple-making—one he's been waiting for us to rediscover. Jesus didn't just

---

4. Todd Wilson, *More: Find Your Personal Calling and Live Life to the Fullest Measure* (Zondervan, 2019), 15.
5. Hugh Halter, *Righteous Brood: Making the Mission of God a Family Story* (100 Movements Publishing, 2023), chap. 5, Kindle.

experiment with different models and methods—he established the laws of disciple-making in his day, repeatedly validated over two thousand years, across cultures, generations, and every revival.

TIMELINE	RHYTHM	OUTCOME
Year 1	Time	Character transformation via relationships
Year 2	Teaching	Learning principles and praxis through training
Year 3	Tactics	Activation and deployment on practical mission

An Overview of Jesus's Three Years

The previous chapter unpacked the *what* and *why* of disciple-making. But the *how of disciple-making is revealed* in the timeline of Jesus's ministry through the three rhythms. The challenge of seeing this clearly is that the New Testament doesn't present his three-year journey in clear chronological order. This is because each gospel writer had a unique purpose in writing, shaping their narratives around theological aims that determined their framework rather than a strict timeline. For example, A. B. Bruce observes that Matthew, as an accountant, groups things together topically.[6] Matthew wanted to present Jesus as the Messiah to a Jewish readership by demonstrating how he fulfilled the Law and the Prophets. Mark shifted from presenting Jesus as the Jewish Messiah to a global Savior, writing to a gentile audience. John wrote evangelistically about the Word, revealing him through conversations. Luke wanted to fill in some of the gaps left by the other gospel writers and produce "an orderly account," yet his gospel falls short of an extensive chronology (Luke 1:3). Because the gospels were written at different times for different audiences, and not as a comprehensive chronological sequence of events, doesn't mean that the chronology doesn't matter. If we want to see what things Jesus did in sequential order to train the Twelve, we have to do some digging. Having a working order of Jesus's ministry provides a mental map of his strategy. Rather than hiding

6. A. B. Bruce, *The Training of the Twelve: How Jesus Christ Found and Taught the 12 Apostles; a Book of New Testament Biography* (1871; Pantianos Classics, 2018), chap. 3, Kindle; Gleason L. Archer, *Encyclopedia of Bible Difficulties* (Zondervan, 1982), 335.

his method, he embedded it in the Gospels—waiting to be rediscovered by those who see his timeline not as a collection of stories but as a framework.

Each gospel writer offers a unique vantage point, but when we harmonize the accounts, a distinct three-year pattern emerges. From beginning to end, Jesus led his disciples through a relational progression of formation in year 1, training in year 2, and deployment in year 3. Each year of Jesus's ministry emphasized one of the core rhythms—time, teaching, and tactics—forming a deliberate progression in how he made disciples.

- Year 1: He spent *time* with a small group of disciples, getting to know them, helping them to become disciples.
- Year 2: He *taught* them on mission, modeling how to reach others and training them for their ministry to be "fishers of people."
- Year 3: He used *tactics* to send them on mission, going out ahead of him.

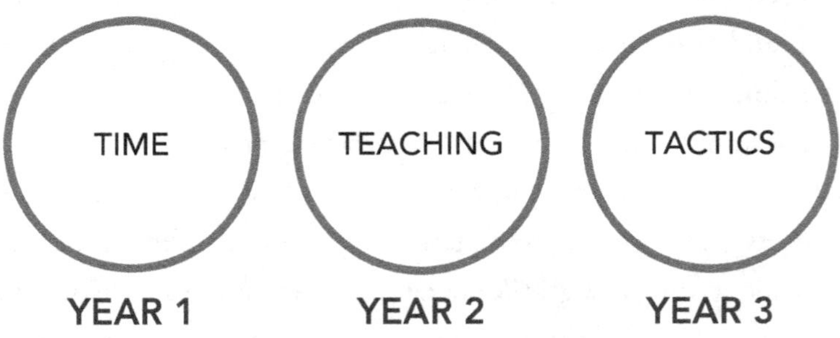

The precise order pieced together from the Gospels is intentional. Jesus crafted an immersive experience for his disciples, with each year building on the last. In the first year, he invited them to simply *be with him*. In the second, he trained them for mission *on the move*. Finally, in the third, he sent them out, *without him*, to tactically practice what he'd modeled in the second year. That's the heart of Discipology and the key to solving the church's mobilization problem.

Jesus designed disciple-making to be a journey—each step moving deeper into the three rhythms. Let's take a closer look at how Jesus lived out Discipology—and how his three-part framework still shapes disciples today.

What follows is a simplified overview of that timeline:

TIME	BEGINNING OF YEAR	MIDDLE OF YEAR	END OF YEAR
Year 1: Time	Jesus meets the first 6 disciples (John, Andrew, Peter, James, Philip, Nathaniel)	Jesus settles into Capernaum to be near the disciples	The first 6 disciples accompany Jesus on the weekends on a preaching circuit in Galilean synagogues
Year 2: Teaching	Jesus calls the 6 to go on mission with him (including the four fishermen who leave their nets). He soon calls Matthew.	Jesus fills the year with preaching the gospel, healing, exorcising demons, and dealing with large crowds	Jesus separates the Twelve from the other disciples, calling them apostles (or "sent ones")
Year 3: Tactics	Jesus sends the 12 apostles out on mission for 3–4 months	Jesus provides opportunities for hands-on miracles to be done by the Twelve	Jesus sends the 72 on mission to Galilee and Judea, then to Samaria

It's important to first step back to see the thirty-thousand-foot overview of Jesus's Discipology rhythm during his incarnation before zooming in on each year in the three sections of the book.

Year 1: The Time Year

Straight after his baptism, Jesus quietly called six of the Twelve and invited them into his life. Instead of rushing into public ministry, he settled into the fishing village of Capernaum, where life moved at the pace of a community of 1,500 people. On weekdays, they lived life together, sharing meals and Jesus's rhythms of normal life. On weekends, they traveled on daylong journeys as Jesus preached in nearby synagogues, fostering friendships, laughing, and learning. Significant events that first year were attending the wedding at Cana and making the pilgrimage to Jerusalem together for Passover. More than anything, this was a year of relationship and presence. Jesus slowed down, not because he was doing less, but because the foundation of disciple-making is built on relationships—and relationships take time. It wouldn't be until year 2 that Jesus started his public ministry as we know it.

Year 2: The Teaching Year

At the dawn of the second year, Jesus announced that he was going on a preaching mission, and he invited the disciples to join him as apprentices. The day before, the four fishermen needed help pulling in the miraculous netload of fish. Jesus would likewise need help pulling in the dragnet of souls over the next year and urged them to leave Capernaum. "Follow me," he said, "and I will make you fishers of people." It was no longer just about being *with* him but about becoming *like* him. The second year would be about their training. Mere spectators that year, they watched miracles unfold, witnessed demons cast out, saw lives restored, and listened as he proclaimed the good news of the kingdom to the lost and the broken. Through every encounter and every moment of that year, watching the Master at work, they learned, not in theory but through real-world situations, how to make disciples,

Year 3: The Tactical Year

Just as it had kicked up a notch in the second year, in year 3 everything accelerated again. At the end of year 2, Jesus picked twelve and called them his "apostles," or sent ones. Their time spectating was done. It was time for them to be activated and sent out to do the things they witnessed. That final year is bookended by two major deployments—two mission journeys—the sending of the Twelve at the beginning, then the sending of the seventy-two at the end. Between these two missionary journeys, Jesus engineered increasingly complex situations for the disciples to step into, such as feeding thousands of people and collecting temple tax from the mouth of a fish. Peter walked on water. Miracles came from their hands. These weren't random moments but intentional on-the-job training—an opportunity to get their feet wet and their hands dirty. Like a mama bird, Jesus pushed them out of the nest to teach them to fly, for in that final year, Jesus was upping their reps to prepare them for what they'd be doing in Acts. The Tactics rhythm was preparing them for Jesus's departure.

The Importance of the Invitation

Those three years would have been a massive ask of anybody, and Jesus didn't expect instant readiness. Instead, he led them step-by-step, at the benchmark of each successive year, making a deeper call of commitment, a deeper invitation. Each year would require greater investment on their part. Each stage more disruptive, more daring, and more transformative than the one before. In *The Training of the Twelve*, A. B. Bruce highlights these three stages of commitment:

> The twelve arrived at their final intimate relation to Jesus only by degrees, three stages in the history of their fellowship with him being distinguishable. In the first stage they were simply believers in him as the Christ, and his occasional companions at convenient, particularly festive, seasons. . . . In the second stage, fellowship with Christ assumed the form of an uninterrupted attendance on his person, involving entire, or at least habitual abandonment of secular occupations. . . . The twelve entered on the last and highest stage of discipleship when they were chosen by their Master from the mass of his followers, and formed into a select band, to be trained for the great work of the apostleship.[7]

Jesus modeled that because of the great sacrifice disciple-making requires, it should never be forced or assumed. Jesus never dragged the Twelve into anything—he *invited* them. "Follow me" was an invitation. Jesus's layers of discipleship and renewed invitations each year demonstrated that the disciple-making relationship should happen only when there is a mutual understanding. Disciple-making starts with the same posture, recognizing that people grow best when they *choose* to step in. Jesus understood that, as in any coaching

7. Bruce, *Training of the Twelve*, chap. 2.

or mentoring relationship, permission must be asked and granted—because without trust disciple-making becomes little more than the white noise of suggestion.

That's why clarity from the outset is essential. Entering a disciple-making relationship presumptuously will lead to resentment. The lack of a mental contract or mutual understanding causes what Patrick Lencioni warns about—unshared expectations that lead to shared frustrations.[8] The disciple-making relationship needs to be defined. For example, Paul and Barnabas treated each other as partners and equals, yet Paul treated Timothy like a son. Different relationships have different dynamics, and these dynamics matter. Permission should never be assumed but rather asked for and granted.

Permission in making disciples does a few things for the person receiving our investment:

1. The permission granted postures the person to receive the necessary assessment, coaching, and training in a non-defensive manner.
2. The permission granted also establishes the disciple-maker as somebody who is, in fact, more experienced or qualified to give advice, and therefore able to speak into the situation of the person being discipled.
3. The permission granted establishes a respectful boundary. Although the time of both parties is valuable, it establishes respect for the disciple-maker's time and knowledge. It allows the person being discipled to recognize that this time is for the disciple's good, and not for the disciple-maker.[9] The disciple-maker is there to develop the disciple, and, therefore, it is different from a friendship. The disciple isn't doing the disciple-maker a favor, and that understanding evokes the gratitude necessary in any student, whether in martial arts, carpentry, or disciple-making.

---

8. Lencioni, writes about the absence of trust in *The Five Dysfunctions of a Team.*
9. Because this also applies to mentorship, it's included under the broader category of permission giving. It should be noted, however, that mentorship and disciple-making are not equivalents, as the book will later explain.

Jesus's Three Invitations

Jesus started with the simple invitation "Follow me"—a low-commitment invitation, similar to "Come and see," raising the stakes each year of what it meant to follow him:

- In year 1, "Follow me" meant "Come spend time getting to know me."
- In year 2, "Follow me" meant "Come train or apprentice with me."
- In year 3, the invitation to follow was to "Go," or "Be sent by me."

In a world where hearts chase social-media-filtered inspiration instead of answering God's unfiltered call, this shift is sacred and essential. There is a give to gain, a sacrifice to secure the win. In *Star Wars*, Jedi trainees begin as padawans, a symbolic braid marking their status. After passing the Jedi trials, they're knighted—and eventually some graduate to masters. Jesus also had rites of passage for his followers, even different names across each year to mark their increasing levels of commitment—learners (or disciple) in year 1, *talmidim* in year 2, and apostles in year 3—each of which we will unpack.

Year 1: The Invitation to Spend Time

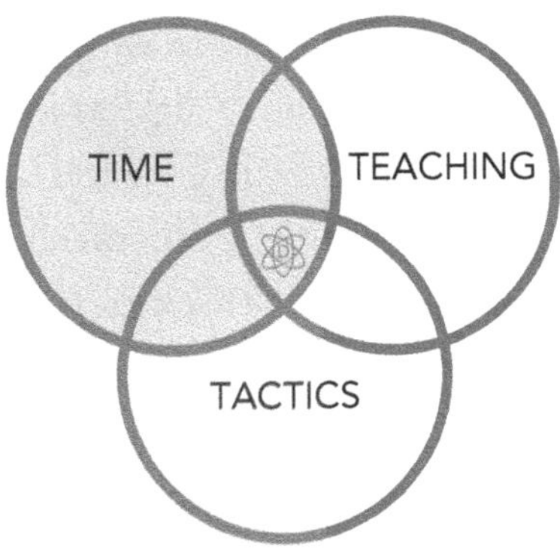

Jesus wasn't weird. He didn't ambush twelve unsuspecting men with an immediate call to global mission. Instead, he started small with a simple invitation: *Get to know me.* That's where Discipology begins—relationship. John's gospel doesn't open with preaching or performing miracles, but with *introductions.* Six young men met Jesus in a string of quiet, relational moments. Effective disciple-making starts not with strategy but with connection. The right thing at the wrong time is still the wrong thing. Therefore, before mission, there must be relationship. Before disciples are sent, they need to be seen. This is why Jesus focused on their knowing him personally before he sent them out to make him known to others.

Knowing and being known is the theme of John 1, which chronicles Jesus's first year of ministry. After John the Baptist publicly identified Jesus as the Lamb of God, John and Andrew trailed behind him—curious and compelled, half stalking and half awestruck—just trying to see what he would do next and where he was headed.

Then Jesus suddenly turned around.

"What are you seeking?" he asked. Maybe it came with a wry grin, but that loaded question stopped them in their tracks either way. That was an unfair question—because at the beginning nobody knows what they're seeking. Not fully, and not yet.

Caught off guard, they fumbled for a response. "Um . . . Rabbi, where are you staying?" It wasn't eloquent, but through the awkwardness of the moment, when they only wanted to know more *about* him, Jesus wanted them to know *him*.

Extending a personal invitation to dinner to accomplish this, Jesus said, "Come and see." They talked late into the night as Jesus demonstrated that disciple-making is not transactional by nature but *relational*. Accepting the invitation to the timeless act of sharing a meal, still one of the most intimate ways to get to know someone, they embarked on the first steps of their disciple-making journey. From there, the invitation expanded to others within their circle as Jesus bid Peter, James, Philip, and Nathanael: "Follow me." As each heeded the simple two-word invitation, they started a chain reaction that would flip their entire lives upside down.

John intentionally weaved the words *know* and *knowing* throughout each encounter as Jesus invited the next four disciples to know him, just as he *already* knew them. When Andrew brought Peter to Jesus, John recorded the moment like this:

> Jesus *looked at him* and said, "You are Simon son of John. You will be called Cephas" (which, when translated, is Peter). (John 1:42, emphasis mine)

That phrase "Jesus looked at him" means more than a glance—it's a studying gaze. After a pause, Jesus spoke: "You are Simon son of John." That alone likely startled Simon. How could this stranger know his name—let alone his father's? But then came something stranger still: "You *will be* called Peter."

Peter meant "rock"—a foundation stone aligned to a cornerstone—one that others could align *themselves* by. But Simon wasn't stable. He was impulsive and volatile—his emotions often got the better of him. That second name didn't describe him as he was. It described him as he would become. Jesus could see that Peter would long to be his closest and most devoted follower, stepping out onto the water to walk toward him, drawing a sword in the garden to defend him, and swearing at the Last Supper that even if all the other disciples denied Jesus, he never would. He was fiercely loyal, albeit flawed. Throughout the Gospels, Jesus often called him "Simon" when correcting him and "Peter" when calling him up. Jesus named both the man he was and the one he was becoming. That's the essence of discipleship—spending time with people with the aim of their transformation. And Jesus didn't do it with Simon alone.

Heading north to Bethsaida, Jesus found Philip, who then brought along Nathanael. Nathanael was skeptical:

> "Nazareth! Can anything good come from there?" Nathanael asked.
>
> "Come and see," said Philip." (John 1:46)

But when Nathanael walked up to Jesus, Jesus greeted him:

> "Here truly is an Israelite in whom there is no deceit."
>
> "How do you know me?" Nathanael asked. (John 1:47–48)

There it is again: How do you *know* me?

Nathanael didn't know Jesus, but Jesus knew Nathanael. That pattern continues: Jesus knows people *before* they know him. And he wants them to know him in return, so he extends the invitation "Follow me," or "Come and know me."

After these first six encounters, Jesus invited John, Andrew, Peter, James, Philip, and Nathanael to walk with him—literally. Inviting them along on a day's journey to a wedding in Cana created margin to become better acquainted. His uncanny knowledge of them must have piqued their curiosity, because they accepted his invitation and went. The day's walk to Cana and the seven-day wedding celebration gave them nine days to talk, walk, eat, laugh, and share stories. Jesus wasn't just recruiting followers; he was making friends. That's where disciple-making starts: *by making friends.*

That first year's investment on the part of the disciples was a low-level ask. Jesus didn't demand they abandon their homes or careers. Not yet. After their nine-day trip, they returned to their nets, and Jesus returned home with them to Capernaum, settling into the community—embedding himself in their world. He lived there for most of that year, traveling to nearby synagogues and journeying to Jerusalem for feasts, spending time as they trekked the dusty Galilean roads.

Up till this point, following Jesus was low pressure and high proximity. Instead of rushing them on mission, he invited them into discovery—giving them space to uncover who he was. Mike Reeves asks, "Have you ever known someone so magnetically kind and gracious, so warm and generous of spirit that just a little time spent with them affects how you think, feel and behave? Someone whose very presence makes you better—even if only for a while, when you are with them?"[10] Jesus allowed the Time rhythm to work the slow burn of transformation, moving at the speed of relationship.

Similarly, the moment someone responds to our invitation to "come and see," they begin to experience the presence and character of Christ up close through us. As they walk with us—just as the Twelve walked with him—they start to believe that they could become more than they are. As Christ reveals

10. Michael Reeves, *Delighting in the Trinity: An Introduction to the Christian Faith* (IVP Academic, 2012), chap. 1, Kindle.

himself through our brokenness, they see that someone like *Simon, son of John*, could actually become *Peter the rock*, giving them hope for themselves.

In summary, Jesus's first-year invitation involved the following:

- An invitation into a relationship
- An invitation to mutual discovery—getting to know him and being known by him
- An invitation to imagine a transformed identity, as with Simon becoming Peter

Year 2: The Invitation to Make Disciples

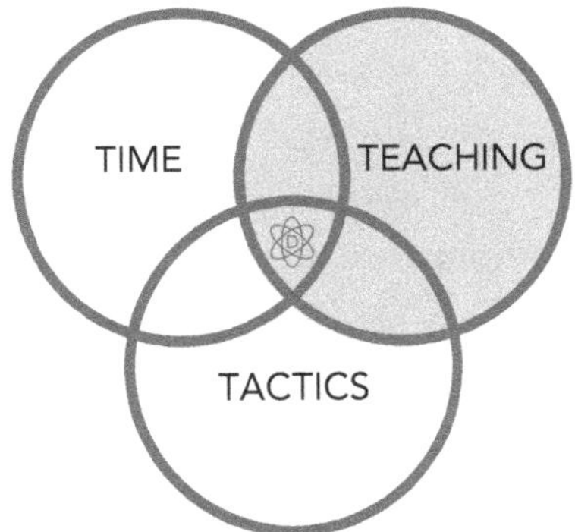

The disciple's second year of following Jesus started with an invitation to go beyond companionship and curiosity and into commitment.

Early one morning, after a long, fruitless night of fishing, four of them—Peter, Andrew, James, and John—were tending their nets on the Sea of Galilee. In the misty gray dawn on the banks of the sea, Jesus called out to them to throw their nets on the other side of the boat. Peter, weary and near exhaustion, yet respectful, hesitated. He remembered the two miracles he'd already seen and responded, "Nevertheless, because you say so . . ." Immediately upon being submerged, the nets exploded with fish—so many the boats began to sink.

Jesus had their attention now.

Then he said the words that changed everything:

> Follow me, and I will *make you* fishers of men. (Matt. 4:19 ESV, emphasis mine)

This wasn't just a call to follow. It was a call to be *formed*—to be made into something.

In Greek, there is just one word for disciple: *mathetes*, or "learner." They'd been learning as they followed him to preach in the synagogues that first year. But now he was offering them the chance to become what the Hebrews termed a *talmid*. Although its root word was "study," it had a deeper meaning—those who left everything to follow a rabbi. This was a different kind of "Follow me," the shift from casual to committed.

Contrast the differing levels of commitment:

- ***mathētēs*:** A Greek word found in the New Testament meaning "disciple," "student," or "learner." It emphasizes someone who is actively learning from a teacher—taking in knowledge and instruction. It's where we get the English word *disciple*.
- ***talmid* (plural: *talmidim*):** The Hebrew concept behind the Jewish disciple. This wasn't just a learner in the academic sense but someone who left everything behind to follow a rabbi, imitate his lifestyle, and one day become like him.

A *talmid* didn't just want to know what the rabbi knew—he wanted to *become who the rabbi was*. It was an immersive, life-on-life paradigm, requiring an utter surrender of all you were to become something else. And Jesus had promised to *make them into something*: "Follow me, and *I will make you* fishers of people."

Becoming a *talmid* was no small thing. It meant leaving your trade, your home, your future. The traditional blessing "*May you be covered in the dust of your rabbi*" described following so closely that the dust he kicked up clung to you. Leaving their nets cost them. Later, Peter would remind Jesus of his sacrifice: "We have left everything to follow you!" (Matt. 19:27; Mark 10:28).

He wasn't exaggerating. They had traded boats for roads, fish for people, and security for uncertainty.

That second-year shadowing Jesus the rabbi was immersive training—a privilege they'd never imagined for themselves. Walking with him through towns and villages as he healed the sick, cast out demons, fed crowds, and preached the kingdom, they were being trained—not in a classroom but on a mobile mission. Stanley Hauerwas and William Willimon put it this way: "Jesus invited ordinary people to come out and be part of an adventure, a journey that kept surprising them at every turn in the road."[11] Every miracle they witnessed served a dual purpose: to bless the person receiving it and to train the Twelve. Jesus ripped open their old paradigms and rebuilt a new framework—one shaped by kingdom thinking and hands-on mission. Jesus provided them a front-row seat to what to do and how to think differently. He unraveled their old assumptions and rewired them with kingdom instincts, preparing them for something they couldn't imagine. Nearly two years would pass before he fully tipped his hand and revealed the stunning truth behind their apprenticeship:

> Whoever believes in me will do the works I have been doing, and they will do even greater things than these. (John 14:12)

Year 2 was for training. But they'd have to wait until year 3 before Jesus unleashed them into the field—no longer just watching the mission but stepping into it.

In summary, Jesus's second-year invitation involved the following:

- An invitation to transition from follower to fisher
- An invitation to be made into something new
- An invitation to leave everything and be trained as *talmid*

---

11. Stanley Hauerwas and William H. Willimon, *Resident Aliens: Life in the Christian Colony*, expanded 25th anniversary ed. (Abingdon Press, 2014), 49.

Year 3: The Invitation to Send Disciples

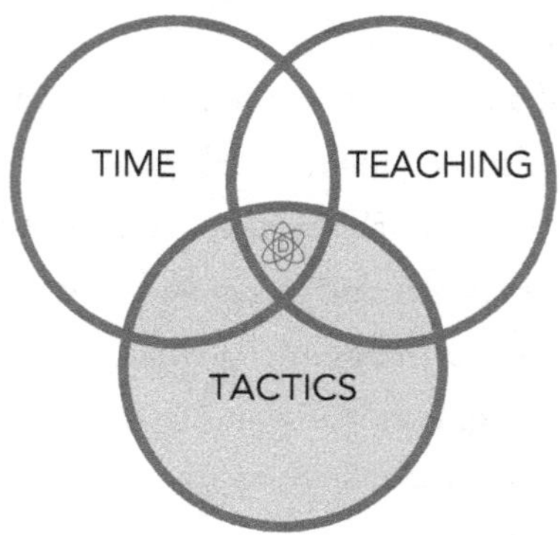

In year 3 the disciples would spend as much time away from Jesus as they spent close to him. That first morning of the final stage of their disciple-making started like any other morning. The dew still clung to the grass. The disciples stirred from sleep, rubbing the crust from their eyes, stretching beneath the early haze of the Galilean sun. Dust floated in the golden light. They blinked, yawned, and reached for cloaks and waterskins, expecting another ordinary day of travel, crowds, and teaching.

Then Jesus jolted them awake.

"No money. No bag. No spare tunic," he said. "You already have everything you need. I'll see you in a few months."

They stood there stunned—jaws slack, hearts pounding. Was he serious? Jesus wasn't just inviting them to follow anymore. He was telling them to *go*.

Jesus had ended the second year by tightening the circle and narrowing the field. The original six—Peter, John, James, Andrew, Philip, and Nathanael (also called Bartholomew)—had been joined by a wider group of disciples. Out of a larger number of disciples, he handpicked twelve of them and gathered them closer so that he could send them out. "He appointed twelve that they might be with him and that he might send them out to preach and to have authority to drive out demons" (Mark 3:14–15).

That one sentence contains all three rhythms of Discipology, revealing that Jesus had now overlapped the third and final rhythm in his training:

- **Time:** "That they might be with him"
- **Teaching:** "To preach and to have authority"
- **Tactics:** "That he might send them out"

This was both a summary of his strategy and a signal that their preparation was nearly complete. Gathering close to train and sending them out to multiply. It also marked a turning point in their identity. In Matthew 10:1–2, the shift is explicit. They are referred to as disciples in verse 1, but in verse 2 they are named "apostles" (*apostolos*, "sent ones" or "missionaries"). The metamorphosis was complete. They had been made into fishers of people, and it was time to push the boats out!

They had spent *time* with Jesus in year 1.

They had learned from his *teaching* in year 2.

Now it was time to learn *tactics* and be sent out.

That timing was no accident. He activated them by sending them—the missional equivalent of parentally nudging grown kids out of the house, knowing that if they stay too long, their maturity stalls. For maturity requires movement, and without that shove from the nest, the Twelve wouldn't have stretched their wings and learned to fly. Fearful and uncertain, they ventured out, but upon returning, they were still in awe of what happened: "Even the demons obeyed us! People were healed!" Their shock betrayed their doubt—they didn't feel ready. And Jesus didn't wait for them to. One of the greatest mistakes people make is waiting for confidence to come. And when it never does, they never go. That's why Jesus put more stock in courage than confidence. As the saying goes, "Courage is being scared to death but saddling up anyway."

Jesus intentionally bookended the third year with two major missionary journeys:

Mission journey 1: Sending the Twelve at the *beginning* of the year
Mission journey 2: Sending the seventy-two at the *end* of the year

These weren't one- or two-week mission trips. According to New Testament scholar Eckhard J. Schnabel, the two missionary journeys that year lasted approximately three to four months each, totaling six to eight months, the majority of Jesus's final year with them.[12] But the tactical focus continued during the intervening four to six months. During the interim, Jesus pulled the Twelve into hands-on supernatural ministry they had only witnessed from the sidelines in the second year.

BEGINNING OF YEAR	INTERVENING MONTHS	END OF YEAR
Sending of the 12	The 12 engage in supernatural ministry	Sending of the 72

The sending of the seventy-two required forming thirty-six more teams of two, in addition to the original six teams of two during the sending of the Twelve. Schnabel suggests these additional recruits may have come from the first missionary journey.[13] The implications? Their mobilization had already resulted in multiplication. The Twelve weren't just being discipled anymore—they were making disciples. Those sixty fledgling disciples were now being sent—shattering any illusion that Jesus's rhythms required a fixed three-year timeline. There is a parallel between Paul's outline of a fourth-generation strategy to Timothy to "entrust to reliable people who will also be qualified to teach others" (2 Tim. 2:2). Considering a level 5 mobilization pattern, four generations emerge:

---

12. Eckhard J. Schnabel, *Early Christian Mission Vol. 1: Jesus and the Twelve* (IVP Academic, 2004), 305–12. The mission of the Twelve would have been longer assuming that they stayed two nights, while the mission of the seventy-two would have covered more ground in a shorter time, despite the larger geographical area covered by the inclusion of southern Judea. Schnabel paints a scenario on the second missionary journey, in which thirty-six towns are visited to prepare "every town and village where he himself was about to go." Schnabel assumes that if Jesus did visit each one, spending one night, it would have been a minimum of thirty-six days (five weeks), not including travel, and if he spent the customary two nights, as he did in Sychar, then it would have been seventy-two days, not counting travel.
13. Schnabel, *Early Christian Mission*, 312.

First generation: Jesus
Second generation: The Twelve
Third generation: The seventy-two added disciples
Fourth generation: Those who would become disciples during the second mission

Jesus was no longer content to show them what he *could do*; he sent them out so they could discover what *God could do through them.* The Master disciple-maker deliberately let the weight of the impossible press on their shoulders so they'd lean on God's power alone. Take the feeding of the five thousand, which happened after the Twelve returned from their first mission. More than a miracle, it was a master class. Jesus let the bread miraculously multiply, not in his hands, but in *theirs.* His jarring command, "You give them something to eat" (Matt. 14:16), injected just enough panic to set in to activate them yet again. That entire year, Jesus worked hard to mobilize them from the sidelines to the front lines, because disciple-making has to eventually go from a spectator sport to a participatory sport. And getting us out of the bleachers and onto the pitch usually takes drastic measures.

In summary, Jesus's third-year invitation included the following:

- An invitation to scatter out
- An invitation to embark on Jesus's mission
- An invitation to rely on the power of the Holy Spirit

Jesus's Sequence of Invitations

TIMELINE	RHYTHM	INVITATION	OUTCOME
Year 1	Time	Invitation to know	Transformation through community
Year 2	Teaching	Invitation to train	Training in principles and praxis
Year 3	Tactics	Invitation to depart	Activation on mission

Where the Flywheel Turns

Dwight Eisenhower once said, "Farming looks mighty easy when your plow is a pencil and you're a thousand miles from a cornfield."[14] Because the Tactics rhythm of Discipology is the hardest, it has become the most neglected. Yet our disciples can't fully develop without hands-on mission. Why? Tactical engagement facilitates the activation of our gifting. Luke couldn't just listen to Obi-Wan's stories on repeat. Eventually he'd have to trust the Force himself and swing a lightsaber. Frodo had to set out from the safety of the Shire and bear the ring to Mordor. In each of these epic tales, the hero must eventually complete the journey after the mentor is gone. The goal of all disciple-makers is that their disciples develop enough to carry the mission forward without them. As with Jesus, it usually takes something drastic to start the flywheel turning to overcome the inertia of inaction. The day I opted to ditch the Sunday gathering in my inner-city church plant in Long Beach for a day, imitating Jesus's sending, they deployed into an urban park and something changed forever. They stopped merely repeating Jesus's words and began mirroring his actions.[15]

That was for adults. But if the flywheel is turning anywhere in your church, the most likely place is the youth group. Carefree and career-free, we don't hesitate to invite youth into deeper levels of commitment as Jesus did. Perhaps we instinctively expect youth ministry to be *formational* in ways we don't expect with adults. Youth ministry may not just be the most *biblical* ministry in our churches, it may also have the most potential.

That may be why Jesus built his movement on teenagers.

Most scholars agree that Jesus began his public ministry at around age thirty, the traditional age for a rabbi to begin formally recruiting disciples. But according to Jewish tradition, the Mishnah states that young men commenced studying Scripture at age five, the Mishnah at ten, and the Talmud at fifteen—at which point they could be selected by a rabbi.[16] If not, they were

---

14. Dwight D. Eisenhower, "Address at Bradley University, Peoria, Illinois," September 25, 1956, American Presidency Project, https://www.presidency.ucsb.edu/node/233210.
15. You can read more about tactical turning points for everyday disciples in my book *Reaching the Unreached: Becoming Raiders of the Lost Art* (Zondervan, 2017).
16. Pirkei Avot 5:21, Dr. Joshua Kulp, Sefaria, www.sefaria.org/Pirkei_Avot.5.21.

apprenticed into a trade. Which means that if Jesus followed Hebrew cultural custom, the disciples he chose were likely between the ages of fifteen and eighteen when he called them. Since eighteen was the age a male got married, and only Peter had a wife (Matt. 8:14), he was likely Andrew's older brother. Likewise, Matthew was likely around Peter's age due to his profession.[17]

If true, then the Gospels aren't just stories of grown men following a rabbi; they're stories of high schoolers flipping the world upside down before they could grow a full beard. It speaks volumes to the value Jesus puts on discipling the next generation. Consider if a disciple started at fifteen as per custom:

- At roughly fifteen, the disciples began following Jesus as learners or *mathētēs* (year 1).
- At roughly sixteen, they left their nets behind to join him on mission as a collective *talmidim* (year 2).
- At roughly seventeen, they went out on two short-term missions as apostles (year 3).
- By the time the Spirt comes upon them at Pentecost, they're roughly eighteen to twenty-one, leaving them to lead the church in Jerusalem—only just considered men by first-century standards.

If the Gospels are about high schoolers, and Acts is about college students, our priority must be on the next generation. And they *are* crying out for discipleship—hungry for practical training, deep community, and meaningful mission. The question is, Will we serve them?

This question will become increasingly important in the shadow of the approaching "silver tsunami," when churches shrink by attrition as the boomers die off, when congregations of thousands become assemblies of hundreds. As a trainer, I've consulted with multiple denominations for planter training, and all of them report dramatically reduced numbers of next-generation planters entering their pipelines. Seminaries report record lows in enrollment. This is a mobilization pipeline issue; the next generation is not being activated in

17. Tom Johnston and Mike Chong Perkinson, *The Organic Reformation: A New Hope for the Church in the West* (PraxisMedia, 2009), 73.

our churches to serve in the world. The danger for any institution is relevant to the church: "If your output exceeds your input, then your upkeep will be your downfall."[18]

Once again, mobilization must precede multiplication. Jesus intended the Discipology flywheel to address this bottleneck. Think of Discipology as a farm system—like in baseball—where the raw talent in young players is intentionally identified and honed for the big leagues. Jesus set up a long-range pipeline, and Paul followed his pattern to mobilize. So did Wesley with his circuit riders, designing the New Room in Bristol to be a circuit-rider factory. He designed the floor above the chapel with lodging rooms ringing the outer edge, joined together by a large central training room. They'd ride in on their horses, get trained between their circuit missions, and be deployed back out on their circuits in regular rhythms. If Wesley could design a building to serve the flywheel, surely we could adopt the rhythms to mobilize the youth in our churches, just like they did in the Great Awakening, the 1904 revival, and the Jesus movement—all youth movements.

The Keys to the Kingdom

They say the best time to plant a tree is twenty years ago—but the second-best time is right now.

So where do you start? Right where you are.

If you're just a Sunday attender, the first step is simple: Add the Time rhythm—commit to deeper community, like a small group where real life-on-life discipleship happens.

If you're already in a discipleship group, add the Tactics rhythm—*step onto the mission field*—even if just for a short-term trip.

It's always about stepping into the next rhythm or the one you're not currently operating in yet. Like Jesus, Discipology doesn't aim to rush people out on the first day, pushing them into awkward conversations with strangers. Jesus had a better way.

---

18. This saying is widely attributed to motivational speaker Jim Rohn.

So imagine with me for a minute what it might look like for you as a leader to start entering the three Discipology rhythms on a three-year track?

What would happen if, for the next year, you gathered twelve people—better yet, young people. Not for a Bible study, but to enter your *life*. You started with opening your home to them in groups. Brought them into the mundane parts of ministry for company in pairs so that you could talk. Invited them to family dinners and social events so that they became part of your everyday rhythms and social obligations, inviting them to watch you, ask questions, laugh and learn . . . just as Jesus did.[19]

Then in year 2 you invited them into ministry. Not just teaching them *about* ministry but letting them contribute as you prepared messages, shadowing you while visiting the sick, counseling the hurting, engaging the homeless. Meanwhile, you debriefed them about the accompanying principles behind your activities.

Then in year 3 you flipped the script. You sent *them*, deploying them to visit the sick and elderly, asking them to lead prayer meetings or open with a five-minute devotional. Preach. Start a home group with their peers. Engage missionally in public space.

What would you have after three years of this experiment?

You already know.

You'd have mobilization . . . because you focused on the flywheel.

---

19. Unfortunately, in today's world, I have to point this out: Always in groups with minors. Never alone. Please hear that this is to protect everyone and should be the norm anyway.

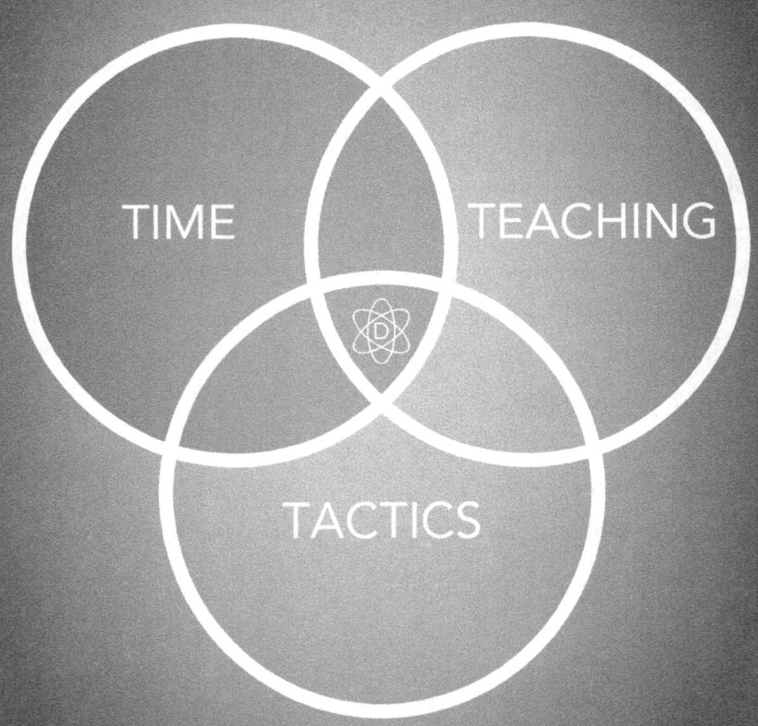
TIME
TEACHING
TACTICS
D

PART II

TIME—WHERE DISCIPLES ARE FORMED

The rhythm of Time is where roots sink deep and where character is shaped in the quiet grind of daily life. If we want to make disciples as Jesus did, we have to follow the pattern of his first year: go small, stay close, build relationships, and let time do its refining work.

In this book, each section focusing on a rhythm is made up of three chapters. The first chapter in a section analyzes what Jesus did that year to establish patterns. The second chapter extracts the principles. The third outlines the practices of that rhythm. For example, section 2 focuses on the Time rhythm in all three chapters, analyzing the patterns, principles, and practices of the Time rhythm. By tracing Jesus's movements, interactions, and priorities during the first year, *patterns* emerge that will reveal the *principles* to inform our *practices.*

The next three chapters will focus on the patterns, principles, and practices of the Time rhythm.

Chapter 3: Patterns of Time
Chapter 4: Principles of Time
Chapter 5: Practices for Time

CHAPTER 3

Patterns of Time

You can create a stronger movement with twelve disciples than with 1,200 consumers.

—ALAN HIRSCH

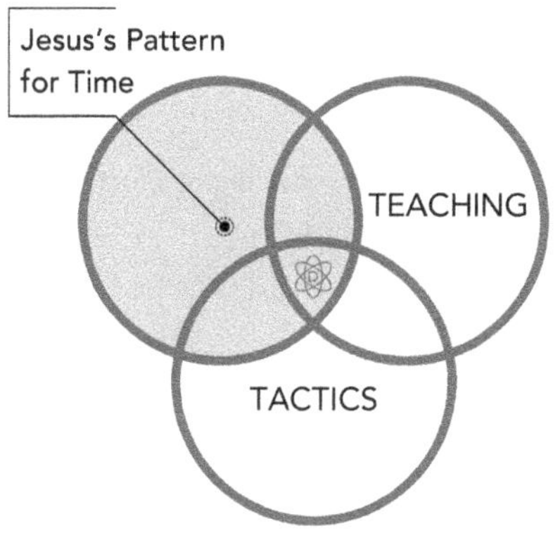

In his first year of public ministry, Jesus focused on the rhythm of spending *time* with the disciples, centering that year around establishing deep relationships with them. Because transformation is slow work, Jesus was in no hurry after his baptism. Rather than run fast or go big, he paced his life low and slow. That's why Jesus's first year of ministry after returning from his wilderness temptation is often called the year of obscurity. Only six of the Twelve—Peter, James, John, Andrew, Philip, and Nathanael—were called that first year. The other six wouldn't join until year 2. Without suggesting that Jesus slacked off that year, it's fair to say his early public ministry wasn't marked by high activity—and that was entirely by design.

This chapter won't unpack everything Jesus did during that year but will focus on what he did *consistently*. If we want to make disciples as Jesus did, we must make time.

Rather than a whirlwind of miracles or massive crowds during this year, the Gospels record Jesus living out the daily rhythms with his first six followers in the quiet fishing village of Capernaum. Schnabel notes, "Capernaum was the center of Jesus' public ministry in Galilee. . . . It was *his own town*."[1] But only recently so, since meeting John and Andrew—this was where they were from. Matthew marveled at Jesus's decision to put down roots in such a religiously obscure town bordering the edge of the gentile world, quoting Isaiah, who himself also marveled at God favoring the area:

> The Way of the Sea, beyond the Jordan,
> Galilee of the Gentiles—
> the people living in darkness
> have seen a great light;
> on those living in the land of the shadow of death
> a light has dawned. (Matt. 4:15–16)

Though Galilee spanned only about thirty miles in radius, most of Jesus's activity in year 1 happened within a four-by-six-mile pocket along the northwestern shores of the Sea of Galilee—a remarkably small footprint for a world-changing movement. In addition to the original six disciples being from this area, Jesus most likely chose this community as an ideal setting to invest in people far from the madding crowds. He settled down, adopting a domestic life, and limited his travels to itinerant speaking in unimpressive local synagogues to small Sabbath gatherings.[2] The few journeys he did take, such as to

1. Eckhard J. Schnabel, *Early Christian Mission Vol. 1: Jesus and the Twelve* (IVP Academic, 2004), 230.
2. Ray Vander Laan, In the Dust of the Rabbi Discovery Guide: Learning to Live as Jesus Lived, That the World May Know Series (HarperChristian Resources, 2015), introduction, Kindle.

the wedding in Cana along with the round-trip journey to Jerusalem and an unnamed feast, were all done with those six, keeping the focus on them.

The chronology and map illustrate how Jesus stayed hyperlocal, prioritizing deep relationships with his six newfound disciples before ever going public.

Mapping Jesus's First Year

Many Christians are surprised to learn that nearly a year passed between Jesus's first meeting with Andrew and John (John 1) and his call for them to leave their nets and follow him full-time (Matt. 4:18–20, Mark 1:16–18, and Luke 5:1–11). That second invitation to "follow me and I will make you fishers of people" came at the dawn of year 2, yet three of the four gospel writers begin at this point. All but John skip the details of the year of obscurity.

For example, Matthew places Jesus in Capernaum right after his temptation in the wilderness, but within six verses he's already leapfrogged into year 2. Mark jumps to Jesus's second year a mere fourteen verses into his gospel (Mark 1:14), and Luke follows suit. All three Synoptic Gospels (Matthew, Mark, and Luke) start with Jesus leaving Capernaum. John alone hits the brakes on the narrative to slow down and capture key moments from that overlooked first year. And it's a good thing he did. In that year, we are privileged with a rare backstage pass to the calling of the first six disciples (John 1), the wedding of Cana (John 2), conversations with Nicodemus during Passover (John 3), the woman at the well on the return journey home (John 4), and various glimpses into the quieter conversations when Jesus spent time walking closely with his first disciples.

The table below gives a chronology of Jesus's first year to place everything in context.

CHRONOLOGY OF JESUS'S FIRST YEAR

1
Dinner with John and Andrew *(John 1:39)* The first recorded moment of connection is a shared meal in the region of Perea.

2
Calling of Peter, James, Philip, and Nathanael *(John 1:40–51)* Jesus begins recruiting, mostly through relational networks, near the Sea of Galilee.

3
Wedding at Cana *(John 2:1)* Jesus brings his disciples to a wedding. He turns water into wine—reluctantly—and his disciples believe in him (John 2:11).

4
Retreat to the Sea of Galilee *(John 4:43–45)* After the wedding, Jesus retreats with his new disciples to decompress and bond.

5
Trip to Jerusalem for Passover *(John 2:13)* A festival pilgrimage leads to his first temple cleansing.

6
Return Through Samaria *(John 4:1–42)* A detour becomes a mission trip. Jesus shares the gospel with a Samaritan woman and spends two days with the locals.

7
Healing in Galilee *(John 4:46–54)* Jesus heals the centurion's servant from a distance in Cana.

8
Settles in Capernaum *(Matt 4:13)* He chooses this fishing village as his home base.

9
Rejection in Nazareth *(Luke 4:16–30)* In his hometown, Jesus refuses to perform miracles and reminds them that God's mercy often reaches gentiles first. They try to kill him.

10
Weekend Synagogue Circuit *(Luke 4:15)* Jesus begins preaching throughout the local synagogues in the region of Galilee, calling people to repent.

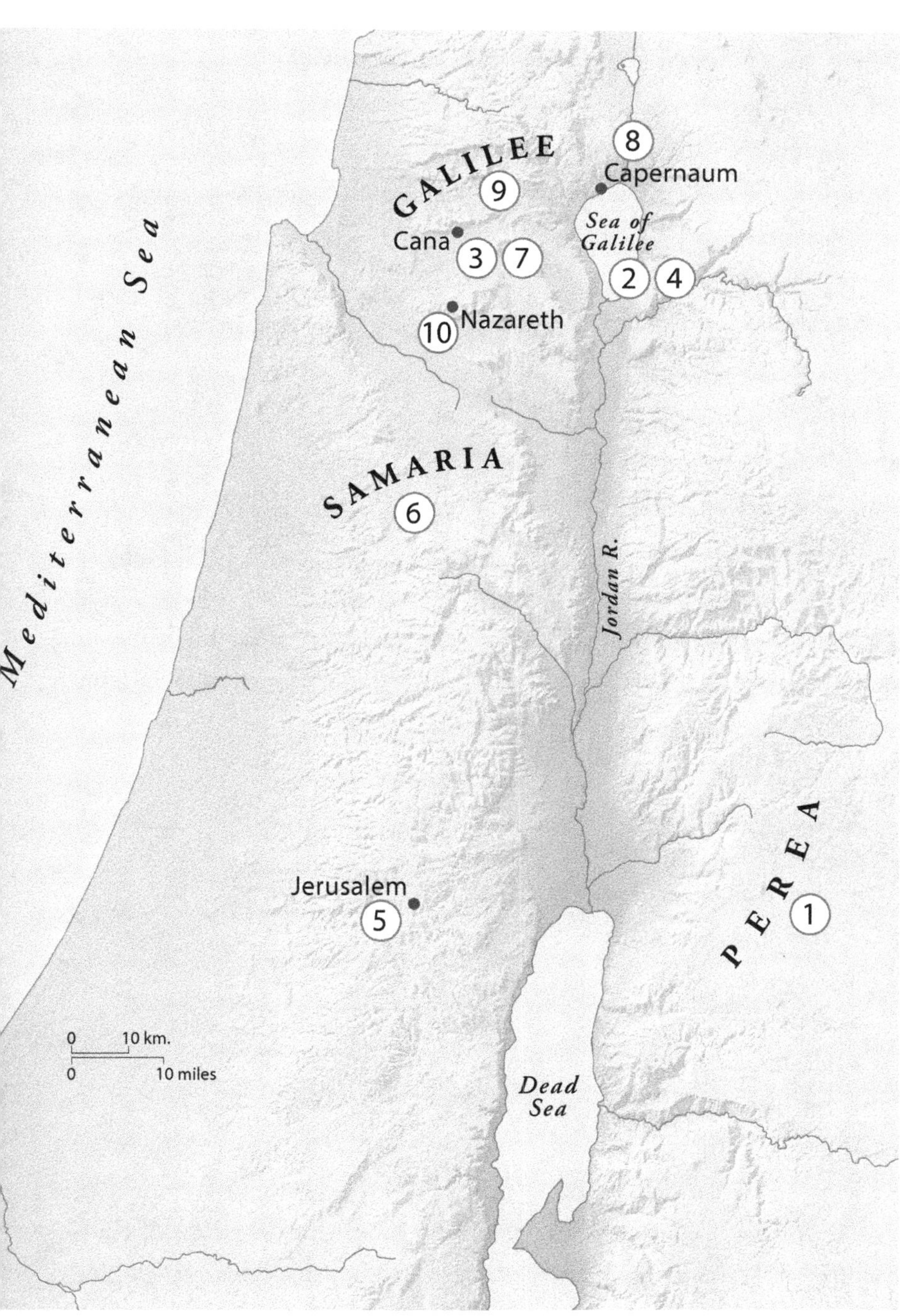
GALILEE
Capernaum
Sea of Galilee
Cana
Nazareth
Mediterranean Sea
SAMARIA
Jordan R.
PEREA
Jerusalem
Dead Sea
0 10 km.
0 10 miles
1
2
3
4
5
6
7
8
9
10

PATTERNS OF THE TIME CIRCLE

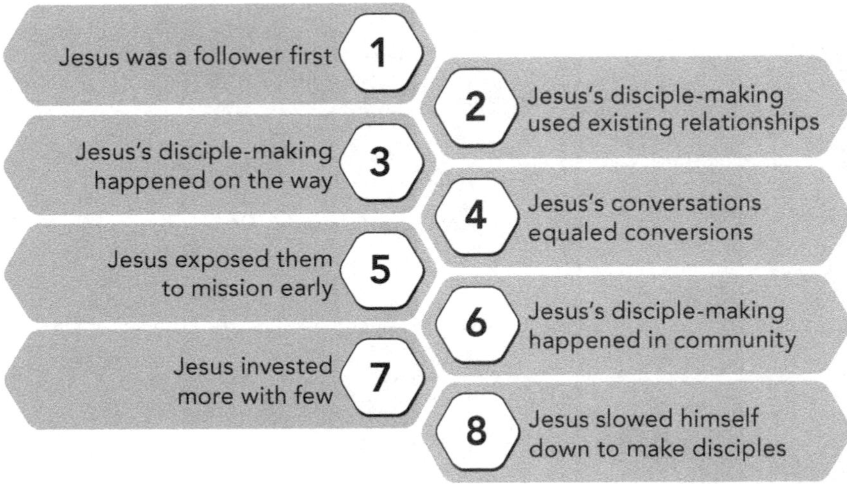

Reviewing the chronological map of Jesus's first year reveals his deliberate intention of starting slower to build deeper. In year 1 we witness Jesus doing the following:

- Eating meals
- Shadowing relationships
- Showing hospitality at a wedding
- Traveling to religious festivals
- Baptizing
- Retreating
- Healing on the road
- Settling in
- Preaching

During the first year, Jesus spent time in all three rhythms of time, teaching, and tactics, but focused on *time*. Those first six disciples gleaned the benefit of a more intimate relational rhythm with Jesus before the crowds and demands intensified in the second year, but that doesn't mean the others missed out—Jesus maintained the Time rhythm in year 2 but *added* the rhythm of Teaching. It was crucial that before sending them to make disciples, Jesus helped them *become* disciples first.

To illustrate, the chart below demonstrates that, although Jesus still operated in the rhythm of *Teaching* and *Tactics* during year 1, his emphasis that year was time:

The Three Rhythms in Jesus's First Year

TIME	TEACHING	TACTICS
Spends time with the Father in the wilderness (Matt 4:1–2, Luke 4:1–2)		
Eats dinner with John and Andrew (John 1:39)		
Travels to Galilee (John 1:43)		
Calls Peter and James (John 1:40–42)		
Travels to Bethsaida (John 1:43)		
Calls Philip and Nathaniel (John 1:45–49)		
Travels to Cana (one day) (John 2:1)		
Wedding of Cana (John 2:1)		Water turned to wine (reluctantly) (John 2:3–11)
Travels to Jerusalem (John 2:13)		Cleanses the temple (John 2:14–25)
Travels to the Jordan	Disciples baptize at Jordan (John 3:22)	
Slows down and sits on the well to talk with the woman	Debriefs on sower and harvester parable (John 4:35–38)	Speaks prophetically to the woman at the well (John 4:10–26)

To understand the strategic pace of Jesus's first year, we need to examine how he prioritized forming followers over compelling crowds.

Time Pattern 1: Jesus Was a Follower First

> Then Jesus was led by the Spirit into the wilderness to be tempted by the devil. After fasting forty days and forty nights, he was hungry. (Matt. 4:1–2)

> But Jesus often withdrew to lonely places and prayed. (Luke 5:16)

This *time* pattern of Discipology teaches us that Jesus's first disciple-making strategy was to pray to his Father. If Jesus's disciple-making was first and foremost relational, his first relationship was with God. Before Jesus ever preached a sermon, healed the sick, or called a single disciple, he spent forty days in the wilderness with his Father, anchoring himself in that relationship. Jesus modeled becoming a disciple before making them. Jesus would later term this "abiding" or "remaining" in him while walking through a vineyard, his hands tracing the vines as he moved, "I am the vine; you are the branches. . . . Apart from me you can do nothing" (John 15:5). Disciple-making doesn't start with our strategy but with surrender. That's why Jesus modeled being a follower before asking anyone else to become one.

The following verses highlight his reliance on the Father as a follower first:

> The Son can do nothing by himself; he can do only what he sees his Father doing. (John 5:19)

> I do nothing on my own authority, but speak just as the Father taught me. (John 8:28 ESV)

> The words I say to you I do not speak on my own authority. Rather, it is the Father, living in me, who is doing his work. (John 14:10)

This provides insight into Jesus's temptation in the wilderness, where Satan zeroed in on Jesus's dependency on his Father: "If you are the Son of God, tell these stones to become bread" (Matt. 4:3). Because self-reliance was at the heart of Satan's downfall, the Enemy tempted Jesus to rely on himself, to act on his own. Whereas Adam and Eve fell for it, Jesus didn't.

Those who desire to follow in Jesus's footsteps of disciple-making must start where he did: *in the wilderness with the Father.* Satan fears men and women who take the posture of fasting and prayer, surrendering their wills to God. Dwight Moody understood this and said, "The world has yet to see what God can do with a person fully consecrated to him. By God's help, I aim to be that person."[3]

Wesley echoed the same:

> Give me one hundred preachers who fear nothing but sin and desire nothing but God . . . and they alone will shake the gates of hell and set up the kingdom of heaven on earth. God does nothing but in answer to prayer.[4]

If the disciple-makers you're catalyzing have the journal, *Journey to Disciple-Making: A Discipology Journal*, this is where they would be asked on their disciple-making journey about prayer, to examine if they're making time to surrender to him.

Scan the QR code to explore the journal.

Time Pattern 2: Jesus's Disciple-Making Used Existing Relationships

> The first thing Andrew did was to find his brother Simon and tell him, "We have found the Messiah" (that is, the Christ). And he brought him to Jesus. (John 1:41–42)

3. Although this is attributed to Moody, it is originally a statement by Henry Varley, which inspired Moody.
4. John Wesley, *Letter to Alexander Mather, August 6, 1777*, in *The Letters of John Wesley, 1777*, Wesley Center Online, accessed September 20, 2025, https://wesley.nnu.edu/john-wesley/the-letters-of-john-wesley/wesleys-letters-1777/.

When Jesus invited those six young men to follow him, he was not starting from scratch but building on a *preexisting network of relationships*. Jesus leveraged a variety of existing relationships:

- Friends
- Family
- Coworkers
- Neighbors

John and Andrew were coworkers. Andrew and Peter were brothers. Philip and Nathanael were friends. The following year, when local taxman and financial touchpoint of the community Matthew joined the group, he added a fifth dynamic: commercial relationships. He was someone they did business with—albeit reluctantly.

Jesus harnessed these connections because relationships take time, and much of the foundational groundwork of these relationships had been established. These weren't strangers off the street but men who had already toiled through long nights at sea and shared real-life burdens together. There was history, trust, and camaraderie. Jesus saved valuable time by using the human threads of friendship and familiarity to weave eternal bonds. As Paul Tripp observes, "Your relationships are a place where the kingdom has come, and they are intended to attract others to the King."[5]

And here's the wild part: *Jesus didn't even recruit all six disciples.* He called three: John, Andrew, and Philip. And they recruited the remaining three:

- John brought James to Jesus.
- Andrew brought Peter to Jesus.
- Philip brought Nathaniel to Jesus.

Peter, James, and Nathanael being invited by other disciples—that's disciple-making in action before any formal training began. In every

5. Timothy S. Lane and Paul David Tripp, *Relationships: A Mess Worth Making* (New Growth Press, 2008), chap. 15, Kindle.

disciple-making relationship I've ever established, someone eventually asks, "Hey, can my brother or friend join us?" That's the natural pull of relational momentum in action.

Time Pattern 3: Jesus's Disciple-Making Happened on the Way

Jesus didn't meet his disciples at a set time every week at the local coffee shop, but rather integrated time with his disciples into the rhythms of what he was already doing. That is to say, he made disciples on the way.

Looking at the map of Jesus's travels, it's evident that he and his first six followers clocked serious mileage on the odometer: approximately 1,000 to 1,500 miles in that first year. After the wedding in Cana, Jesus and his small band traveled to Jerusalem to observe the Passover—a 180-mile round-trip journey from Galilee to Jerusalem, back through Samaria, and all throughout the Galilean region to arrive back in Cana. Traveling together created space for bonds to quickly form as they do when you walk a path for days, swapping stories and huddling around the same campfire. Jesus must have calculated the mileage in both distance and the value of intentional time together. Their journey was more about what happened *on the way*, their travels creating margin for disciple-making.

The chart below calculates the staggering number of estimated days they traveled that first year:

JOURNEY	ESTIMATED MILES	ESTIMATED DAYS	SCRIPTURE REFERENCES
From Nazareth to the Jordan River for baptism	30–60 miles	2–4 days	Matthew 3:13, John 1:29–34
From the wilderness to Galilee after temptation	60–70 miles	3–5 days	Luke 4:14, John 1:43
Ministry tour around Galilean towns and synagogues	150–200 miles	8–13 days	Luke 4:31–44, Matthew 4:23

JOURNEY	ESTIMATED MILES	ESTIMATED DAYS	SCRIPTURE REFERENCES
Trip to Jerusalem for Passover	85–90 miles (one way)	5–6 days	John 2:13
Return to Galilee via Samaria	90 miles	5–6 days	John 4:3–42
Ongoing movement around Galilee	100–200 miles	7–13 days	Matthew 8–9

They spent thirty to forty-seven days on foot that first year alone. That's *one to two months of their lives* simply walking from town to town together. Every step, every mile was time to talk, laugh, question, teach, and bond, as much by throwing things at the campsite snorer, as by having spiritual conversations on the road. Road trips like these ensure that dumb comments become inside jokes for the next hundred miles. As a former firefighter, I can testify that groups of men confined together for days is a formula equal parts chaos and comedy. To illustrate the bonding nature of their humor, the group picked up a disciple named Judas in the second year. One can imagine that he kept answering when the other Judas was called, so he was given the nickname "Thaddeus." Despite the etymology of the name being uncertain, it comes from the Aramaic *taddā'*, meaning "heart" or "breast." Today, we might say "milk baby." And in a group of teenage boys, that would stick, especially if he had a baby face or an idiosyncrasy that made him an easy target of ribbing. Another later disciple was nicknamed Didymus, which means "the twin." Scholars surmise he looked identical to another disciple or even Jesus himself, but we know him more commonly as Thomas. From a distance you can hear the laughter and jokes flying as the disciples approached, kicking up dust. As C. S. Lewis remarks about people who read into everything as serious, "Say what you like . . . the world is sillier and better fun than they make out."[6] The same applies to the Gospels.

In the Greek, the Great Commission—to go and make disciples—is actually

6. C. S. Lewis, Letter to Owen Barfield, April 4, 1949, in *Letters of C. S. Lewis*, ed. W. H. Lewis and Walter Hooper (HarperOne, 2017).

an aorist participle, which more literally conveys the idea "as you are going" or "as you go."[7] This participle sets the scene, showing when or how we make disciples: while we're on the move, in the marginal spaces between religious dealings. The Time rhythm often feels more like "hanging out" than spiritual work, but appearances can be deceiving. My own discipleship took place in the home of my youth pastor who (between the spaces of radical mission reaching the LGBTQ community and hosting punk shows for kids with broken lives, where we witnessed miracles and exorcisms) opened his home, fridge, and life. Those late-night hours decompressing on his sofa, in between busting a gut heckling music videos on TV before Beavis and Butt-Head ever existed, were as formative in my disciple-making as any front-line mission. When Steve Jobs was between intense sessions of changing the world of technology, he would take off his shoes and walk through the gardens daily—because when his brain was at rest, his biggest breakthroughs happened. Similarly, the transformation of discipleship happens in the marginal spaces, on the way, or in the everyday rhythms of life as we spend time together. As Tish Harrison Warren has observed, "The crucible of our formation is in the anonymous monotony of our daily routines."[8]

Time Pattern 4: Jesus's Conversations Equaled Conversions

Words hold unimaginable power. For every word in Hitler's seven-hundred-page manifesto *Mein Kampf*, five hundred people died. Words can be a destructive force, but words can also redeem. That's how John chose to open his gospel—with Jesus, the Word, or Logos, made flesh. While the Synoptic Gospels focus primarily on Jesus's actions, John's zooms in on his words. His gospel is built around conversations—personal one-on-one encounters that reveal Jesus. In fact, John has more red-letter real estate than any other gospel—77 percent dialogue. For that reason, the gospel of John should be subtitled *Conversations with Jesus*. John knew what all evangelists know: Conversations equal conversions. No wonder his gospel is considered

---

7. Donald A. Hagner, *Matthew 14–28*, vol. 33B, *Word Biblical Commentary*, ed. Bruce M. Metzger et al. (Word, 1995), 886.
8. Tish Harrison Warren, *Liturgy of the Ordinary: Sacred Practices in Everyday Life* (IVP, 2016), 33.

the most evangelistic book of the New Testament. Some of those exclusive conversations include the following:

- Nicodemus in the dead of night
- The Samaritan woman at the well
- The man born blind
- Mary Magdalene at the empty tomb
- Pilate in the governor's palace

After the wedding in Cana, Jesus traveled to Jerusalem for the Passover for one of the most famous conversations ever recorded. "Rabbi, we know that you are a teacher who has come from God" (John 3:2). Nicodemus opened the dialogue under the cover of darkness, unwilling to be seen with Jesus in public. Rather than shaming him for sneaking around like Nic at Night, Jesus heard him out—and dropped the most quoted line in history: "For God so loved the world . . ." (v. 16). That single conversation has led millions to Christ over the past two thousand years—all because Jesus was willing to slow down and take time to talk. Jesus knew his time was limited to three years. If you had only just over one thousand days to minister, would you prioritize private conversations as he did?

Henrietta Mears also understood that time was a valuable part of discipleship. On Sunday mornings at her Hollywood home, she would flip her famous blueberry pancakes for scores of eager young students, creating an atmosphere of warmth and welcome before opening Scripture. Those breakfast gatherings—equal parts fellowship and Bible study—became legendary as they ate breakfast, formed relationships, and talked together. From them emerged a generation of leaders who would shape evangelicalism worldwide, including Bill Bright (founder of Campus Crusade for Christ), Dawson Trotman (founder of The Navigators), Richard C. Halverson (chaplain of the US Senate 1981–1995), and even Billy Graham, who considered Mears one of his most important influences.[9]

---

9. Arlin C. Migliazzo, *Henrietta Mears and How She Did It: A Biography of a Visionary Educator* (Baker Books, 2007), 135–38.

We may never fully know the ripple effects of just one conversation in the lives of others beyond one single conversation. Charles R. Swindoll wrote about "hinge people," individuals whose small conversations lead to significant spiritual movements, like big doors turning on small hinges. Edward Kimball was a Sunday-school teacher who, despite his own apprehensions, visited a young shoe salesman at his workplace to share the gospel. That one conversation led to the conversion of shoe salesman Dwight L. Moody, who would go on to become one of the most influential evangelists of the nineteenth century. Millions of souls hinged on that one conversation, yet few even know hinge person Edward Kimball's name. You might be one conversation away from changing the world. Driving with his secretary E. T. Rees, Martyn Lloyd-Jones pointed and said, "That's the village where Rhys Peg-leg was born. They say he had only one child, but a thousand grandchildren."[10] Hinge people have hinge conversations, upon which the door of someone's eternity swings, because conversations lead to conversions.

Time Pattern 5: Jesus Exposed His Disciples to Mission Early

> Now Jesus learned that the Pharisees had heard that he was gaining and baptizing more disciples than John—although in fact it was not Jesus who baptized, but his disciples. So he left Judea and went back once more to Galilee. *Now he had to go through Samaria.* (John 4:1–4, emphasis mine)

After the Passover in Jerusalem, Jesus and his disciples journeyed to where the Jordan River runs through the countryside of Judea, where they baptized for a couple of days. But when the crowds swelled and Pharisees started sniffing around, Jesus packed up and left Judea. On his journey back to Galilee, Jesus didn't take the traditional detour around Samaria. Instead, he pressed straight through it. John's statement in 4:4, "He had to go through Samaria," isn't about geography. No self-respecting Jews *needed* to go through Samaria

10. This anecdote is from a personal account told to me by a parishioner at Lloyd-Jones's former church, Bethlehem, Sandfields.

but avoided it at all costs, skirting east along the Jordan River to bypass the region. But Jesus's need to go there was twofold: to save a woman (and a village) and to give his disciples a taste of mission.

Arriving near the outskirts of Sychar, the disciples continued into the village to buy food, but Jesus lingered behind and sat on the edge of Jacob's well in the hot sun. When the Samaritan woman approached to fill her bucket, Jesus started a conversation that would ripple like water through the entire community. Returning, the disciples were shocked to find Jesus talking with a Samaritan . . . and a woman no less:

> Just then his disciples returned and were surprised to find him talking with a woman. But no one asked, "What do you want?" or "Why are you talking with her?" (John 4:27)

They didn't dare interrupt, but you could practically see their eyebrows hitting their hairlines. That conversation's prophetic nature cracked something open in her and changed her life forever. Burdened by shame, her modus operandi of avoiding others and doing whatever it took to protect the last shreds of her privacy, shifted on a dime. She dropped her bucket and rushed into the village, inviting everyone, including the people she'd been avoiding, to meet Jesus—declaring, "Come, see a man who told me everything I ever did" (v. 29). She was not only the first missionary to her people, but she was also the first foreign missionary of Jesus—ever.

And here's the brilliant part: Jesus, the Master disciple-maker, simply sat and let the Holy Spirit work. He didn't rush the moment or orchestrate a spectacle but entered the existing rhythm of the community, modeling with effortless choreography every part of the Discipology flywheel. The genius of a flywheel is that, unlike a formula, it can be engaged at any point—so Jesus switched up the order to Tactics, Time, Teaching.

Tactics: Jesus went.

> Now he had to go through Samaria. (John 4:4)

Time: Jesus waited and conversed.

> Jacob's well was there, and Jesus, tired as he was from the journey, sat down by the well. It was about noon. When a Samaritan woman came to draw water, Jesus said to her, "Will you give me a drink?" (John 4:6–7)

Teaching: Jesus artfully pressed the woman's need for a Savior.

> "Woman," Jesus replied, "believe me, a time is coming when you will worship the Father neither on this mountain nor in Jerusalem. You Samaritans worship what you do not know; we worship what we do know, for salvation is from the Jews. Yet a time is coming and has now come when the true worshipers will worship the Father in the Spirit and in truth, for they are the kind of worshipers the Father seeks. God is spirit, and his worshipers must worship in the Spirit and in truth."
>
> The woman said, "I know that Messiah" (called Christ) "is coming. When he comes, he will explain everything to us."
>
> Then Jesus declared, "I, the one speaking to you—I am he." (John 4:21–26)

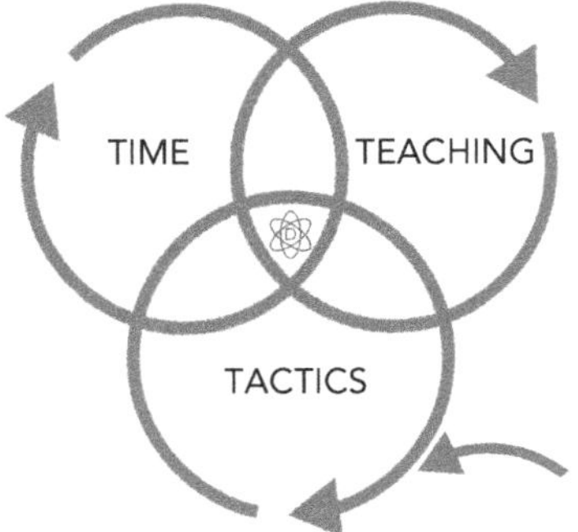

Whereas Jesus started in the Time rhythm with his six disciples, with the Samaritan woman he started with Tactics. The lesson? *Mission always*

determines method. For example, C. S. Lewis broadcast a series of lectures called *Mere Christianity*. Because he was attempting to reach the dechurched post-Christian listeners of Great Britain with an apologetic gospel, his entry point was the Teaching rhythm.

Now, observe that once the Samaritan woman believed, she herself responded with the three rhythms in yet *another switched order*. Her approach of reaching her village with the Discipology flywheel was Tactics, Teaching, Time.

Tactics: She went to her village on a mission.

> Then, leaving her water jar, the woman went back to the town and said to the people, "Come, see a man who told me everything I ever did. Could this be the Messiah?" They came out of the town and made their way toward him. (John 4:28–30)

Teaching: She told them about Jesus.

> Many of the Samaritans from that town believed in him because of the woman's testimony, "He told me everything I ever did." (John 4:39)

Time: They spent two whole days with Jesus.

> So when the Samaritans came to him, *they urged him to stay with them, and he stayed two days*. And because of his words many more became believers. They said to the woman, "We no longer believe just because of what you said; now we have heard for ourselves, and we know that this man really is the Savior of the world." (John 4:40–42, emphasis mine)

As previously mentioned, Rick Warren's baseball diamond of discipleship worked well for people already inside the church, but outside the church, in

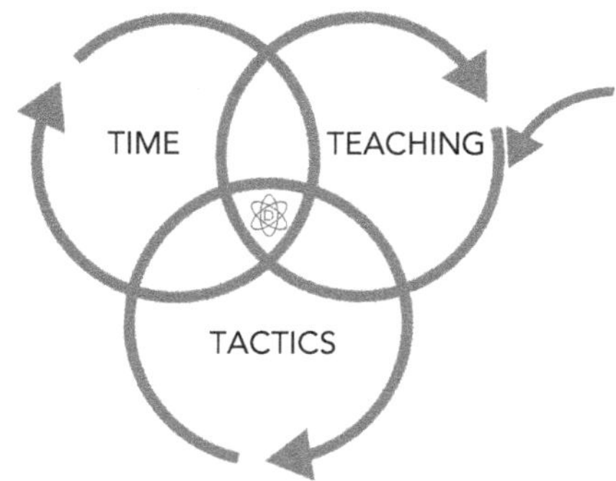

places like Samaria, it often works in reverse. When we were planting in an economically deprived neighborhood in urban Long Beach, the local principal asked whether we could serve Sunday breakfast for kids who would otherwise go hungry. Soon word spread and people showed up—not for Jesus but to help with the mission. As non-Christians served alongside us, the Tactics rhythm overlapped the Time rhythm of community. Over time, they heard the Teaching, and slowly, they followed Jesus. They entered through tactical mission, but the flywheel kept turning.

Mission is messy, and disciple-making doesn't always follow a tidy, linear path. But Jesus never expected it to. Understanding the variable order of the Discipology flywheel of *Time, Teaching,* and *Tactics* prevents us from degrading it to a checklist or a rigid step-by-step program, committing what J. D. Greear calls "the heresy of sequentialism."[11] Blessed are the flexible, for the Holy Spirit blows like the wind.

Different Orders on the Flywheel

DISCIPLES	SAMARITAN WOMAN	THE VILLAGE
Time	Tactics	Tactics
Teaching	Time	Teaching
Tactics	Teaching	Time

11. Leonardo Blair, "Pastor With 9,000-Member Congregation Says Churches Should Stop Focusing on Numbers," *Christian Post*, September 24, 2013, www.christianpost.com/news/pastor-with-9000-member-congregation-says-churches-should-stop-focusing-on-numbers.html?page=3.

Just days earlier, Jesus told Nicodemus that the Holy Spirit blows like the wind, doing what he pleases. A few days later in Samaritan Sychar, Jesus demonstrated that those on mission are perpetually late to the party, for the Holy Spirit always gets there first. John recounts Jesus's first mission debrief in Sychar:

> "Don't you have a saying, 'It's still four months until harvest'? I tell you, open your eyes and look at the fields! They are ripe for harvest. Even now the one who reaps draws a wage and harvests a crop for eternal life, so that the sower and the reaper may be glad together. Thus the saying *'One sows and another reaps' is true.* I sent you to reap what you have not worked for. Others have done the hard work, and you have reaped the benefits of their labor." (John 4:35–38, emphasis mine)

Who were the "others" Jesus referred to, who had "done the hard work"?

- The villagers who ridiculed the woman prepped her to be receptive to Jesus's words.
- The men who abandoned her had made her ache for a love that would never run dry like an old well.
- The woman evangelized the villagers, who believed because of her testimony.

Jesus's first rabbinic lesson to the disciples was that God is often at work in people's lives long before you and I arrive. Paul quoted this maxim to the Corinthians, illustrating again how dependent Paul had become on Christ's model of disciple-making (1 Cor. 3:5–9).

Along the lines of Jesus's disciple-making strategy in Samaria, I was initiated into a brief but early exposure to mission. My discipler took me to the same beach that Lonnie Frisbee frequented to witness to complete strangers. It's not my favorite tactic, to be honest, but that simple act, like a cold plunge, stirred mission deep in my soul. To replicate that, part of my disciple-making process involves asking someone who has just been baptized to help baptize the next person coming into the water immediately after getting their feet wet on mission (literally) from the start. It's on the label: "*Go* and make disciples . . . *baptizing them* in the name of the Father and of the Son and of the Holy Spirit" (Matt. 28:19, emphasis mine). It communicates two things: (1) You're a part of this, and (2) the best time to start fulfilling the Great Commission is *right now*. If Jesus's disciple-making strategy involved early exposure to mission, then we should get creative to foster similar scenarios.

Time Pattern 6: Jesus's Disciple-Making Happened in Community

Jesus discipled a team. John Mark Comer writes, "Jesus didn't have a disciple; he had disciples, plural. He called people to apprentice under him in community."[12] The first six disciples followed him *together*. When Matthew joined as the seventh disciple, Jesus dropped him straight into a mess of six other well-acquainted men, so their rough edges rubbed up against one another. Jesus knew that you not only learn faster in community, you also struggle better. Community itself is an invisible secondary trainer, and the statistics regarding peer-to-peer learning that back this up are impressive:

1. The Center for Creative Leadership reports that 70 percent of learning happens informally, through experience, peer conversations, and collaboration often referred to as the 70/20/10 model:[13]
   - 70 percent experiential
   - 20 percent peer/social learning
   - 10 percent formal education
2. Workplace learning research has found that when employees work together, their individual performance increases.[14]

---

12. John Mark Comer, *Practicing the Way: Be with Jesus. Become Like Him. Do as He Did.* (WaterBrook, 2024), Goal #2, Kindle.
13. "The 70-20-10 Rule for Leadership Development," CCL, September 20, 2025, https://www.ccl.org/articles/leading-effectively-articles/70-20-10-rule/.
14. Kenju Kamei and John Ashworth, "Peer Learning in Teams and Work Performance: Evidence from a Randomized Field Experiment," *Journal of Economic Behavior & Organization* 207 (2023): 413–32, https://doi.org/10.1016/j.jebo.2023.01.015.

3. Companies that use peer learning programs see a 30–50 percent increase in engagement and retention.[15]
4. Research suggests that employees who teach or share knowledge with others tend to see higher productivity, often markedly so in field studies of peer effects.[16]

It's no wonder that Jesus, as the designer of the cerebral cortex, understood the group as the ideal environment for learning.

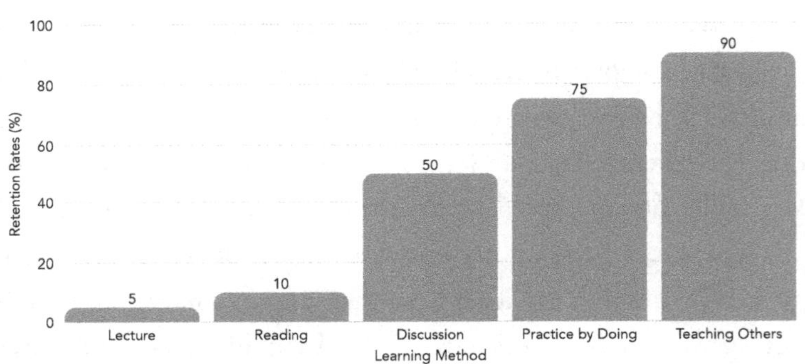

Jesus didn't invent his disciple-making model during his incarnational ministry. He merely perfected it. Drawing from the ancient rabbinical *haverim* model, Jesus infused it with kingdom dynamics.[17] *Haverim* described tight-knit bands of disciples who studied the Torah together under a rabbi. These groups were a less casual, more bonded platoon—akin to a company of firefighters willing to lay down their lives for each other. Such relationships forge a bond stronger than death. In the *haverim* learning environment, iron sharpened iron through Scripture, discussion, and real-life application. As they trekked long distances, it was in the shadow of a rabbi—walking that they talked. Talking, they bonded—the same kind of bond formed on a winning

15. *Workplace Learning Report 2025: The Rise of Career Champions*, LinkedIn Learning, https://learning.linkedin.com/resources/workplace-learning-report.
16. John J. Horton, "Employer Expectations, Peer Effects and Productivity: Evidence from a Series of Field Experiments," arXiv preprint, August 2010, https://doi.org/10.48550/arXiv.1008.2437.
17. Vander Laan, *Dust of the Rabbi*, session 1.

sports team. All the sacrifice, all the grueling challenges bond them together. It's what Alan Hirsch speaks of when he cites *communitas*; not coffee-shop acquaintances but a band of brothers.[18] Hirsch elaborates, "*Communitas* is the kind of community that develops among a group of people who find themselves in a dangerous or challenging situation together—like a platoon in combat or a team climbing Everest."[19]

That description is a far cry from our modern disciple-making practices. Imagine if the Gospels chronicled nothing more than Jesus meeting with his disciples for one hour every week in a coffee shop—sipping hot caffeinated beverages and sharing ideas from their reading. At the end of the hour, Jesus smiles and says, "Now go be the church," scattering them to figure out the remaining 167 hours left in their week.

Some can remember when the missional circles boasted of logging four or five hours of community midweek, eating dinner or grocery shopping together, while criticizing the established church and congratulating themselves for doing it "the Jesus way." Admittedly, it was progress in the Time rhythm, but *progress does not equate to arrival.* "Doing life together" looks very different between the modern missional and a member of Jesus's *talmidim.* In the 168 hours allotted to all of us in the span of a week, spending 56 hours sleeping leaves 112 waking hours on the table. Five hours together doth not a *talmidim* make. Thankfully, we are not held to the requirements of a *talmidim* in our disciple-making. However, it is a caution that our modern hubris may not be warranted as much as humility. Legend has it that after painting the Sistine Chapel and shaping the skyline of Florence, Michelangelo uttered the phrase *Ancora imparo*, "I am still learning." There is a similar sounding phrase in Italian, "*Agora impero*," meaning just the opposite, "Now I rule." Far too many times I've whispered *Agora impero* to myself when I should have been echoing Michealangelo's *Ancora imparo* instead.

---

18. *Communitas* is a term popularized by Victor Turner, an anthropologist who studied how groups bond through shared challenges and liminal experiences (moments of transition and transformation). Communitas isn't just being together—it's being forged together in mission.
19. Alan Hirsch, *The Forgotten Ways: Reactivating the Missional Church* (Brazos Press, 2006), 220–23.

Time Pattern 7: Jesus Invested More with Few

Jesus embraced all the limits of his humanity; one of the most frustrating being an inability to be in more than one place at a time. There was only so much of Jesus to go around. He didn't attempt to disciple everyone in a crowd with a one-size-fits-all approach, but created layers of access. As Joe Myers observes, "When we look through Jesus's relationships, we find that he is comfortable having people belong in multiple ways."[20] Myers is referring to crowds of five thousand—and various *haverim* of differing sizes: seventy-two, twelve, and three.

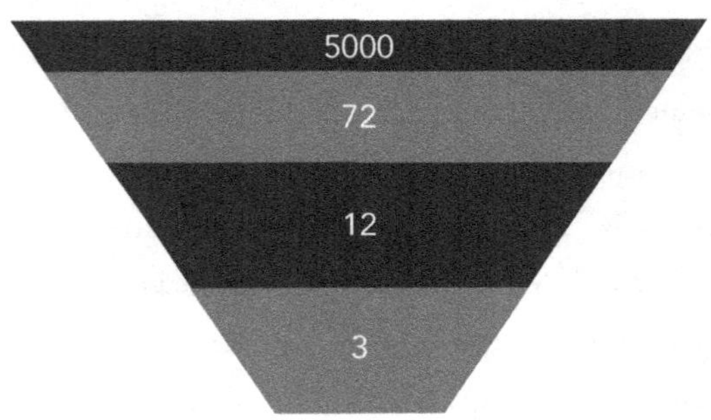

Jesus's rule being that the larger the group, the less intimate the contact. Conversely, the smaller the group, the more intimate the contact. He reserved the bulk of his time for his *talmidim* of twelve, while investing even more strategically into three: Peter, James, and John. In Jesus's approach there was both breadth and depth, consistent with the research of British anthropologist Robin Dunbar, who proposed that the average person can maintain stable social relationships with about 150 people (known as Dunbar's number). Dunbar's research identified these concentric circles or layers of intimacy:

- 1,500 names (faces you can recall)
- 500 acquaintances (recognizable but not close)

20. Joseph R. Myers, *The Search to Belong: Rethinking Intimacy, Community, and Small Groups* (Zondervan, 2003), 112.

- 150 meaningful contacts (stable social relationships)
- 50 good friends (you'd invite to a party or depend on in a pinch)
- 15 close friends (people you can confide in regularly)
- 5 intimate friends (your inner circle of deep trust)[21]

Jesus's layers fall within this framework. He understood that human capacity is limited by design, forcing us to be intentional about where we go deep and avoid spreading ourselves too thin. Learning how Jesus segmented his disciple-making groups will assist us in contextualizing disciple-making at these various levels in the real world.

The Five Thousand

The crowds flocked to Jesus as spectators, gathering for bread and spectacle like rubberneckers at the scene of an accident, drawn more by curiosity than commitment. In response, he taught, fed, and healed many, but with limited access beyond the healing. No matter who you are, quality time with five thousand people is out of the question. For crowds, Jesus applied the metaphor of farming, spreading seed widely across the fields. According to the parable of the sower, 75 percent of what lands in a crowd never bears lasting fruit, and if Jesus didn't escape those odds, neither will we.

Across the spectrum, Jesus neither encouraged nor forbade large numbers, knowing that "crowds happen." Crowds become a *bad thing* only when you think they're the *main thing.* Rather than pander to packs of people, Jesus preached hard things to disperse crowds turned mobs. One only does that when they aren't your aim. This is "giving yourself to the crowd," and Jesus knew better: "But Jesus would not entrust himself to them, for he knew all people" (John 2:24). That didn't prevent him from addressing crowds in the Teaching rhythm so he could funnel them into the next rhythm of his Discipology flywheel.

---

21. Robin Dunbar, *How Many Friends Does One Person Need?: Dunbar's Number and Other Evolutionary Quirks* (Faber & Faber, 2010).

The Seventy-Two

Not to be confused with the Twelve, the seventy-two short-term missionaries were sent out toward the end of the third year of Jesus's ministry. As the clock ran down on the scoreboard, these former spectators from the stands got into the game. The mission field wasn't only where they went but where they were forged. No matter how much leaders desire to see an entire congregation mobilized, not all step up from the crowd. As they responded to Jesus with deeper commitment, he opened access to a preliminary training (Luke 10:1–16) and an exclusive debrief (Luke 10:17–24). Possibly from this very group, Matthias would rise to take Judas's place among the twelve apostles.

The Twelve

From a greater number, Jesus chose a ragtag band of twelve ordinary young people, six of whom were the first year crew. Far from disciple-makers at the outset, they were unreliable by most standards. The Gospels don't hide their inconsistencies, impulsiveness, and clueless comprehension. Thankfully, Jesus was looking not for perfection but for *participation*. The more they participated, the more 24/7 access Jesus gave. In return, he inherited a front-row seat to their immaturity, ego clashes, and failures. His "sent ones" were still-growing ones. Moldable missionaries aren't we all.

The Three

Among David's mighty men there were the three. Similarly, while not legendary warriors of renown, Peter, James, and John became Jesus's closest companions and future network leaders in their own right. Paul noticed that they stood out from the Twelve, writing of "James and Cephas [Peter] and John, who seemed to be pillars" (Gal. 2:9 ESV). Each of them would play a unique and essential role in the future of the church:

- **James** would become the first of the Twelve to be martyred (Acts 12:2), his death igniting courage in others. Prior to that, he'd oversee the Jerusalem hub at ground zero.

- **Peter** would be the first to preach at Pentecost, the first to lead the church in Jerusalem until he became itinerant, and the first to open the kingdom to the gentiles (Acts 2, 10).[22] He would also oversee the Judean network. According to tradition, Peter would move to Rome to oversee the hub movement.
- **John**, the last surviving apostle, would serve as a theological anchor through the persecution of the church, writing the gospel of John, his epistles, and Revelation, and serving in the Ephesus hub.

Because Jesus foresaw them as network leaders, he strategically gave them access that no one else had.

- They were the only ones in the room when Jesus raised Jairus's daughter (Mark 5:37).
- They were the ones who saw him transfigured on the mountain (Matt. 17:1–2).
- They were the three he asked to stay closest in the garden of Gethsemane (Mark 14:33).

This greater access was not for privilege but for preparation. Because they would give more of themselves, Jesus gave more of himself, reflecting the pattern at the heart of disciple-making: *You must learn to give more time to fewer people and less time to more.*

The early Methodist movement of the eighteenth century based its structure on how John Wesley and Howell Harris systematized Jesus's practices in the

22. While the Bible does not explicitly state that Peter was in Rome, some scholars interpret 1 Peter 5:13—where Peter refers to "Babylon"—as a coded reference to Rome, a common early Christian practice (also seen in Revelation 17:5, 18). Early church writings strongly support the tradition of Peter's ministry and martyrdom in Rome. Clement of Rome (ca. 96), in *1 Clement*, mentions Peter's and Paul's martyrdoms, likely referring to Rome. Ignatius of Antioch (ca. 110), in his *Letter to the Romans*, suggests Peter had a significant role in the church there. Irenaeus (ca. 180), in *Against Heresies 3.3.2*, states that Peter and Paul founded the Roman church and appointed Linus as its first bishop. Eusebius (ca. 325), in *Ecclesiastical history 2.25*, explicitly records that Peter ministered in Rome for years before being martyred under Nero, aligning with earlier Christian tradition.

Gospels.[23] Wesley's success in organizing people into groups of various sizes—modeled on the Discipology patterns of Jesus—demonstrates the universality of his practices. Like Jesus, Wesley preached to the crowds of five thousand, treating mass evangelism as a gateway rather than the goal. The goal Wesley sought was to make disciples, and, like Paul, he distilled his practices from the Master disciple-maker.

To mirror Jesus's group of twelve disciples, Wesley formed classes: midsize discipleship groups of about twelve people, in which members were instructed, encouraged, and held accountable in their walk with Christ by their peers.

To replicate Jesus's inner circle of three, Wesley created bands: small groups of three to five people, divided by gender and spiritual maturity. These were intimate circles for confession, accountability, and deep spiritual formation. Members met weekly to share struggles, confess sins, and pray for one another.

JESUS MODELED	WESLEY SYSTEMATIZED	PURPOSE
5,000	Preaching circuits (thousands)	Proclamation (Teaching and Tactics)
72	Societies	For seekers (Teaching and Tactics)
12	Classes (10–12)	Transformation (Time)
3	Bands (4–5)	Accountability (Time)

Each of the groups accomplished a different objective—Wesley's entire system (societies, classes, and bands) scaled from crowds to close companions.

Time Pattern 8: Jesus Slowed Down to Make Disciples

Disciple-making legend Ralph Moore has said, "If you do your homework, you will come to see that virtually every culture-bending spiritual breakthrough happened because someone took time to make a few disciples."[24]

23. Peter Jeffrey, *Christian Handbook: A Straight Forward Guide to the Bible, Church History and Christian Doctrine* (Evangelical Press, 1988).
24. Ralph Moore, *Making Disciples: Developing Lifelong Followers of Jesus* (Baker Books, 2012), 78.

After their brief foray on mission in Samaria, Jesus headed home toward Capernaum by way of Cana, the site of his first miracle (John 4:46–54). Word spread, and upon his arrival in Cana he was asked once again to miraculously intervene. A Herodian official had traveled all the way from Capernaum to beg Jesus to return and save the life of his dying son. Yet Jesus refused to make the trek to Capernaum, calmly telling the man, "Your son will live." It almost seems cold in the face of a dying child. So why did Jesus refuse to go? Unlike a leader with a messiah complex who flies off to save the day, Jesus, the actual Messiah, resisted the pull of the urgent to stay committed to the relational development of his disciples. The child was healed immediately from afar, but the lesson was clear; Jesus wasn't ready yet for crowds. He was still building community.

This echoes the only other miracle Jesus did earlier, ironically also in Cana. Jesus wasn't ready to shift outside of the Time rhythm then either, and only reluctantly performed the miracle at a wedding for family friends after the persistence of his mother. Mary asked Jesus to intervene miraculously, receiving the response, "Woman, it's not yet my time." *Not yet my time.* Jesus knew that every miracle would attract crowds, and it wasn't time for that . . . yet.

Unlike so many leaders today, Jesus wasn't in a hurry to build a platform. Mike Chong Perkinson and Tom Johnston observe, "The Rabbinical process of Jesus teaches us that if you want to start an organization, make your focus large, on the crowd. If you want to start a movement, make your focus small, on the disciples or leadership community."[25]

Spending more time with fewer people = disciple-making

Spending less time with more people = Sunday morning

Be careful here. The contrast positions them next to each other strategically, not against each other. As we've already established, crowds were part of Jesus's funnel, but chasing crowds as a priority often comes at the expense of

25. Tom Johnston and Mike Chong Perkinson, *The Organic Reformation: A New Hope for the Church in the West* (PraxisMedia, 2011), chap. 5, Kindle.

not making disciples at all. One tracks numbers, while the other creates movement. That's why Jesus chose twelve, not twelve hundred, because disciples can't be mass-produced. They must be handcrafted. Regi Campbell states, "More time with fewer people equals greater kingdom impact."[26]

Bigger isn't better, any more than faster is. Aesop's fable "The Tortoise and the Hare," debunks the faster-is-better fairy tale we often believe. Jesus and Paul both modeled slowing down to invest more time into fewer people. Yet this tortoise-style disciple-making catalyzed movements, bypassing the hares who merely build crowds. In reality, the kingdom reads like a Cinderella story, in which the lowly stepchild becomes the belle of the ball, as evidenced by John Wesley, Henrietta Mears, and living legend and Discipology team member Ralph Moore. Each of them embodied the Discipology practices of Jesus, not rushing but changing the world one person at a time.

H. Richard Niebuhr once quipped, "Christianity has achieved apparent success by ignoring the precepts of its founder."[27] But I'm willing to go out on a limb here and risk saying something crazy. Perhaps, just maybe, Jesus knew what he was doing.

And if so, we should pay more attention to his strategy going forward—making space for long roads, long tables, and long-lasting relationships. That's what it takes to make time to make disciples.

For help with the Time rhythm, use the QR code and register for our free Discipology course.

26. Regi Campbell, *Mentor Like Jesus: His Radical Approach to Building the Church* (RM Press, 2016), chap. 1, Kindle.

27. H. Richard Niebuhr, *The Responsibility of the Church for Society and Other Essays* (Westminster John Knox Press, 2008).

CHAPTER 4

Principles of Time

My idea of God is not a divine idea. It has to be shattered time after time. He shatters it himself. He is the great iconoclast.

—C. S. LEWIS

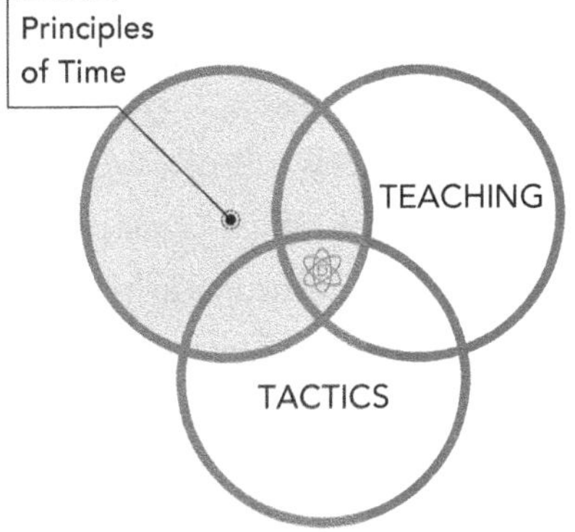

Now that we've traced Jesus's patterns within the Time rhythm, it's time to draw out the timeless principles behind them. The overriding principle is simple: True transformation is distilled over time, slow-brewed in the company of others. Transformation doesn't happen through self-help isolation but when time and community intersect. Growing older in Christ is not the same as growing up in Christ. If we were scratching out a formula, it would read like this: time + community = transformation. But *what exactly are we being transformed into*? If transformation is the game, what's the win?

Dawson Trotman, founder of the Navigators, wrestled with this question. Driving late one night along the Pacific Coast Highway, Trotman picked up a hitchhiker. Climbing into the car, the hitcher swore using the Lord's name, expressing how hard it was to catch a ride. Trotman witnessed to him about Christ, eliciting a contrite prayer of conversion before dropping the man off. Approximately one year later, Trotman once again picked up a hitchhiker, who got into the car swearing about how hard it was to get a ride. Trotman's déjà vu led to him doing a double-take at the man. Trotman realized he'd picked up the same hitchhiker he'd prayed with—except there'd been no change in the man's life. It was a wake-up call for Trotman, who concluded that the man's lack of transformation was due to lack of discipleship. From that night forward, Trotman devoted himself to spending the time necessary to disciple people. Trotman often quipped, "You can lead someone to Christ in 20 minutes to a couple of hours, but it takes 20 weeks to a couple of years to adequately follow them up."[1]

I know, I know . . . we all want to rush straight to the disciple-making part, but if Jesus didn't, neither should we. Before we make disciples, we must first become disciples. Before disciple-making comes discipleship. This chapter will lay the foundational principles for discerning what a mature disciple looks like. Unfortunately, there's no formula or magic number of conversations, sermons, or quiet times that mark the maturity of a disciple. There's no magic time frame. When baking cookies, the recipe gives a range of twelve to fifteen minutes or "until slightly browned." Even Betty Crocker knows that there's not a one-size-fits-all formula—everybody's equipment and ingredients vary. When making disciples, you still need to peek through the window. You watch and wait, assessing the character of those discipled to see whether they're lightly browned around the edges. Time is still the *quantitative* magic ingredient, but you're looking for a *qualitative* result.

Even after three years, Jesus's disciples were still slightly doughy in the center, despite being up close and personal with him. When a Samaritan village rejected Jesus's message, James and John went full scorched-earth: "Lord,

1. Betty Lee Skinner, *Daws: A Man Who Trusted God* (NavPress, 1974), 70.

do you want us to call fire down from heaven to destroy them?" (Luke 9:54). Three years in and firebombing Samaria was still on the table as a missionary strategy. Yet Jesus didn't give up on "the Sons of Thunder." They just needed more cook time to grow into to their names, for Zebedee means "gift of God" or "grace." It's comforting that Jesus laughed it off by giving them nicknames. We all need to learn to laugh at ourselves and our frustratingly slow rate of progress as disciples. If Jesus didn't expect overnight transformation in the Twelve, neither should we.

Before setting out to reproduce ourselves in others, we must examine our own transformation as disciples. Becoming disciples is the prerequisite to making them. Within the rhythm of Time, community shapes our characters—slowly, quietly, and even painfully. The curated version of ourselves presented to others is quickly burned as an effigy in the fires of community, and our real self, the one God sees, emerges—the person we are when no one else is watching. Robert Redford was asked by someone getting into an elevator, "Are you the real Robert Redford?"

"Only when I'm alone."[2]

According to the Sermon on the Mount, that's the inner part of us that the Spirit is transforming—the real us. I can modify my external behavior, but the inner transformation of my character remains outside my grasp, requiring the power of the Holy Spirit. "To this end I strenuously contend with all the energy Christ so powerfully works in me" (Col. 1:29).

Evaluating Our Metrics

If transformation takes time in community with others, that presents a problem for leaders. Time is a commodity that we possess so little of. A constraint to beat at best, or a burden to manage at worst. Yet time is a gift to embrace. The values of leadership culture in general work against slowing down and carefully crafting quality. Everything marketed to leaders promises

2. Kris Shearer, "Are We Our Real Selves?," *Daily Record*, November 11, 2010, www.the-daily-record.com/story/news/2010/11/11/are-we-our-real-selves/19639355007.

life hacks, maximization, and fast tracks for an increased quantitative yield. As a result, our values have shifted. When I left for the mission field in 1999, the metric of the church growth movement taught that *bigger is better.* Yet, returning home twelve years later, the message of the multiplication movement is that *faster is better.* If Jesus's use of time teaches us anything, however, it's that *better is better.*[3] And better takes time.

When the metrics of ministry are quantitative rather than qualitative, the result is a rush to hit those benchmarks. But transformation can't be rushed—*won't* be rushed. Transformation is qualitative, where spending time with God results in becoming like him, just as Moses spent time with God face-to-face and became the humblest man on earth. He carved out the necessary time for transformation. The irony is that the process starts with establishing qualitative priorities that lead to quantitative results. For some of us, it takes nothing less than disaster to shatter our old paradigm of ministry and finally set us on the path of true transformation. At least, that's what it took for Paul.

Paul's Learning Curve

For all his brilliance and boldness, Paul struggled early on with the slower pace of transformation. If anyone had begun believing that faster was better, it was Paul. He expected the spiritual growth of his disciples to match the urgency of his mission, but the Galatians would teach him otherwise. They had a discipleship problem, one that Paul himself had inadvertently created on his first missionary journey. While planting in Galatia, Iconium, Lystra, and Derbe, he moved quickly, spending a paltry three to four months in each place, expecting those new believers to stand strong after he'd left. After returning to Antioch, however, Paul received troubling news: The Galatians had quickly fallen into heresy. Agonizing over the catastrophe caused by his premature departure, he wrote, "I am again in the pains of childbirth until Christ is formed in you" (Gal. 4:19).

The Galatians couldn't have had a better teacher than Paul, so what went wrong?

---

3. I owe Mike Chong Perkinson for concluding "Better is better" after I shared my observations about bigger/faster metrics during a conversation. This is why we say he drops MCP nuggets.

Paul had focused on the Teaching and Tactics rhythms but neglected the Time rhythm.

Movement scholar Gene Wilson notes that "rapid multiplication is desirable in that many enter the kingdom of God in a short period of time. But leader maturation takes time and character is chiseled gradually. When discipleship does not produce enough mature leaders, the movement will struggle, falter, or become shallow."[4] Even in the Southern Hemisphere, where movements are spreading at breakneck speed, heresy and theological error often spread just as fast, just as they did in Galatia. Unfortunately, many of the movements that we hear whispered about are not experiencing true mobilization. Many have leaned into the Tactics rhythm on the flywheel but left the Time and Teaching rhythms neglected, negating the designation as true mobilization.

Despite apparent forward progress, a movement operating in the Tactics circle alone produces only activation. But activation of *what*? David Garrison, a respected authority on church-planting movements, doesn't shy away from asking, "Are Church Planting Movements capable of conveying heresy? Absolutely. . . . People can multiply truth or error."[5] It explains why heresy runs rampant in some regions of the developing world where disciple-making "movements" are said to occur. Yet Paul would not be any more pleased with it than he was with the Galatians. Faster is not always better.

How Paul Fixed the Problem

After the Galatian fiasco, Paul learned Trotman's lesson: Evangelism without investment is like scattering seeds across topsoil but abandoning them before they root, neglecting the watering stage. Paul's weakness was going too fast, but flooring the gas pedal to a stoplight is never fun, so Paul shifted gears. He slowed down to speed up in the long run. His second missionary journey was a return to Galatia to fix what was broken, telling Barnabas, "Let us go back

4. Gene Wilson, *Emerging Gospel Movements: The Role of Catalysts* (Wipf & Stock, 2021), chap. 3, Kindle.
5. David Garrison, *Church Planting Movements: How God Is Redeeming a Lost World* (WIGTake Resources, 2004), 240, https://www.scribd.com/document/78434678/Garrison-Church-Planting-Movements.

and visit the believers in all the towns where we preached the word of the Lord and see how they are doing"(Acts 15:36). *See how they are doing.* Paul knew they were a mess, but wanted to see if his letter had led to a course correction. It had certainly changed Paul's entire MO. He down-shifted from trying to plant churches to planting people; from leaving converts in his wake to making disciples. In short, Paul started paying attention to Jesus's strategy and practices and embraced the Discipology rhythms.

As is always the case, however, the best laid plans of mice and men often go awry. The circumcision group, hot on Paul's tail for the entire second missionary journey, deprived him any time to catch his breath. Every time he set foot in a city, persecution drove him out before he could spend the necessary time to make disciples. This pattern repeated in Iconium, Lystra, Derbe, Thessalonica, and Berea during his second missionary journey. His only option, therefore, was to *leave people behind*, entrusting his missionary companions to stay and develop the disciples in his place. Circumstances forced Paul's disciples to make disciples.

Finally, he landed in Corinth worn out, beat up, and ready to collapse. There, Paul lay low for six months, waiting for his team to arrive before preaching the gospel. After his team caught up to him, they stayed another year, totaling eighteen months in Corinth. That one pivotal decision to slow down, stay put, and invest in one place paved the way for the greatest expansion strategy of the first century, for during those six months of waiting, Paul forged a deep and lasting partnership with two disciples he made there: Aquila and Priscilla. They established a tentmaking empire that would help fund Paul's bivocational missionaries to spread the gospel throughout the known world. And when he departed Corinth? They discipled Apollos in his absence, spinning the flywheel. Again, disciples making disciples—all because Paul slowed down, investing in the Time rhythm. And when he couldn't—his disciples could.

When Paul's Discipology Flywheel Screamed

By Paul's third missionary journey, all three cogs of the Discipology flywheel were catalyzing the mobilization that Paul dreamed of. But it wasn't just Paul's strategy that had changed. *Paul himself* had changed. He was now a disciple-maker with focused intentionality.

Time: For the first time, Paul made the bold decision to stay in one place during the entire missionary journey, investing three years of time into reproducing himself in others.

Teaching: Paul laid a strong doctrinal foundation. "Therefore be alert, remembering that for three years I did not cease night or day to admonish every one with tears" (Acts 20:31 ESV).

Tactics: Paul forged Ephesus into a mobilization hub, deploying the seven churches of Asia outward from the Ephesian epicenter. "He took the disciples with him and had discussions daily in the lecture hall of Tyrannus. This went on for two years, *so that all the Jews and Greeks who lived in the province of Asia heard the word of the Lord*" (Acts 19:9–10, emphasis mine).

Paul had reproduced himself so effectively in the disciples he'd made that they planted the *six other churches of Asia* while he stayed put training others from the Ephesus hub. It's the tortoise and the hare all over again—slowing down to increase efficiency builds what lasts. His earlier mistakes gave him the humility to fully embrace Jesus's master model, pouring into a small group of leaders who would carry the mission forward after he left. In a world chasing quick results, Paul reoriented himself to Jesus's slow, steady, and transformational approach. Therefore, when Paul left Ephesus after three years, he didn't leave with mere travel companions—he left with *disciple-makers*. Luke lists seven of them by name:[6]

> He was accompanied by Sopater son of Pyrrhus from Berea, Aristarchus and Secundus from Thessalonica, Gaius from Derbe, Timothy also, and Tychicus and Trophimus from the province of Asia. (Acts 20:4)

---

6. Interestingly, Luke separated them by people groups, indicating that Paul had become even more strategic in sending at the end of his third missionary journey.

Not only did Paul group them in teams of two (paired by their ethnicity), but he also spent three years in Ephesus discipling his disciple-makers. Three years? Sounds familiar. Is it coincidental, or does Acts 19 give us a glimpse into how closely Paul was imitating Christ's model of Discipology by his third journey? Consider how the flywheel is presented during those three years:

Years 1 and 2: According to Luke, Paul trained daily in the hall of Tyrannus for two years, emphasizing Time and Teaching. "He took the disciples with him and had discussions daily in the lecture hall of Tyrannus. This went on for two years" (Acts 19:9–10).

Year 3: In year 3, Paul deployed his disciples on mission, "so that the word of the Lord spread throughout all Asia" (Acts 19:20). It's remarkable that the mighty church planter Paul didn't plant any of the six other churches of the seven churches of Asia but deployed those he trained for two years. Colossae was planted by Epaphras (Col. 1:7), a Colossian himself (4:10). It's likely that after his planting ministry in Colossae, Epaphras evangelized the sister cities Laodicea and Hierapolis (v. 13).[7] Arguably, Paul went further by staying in one place and reproducing himself.

Most of us need a similar course correction if we ever hope to spark a disciple-making movement in our own ministries.

The Imitation Game

This brings us back to our original question: How would Paul or his companions know when it was time to leave? When their disciples were ready to stand on their own—when the cookies were browned around the edges.

What *does* a transforming disciple look like? Paul certainly had an idea in mind. Having left his disciples behind, Paul repeatedly reminded them of God's character revealed by his life:

7. Mark R. Fairchild, *Christian Origins in Ephesus and Asia Minor*, 2nd ed. (Hendrickson, 2017), 64.

- “Therefore I urge you to imitate me” (1 Cor. 4:16).
- “Join together in following my example, brothers and sisters, and just as you have us as a model, keep your eyes on those who live as we do” (Phil. 3:17).
- “Follow my example, as I follow the example of Christ” (1 Cor. 11:1).
- “And you became imitators of us and of the Lord when you welcomed the message with the joy of the Holy Spirit, in spite of your great suffering” (1 Thess. 1:6 ESV).
- “Whatever you have learned or received or heard from me or seen in me—put it into practice. And the God of peace will be with you” (Phil. 4:9).
- “For you yourselves know how you ought to follow our example. We were not idle when we were with you, nor did we eat anyone’s food without paying for it. On the contrary, we worked night and day, laboring and toiling so that we would not be a burden to any of you. We did this, not because we do not have the right to such help, but in order to offer ourselves as a model for you to imitate” (2 Thess. 3:7–9).
- “For you, brothers and sisters, became imitators of God’s churches in Judea, which are in Christ Jesus: You suffered from your own people the same things those churches suffered from the Jews” (1 Thess. 2:14).
- “You, however, know all about my teaching, my way of life, my purpose, faith, patience, love, endurance, persecutions, sufferings” (2 Tim. 3:10–11).

Paul even urged Timothy, who was tending the most strategic hub of the first century, “Watch your life and doctrine closely” (1 Tim. 4:16). Perhaps it’s peculiar to us that Paul didn’t mention gifting, when modern ministry prizes gifting above all else, often at the expense of character. Yet, as Wayne Cordeiro warns, “Your gifts will only go as far as your character can take you.”[8] Paul wanted Timothy to go further than himself; therefore, behind Paul’s advice

8. Wayne Cordeiro, “Rebuilding Character,” *Life Journal Daily with Pastor Wayne*, New Hope West, accessed April 16, 2025, https://newhopewest.com/life-journal-daily-with-pastor-wayne/rebuilding-character.

was this principle: *Whether we realize it or not, we are always making disciples.* Our lives shape others intentionally or unintentionally by divine design. The real question is this: Are we modeling *Jesus* to them?

If that question makes you nervous, remember that disciple-making isn't something reserved for the flawless. Running from it because you feel unqualified doesn't mean you're not making disciples; it only means that you're avoiding the opportunity to do it *better*. We are all radiating something through our lives already. The question is, What?

Go deep with me for a minute, to the beginning of the Bible, to trace the thread of radiating God's glory to the world. In the garden of Eden, discipleship wasn't needed. Adam and Eve glorified God by simply existing. Made in his image, they reflected God's character throughout creation. Therefore, the mandate to be fruitful and multiply produced more image bearers of God, spreading his glory throughout the earth, lighting up the world like the moon reflecting the light of the sun. This is what made the serpent's deceptive promise so tragic—that they would "become like God." Satan offered God's image bearers a likeness they already possessed, and in grasping for it, they lost it.

Satan's mission accomplished, the plan to glorify God through reproduction stopped short. But thousands of years later, through the death and resurrection of Christ, that plan was restored. The Holy Spirit restores Christ's image within us, restoring us as image bearers. The Great Commission to "Go make disciples" is the New Testament equivalent of "be fruitful and multiply." When we multiply disciples, Christ's glory radiates through the lives of those being transformed. And as we've witnessed in the Sons of Thunder, those who are transformed are still transforming. Always.

Through disciple-making, Jesus intentionally reproduced his character in twelve flawed disciples, who reproduced it in others. Barnabas modeled Christ's character to Paul, who in turn glorified him to other broken people. Despite our flaws, the treasure of Christ's glory still shines through our cracked jars (2 Cor. 4:7). And in his wisdom the all-wise Creator entrusted imperfect vessels to reflect his glory. That's why Paul never pointed to himself as the model but fixed his eyes on Christ himself, hoping that others would glimpse Jesus through his own flawed reflection. Paul's humble call was, "Be imitators of me, as I am of Christ" (1 Cor. 11:1 ESV). Gazing at Christ's glory leaves us little time to fixate on ourselves. If Paul could swing their gaze toward Christ, he knew that they would also be transformed into his likeness. Paul didn't look for perfection but the presence of the process. And this is exactly what was missing on the island of Crete when he left Titus behind to finish the work of disciple-making there.

The Call for Character

The salty air whipped across the docks as the Mediterranean waves slapped against the wooden hull of their ship. Paul stood with Titus at the water's edge, his cloak billowing behind him, the scent of fish and brine thick in the air. The ship creaked as the crew prepared to set sail for Antioch, ropes groaning under the weight of the mast. Paul exhaled, his brow furrowed. This wasn't an easy ask. Turning to Titus, he placed a firm hand on his shoulder, looking him square in the eye. "Titus," he said, his voice steady but heavy with the weight of leadership. "I need you to stay." Titus blinked, glancing back at the island behind them. Crete was rough, known for its liars, drunks, and lawlessness. Titus knew that this wasn't just an assignment; it was a *battleground*. Surely there were enough believers here to get the job done. After all, he and Paul were just passing through. As if reading his thoughts, Paul's grip tightened. "Titus, these people need more than a quick sermon and a wave goodbye. They need shepherds—mature disciples who look like Jesus and can lead others." He paused, scanning Titus's face, searching for hesitation. "I can't stay, but you can."

The sea breeze carried the shouts of fishermen as Titus looked back at the town, let out a breath, and nodded. He'd been with Paul long enough to know that Paul wouldn't have asked if it wasn't necessary. Paul gave a faint smile, patting his shoulder. "Good. Now go find others—faithful men and women who will embody Christ Jesus on this island." With that, Paul turned and boarded the ship, leaving Titus standing on the dock watching the sails fill with the wind, knowing that the hard work was just beginning.

Months passed, and Titus found himself standing on that same dock awaiting an inbound ship with word from Paul, answering Titus's last letter requesting advice. In response, Paul wrote:

> The reason I left you in Crete was that you might put in order what was left unfinished and appoint elders in every town, as I directed you. An elder must be blameless, faithful to his wife, a man whose children believe and are not open to the charge of being wild and disobedient. Since an overseer manages God's household, he must be blameless—not overbearing, not quick-tempered, not given to drunkenness, not violent, not pursuing dishonest gain. Rather, he must be hospitable, one who loves what is good, who is self-controlled, upright, holy and disciplined. He must hold firmly to the trustworthy message as it has been taught, so that he can encourage others by sound doctrine and refute those who oppose it. (Titus 1:5–9)

There it was. A description of the transformed character of a disciple.

Paul reminded Titus that his mission on Crete was to raise up elders in "every town"—an insurance policy against a repeat of the Galatian fiasco. If Paul had left Timothy with a hard job of leading the disciple-making efforts in Ephesus, he'd just multiplied that difficulty for Titus by as many towns. Interestingly, the lists of the qualifications of those who would lead, written to Timothy and Titus, were very similar. These are the qualities Paul required for leaders, but why did Paul choose these qualities? Where did he get them from? Surely Paul the Pharisee didn't invent them out of thin air. He must have been working from a template for a mature disciple.

That template was Jesus himself. Paul's lists are simply descriptions of Christ's own character. To lead others, Paul required only this: that you walked, spoke, loved, and lived in a way that made people think, *This person has been with Jesus, has been transformed by him*. Put all those traits together and you've painted a composite portrait of Jesus. Not arrogant, not greedy, holy, disciplined, not a drunkard. A life like that will reveal him to others. Therefore, *the only suitable answer to the question of what a mature disciple looks like is Jesus.*

Traits of a Mature Disciple in Timothy and Titus

QUALITIES	1 TIMOTHY 3:1–7	TITUS 1:5–9
Above reproach	☑	☑
Husband of one wife	☑	☑
Not be arrogant		☑
Not be quick-tempered		☑
Sober-minded	☑	
Self-controlled	☑	☑
Respectable	☑	
Hospitable	☑	☑
Able to teach	☑	☑
Not a drunkard	☑	☑
Not violent but gentle	☑	☑
Not quarrelsome	☑	
Not a lover of money	☑	☑
Manage his own household well	☑	☑
Lover of good		☑
Not be a recent convert	☑	
Well thought of by outsiders	☑	
Upright		☑
Holy		☑
Disciplined		☑

The qualifications listed in the chart aren't exhaustive but are drawn from a much larger tapestry. Note where the traits overlap in 1 Timothy and Titus are listed in the chart, assuming that the single-use traits were more likely specific to their unique assignments. Some traits in Titus's larger list may speak directly to the cultural dysfunction on Crete, while others in Timothy's reflect specific challenges in Ephesus. *But both lists mirror the character of Jesus himself.* Therefore, Paul's requirement for someone who *leads* is someone who's *following* first. To Paul, a leader must be more than competent—a leader must be *Christlike.* That's why all but one trait are about character rather than skill. Johnston and Chong Perkinson label the traits as "capacities of being rather than capacities of doing."[9] The list gives only the briefest nod to the gifting "able to teach." The conclusion from both lists? Character trumps gifting every time. Prior to his conversion, Saul was the embodiment of someone with impressive gifting that outpaced his character. Paul wasn't impressed by talent anymore and knew the destructive path religion could take a person down if their character was out of alignment with God's.

Relearning God's Character

Saul of Tarsus had all the credentials, knowledge, and zeal required to take him to the top but was dead wrong about the character of the God he claimed to serve. He was of the ilk of Pharisees that Jesus rebuked: "You study the Scriptures diligently because you think that in them you have eternal life. These are the very Scriptures that testify about me" (John 5:39). Nobody had studied like Saul, a Pharisee of Pharisees. Nobody had studied like Saul—relentlessly driven to outpace his peers, scouring the Torah like a man starving for holiness, chasing the shadow of the divine between the lines of Hebrew ink. Describing this period, he wrote,

> I was advancing in Judaism beyond many of my own age among my people and was extremely zealous for the traditions of my fathers. (Gal. 1:14–15)

Sitting under the legendary Rabbi Gamaliel, he soaked in orthodoxy like a sponge, mastering the ancient texts of Scripture like windows into the very nature of God. So why did God still feel so distant? Saul thought himself an expert on Yahweh, but when Jesus tore through Paul's religious ceiling on the

9. Tom Johnston and Mike Chong Perkinson, *The Kingdom Quest: Preparing to Church Plant in the Post-Christian West* (PraxisMedia, 2019), chap. 2, Kindle.

road to Damascus, that illusion was wrecked as Paul found himself like Isaiah beholding God's glory—undone. Crawling blindly through the dust and a world of shadows, Saul realized he'd been *blind* about God himself.

And that broke him.

Prostrate at the feet of the risen Christ on the road to Damascus, Paul, though physically blind, realized that his eyes were open to God for the first time in his life. His journey to Damascus as a Pharisee interrupted, his journey of relearning the character of God as a disciple of Christ was just beginning. Paul's physical sight was instantly restored at his baptism, but learning to truly *see* God would take another lifetime. Looking back, Paul was horrified that his misunderstanding of God allowed him to justify atrocities such as imprisoning people, even condoning murder all in the name of God. *Paul learned then that the God we gaze upon determines who we ourselves become*; who we think God is determines the character we'll reflect. In *The Source*, James Michener captures this dynamic through the story of a grieving Canaanite woman, forced by her culture's gods to sacrifice her firstborn son in a fertility ritual. Embittered by the sacrifice of her son and her husband's regular "worship" with temple prostitutes, "she walked slowly homeward, seeing life in new and painful clarity; with different gods, her husband, Urbaal, would have been a different man."[10] Michener is asserting that the gods we worship determine the character of the worshiper. As Tozer puts it, "What comes into our minds when we think about God is the most important thing about us."[11]

Paul returned to the same Hebrew Scriptures, but now its pages revealed *Christ* himself, the warp of the old weaving with the weft of the new. In the process, Paul became the living embodiment of Jesus's statement that "every teacher of the law who has become a disciple in the kingdom of heaven is like the owner of a house who brings out of his storeroom new treasures as well as old" (Matt. 13:52). Paul now saw Jesus as the writer of Hebrews described him: "the radiance of God's glory and the exact representation of his being" (Heb. 1:3).

The holiness Paul once tried to find through the law Jesus embodied with

10. James Michener, *The Source* (Harper Perennial, 2004).
11. A. W. Tozer, *The Knowledge of the Holy* (Harper & Brothers, 1961), 1.

incarnational love. The law had principles, but it lacked a face, until Jesus gave it one. Paul had never *grasped* the importance of Mosaic concepts like mercy, covenant love, and enduring faithfulness until he saw them so vividly lived out; walking, weeping, bleeding, forgiving, and embracing sinners. Slowly, Jesus transformed Paul's character until the memory of Saul of Tarsus felt like another person, a stranger even—like a ghost from a past life.

God's Character Transforms Our Own

Like Paul, anyone in a head-on collision with the Holy One experiences the "Moses effect," where Moses's face-to-face encounters gazing on God transformed his character until he was the humblest man on earth (Ex. 33:11; Num. 12:3). But Moses's inward character was not the only thing that shone out—his face physically radiated the glory of God like an atomic tan—an external picture of how God's glory changes us inwardly. Paul compared this to our own experience of Jesus was we gaze into his glorious face:

> And *we all*, with unveiled face, beholding the glory of the Lord, are being transformed into the same image from one degree of glory to another. (2 Cor. 3:18 ESV, emphasis mine)

Going from one degree of glory to another is the goal of discipleship, *becoming like him as we behold his glory. God's glory, after all, is the uncontainable majesty of his character, the afterburn that radiates from his awesomeness.* As Moses demonstrates, basking in the presence of God means inevitably radiating and reflecting his glorious character to the world, which is *our purpose according to* the Westminster divines who concluded, "The chief end of man is to glorify God and enjoy him forever."

There is no candy-coated detour or shortcut through Gumdrop Forest on the journey to transformation. Beholding his glory and gazing upon his face requires slowing down and taking the shoes off our feet and sitting at his until the image of Christ is seen not only *in* us but *through* us. Jessie Cruickshank notes, "By looking at God, we mirror God and become more like him. . . .

You may be able to instruct others effectively, but it is *who you are* that has the greatest impact."[12] However, as Wright Thompson observes, "We are so obsessed with doing that we have no time and no imagination left for being."[13]

Learning Christ

If transformed lives radiate Christ's glory, our starting point can't begin with focusing on our own character. We must begin with *Christ's*. Nor will we ever become like Jesus by admiring him from a distance—it happens through inching up closely behind him as a *talmid* on the dusty road, walking close, studying his every movement, hanging on his every word. That proximity to Jesus was what Paul described to Timothy as "learning" Christ.

> *But you have not so learned Christ*, if indeed you have heard him and have been taught by him, as the truth is in Jesus: that you put off, concerning your former conduct, the old man which grows corrupt according to the deceitful lusts, and be renewed in the spirit of your mind, and that you put on the new man which was created according to God, in true righteousness and holiness. (Eph. 4:20–24 NKJV, emphasis mine)

"But you have not so learned Christ . . ."

In that passage, one thing becomes clear: Our modern definition of learning is not the Bible's definition of learning. Learning information is not *transformation*. Biblically speaking, to learn is not to know something but to *live it*. Paul echoed the same truth to Titus:

> For the grace of God has appeared that offers salvation to all people. It *teaches us* to say "No" to ungodliness and worldly passions, and to live

12. Jessie Cruickshank, *Ordinary Discipleship: How God Wires Us for the Adventure of Transformation* (NavPress, 2023), 70.
13. Wright Thompson, *Pappyland: A Story of Family, Fine Bourbon, and the Things That Last* (Penguin Press, 2020), 165.

self-controlled, upright and godly lives in this present age. (Titus 2:11–12, emphasis mine)

Every attribute of God, from his grace to his holiness, appeared as a person rather than a doctrine. Therefore, learning Christ means learning a person, for Paul, the former Pharisee, could never again separate religious character from Christ himself. Jesus wasn't a break from the Old Testament but the full picture. He no longer separated the Lord of the Old Testament from Jesus as Lord. For the God of Sinai was the man from Galilee. And this time around, Paul determined to reflect God's character as he really was—Christlike—and expected all disciples to reflect God's glory through transformed lives.

THE CHARACTER OF GOD:
EXPRESSED THROUGHOUT THE BIBLE

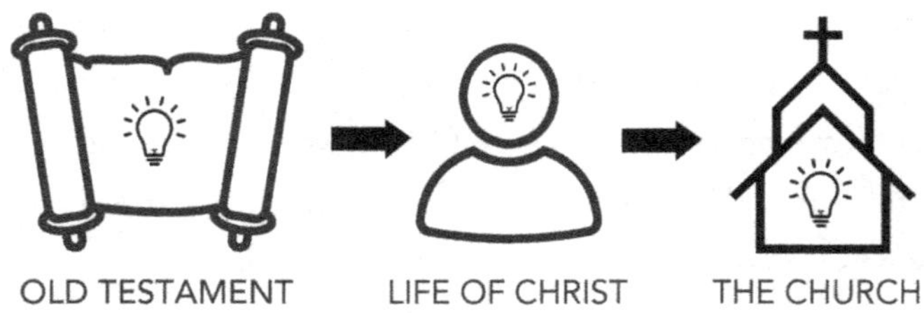

OLD TESTAMENT LIFE OF CHRIST THE CHURCH

The Continuity of God's Character

As a disciple of Jesus himself, Paul could now behold the panoramic scope of the triune God radiating his glory as Father, Son, and Holy Spirit.

The triune God revealed himself in three ways:

- In the Old Testament, the Father revealed himself through his word.
- In the incarnation, the Son revealed himself in the flesh.
- In the church, the Spirit reveals himself through us.

The marks of a mature disciple in Paul's lists to Timothy and Titus were the character not only of Jesus but of Yahweh revealed in the scrolls of the Torah. They were lived out by his Son, Jesus during his incarnation, and now reproduced in our lives through the indwelling of the Holy Spirit.

He has desired to be known and have his glory spread throughout the world again. Throughout the ages, there has always been one epicenter of this activity: the temple. The temple was a physical reminder that the infinite God of the heavens was retaking earth. Beginning in the garden of Eden, God chose to dwell amid his creation, where he walked regularly with Adam and Eve.[14] The tabernacle, a forerunner to the temple, was called the "the tent of meeting" because it existed to restore relationship with God himself. Across the panoramic spectrum of redemptive history, it looked like this:

- In the Old Testament, God revealed his glory in a building.
- During the incarnation, Jesus was the temple.
- Since Christ's ascension, we are the temple of the Holy Spirit.[15]

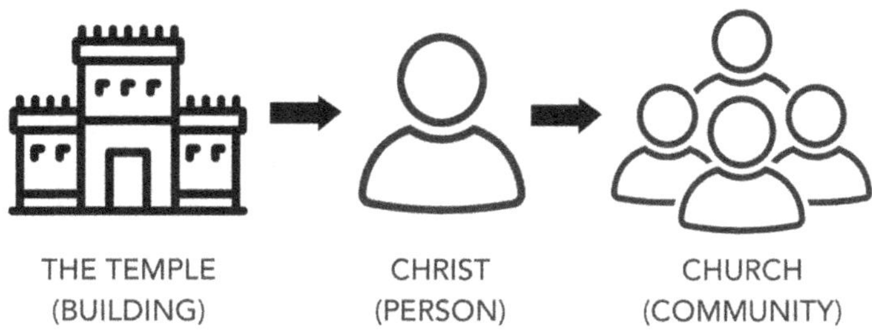

God's Physical Temple Revealed God's Character

Designed with heavenly blueprints yet constructed with earthly materials, the temple in Jerusalem stood as the crown jewel, unlike any other building on earth. Every detail represented a deeper spiritual symbolism. Every surface was crafted with intention, built from the finest stone and cedar, with walls inlaid with gold, all resonating with a sense of holiness. Every cubit was carefully

14. G. K. Beale and Mitchell Kim, *God Dwells Among Us: A Biblical Theology of the Temple* (IVP Academic, 2021), 6.
15. Many people erroneously believe that Christians were indwelt for the first time at Pentecost. However, Jesus breathed on the disciples in John 20, saying "Receive the Holy Spirit" (John 20:22).

measured, every vessel painstakingly consecrated, from the altar ablaze with sacrifice to the lampstands perpetually burning to radiate light like hope. More than a building, the temple's every beam and curtain declared that *the glory of God lives here.*

Those who stepped beyond the outer courts noticed the change in the air—thicker, heady with smoke and mystery. The scent of incense, sweet, spicy, rising in slow, swirling ribbons mingling with the acrid sting of blood and the rich aroma of roasting meat, still crackling on the altar; the scent of sacrifice, of a life given in place of another. The stone floor beneath the feet was cool to the touch, but the heat of burning offerings warmed the space. Somewhere deep within, priests chanted ancient prayers, their low murmuring voices hushed but resolute in worship. More sounds—the echoing shuffle of sandals, and the occasional bleat of a lamb before silence falls again. The holiness of God could almost be felt through all five senses—sight, sound, smell, hearing, and touch—each immersing the worshipper into an experience.

And there behind the sacred space of heavy woven curtains dyed deep in blue and scarlet lay the holy of holies, the innermost room, where heaven overshadowed earth. There the very presence that split seas and silenced armies rested just beyond that curtain, God's glory veiled by thick cloud. But the creator of the universe could not be confined within walls of stone. Even Solomon, dedicating the temple in all its splendor, confessed: "The heavens, even the highest heaven, cannot contain you. How much less this temple I have built!" (1 Kings 8:27). The physical temple, for all its beauty and precision, was never the final destination but a temporary *placeholder.* A symbolic shadow cast by a far greater reality. For the temple was always pointing forward to the day when glory would no longer rest behind a veil but would walk among us with cracked feet and eyes that burned like the coals on the altar, not with judgment but with the compassion lit by sacrifice.

If a worshipper stepped away and examined the instructions for the tabernacle carefully, they could see that the pattern transmitted in Exodus resembled *a human body.* Scarlet, blue, and purple threads woven into cords, running through the curtains, intertwined like living blood vessels. Scarlet cords to represent oxygen-rich blood. Blue cords to represent the appearance of blue veins returning our unoxygenated blood under our skin.[16] Finally, purple cords for the appearance of capillaries containing the mingling of gases in our lungs and elsewhere. And outside, draped over the tabernacle, the design called for a wrapping, not of cloth but of animal skin, smooth and taught. The entire structure began to resemble something, someone. No wonder John reached for tabernacle imagery when describing the mystery of Christ's incarnation:

> The Word became flesh and [tabernacled] among us. (John 1:14)

Jesus was the living temple where man met with God through the atonement of sacrifice. He was the temple veiling God's glory, and like the stone temples before him, this temple of flesh would also be destroyed:

> Jesus answered them, "Destroy this temple, and I will raise it again in three days." They replied, "It has taken forty-six years to build this temple, and you are going to raise it in three days?" *But the temple he had spoken of was his body.* (John 2:19–21, emphasis mine)

But the resurrection proved that God wasn't finished radiating his glory to a dark world. And the God of the tabernacle, who delighted to dwell in the midst of his people, would continue to have a temple to display his glory—through us. This was no abstract theology for Paul, who prayed,

> I pray that out of his glorious riches he may strengthen you with power through his Spirit in your inner being, so that Christ may dwell in your hearts through faith. (Eph. 3:16–17)

And

> In him you too are being built together to become a dwelling in which God lives by his Spirit. (Eph. 2:22)

16. Despite all blood being red, the appearance changes depending on the effect of light, oxygen levels, and skin tissue.

The metaphor would not have been lost on the Ephesians, whose skyline was dominated by one of the Seven Wonders of the Ancient World—their pride and joy, the Temple of Artemis. Paul brought to mind the language of measuring the temple by cubits to describe the love of God, as he continued: "That you . . . may have strength to comprehend . . . what is the breadth and length and height and depth, and to know the love of Christ that surpasses knowledge, that you may be filled with all the fullness of God" (vv. 17–19 ESV). Yet Paul was pointing to a different kind of temple. Not a temple of stone, but a living temple, as he also told the Corinthians:

> Do you not know that your bodies are temples of the Holy Spirit, who is in you, whom you have received from God? You are not your own; you were bought at a price. Therefore honor God with your bodies. (1 Cor. 6:19–20)

1. The Father, who built a temple that was *beyond us*

   > My house will be called a house of prayer. (Matt. 21:13; Isaiah 56:7)

2. The Son, who tabernacled in the flesh *among us*

   > The temple he had spoken of was his body. (John 2:21)

3. The Spirit, who now makes his home *within us*

   > Your bodies are temples of the Holy Spirit. (1 Cor. 6:19)

Jesus told his disciples that his indwelling and their character transformation were connected: "Anyone who loves me will obey my teaching. My Father will love them, and we will come to them and make our home with them" (John 14:23). This is the essence of discipleship: Christ formed *in us* (Gal. 4:19) so that his glory radiates *out of us*. The character of God, once as the law on tablets of stone, is now engraved on our hearts through the Holy Spirit. Paul's lists in 1 Timothy 3 and Titus 2 are more than leadership checklists—they are sacred echoes of God's triune character traced from Yahweh, through Christ, to us in the Spirit.

OLD TESTAMENT	NEW TESTAMENT	TODAY
Father	Son	Holy Spirit
Temple	Incarnation	Church
Building	Person	Community

Reverse Engineering God's Character

Knowing the continuity of God's character across the three persons of the trinity, the New Testament writers drew from the Old Testament like a well of wisdom. They quoted it directly over three hundred times, while alluding to it six hundred. When Paul told Timothy that ministers have a right to financial support, he quoted Deuteronomy: "Do not muzzle the ox while it treads the grain," then asked, "Was it oxen God was concerned about?" Paul was drawing out something deeper, a glimpse of God's character. If God cares for animals, then he certainly cares for people.[17] This leads to one of the chief character traits of God revealed throughout all of Scripture: God cares about everything.

When the Old Testament passages quoted or alluded to in the New Testament are distilled into themes, six character traits emerge:

- God alone is king.
- God cares about everything.
- God is a missionary.

17. In *Church Plantology,* I point out that Paul's understanding of four major principles from the Old Testament informed his mission: (1) the wisdom of the Holy Spirit diffused throughout the known world, (2) the missional mandate to spread God's glory throughout the created world, (3) the influence of Israel in the Old Testament to the nations around it as a precursor to global mission, and (4) a model community of "the people of God"; Peyton Jones, *Church Plantology: The Art and Science of Planting Churches* (Zondervan, 2021), 51–54.

- God alone is wise.
- God is relational.
- God allows suffering.

These verses reveal God's character in the Old Testament, embodied in Christ, and now expected of us.

The following chart demonstrates how the character traits of God were embodied by Jesus and inform Paul's marks of mature disciples. For example, if God alone is king, and Jesus surrendered to his Father in response, then mature disciples yield to the will of the Holy Spirit, resulting in holiness (Rom. 6:13, 19). Between Yahweh's character and our own, Christ is the linchpin.

THE CHARACTER OF GOD	LIFE OF CHRIST	MATURE DISCIPLE
God alone is king	Surrendering to God in the wilderness	Holy
God cares about everything	Wedding at Cana	Respectable Self-controlled
God is relational	Presence of the Trinity at Christ's baptism	Faithful to spouse Manage family well
God alone is wise	Asks questions in the temple	Able to teach
God is a missionary	Incarnation	Hospitable Well thought of
God allows suffering	Difficult childhood	Sober-minded

The following section walks through each of the character traits of God carried over from the Old Testament, examines how they were lived out by

Jesus, and shows how they transform our own character, leading to the marks of a mature disciple. Each trait follows this template:

1. How God the Father revealed this part of himself
2. How Jesus reflected this aspect of God's character in his life
3. How the Holy Spirit transforms us to reflect the glory of God's character in this way

PRINCIPLES OF TIME

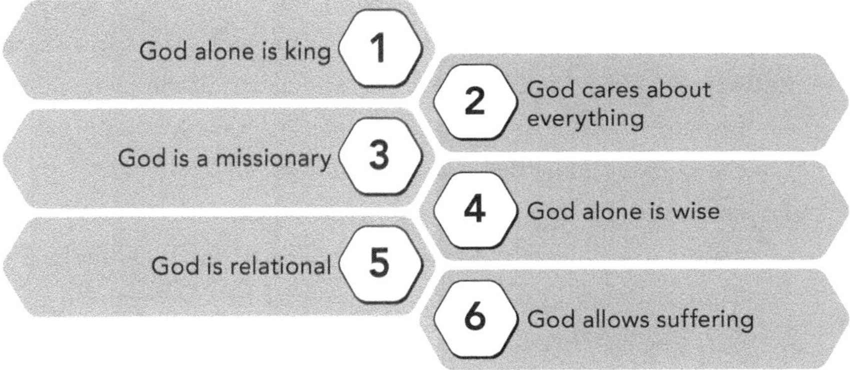

Character Trait 1: Because God Alone Is King, Mature Disciples Live Spiritually Holy

Revealed by the Father: Because God created time, space, and matter, he defines existence itself. As the eternal king, he does not need our permission to rule, for he already reigns, and our self-rule is only an illusion.

Reflected by the Son: Because Jesus surrendered perfectly to the Father's rule and reign during his incarnation, he modeled perfect worship, reliance, and surrender (even unto death).

Transformed by the Spirit: Because God alone is king, mature disciples live submitted to God's rule, they yield to the Holy Spirit as he conforms their character to Christ (Romans 8:29) imparting *holiness* (Titus 1:8). This consecration surrenders self-rule daily, praying,

"Your kingdom come, your will be done, on earth as it is in heaven," giving the world a glimpse of a kingdom worth belonging to.

Character Trait 2: Because God Cares About Everything, Mature Disciples Live Honorably in All Things

Revealed by the Father: Because God created all things, he does not divide the sacred and secular. Therefore, everything matters, from worship to work; from oxen to overlooked neighbors. The Hebraic worldview expressed in Proverbs teaches that God is present in all—how we worship, work, play, rest, and relate—and all glorify God.

Reflected by the Son: Because Jesus cared about the mundane things, like turning water to wine at a wedding, Christ modeled caring about the everyday things that concern us (1 Peter 5:7).

Transformed by the Spirit: Because God cares about everything, mature disciples are *respectable* and *self-controlled*, (1 Timothy 3:2, Titus 1:8) working with integrity, caring for their communities, and honoring their responsibilities, which glorifies the God who sees, values, and redeems every part of life.

Character Trait 3: Because God Is Relational, Mature Disciples Are Affectionate

Revealed by the Father: Because God exists in an eternal triune relationship of love, God desired to share that love with other beings, saying, "Let us make man in our image," creating man for relationship rather than servitude. As Reeves states, "God is love because God is a Trinity."[18]

Reflected by the Son: Because the Father loved the world, Jesus, the eternal Son of God, honored the Father, just as the dove descended at his baptism, and the voice of the Father thundered with joy, "This is my Son, whom I love; with him I am well pleased" (Matt. 3:17). Jesus

---

18. Michael Reeves, *Delighting in the Trinity: An Introduction to the Christian Faith* (IVP Academic, 2012), Introduction, Kindle.

loved God with all his heart and modeled faithful, loving affection for God and others.

Transformed by the Spirit: Because God is relational, mature disciples demonstrate God's affections, being faithful to their spouses and loving their children, understanding that they who would reveal Christ to others must first reveal him in their closest relationships (1 Tim. 3:4–5).

Character Trait 4: Because God Alone Is Wise, Mature Disciples Are Always Learning

Revealed by the Father: Because God's blueprints wisely laid the foundations of the earth, all wisdom lies with him, undergirding every unseen detail of our lives.

Reflected by the Son: Because divine wisdom took human form, Jesus's words astound us now, as they did others, starting with the teachers of the law at the temple. He continues to challenge conventional wisdom and stun those who listen.

Transformed by the Spirit: Because God alone is wise, mature disciples must be *able to teach* (1 Tim. 3:2): learning, wisely understanding, and applying God's Word to real life.

Character Trait 5: Because God Is a Missionary, Mature Disciples Welcome Others

Revealed by the Father: Because God has been on a mission from Genesis 3 onward, he called Abraham to bless the world through him. His relentless pursuit of people reveals a missionary heart.

Reflected by the Son: Because Jesus crossed the infinite divide between heaven and earth, he modeled the missionary heart of God—his life a mission in motion, a daily journey to seek and save the lost and walk among the broken.

Transformed by the Spirit: Because the Spirit within us is a missionary, mature disciples are hospitable (1 Tim. 3:2, Titus 1:8), opening their homes and hearts on mission so outsiders can glimpse the glory of *the God who goes.*

Character Trait 6: Because God Allows Suffering, Mature Disciples Mentally Persevere

Revealed by the Father: Because the world is broken, God allows suffering while working all things to his own glory and purposes.

Reflected by the Son: Because being loved by God does not shield us from suffering in a broken world, God's beloved Son was not spared. From the cradle in Bethlehem to the cry in the garden of Gethsemane, he was never outside the love of the Father yet was a man of sorrows, acquainted with grief.

Transformed by the Spirit: Because suffering is not a sign of God's absence but a space where trust deepens, the mature disciples mentally persevere in sober-mindedness (1 Tim. 3:2, Titus 1:8). They allow *suffering to produce perseverance, and perseverance, character.* God's love allows them to sing through scars and echo eternity amid the ache, awaiting a world without end.

You Have One Job

All of these character traits of God funnel through Christ to us, through the Spirit. Imagine the power of a life so transformed by the glory of God, so shaped by and surrendered to Christ, that when people look your way, they catch glimpses of him through you. In that sense, every disciple's life should echo the words of Jesus: "If you've seen me, you've seen the Father." God restores his image in us so that we look like Jesus and people can see the heart of God. Disciple-making is merely the vehicle.

So how do you know when a disciple is formed? Simple. It means that they're ready to make their own disciples. That's how Jesus left the Twelve. It's how Paul left Titus, Timothy, and others. Rather than telling them to look for browning edges, he gave them the lists of character traits that would show Christ forming in someone. And when they could peek through the glass and see the process of transformation in full swing, they looked less like balls of dough and more like cookies. Then they had transformed enough to make disciples themselves.

CHAPTER 5

Practices for Time

I can promise you none of these things. No sphere of usefulness: you are not needed there at all. No scope for your talents: only forgiveness for having perverted them. No atmosphere of inquiry for I will bring you not to the land of questions but of answers, and you shall see the face of God.

—C. S. LEWIS

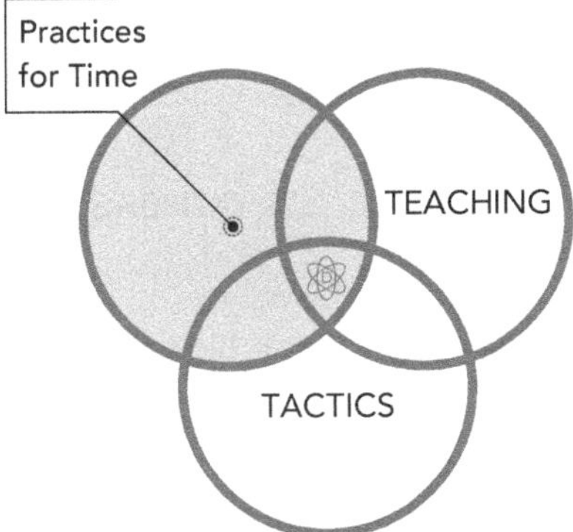

Chapter 3 explored the patterns of Time, as modeled by Jesus. Chapter 4 explored the principles of Time, showing how discipleship transforms us. Now chapter 5 moves into the practices for Time—the practical rhythms to form intentional, repeatable patterns to shape the formation of disciples.

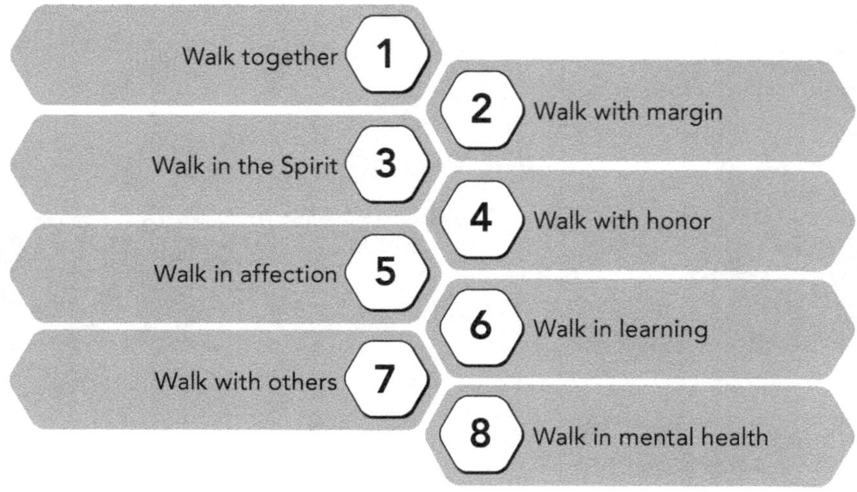

The Heart of Discipleship

Disciple-making begins with relationship—not focusing on plans, pathways, or programs but on people. Jesus came near through his incarnation, so to reach people, we must risk getting close. And above all, we must love them.

- ☐ **A LOVE FOR GOD**
- ☐ **A LOVE FOR OTHERS**

Everything Jesus did, including making disciples, was motivated by love—a love for God and for others. In the Great Commission, Jesus asks his followers to bridge the gap between them—God and people (Matt. 28:19). We love God, but other people don't. But that doesn't stop God from loving them. Therefore, disciple-making is driven by our love for God and his love for them.

Aware of these dynamics, John wrote,

> That which was from the beginning, which we have heard, which we have seen with our eyes, which we have looked at and our hands have

> touched—this we proclaim concerning the Word of life. . . . We proclaim to you what we have seen and heard, so that you also may have fellowship with us. And our fellowship is with the Father and with his Son, Jesus Christ. (1 John 1:1–3)

John pictures himself in Jesus's inner circle of fellowship. They had witnessed the Son of God up close, eating, laughing, weeping, reclining at the table: ". . . which we have seen with our eyes, which . . . our hands have touched . . ." The Word made flesh was approachable, and John couldn't help but want others to experience him too. "We proclaim to you what we have seen and heard, so that you also may have fellowship with us. And our fellowship is with the Father and with his Son, Jesus Christ" (1 John 1:3–4).

But here's the catch: You can only invite others into the circle you inhabit yourself. You can't lead people into a relationship you don't enjoy. John, a former "Son of Thunder," understood all too well that if you walk closely with Jesus, soon enough you'll love *who he loves*. And Jesus always loved people *outside the circle*. John learned from Jesus that a love for God and love for others are inseparable. He made that point repeatedly in the same letter:

> Anyone who claims to be in the light but hates a brother or sister is still in the darkness. . . . But anyone who loves their brother and sister lives in the light. (1 John 2:9–11)

> Let us love one another, for love comes from God. . . . This is love: not that we loved God, but that he loved us and sent his Son. . . . No one has ever seen God; but if we love one another, God lives in us. (1 John 4:7–12)

> Whoever claims to love God yet hates a brother or sister is a liar. . . . Anyone who loves God must also love their brother and sister. (1 John 4:20–21)

The degree to which you love God will be directly reflected by how you love others. That's where disciple-making bridges the gap. The intersection of disciple-making is where your relationship with Jesus and others meet. Think of two circles. One is your fellowship with Christ. The other is your fellowship with people. Disciple-making occupies the space where those two circles overlap—that sacred middle ground where your relationship with God touches the life of someone else, helping that person to know him better.[1]

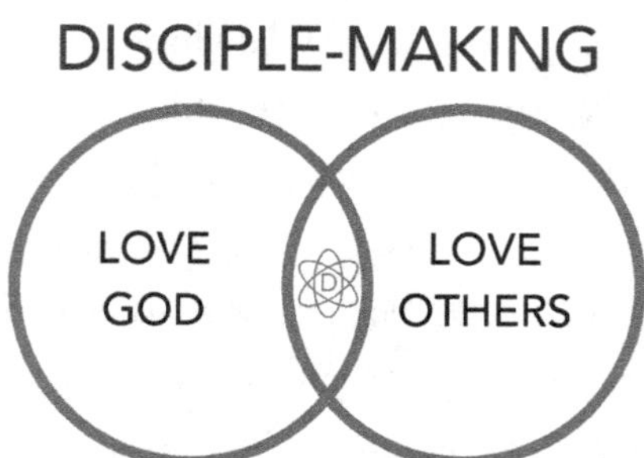

Like any good story, Jesus's disciple-making journey has an epilogue. By the end of John 20, the resurrected Christ had completed his mission. Like a Marvel post-credits bonus scene, John gives us John 21, containing a solitary conversation between Peter and Jesus as they walked down the beach. On that walk, Peter was told that his love for Jesus would work itself out by loving others—others whom Jesus also loves.

After Peter's denial and failure, Jesus stood on the beach that morning cooking breakfast for his friends and toying with them with the all-too-familiar "Friends, haven't you any fish?" It was half invitation, half holy trolling. The voice from the shore continued: "Throw your net on the right side of the boat." Peter froze. It was the same line Jesus had spoken years ago, when he first called them to follow. Jesus was intentionally bringing Peter back to that day, as if he was restoring him . . . even after all his failures. But Peter had one final lesson to learn, so after they'd eaten breakfast, Jesus pulled Peter aside to take a long walk down the beach, just the two of them.

Three questions. Three chances to say what he couldn't that awful night.

1. It's what Tom Johnston and Mike Chong Perkinson call "the irreducible core"; Tom Johnston and Mike Chong Perkinson, *The Organic Reformation: A New Hope for the Church in the West* (PraxisMedia, 2011).

"Simon . . . do you love me?"
"Yes, Lord. You know I love you."
"Feed my lambs." (v. 15)
Each time Peter answered, Jesus followed up with a variation. "Tend my sheep" (v. 16). "Feed my sheep" (v. 17).

Jesus wasn't just restoring Peter; it was like he was recommissioning him to a new kind of work—*to care*. Tend the weak. Feed the wandering. Love those who keep getting stuck like sheep, who keep getting dirty . . . just like Peter. The overlap of loving God and loving people is unmistakable: "Peter, if you love me, feed my lambs." Tend those I love. Disciple-making starts by going after the wanderers, tending the sheep, feeding the lambs. Disciple-making is always about others.

Time Practice 1: Walk Together

There are many ways we're like Peter: thick-headed, hard-hearted, and fast to forget. And because of that, Jesus doesn't call us to reach others without taking others with us. For people like Peter, it's quite the relief that we're not in this alone. Many imagine disciple-making as a solo sport, but it's a team sport. Lonnie Frisbee echoes what all disciple-makers can attest to: "I never accomplished anything of real significance for God as a lone ranger. Any good fruit from my calling and ministry always came out of a team effort."[2] Ecclesiastes gives us the wisdom behind such experience, "Two are better than one. . . . For if they fall, one will lift up his fellow. But woe to him who is alone when he falls and has not another to lift him up!" (Eccl. 4:9–10 ESV).

Therefore, from the beginning, disciple-making has always been shoulder to shoulder, step-by-step. Jesus never called individuals into isolation; he called them into community through the rhythm of Time. Then he sent the disciples out two by two because, as we've already learned, transformation happens in community. Think of becoming like Jesus as a type of community-based

2. Lonnie Frisbee with Roger Sachs, *Not By Might Nor By Power: Set Free*, rev. ed. (Freedom Publications, 2019), chap. "Colorado," Kindle.

fitness group for mission, in which you journey with someone to *develop* as disciples as you *make* disciples. As the African proverb goes, if you want to go fast, go alone. If you want to go far, go together. It's easier to stay committed when you're connected to someone. Not all of us can be like Pee-wee Herman, who could boast, "I'm a loner, Dottie . . . a rebel."

And as you shift from discipleship to disciple-making, your own journey of transformation is far from finished. So the first question to ask yourself is, *Who is my "two"?* Or, who will go two by two with you to make disciples? Your "two" is your disciple-making partner—the one who will walk beside you, shoulder to shoulder, on your two-person-team. With your "two," you will do the following:

1. Train together in the Discipology journey on the Through the Word app to learn more about the three rhythms of Discipology.
2. Start praying for one of your contacts who doesn't know Jesus. We call this person your "who"—the person you're discipling.
3. Invite your "who" to walk beside you and your "two" as you follow Jesus, using the gospel of John on the Through the Word app, forming a triad. Together you will walk in the Time, Teaching, and Tactics rhythms.

4. An optional third step is to go through *Journey to Disciple Making: A Discipology Journal* and record your journey of transformation together.

But what qualities should you look for in your "two," or disciple-making partner? It might be more helpful to talk about what you shouldn't be looking for. The section below lists the mistakes we make when recruiting our twos who need to be training alongside us:

- We recruit only people like ourselves—people who fit with our own particular personality.
- We recruit the flashy, outgoing young superstar rather than the person of real character and substance.

- We don't let people escape from the box into which we've put them; we don't let them outgrow the first impressions we have of them.[3]

The important question to ask is, Does this person reflect Jesus? You're both shining brightly but in different places. Maybe even in different ways.

When you come together, the light magnifies its effect. Have you ever noticed that lights are often grouped together? Whether a ceiling fan or a streetlight, more lights together are more powerful.

3. Colin Marshall and Tony Payne, *The Trellis and the Vine* (Matthias Media, 2024), chap. 11, Kindle.

Time Practice 2: Walk with Margin

If Jesus hadn't modeled slowing down to invest in others, we'd never see the value in it, especially with our limited time. The chart below shows how much time we have in months, assuming a ninety-year life expectancy.

We're all losing seconds at the same rate. By the time an average American is eighteen, 25 percent of the their life is already gone. An eighteen-year-old has only 312 months separating him from the age of ninety.[4]

A HUMAN LIFE IN YEARS

(assuming a ninety-year life expectancy)

1 row = 36 months (3 years)

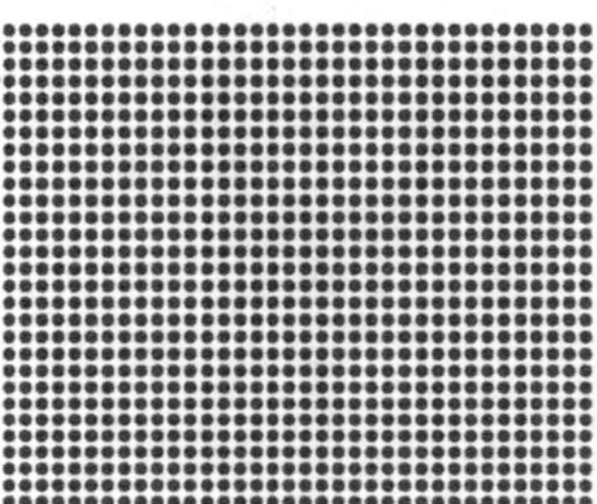

In *The Hobbit*, Gollum once riddled Bilbo Baggins about time:

> This thing all things devours;
> Birds, beasts, trees, flowers;
> Gnaws iron, bites steel;
> Grinds hard stones to meal;
> Slays king, ruins town,
> And beats high mountain down.

Bilbo answered, "Time! Time!"

His frustrated cry for more time answered the riddle, yet we could all cry the same. Time—our most precious commodity—is so easily traded away for everything else: success, stimulation, or screens. In wasted hours, we amass the equivalent of Satan's ultimate economic design, the Chuck E. Cheese ticket,

4. Around 25–30 percent of global deaths occur when people are in their seventies, and roughly 20–25 percent in their eighties. That leaves about 5–10 percent of people who die in their nineties.

redeemable for a plastic whistle or a sticky hand that doesn't even stick. It's the worst exchange rate this side of hell—yet we barter our time for things that don't add value to our lives. The reality is that time is a finite, nonrenewable resource—extra quantities can't ever be purchased or earned. We can only choose *where to spend it.* Jesus spent his limited three years of borrowed time investing in making disciples.

Jesus knew the time investment that disciple-making required, so when he called them to train as "fishers of people," he completely derailed their routine, calling them away from their day jobs and busting their schedules wide open. They accepted the commitment to walk in the margin that disciple-making takes. At some point all disciple-makers commit to give up the sands of time sifting through their fingers to gain what lasts for eternity, sowing the seeds of the temporal for a harvest of eternal value.

The chart below shows the total of ninety years in months, but, admittedly, most of us won't make it that far. It's not a question of *how long you have* but of *what you'll do with what's left.*

AN EIGHTEEN-YEAR-OLD'S REMAINING MONTHS

(assuming a ninety-year life expectancy)

Occupied time = 531 months

○ Sleep (288 months)
▲ Work/school (126 months)
◆ Driving (18 months)
▼ Cooking/eating (36 months)
✦ Chores/errands (36 months)
● Hygiene (27 months)

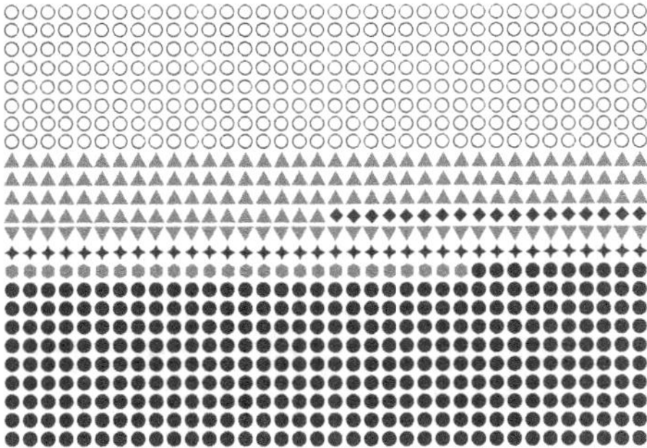

Ralph and Ruby Moore knew the answer to that question. They didn't plan on sparking a global movement. They merely committed to discipling three people at a time for fifty years, creating margin for disciple-making, refusing to allow the opportunities to slip away with every lunar cycle. No matter who you are, time marches on relentlessly, but you must value it to make kingdom impact.

312 MONTHS = 26 YEARS = 227,000 HOURS

By the 10,000 hour rule, you could master 22 skills

Alternatively, you could:

Sail around the world 214 times

Walk 264% of the distance to the moon

Or read over 26,298 books

As the saying goes, you gotta take time to make time. Consider how you'd spend your time if a price was put on every hour of it. If you value your time at $20 an hour and spend the two hours a day the average American spends on social media, you'd be wasting $1,200 a month. That's the sound of more than money drifting away—it's opportunity for mission drifting away one reel at a time. Any marathon runner will tell you that we don't wake up one morning suddenly able to run twenty-six miles, nor do we stumble into benching our own body weight. We prioritize our time by setting an alarm, showing up when it hurts, prioritizing the schedule, saying no to lesser things, and training like we want to win (1 Cor. 9:24). Disciple-making won't magically squeeze itself into your schedule; you must create margin for it. Making disciples starts with making time.

Nobody can tell you what rhythm is going to work for you, but here are some suggestions for disciple-making:

Daily Rhythms of Disciple-Making

- Pray for the person you're discipling
- Use the Discipology app to walk with someone to help them know Jesus

Weekly Rhythms

- Keep in regular contact with the person you're discipling, sending texts or making phone calls
- Get together for coffee, meals, social events, or hobbies with the person you're discipling

- Gather as families

Monthly Rhythms

- Reflect and strategize your disciple-making approach
- Retake the SHALOM assessment to track your progress

What's the SHALOM assessment? Glad you asked.

The next six practices of the Time rhythm are packaged together in a discipleship tool called the SHALOM Star. The Hebrew word *shalom* is a pregnant word often translated as "peace," while the exact meaning is closer to "wholeness." *The Complete Word Study Old Testament* defines the root word as "complete, wholehearted, perfect" but notes that it also conveyed the act of blessing "to restore, to repay, to make restitution, to reward."[5] In Jesus's day, saying "*Shalom aleichem*," or "Peace be upon you," was the customary greeting, but it also doubled as a pronouncement of blessing—for life as the Creator intended. Wishing someone "*Shalom*" carried the profound promise that one day all the blessings of Eden would be restored to the world, while also asking God to grant them a glimpse of that peace in the present.

The *shalom* greeting harkened back to when God formed humankind from dust. He wove humankind's mind and body, heart and soul, and spirit together to function as an integrated whole. Every aspect of our humanity in tune with another—thoughts, emotions, work, rest, worship, and relationships all drawing their source from the peace of being in harmony with God. Our cosmic fall disrupted the balance God designed, causing us to be out of harmony with God and ourselves, fragmenting and disjointing our psyche. The root word for "anxiety" conveys the opposite of *shalom,* meaning "to be pulled apart or stretched in different directions," leaving us feeling drawn and quartered. As with a pinched nerve in the spine, imbalance in one area can ripple across the whole frame. Today, medical experts are trained to view patients as integrated bio-psycho-social-spiritual beings.[6]

---

5. Warren P. Baker and Eugene Carpenter, *The Complete Word Study Old Testament* (AMG Publishers, 1994), 2608.
6. Taken from Sister Calista Roy's Adaptation model.

Jesus's greatest commandment speaks to the integrated parts of our humanity, body, soul, mind, and spirit:

> You shall love the Lord your God with all your heart and with all your soul and with all your strength and with all your mind. (Luke 10:27 ESV)

- Heart: Your emotional and mental life
- Soul: Your spiritual life
- Strength: Your physical body
- Mind: Your intellect and thought life

To love God with all our heart, soul, mind, and strength is not only the greatest commandment—it brings the greatest blessing. When every aspect of our humanity orients its faculties toward God in love, the blessing of peace within can quiet the chaos of the storms without. Being perfect, Christ balanced every area effortlessly. Likewise, as the Spirit forms Christ within us, the relational, emotional, spiritual, and intellectual aspects become increasingly balanced. Christ, the source of our peace, inhabits the center, restoring *shalom*—or wholeness. Hans Urs von Balthasar has said, "Only in Christ are all things in communion. He is the point of convergence of all hearts and beings and therefore the bridge and the shortest way from each to each."[7]

The SHALOM Star uses the acronym "SHALOM" for the six aspects of our lives that find balance only as we allow God to permeate them:

Spirit: Your soul's connection to God
Honor: The areas of life you steward
Affections: Your family and friendships
Learning: Your intellect and creativity
Others: Your allies on mission
Mental: Your emotional well-being

---

7. Hans Urs von Balthasar, *The Grain of Wheat: Aphorisms* (Ignatius Press, 2011), chap. "Christ," Kindle.

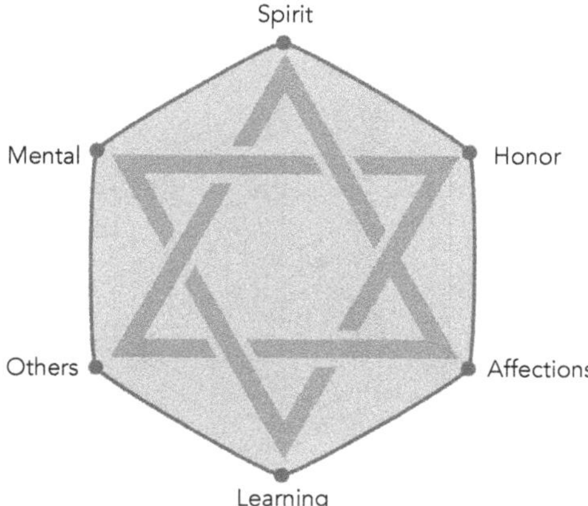

The SHALOM Star is designed as a simple assessment you can revisit weekly on your own, or monthly with your disciple-making partner (your two). It tracks your maturity and growth as a disciple in these six areas, functioning like a wholistic dashboard to track balance.

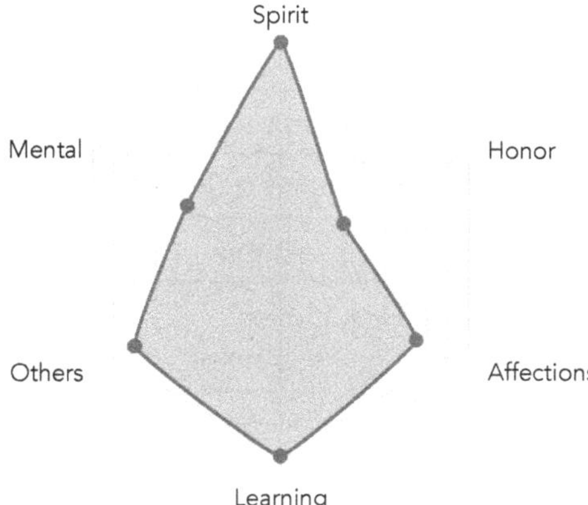

Shalom isn't some Zen-like state in which everything feels calm and under control. Nor is it balance for balance's sake but something much deeper. The SHALOM Star mirrors the marks of mature disciples from the previous chapter as demonstrated in the table below.

Our soul, responsibilities, relationships, intellect, and mental health are all integrated into our *transformation journey,* woven into the very fabric of a Christlike character. Transformation doesn't happen in the abstract, but takes place in the rhythms of our mundane everyday lives. These aren't just life categories—they're signposts for maturity, markers that help us trace the contours of Christ being formed in us.

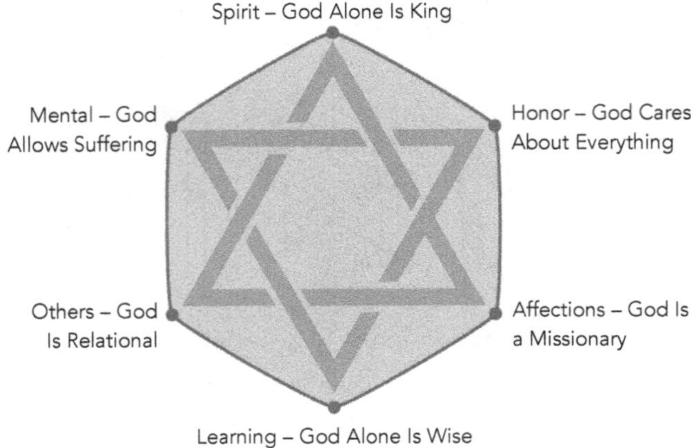

SHALOM STAR	MATURE DISCIPLES
Spiritual	Holy
Honor	Respectable, self-control led
Affections	Faithful to spouse, able to manage family well
Learning	Able to teach
Others	Hospitable Well thought of
Mental	Sober-minded

The rest of this chapter will unpack each of these six areas to help you track the transformation, both in yourself and in the disciples you make, to discover practical ways to walk in step with the Spirit through every part of your life.

Time Practice 3: Walk in the Spirit

Paul said that a mature disciple should be holy, and that can only come from the Spirit. The *S* in the SHALOM tool stands for "spirit," and our spiritual life is gauged by our alignment and surrender to God's will. It encapsulates everything present in the Lord's Prayer: reverence, worship, adoration, surrender, confession, forgiveness, and reliance on God. Despite what others tell you, there's more to our spiritual lives than prayer times and Bible reading plans. The pulse of our inner lives centers on meeting with God relationally. Our connection with God isn't based on what *we* do for him but in what *he's* done for us. Everything should be built on the foundation of God's immeasurable love for us as demonstrated by Christ's finished work on the cross. Immersing ourselves daily in his love, basking in his grace, we discover the counterintuitive secret of walking with God—that abiding in Christ means not trusting in yourself but hiding yourself in him, allowing him to be your all-sufficiency.

Be careful that you don't allow this part of the SHALOM tool to become a metric for your worth or value, as your value to God was demonstrated by Christ's loving sacrifice for you. This tool should only gauge your soul's surrender to God's will, not your righteousness, for that is found in Christ alone.

When using the SHALOM Star, remember that spiritual health doesn't mean the absence of struggles or wrestling against your flesh; it simply means you know where to bring them. All your fears, joys, weariness, and brokenness are all a part of your sacred connection with God. Because God alone is king, we surrender everything to him, yielding to the Holy Spirit. To prioritize his spiritual life, Jesus regularly rose early to be alone with his Father, making that a must for all disciple-makers to establish this relationship first.

Time Practice 4: Walk with Honor

Paul said that a mature disciple should be respectable and self-controlled. This is the outward, physical part of our lives, where we model outwardly what is going on inwardly. If Proverbs teaches us anything, it is that the physical and mundane aspects of our lives should not be compartmentalized from the spiritual. In Proverbs, the law of God is applied to work, domestic affairs, business dealings, and even how we treat our animals. Mature disciples honor what they've been entrusted with as good stewards. Paul addressed this with the Thessalonians: "Make it your ambition to lead a quiet life: You should mind your own business and work with your hands, just as we told you, so that your daily life may win the respect of outsiders and so that you will not be dependent on anybody" (1 Thess. 4:11–12).

We were designed to be physical beings that interact with the physical world, a world we were instructed by God to manage and steward. The SHALOM tool brings the physical aspects of our lives back into balance, rescuing us from poor dualistic theology that teaches us to think about God only when engaging in spiritual activities, such as attending church but leaving him at the door as we exit. Mature disciples bring the presence of God with them everywhere and seek to honor God by stewarding everything well—mundane responsibilities, physical health, financial obligations, household chores—because God cares about everything.

Jerry Trousdale and Glenn Sunshine speak to the integrated nature of the spiritual and physical in the way the church honors their responsibility in the world:

> Christians are not to be concerned only with people's souls; they are also to been concerned with their wellbeing in this world. Christians have always tended to the sick and built hospitals; they have always fed the hungry; they began the first charitable institutions in human history. Why? Because Christians have always believed that the body is important. Christians have always opened schools; in fact, most of the major universities in the world, historically, were founded by Christians. Why? Because Christianity is concerned with the mind. Christians were the first to develop technologies that make the laborer's work better, easier, and more productive. Why? Because work is a positive good, given to us before the Fall. The Fall brought with it drudgery and painful toil, but Christ came to redeem us from the effects of the Fall, and so we are to restore dignity to work. As Christians, we are to bring joy back to the work we do. Christians invented the idea of universal human rights. Why? Because the Bible tells us about human dignity founded on the image of God and on the Incarnation of Christ.[8]

---

8. Jerry Trousdale and Glenn Sunshine, *The Kingdom Unleashed: How Jesus' 1st-Century Kingdom Values Are Transforming Thousands of Cultures and Awakening His Church* (DMM Library, 2018), chap. 2, Kindle.

The neglect of the physical world around us does not demonstrate the virtue of being filled with the Spirit. Quite the contrary. It won't impress your neighbors that you don't mow your lawn because you're "doing important God stuff." Neither is it a sign of virtue to neglect the stewardship of your physical health because you "care so much about the soul." To everyone looking on, it demonstrates that something is out of balance, and it won't "win the respect of outsiders." Honoring the stewardship God has entrusted to us does that. It also leads to the balance of shalom—life as the Creator intended it.

Paul used the very word *honor* writing to the Corinthians: "Do you not know that your bodies are temples of the Holy Spirit, who is in you? . . . You are not your own; you were bought at a price. Therefore, *honor* God with your bodies" (1 Cor. 6:19–20, emphasis mine). God didn't just create your soul; he knit your body together in your mother's womb fearfully and wonderfully, breathing your soul into it. Therefore, your body isn't an afterthought but a sacred space, a temple. God's image is still stamped on our humanity, meaning that we are responsible to steward our physical health. While the Bible doesn't directly command workouts or weight training, it affirms the value of physical fitness. "Physical training is of some value," Paul told Timothy, "but godliness has value for all things" (1 Tim. 4:8). Like everything we possess, it is on loan to us. Therefore, how we treat our bodies matters—the food we eat, the rest we get, the pace we run, the care we neglect. These aren't neutral choices but acts of worship or warning signs of imbalance. Honoring the stewardship of our bodies isn't about chasing the mirror's approval either; it's about stewarding our strength for mission. Robbing your health is robbing God of the opportunity to fully work through you. This is why Wesley wrote a book on physical health for his circuit riders, writing, "Observe all the time the greatest exactness in your regimen or manner of living. Abstain from all mixed, all high seasoned food. Use plain diet, easy of digestion. . . . Use as much exercise daily in the open air, as you can without weariness. . . . Above all, add to the rest . . . that old unfashionable medicine, prayer."[9] For Wesley, these things were all interrelated.

9. John Wesley, *Primitive Physick; or, An Easy and Natural Method of Curing Most Diseases*, 14th ed. (Bristol, 1770).

This includes rest as well, a too often neglected part of our stewardship. Rest is so crucial that God sanctified rest with the Sabbath in the Old Testament to ensure that the Israelites maintained balance. Even Jesus didn't work against the limits of his physical body but honored it. If he got tired, he took naps. Walking hundreds of miles, he became familiar with the ache of physical exhaustion. When we're exhausted, inflamed, anxious, or out of rhythm, it affects how we disciple others. When we're healthy, present, and physically grounded, we have margin to serve, listen, and love well. Unfortunately, disciple-makers tend to pour themselves out for others while neglecting themselves. But you can't sustain ideal soul care without caring for your health. Burnout, anxiety, and fatigue don't come out of nowhere but are warnings from the dashboard that your rhythms are out of sync.

Mature disciples honor everything they have been entrusted with, from their work ethic, to their neighbors, to mundane chores. All of it truly matters, for God cares about everything.

Time Practice 5: Walk in Affection

Paul says that a mature disciple is faithful to their spouse and gives attention to their *oikos*, or "household." The family is a leader's first congregation, primary mission field, and the testing ground of their character. For Paul, saving the world began at home, "for if someone does not know how to manage his own household, how will he care for God's church?" (1 Tim. 3:5 ESV). This means we should disciple our children first, before anyone else. For in the home, the gospel takes on flesh, incarnating God's love. Or, if neglected, home is where it all falls apart behind closed doors. Building on the Honor part of the SHALOM Star, our family responsibilities shouldn't be background noise to disciple-making but the soundtrack. The Spirit himself teaches us to honor our spouses and to parent with grace, because if the gospel doesn't work at home, it won't work anywhere. If we neglect the responsibilities to love and care for our own households, Paul said we are "worse than an unbeliever" (1 Tim. 5:8).

But when we invest in our household, imperfectly but intentionally, we build a sanctuary where the Spirit dwells, where discipleship breathes, and where the glory of God quietly radiates out from the living room into the world. Personally, in the Jones house, it means saying sorry to each other a lot, not just as spouses but to our kids. That's what it sounds like when a family truly embodies the grace of a relational God who laid down his own life to cover our sins.

Time Practice 6: Walk in Learning

Paul said that a mature disciple should be able to teach. In the SHALOM Star, *learning* represents the development of our thinking, our willingness to deepen our knowledge and gain wisdom about the world around us. God gave us a mind, and he meant for us to use it. In fact, loving God with your *mind* is part of the Great Commandment: "Love the Lord your God with all your heart and with all your soul and with all your strength and with all your *mind*" (Luke 10:27, emphasis mine). In rabbinical style, Jesus trained the Twelve to think deeply. He asked 307 rabbinical questions, and out of the 157 questions he was asked, he answered only 3 directly. The intended consequence was to make his followers work hard for the answers—to think.

The role of our intelligence and critical thinking often gets overlooked, but it's an essential aspect of our makeup, therefore it's essential to our pursuit of God. Being made in the image of God means we reflect a God who thinks and reasons—the Logos himself. Therefore, a maturing disciple doesn't stop at belief but presses into understanding to not merely *know* about God but to think like him as well. Although Proverbs warns, "Lean not on your own understanding" (Prov. 3:5), the Spirit of God doesn't bypass the mind, he transforms it. This means renewing our minds (Rom. 12:2) by allowing God's Word to demolish arguments and opinions in our thinking that oppose the wisdom of God (2 Cor. 10:5). Church history boasts an incredible host of thinkers, intellects who loved and glorified God with their reason and imaginations: R. C. Sproul, Tim Keller, Martyn Lloyd-Jones, J. R. R. Tolkien, Flannery O'Connor, Charles Spurgeon, Dorothy Sayers, Madeleine L'Engle, and C. S. Lewis, to name a few.

Peter also exhorted us to pursue learning: "Make every effort to add to your faith goodness; and to goodness, *knowledge*" (2 Peter 1:5, emphasis mine). Rather than being honored by lazy thinking, God is glorified whenever we engage truth deeply, study Scripture, and wrestle with difficult questions. But he is also honored when, butting up against the limits of our intellect, we declare with one of the most brilliant minds in history, Saint Augustine, "Let others wrestle. I will wonder." When easy answers don't come, questions are converted to worship.

Finally, the discovery of neuroplasticity affirms that the renewing of our minds is a physical phenomenon. Rather than our minds being fixed, they are capable of forming new neural pathways, adapting and expanding with learning and experience. Our reasoning skills can strengthen, our understanding can deepen, and our imaginations can awaken. Maturing disciples should become not increasingly brainless over time but increasingly intellectually alive because an all-wise God is the fount of all knowledge.

Time Practice 7: Walk with Others

We were never meant to walk alone. From humanity's first breath in Eden, we were hardwired for connection. "It is not good for the man to be alone" (Gen. 2:18) wasn't a statement about marriage but a divine commentary on the human condition. Designed by a triune God to thrive in relationships, we were created in the image of a God who joyfully exists within an eternal relationship of Father, Son, and Spirit. We wither socially, mentally, and spiritually without deep meaningful relationships with people in our corner. We need others, as Bono sang, "Sometimes you can't make it on your own."[10]

For this reason, Jesus surrounded himself with twelve, drew close to three, and modeled disciple-making in community. Your allies—who encourage, challenge, and walk beside you—are vital to your disciple-making journey. The joke that Jesus's greatest miracle was that at age thirty-three he still had

10. U2, "Sometimes You Can't Make It on Your Own," *How to Dismantle an Atomic Bomb* (Interscope Records, 2004), compact disc.

eleven close friends painfully hits home. Despite the tendency of leaders to try and "go it alone," disciple-making requires the support of others inside our circle to reach others outside it. Support systems aren't a luxury in life but sometimes the lifeline itself. Paul's allies kept him going, from his deep bond with Timothy, whom he called "my true son in the faith" (1 Tim. 1:2), to his affection for Titus, his "true child in our common faith" (Titus 1:4). Paul's ministry associates were more than companions—they were mental ballasts in turbulent waters. David's soul being knit to Jonathan's "helped him find strength in God" (1 Sam. 23:16). Elijah had Elisha. Ruth had Naomi. Moses had Aaron and Hur to hold up his arms when they grew too weary to lift. Even Jesus leaned on the companionship of his disciples in Gethsemane, and though they failed him, his last request from them was friendship: *Stay with me* (see Matt. 26:38).

Church history provides a rich roster of legendary allies: Augustine and Ambrose, Luther and Melanchthon, Tolkien and Lewis. When your relationships are thriving, your soul breathes deeply, and "as iron sharpens iron, so one person sharpens another" (Prov. 27:17). Because God is a missionary, mature disciples are others oriented; they build strong circles around them, while constantly seeking to bring others into it, just like Jesus did.

Time Practice 8: Walk in Mental Health

Estimates suggest that over 50 percent of people experiencing poor mental health symptoms do not access formal treatment.[11] As a former psych nurse, I've learned to read the pain behind the eyes of individuals who present fine on the outside but are barely holding it together. Anxiety, depression,

11. In 2022 only 50.6 percent of US adults with any mental illness received treatment; "The State of Mental Health in America," Mental Health America, accessed September 20, 2025, https://mhanational.org/the-state-of-mental-health-in-america/. The World Health Organization indicates that 35–50 percent of mental illnesses in high-income countries and 76–85 percent in low- and middle-income countries go untreated; "Prevalence, Severity, and Unmet Need for Treatment of Mental Disorders," World Health Organization World Mental Health Surveys, *Journal of the American Medical Association* (June 2004).

burnout—none of these is a failure of faith; it's a part of living in a broken world. Just as bodies can be broken, the tissue and function of our brains can take a beating. You're not alone if you've felt overwhelmed, numb, stuck in fear, or unable to get out of bed. You're also not any less a disciple or disciple-maker if you have had these symptoms. Jesus himself was "a man of sorrows and acquainted with grief" (Isa. 53:3 ESV). Matthew quoted Isaiah regarding Jesus's gentle compassion toward those who struggle mentally: "A bruised reed he will not break, and a smoldering wick he will not snuff out" (Matt. 12:20). During a dark time of deep depression, D. Martyn Lloyd-Jones found an exposition of this verse to be a lifeline.

> I shall never cease to be grateful to . . . Richard Sibbes who was balm to my soul at a period in my life when I was overworked and badly overtired, and therefore subject in an unusual manner to the onslaughts of the devil. In that state and condition to read theology does not help, indeed it may be well-nigh impossible; what you need is some gentle tender treatment for your soul. I found at that time that Richard Sibbes, who was known in London in the early seventeenth century as "The Heavenly Doctor Sibbes" was an unfailing remedy. His books *The Bruised Reed* and *The Soul's Conflict* quietened, soothed, comforted, encouraged and healed me.[12]

The Bible may not use the term "mental health," but it speaks straight to the souls of those who suffer. "The Lord is close to the brokenhearted and saves those who are crushed in spirit" (Ps. 34:18). And Jesus? He came not for the healthy but for the sick. He said, "Come to me, all you who are weary and burdened, and I will give you rest. . . . For I am gentle and humble in heart, and you will find rest for your souls" (Matt. 11:28–29). Rest. Not pressure. Not shame. Just the promise of a restful place in him that makes healing possible.

Elijah, a spiritual baller, hit a wall in what could be described in modern

12. D. Martyn Lloyd-Jones, *Preaching and Preachers* (Zondervan, 1971), 186–87.

terms as a mental breakdown. After his showdown on Mount Carmel, Elijah ran for his life, collapsed under a tree, and begged God to end his life. Unlike Job's friends, God didn't scold. God is not threatened by our mental health struggles, neither is he afraid of our darkness. Rather, he comes into it and meets us there. God prescribed sleep to Elijah and sent him food and, after he'd rested physically, talked him through it. His physical and mental states were interconnected, reflecting the wholistic balance of our design.

Our emotional states play a powerful role in our design; God wired us for both joy and sorrow, celebration and lament. The heart, in Hebrew thought, is the center of our entire inner life: our thinking, our feeling, and our willing. Proverbs says, "Above all else, guard your heart, for everything you do flows from it" (Prov. 4:23). Guarding your heart means tending and nurturing it, but how? As bio-psycho-social-spiritual beings, the way back to mental health often comes through balancing the points on the SHALOM Star. For example, restoring our mental balance can come through movement, running, swimming, or dancing. As with Elijah, restoration can come through rest and creating margin to play. Recreation can be re-creation. Sometimes healing happens through the Learning sector: creating things or reading something restorative, as in Lloyd-Jones's case. It can come through laughing with friends in the Affection sector, or sitting with God in the Spiritual sector to reduce anxiety. Lastly, there are times when professional medical care is required. No shame or stigma should be placed on a disciple for needing help with their mental state any more than seeking cardiac surgery when needed.

Years ago, I wept as I read about the eighteenth-century British poet William Cowper and his struggle with depression. Cowper was the best friend of John Newton, as well as Newton's cowriter of the hymn "Amazing Grace." This man of God had written so many beautiful hymns and poems that had blessed so many, yet few knew of the horrific struggles that beset his life and served as the crucible that forged his words. Cowper suffered a nervous breakdown, and, as a result, walked with a mental limp for the rest of his life. Considered the greatest poet of his day by Wordsworth, Coleridge, and Austen, many felt that his great talents were squandered when he stopped publishing poetry and focused instead on glorifying Christ with his craft. Unknown to many at the time, "God Moves in a Mysterious Way" was penned about how God miraculously intervened in his multiple suicide attempts. Newton would physically hold and restrain Cowper through his manic fits of raving and foaming at the mouth when he was suffering strong delusions and hallucinations. Cradling Cowper in his arms, Newton would pray over him, whispering soothingly to him until the fit passed. Because the wolf was always at the door, Cowper began to surround himself with things that brought him peace and reduced his anxiety. You can visit his house in Olney, England, and stand at the small six-foot "Summer House" (or, as he called it, the "verse manufactory"), where he penned his poems and hymns, nestled in a picturesque English walled garden, surrounded by flowers, bees, and, eventually, three pet hares. Cowper took in the first hare when it failed to thrive under the care of a friend's child. Cowper felt that the hare might help aid his mental state, which it did. He wrote, "How cheerful they are in their spirits, what enjoyment they have of life."[13] Cowper teaches us that peace can come from the most unexpected places.

Cowper also reminds us that despite our brokenness, God can use us powerfully. Our mental state matters to God, and he loves us far more than anything we can ever do for him. The Great Physician knows how to send his Spirit to do what no human help can do. Paul seemed to have intimate experience with mental exhaustion, having experienced burnout in Corinth, testifying, "We almost despaired of life." It takes a man who has been ripped apart by anxiety to prescribe receiving "a peace that surpasses understanding" (Phil. 4:7). Paul's warfare of the mind taught him to "take every thought captive to the obedience of Christ Jesus" (2 Cor. 10:5), which positions the mind as a potential battlefield. So if your mind and emotions are struggling, hear this: You're not broken beyond repair. You're human. You're loved. And you're not alone.[14]

---

13. William Cowper, letter to *The Gentleman's Magazine*, May 28, 1784, in *Works of William Cowper* (London, 1849), Project Gutenberg, www.gutenberg.org/files/47790/47790-h/47790-h.htm.
14. For those struggling, I wholeheartedly recommend *Radically Living, Quietly Dying* by Mike Chong Perkinson (Light and Life Publishing, 2024).

Tying It All Together

Each of these six areas reflect who *you* are because of who *God* is. Using the SHALOM Star is about revealing how his character has shaped your own—spiritually, physically, relationally, intellectually, missionally, and emotionally.

SHALOM STAR	GOD'S CHARACTER	MATURE DISCIPLES
Spirit	God alone is king	Holy
Honor	God cares about everything	Respectable, self-controlled
Affections	God is a missionary	Hospitable, well thought of
Learning	God alone is wise	Able to teach
Others	God is relational	Faithful to spouse, able to manage family well
Mental	God allows suffering	Sober-minded

How does God's character shape our *shalom*, our integrated wholeness?

Walking in the Spirit: We surrender to the Holy Spirit, surrendering to *God as king,* like Jesus did.

Walking with honor: We honor what God has physically entrusted to us, like Jesus did, knowing that *God cares about everything.*

Walking in affection: We are faithful to our spouses, children, and friends, as those adopted by Christ into the family of a *relational* God.

Walking in learning: We humbly pursue growth in wisdom to better worship the *all-wise God*, whose wisdom was on full display in Christ.

Walking with others: We welcome others because *God is a missionary* who sent his Son as the ultimate missionary.

Walking in mental health: We value soul care and endure suffering, knowing that God allowed sorrow and pain in the life of his beloved Son.

Walking It Out Together

Discipleship, like disciple-making, is a journey. We walk with others.

Imagine meeting regularly with a tight circle of friends and fellow disciple-makers on the same journey using the SHALOM Star. Imagine how your transformation might accelerate if you created the community Jesus did with the Twelve. What would happen if you regularly checked in, prayed hard, laughed harder, and held each other to the fire? I belonged to a group like that for years. In our journey together, our lives fell apart; one lost a child, another had his dreams of his son ever speaking shattered, another nearly lost a spouse to cancer, and one has since gone home. And slowly, over time, we were transformed through the power of walking with Jesus together, through the grace and grit of real life.

The SHALOM Star is like a compass on your journey, helping you navigate your way as you aim to thrive together. Use it monthly at a minimum, setting a rhythm with your "two"—your disciple-making partner. Don't run and hide from the imbalances in your life, but turn and face them with others. And under God's grace, invite the gentle power of the Holy Spirit into the broken places. Discipleship, like disciple-making is about progression, not perfection. That's why it's a walk—we walk together in community with Jesus until we become like him.

It may be easier to download a copy of the SHALOM Star that can be reused, rather than writing in this book or ripping out pages. You can download a digital version of the SHALOM Star for free.

As you walk together, may you encourage each other to stay focused on Jesus, never losing sight of him. Let the SHALOM tool guide you to focus not on yourselves but on Jesus, that you might be inspired by those who have gone before us:

> Therefore, since we are surrounded by so great a cloud of witnesses, let us also lay aside every weight, and sin which clings so closely, and let us run with endurance the race that is set before us, looking to Jesus, the founder

and perfecter of our faith, who for the joy that was set before him endured the cross, despising the shame, and is seated at the right hand of the throne of God.

Consider him who endured from sinners such hostility against himself, so that you may not grow weary or fainthearted. In your struggle against sin you have not yet resisted to the point of shedding your blood. (Heb. 12:1–4 ESV)

A walk of faith like that is a walk worth taking.

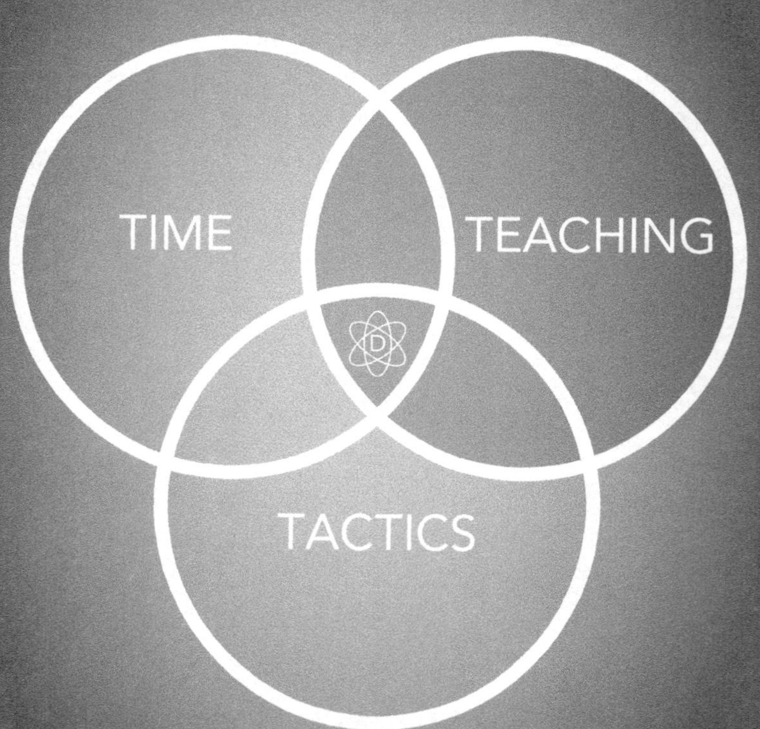
TIME
TEACHING
TACTICS
D

PART III

TEACHING—WHERE DISCIPLES ARE TRAINED

Jesus didn't just spend time with his disciples; he trained them. As the book moves into the Teaching rhythm, we will observe how Jesus moved from friendship to formation. In the second year, his focus on the Teaching rhythm rewired their thinking and prepared them for kingdom mission. He taught with power and modeled truth in action powerfully. He demonstrated that making disciples isn't merely learning what to believe but also how to live it out.

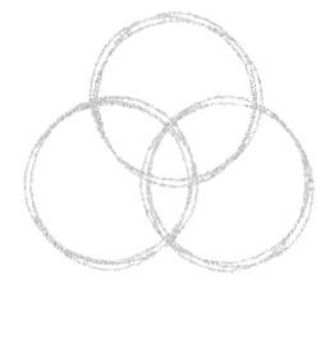

CHAPTER 6

Patterns of Teaching

You cannot understand *what* Jesus taught unless you understand *how* he taught.

—**DALLAS WILLARD**

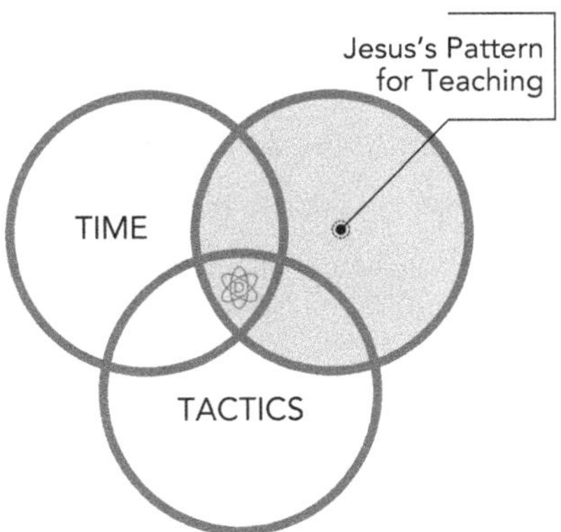

Peter thought back to what a crazy week it had been and wondered, *How could everything shift so fast in so short a time?* It had all begun over a week ago, on familiar dusty roads, winding back to Nazareth, his hometown, during their routine synagogue stop, as on so many Sabbaths before. Jesus stood to read, as he had dozens of times, but this time he turned to a different passage, reading from Isaiah, about the Messiah. His voice carried like thunder: "Today this Scripture is fulfilled in your hearing" (Luke 4:21).

The immediate silence fell heavy, then exploded into fury. The scroll had barely been rolled before they were dragging him to the edge of town, hands trembling with rage, hearts burning with disbelief. They meant to throw him off a cliff—but something stopped them. They parted like the Red Sea before Moses, and he walked right through them, untouched. When they asked him later, Jesus just laughed. But behind the humor, they caught something new in his eyes—an ache, quiet and deep. The first flicker of Isaiah's shadow: *a man of sorrows, acquainted with grief.*

Still, something had shifted. It felt strangely catalytic, almost like his rejection had lit a match inside him.

Was it also why the atmosphere was so electric at the synagogue in Capernaum yesterday? Jesus had barely begun teaching when a man, wild-eyed and unhinged, collapsed on the floor—terrified. Possessed. The demon inside him screamed, naming Jesus with ancient dread: "The Holy One of God!" It was a title meant for Messiah—the very thing Jesus had claimed in Nazareth.

Shock rippled through the room. Whispers stirred. And, in a town like Capernaum, whispers could start wildfires. So, Peter, trying to shield Jesus from the swirl, invited him home to lay low for the afternoon. But peace doesn't last long when heaven touches earth. Jesus healed Peter's mother-in-law, and by sunset the whole town of fevered, crippled, and possessed stood outside their door.

Jesus didn't turn them away. One by one, he laid hands, whispered life, and drove out darkness. Demons shrieked his name—"Son of God!"—but he silenced each one, commanding them not to speak. Jesus healed long into the night, the flicker of oil lamps catching glimpses of hope in the eyes of the desperate.

Then came the morning. Peter didn't remember when he slipped away to drift off to sleep, but a fisherman, he woke up in darkness just as he did every day. It was hours before sunrise, a perfect time for fishing, but he went to check on Jesus in the spare room before he left.

Jesus was gone.

He found him at last by the water's edge, sitting alone in the darkness, lips moving in prayer, eyes lost in the shimmer of the predawn sea.

When they approached, Jesus startled as if pulled from another world. "The time has come . . . I have to go. I'm leaving Capernaum," he said quietly.

Peter tried to stop him, confused. Why leave now, when momentum had just begun? But Jesus simply said, "I must proclaim the good news of the kingdom of God to the other towns also, because that is why I was sent" (Luke 4:43).

That was yesterday. Peter still felt the ache of it—Jesus was leaving. He didn't quite understand why, but, then again, Jesus was often like that: cryptic, layered, always one step ahead in meaning. That mystery was part of what made following him so compelling. Their weekend Sabbath trips from town to town had become Peter's favorite rhythm, like walking on the edge of something eternal. He needed that feeling today. Needed it to lift the bitter weight of a fruitless night as he cleaned his empty nets with wrinkled fingers and a tired heart.

They'd been out fishing the entire night, but the nets came back empty, whispering disappointment with every pull. Casting their nets under a moonlit sky, dragging in nothing but silence and seaweed, they knew it was one of those nights when the sea kept its secrets. Fishermen by trade, Peter, John, James, and Andrew knew that if they didn't catch, they didn't eat. Exhausted, they made for shore. After hauling in the boats, they stretched out the nets and cleaned them, only adding to the resentment that the water gave them nothing but a cold shoulder.

Then, through the corner of his eye, he saw him—Jesus, striding down the shoreline with a crowd swelling behind him, hanging on his every move, just as Peter and the others had done a year ago. They followed, breathless with wonder, until Jesus's sandaled feet met the water's edge. He turned, locked eyes with Peter, and grinned—a wordless request hanging between them: *Help me out here, will you?*

Looking back years later, Peter understood that this had been a premeditated encounter. He had come by at this hour to find the boys coming in. After spending a year getting to know them, he was aware of exactly when they'd hit the shore.

Jesus said, with playful formality, "I need your boat, sir."

Peter chuckled, catching the spark in his eye. "Lads," he called, "looks like we're ferrymen today."

John, James, and Andrew smiled as they flipped the boat and shoved it into the shallows. Jesus climbed in and made his way to the stern. From there, he began to teach, his voice dancing across the surface of the sea as the crowd hushed to listen.

James leaned over with a smirk. "I suppose if we keep having nights like this one, we could start a water taxi for wandering teachers?"

When Jesus had finished, he turned to Peter with that familiar tone that sounded like suggestion but landed like command: "Put out into the deep water and let down your nets for a catch."

Peter blinked, caught off guard. "Rabbi," he sighed, "we were out all night. Not a single fish . . ." His voice trailed off. Then he added with a reluctant smile, "But because it's you, I'll do it."

He called him *Master*—not casually. Not flippantly. That word meant something. It meant obedience. Submission. Trust. It meant following—even when it made no sense.

Peter had been playacting at discipleship, following Jesus here and there like a weekend traveler. But deep down he knew the road was about to shift. Jesus was becoming a true rabbi, gathering real disciples—the kind that would walk behind him, live like him, and one day carry what he started.

Peter wasn't sure he belonged in that group. But this . . . this moment . . . maybe it was his chance to learn something from Jesus one last time. A last lesson. One last moment to pretend his life had been different, had mattered.

The net hit the water with a familiar slap, sinking into the deep as it had a hundred times before. Peter gave it a token tug, half expecting it to drag in the same silent disappointment. But then it jolted. Hard. Like the sea itself had clenched its fist around it. The rope tightened, screamed against his calloused palms. Peter shouted, and the others leaped to help as the boat lurched sideways under the weight. Fish—too many to count—thrashed and shimmered like silver fire beneath the surface. The net strained, bulging like a lung full of wind, on the brink of bursting. Another boat was signaled, and they came fast, both vessels groaning with the load, sinking under the sheer glory of it.

And right there—knee-deep in fish and salt water—Peter fell to his knees, eyes wide, breath stolen, and said, not "Thank you," but "Go away from me, Lord, for I am a sinful man." Because sometimes, when grace floods the boat, the first thing you feel isn't worthy—it's undone. Peter thought Jesus had the wrong person, but the right people always feel that way.

The boats groaned under the weight of the miracle, but Peter—kneeling in fish, breathless from glory—barely noticed. Then came the words that changed everything. Jesus didn't say "Follow me and try harder." Or "From now on you'll have to do better, Peter." He didn't say "Follow me and prove yourself." He said, "Follow me, and I will make you . . ." The call wasn't to earn something but to become something . . . *something he wasn't yet.* Fisherman? Yes. But not a fisher of men. Not yet. This wasn't a job offer. It was a summons to train with Jesus. A lifetime apprenticeship with the Son of God himself, "to train them as 'fishers of people,' coworkers in his own missionary activity."[1] For Peter, this wasn't just a chance to follow a rabbi—it was the fulfillment of a dream he'd never dared to say out loud. He would no longer be a Pinocchio-like little wooden boy in a game of make-believe held back by the strings of reality; he would become a "real boy," as if he'd wished upon a star. During that second year, he sometimes had to pinch himself to see whether it was really happening. To follow God. Really follow him. Full-time. No nets. No fallback plan. Just Jesus—and a new identity being forged in the fire of obedience.

"Follow me, and I will make you fishers of men."

Jesus's second invitation to hit the road with him prompted the disciples to cut all ties. Each would no longer be a *mathetes* or part of a large crowd of loosely connected followers who simply listened to and admired a rabbi's teaching. By accepting Jesus's deeper invitation to become *talmidim*, they were committing to hit the road so that the real *teaching* could begin.

Peter and company dropped their nets just like that. Left behind their trade, their boats, and the only life they'd ever known in Capernaum. With hearts pounding and eyes fixed on the Rabbi who had called them, they

---

1. Damian Emetuche, "Church Planting: Biblical, Theological, and Missiological Considerations," *Global Missiology*, January 2012, https://www.globalmissiology.org.

stepped onto the path that required them to adjust their gait to the Teaching rhythm, and they'd never be the same again. Jesus had promised.

This was the beginning of the second year, when Jesus moved into the Teaching rhythm, focusing on bringing the message and methods of the kingdom to the masses. The year of quietly building relationship was over. Now those six would be trained, along with a few other disciples Jesus would recruit to the cause. This was the year of their training as disciple-makers.

The Nature of the Teaching Rhythm

In the 1970s TV show *Kung Fu*, set in the American Wild West, Shaolin monk Caine drifts from town to town, bare feet, shaved head, searching for his father. Dedicated to a life of peace, Caine is always ready to step into injustice with ancient calm and steely resolve. Every time he faces a challenge, a flashback to the monastery of his youth shifts to scenes of the waxy temple floors and incense smoke of the temple. In his reverie, Caine recalls a lesson of Master Po. And in those quiet halls of his memory, a single lesson would come alive; the wisdom of his master, spoken in the past, guides his hands in the present. Caine carries no scrolls or notes—only the master's voice in his soul.

A Jewish rabbi's aim wasn't merely information but transformation. Caine had been shaped into a living weapon with kung-fu reflexes. Similarly, Jesus was training his disciples to fall back on their training when he would no longer be at hand. Like Shaolin monks, their minds would flash back to what they'd learned from their Master during their second year, observing him preach, perform miracles, and exorcise demons. It was their monastery training. Master Yoda exhorted Luke to "remember your training. Save you it can." Non-Jedi Steve Smith adds, "Teaching conveys the idea of transferring knowledge, but training conveys the idea of changing behavior."[2]

Rabbis didn't confuse talking with teaching. Nor did Jesus merely *teach* about the kingdom—he *brought* it. When Jesus told a parable about grace, he

---

2. Steve Smith with Ying Kai, *T4T: A Discipleship Re-Revolution* (WIGTake Resources, 2011), chap. 2, Kindle.

illustrated grace by freeing a demoniac. When he claimed the power to forgive sin, he proved his power to do so by healing a paralyzed man. Thinking thoughts is great, but only actions change the world. Jesus wanted the disciples to observe, absorb, and begin to understand how the kingdom moves through real people in real life.

In short, year 2 involved the disciples observing Jesus in action, preparing them for the hands-on mission he had planned for them in year 3. When their training was complete, Jesus would send them out with a promise: You "will do greater things than I have done" (John 14:12). Year 2 may have started with them dropping physical nets from their hands, but Jesus the King Fisher would make good on his promise to make them "fishers of people." Then he would pass the metaphorical net back to them in year 3. In year 2, however, the disciples stood back, observing Jesus demonstrate the same mastery over souls that he had shown with fish that day in the boat.

This chapter will primarily focus on the patterns of the Teaching rhythm during that second year. Because Jesus shifted gears, speeding up, and increasing his rpm's, it was a packed-out year. Therefore, an overview of all he did in year 2 is useful to get our bearings.

Overview of Year 2

Immediately after receiving the news that John the Baptist had been imprisoned, Jesus kicked off the second year with an announcement: "The time has come. The kingdom of God has come near. Repent and believe the good news" (Mark 1:15). The Baptist's lockup seemed to shift something in Jesus: Right as "the voice" was being silenced, Jesus decided to raise his own. In the previous year, Jesus had lain low. And when his mom asked him to do a miracle at the wedding, he said, "It is not yet my time." Now it wasn't about Time anymore; it *was* time.

It was like the shot of a starting gun. At the dawn of the second year, Jesus hit the road like a band on tour to sell a record. Year 1 is called the year of obscurity, but year 2 is known as the year of popularity. From the second Jesus started healing without reservation, his popularity skyrocketed, swelling crowds and multiplying followers. Jesus went public.

Jesus didn't cloister his disciples in a synagogue (*beit midrash*) like most rabbis, but rather pressed them onto the highways, byways, and busy trade routes, taking his training on the road. Every dusty path and crowded village was their classroom. Every awkward encounter a curriculum.[3] Jesus told the disciples, "Let us go somewhere else—to the nearby villages—so I can preach there also. That is why I have come" (Mark 1:38). And he proclaimed it—everywhere. Like a divine Dr. Seuss, Jesus trained on roads, fields, and graveyards, in a box with a fox, on a train in the rain, and in a boat that would float.

Jesus planned a preaching circuit that would make John Wesley proud. The route that second year was carefully mapped, strategically designed to train his disciples for where he would send them in the third year. Later, Paul adopted a similar approach during his second missionary journey, leaving disciples behind to continue the work throughout Galatia.

This map traces his message, miracles, and movement during year 2:

3. As Martyn Lloyd-Jones noted, Paul's epistles follow a consistent pattern: first the doctrine—who Jesus is, what he's done through his life, death, and resurrection—then the implications for how we live. Romans 1–8 lay the foundation; Romans 12–15 build the life. Same with Ephesians: Chapters 1–3 ground us in identity, while 4–6 call us to live it out. Jesus and Paul shared the same rhythm: doctrine, then discipleship. As Jesus said in the Sermon on the Mount, "Everyone who hears these words of mine and puts them into practice . . ." Principles always preceded praxis.

CHRONOLOGY OF JESUS'S SECOND YEAR

1 **Jesus heals the demoniac** *(Mark 1:21–28; Luke 4:31–37)* Jesus demonstrates his authority over demons in the Capernaum synagogue.

2 **Jesus heals Peter's mother-in-law** *(Matthew 8:14–15; Mark 1:29–31; Luke 4:38–39)* Jesus heals Peter's family, extending his ministry into his disciples' homes.

3 **Jesus heals many at sundown** *(Matthew 8:16–17; Mark 1:32–34; Luke 4:40–41)* Crowds gather as Jesus heals sicknesses and casts out demons late into the night.

4 **Jesus recruits the four fishermen** *(Matthew 4:18–22; Mark 1:16–20; Luke 5:1–11)* Jesus recruits Peter, Andrew, James, and John to leave their nets and follow him.

5 **Jesus preaches and heals across Galilee** *(Matthew 4:23–25; Mark 1:35–39; Luke 4:42–44)* Jesus goes on a preaching tour, healing diseases and casting out demons across the region.

6 **Jesus heals paralytic** *(Matthew 9:1–8; Mark 2:1–12; Luke 5:17–26)* Jesus forgives and heals a paralyzed man, dropped through a roof in Capernaum, shocking the crowd with his authority.

7 **Jesus recruits Matthew** *(Matthew 9:9–13; Mark 2:13–17; Luke 5:27–32)* Jesus invites a despised tax collector from Capernaum to join his disciples.

8 **Jesus eats at Matthew's house** *(Matthew 9:10–17; Mark 2:15–22; Luke 5:29–39)* Jesus rocks the house party and then gets questioned by the Pharisees about fasting.

9 **Jesus goes to the feast in Jerusalem** *(John 5:1)* This is second time since his public ministry that he's traveled to Jerusalem.

10 **Jesus heals at the Pool of Bethesda** *(John 5:2–15)* Jesus heals a man in Jerusalem who had been disabled for 38 years.

11 **Jesus's disciples pluck grain on the Sabbath** *(Matthew 12:1–8; Mark 2:23–28; Luke 6:1–5)* Jesus defends his disciples' actions in Jerusalem, declaring himself Lord of the Sabbath.

12 **Jesus heals the man with a withered hand** *(Matthew 12:9–14; Mark 3:1–6; Luke 6:6–11)* Jesus heals in the synagogue, provoking the religious leaders' anger.

13 **Jesus returns to Capernaum** *(Matthew 4:13)* There is a garrison there because of the trade route.

14 **Jesus heals the centurion's servant** *(Matthew 8:5–13; Luke 7:1–10)* Jesus heals from a distance, marveling at the centurion's faith.

15 **Jesus raises the widow's son at Nain** *(Luke 7:11–17)* Jesus raises a widow's only son from the dead, filling the town with awe.

16 **Jesus anointed by a sinful woman** *(Luke 7:36–50)* A woman in Nain washes Jesus' feet with her tears, and he forgives her sins.

17 **Jesus heals a demon-possessed man in the Gerasenes** *(Matthew 8:28–34; Mark 5:1–20; Luke 8:26–39)* Jesus casts out a legion of demons and sends them into pigs.

18 **Jesus heals two blind men and a mute demoniac** *(Matthew 9:27–34)* Jesus restores sight and speech, leaving the crowds in Capernaum amazed.

19 **Jesus heals Jairus's daughter and a bleeding woman** *(Matthew 9:18–26; Mark 5:21–43; Luke 8:40–56)* Jesus heals a woman suffering for 72 years and raises a young girl from the dead.

20 **Jesus calms the storm** *(Matthew 8:23–27; Mark 4:35–41; Luke 8:22–25)* Jesus rebukes the wind and sea in the Sea of Galilee, leaving his disciples in awe of his power.

21 **Jesus's second rejection in Nazareth** *(Matthew 13:54–58; Mark 6:1–6)* Jesus is rejected again in his hometown when they question his authority.

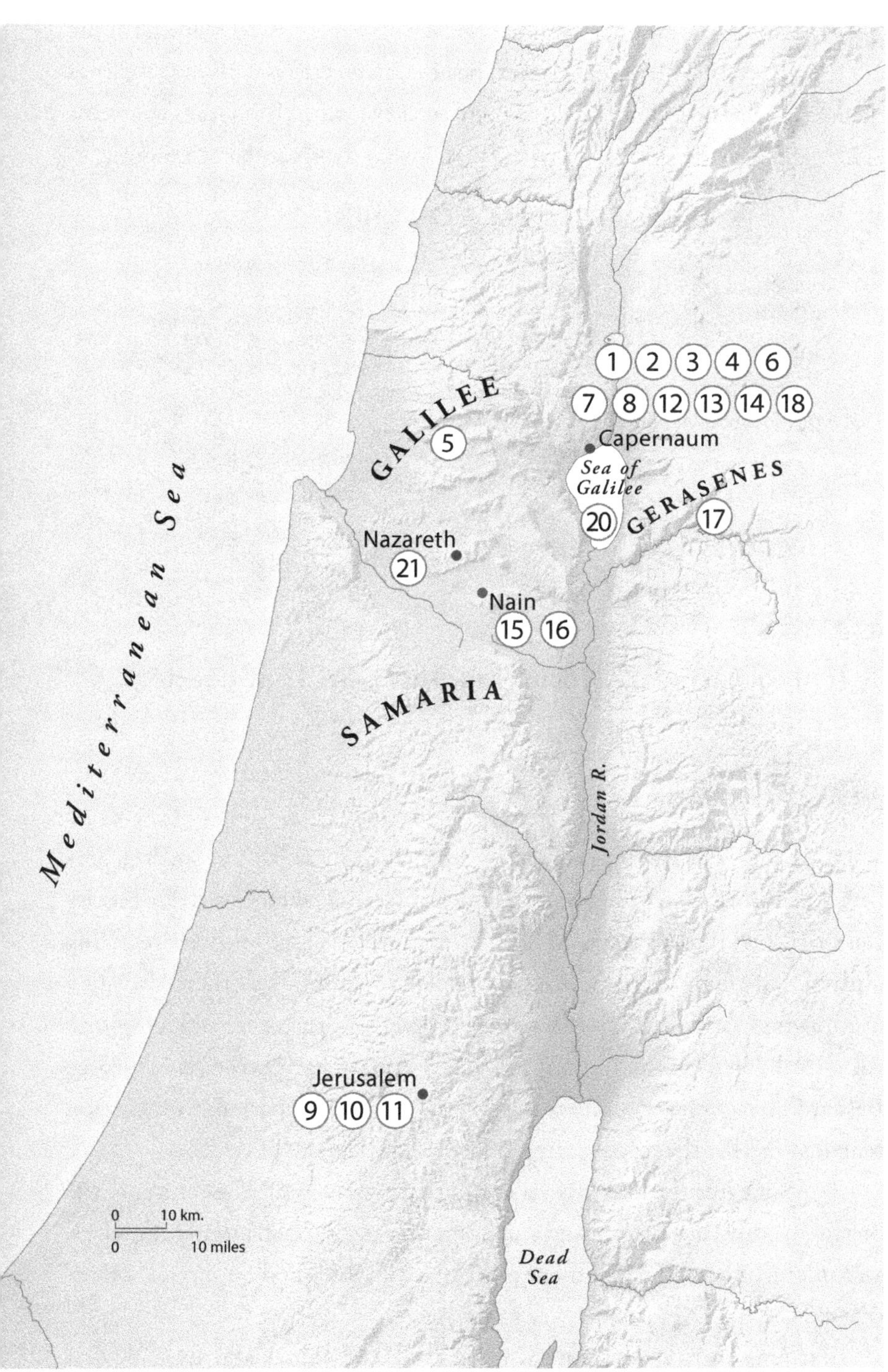

GALILEE
5
1 2 3 4 6
7 8 12 13 14 18
Capernaum
Sea of Galilee
GERASENES
20
17
Nazareth
21
Nain
15 16
SAMARIA
Mediterranean Sea
Jordan R.
Jerusalem
9 10 11
0 10 km.
0 10 miles
Dead Sea

As we trace the movements and moments of year 2, patterns emerge in the master-class training Jesus delivered. The next chapter deals with the teachings themselves, but this chapter focuses on what they learned from Jesus's patterns as he walked in the Teaching rhythm—and what they learned as a result.

PATTERNS OF TEACHING

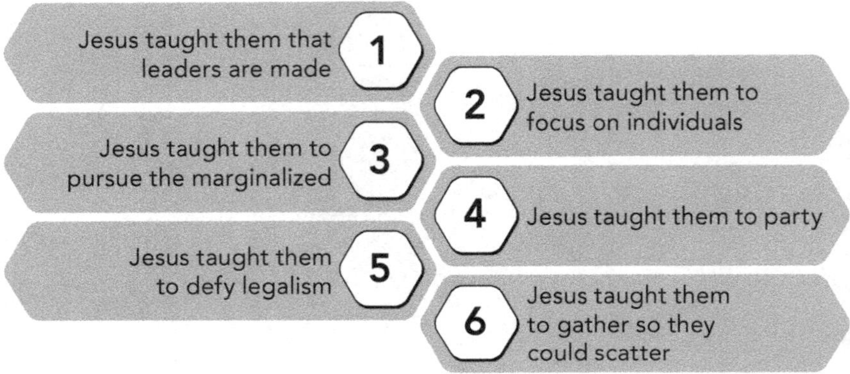

Teaching Pattern 1: Jesus Taught Them That Leaders Are Made

"Follow me, and I will make you fishers of men." (Matt. 4:19 ESV)

Trading Places was a comedic film set in 1983 in which two wealthy brokers make a bet on nature versus nurture, wagering whether a street hustler can be turned into a successful businessman while simultaneously reducing a privileged financier to nothing. The comedy unfolds as these two men unknowingly swap lives, one rising to refinement, the other plunging into ruin. Drawing from the film *My Fair Lady* (1964), itself taken from George Bernard Shaw's play *Pygmalion*, a story about transformation, the question remains whether the teacher can produce a diamond out of coal.

Now imagine the heavenly version of that wager. Satan, the accuser of the brethren, points at a broken and stubborn candidate, rough around the edges, and impulsively scoffs, "I'll make a bet that you can't make a disciple out of that one."

But Jesus leans in, eyes on the unqualified individual, and says, "Really?

That's the highest stakes you can play? I was expecting more of a challenge. I'll up the stakes. I won't just make that person a disciple; I'll make that one a disciple-maker. In fact, I'll bet you I can make anyone you give me a fisher of people."

While the worst players always get picked for the team, Jesus's draft picks work in reverse. He didn't wait for the cream to rise but scoured the bottom of the barrel. Nor did he scout talent—he *developed* it. "I will make you fishers of people" is a strategy wrapped in a promise. Jesus intentionally poured himself into lost causes, such as his dirty dozen—a motley crew of misfits who would break the Roman Empire—to prove a point: Disciple-makers aren't born, they're made. That's why it's called disciple-*making*, not disciple-*discovering*.

Jesus didn't pick any of us because we have what it takes. In the Gospels, he picked *ordinary, unschooled men*, not rabbis or scholars. A. B. Bruce observes that "an ex-zealot was not a safe man to make an apostle of, for he might be the means of rendering Jesus and his followers objects of political suspicion. But the Author of our faith was willing to take the risk. He expected to gain many disciples from the dangerous classes as well as from the despised, and he would have them, too, represented among the twelve."[4]

Cue the kung-fu flashback. I learned this the hard way when planting churches in Long Beach. After launching multiple churches, we hit a wall fast. The problem? We kept sending out waves of church-planting teams, emptying our dugout of trained leaders. Soon we were sucking air. But like George Bailey desperate to escape Bedford Falls, I needed someone to hand the ol' Building and Loan over to, but I had failed to train enough disciples to replace all the leaders we kept sending out. One day, during a baptism, a man came up out of the water with a full-back tattoo of a pornographic succubus. I heard God whisper, *That's your next church planter.* Next came a kid with a DUI doing community service, and again: *That one too.* Everyone that day was followed by that same prophetic whisper. It felt like the knock-knock banana joke—I kept waiting for the "orange you glad" punchline. Then God said, *Just disciple*

4. A. B. Bruce, *The Training of the Twelve: How Jesus Christ Found and Taught the 12 Apostles; a Book of New Testament Biography* (1871; Pantianos Classics, 2018), chap. 4, Kindle.

the people right in front of you like they're your next church planter, and they'll become the best leaders you've ever had.[5] And they were.

That's the beauty of Jesus's words "I will *make* you fishers of men." It's not just about making disciples—it's about *being made* into something we're not . . . yet. He can take any mess or misfit and make them heft kingdom nets. And he can do it with you. As the saying goes, "'When God put a calling on your life, he already factored in your stupidity.' Most comforting thing I've ever heard."

Teaching Pattern 2: Jesus Taught Them to Focus on Individuals

> Very early in the morning, while it was still dark, Jesus got up, left the house and went off to a solitary place, where he prayed. Simon and his companions went to look for him, and when they found him, they exclaimed: "Everyone is looking for you!" Jesus replied, "Let us go somewhere else—to the nearby villages—so I can preach there also. That is why I have come." (Mark 1:35–38)

After Jesus's fame exploded like wildfire, there was no looking back. They brought the sick to him in droves at the early hours of the morning, even prying the tiles off a roof to lower a paralytic man to him. Mark records, "Jesus could no longer enter a town openly but stayed outside in lonely places. Yet the people still came to him from everywhere" (Mark 1:45). The crowds swelled to unmanageable sizes, making it impossible for him to enter towns without being mobbed. Matthew notes that this followed them everywhere:

> Jesus went throughout Galilee, teaching in their synagogues, proclaiming the good news of the kingdom, and healing every disease and sickness among the people. . . . Large crowds from Galilee, the Decapolis, Jerusalem, Judea and the region across the Jordan followed him. (Matt. 4:23–25)

---

5. You can read about this team in my book *Reaching the Unreached* (Zondervan, 2017) to hear the resolution to this story.

Jesus was, by every modern metric, a phenomenon, but he wasn't intoxicated by the fumes of his own popularity. Rather, he withdrew when the crowds pressed in. Jesus knew that a big crowd doth not a disciple make. Nor was a crowd a stat—to him it was a sea of individuals. Every face had a story. Every need had a name. The disciples watched closely and learned.

One day his disciples watched as a lone figure knelt in the dust—a leper. His voice trembling, a garbled whisper escaped through what lips remained: "If you want to, you can make me clean." In moments like these, everything stopped for Jesus. The crowd faded as he reached out a hand and touched the untouchable. A man who hadn't felt human touch in years. The disciples couldn't believe it: He *touched* a leper. He didn't have to—he wanted to. From within Jesus's soul, compassion kindled like fire. "I want to," he said. "Be clean." But then: "Don't tell anyone" (Mark 1:40–43). The truth is, every time Jesus healed someone, it created more logistical problems, interrupting access. Fame interfered with the mission. And Jesus's miracles were acts of mercy rather than marketing.

As ministers, we run the risk of chasing crowds, attaching our inflating ego to the swelling numbers, SEO, algorithms, and viral moments. However, mature disciples know that large platforms never fill the consuming void in our soul. Open wounds become bottomless black holes. Bono, the frontman of U2, confessed the weakness of rock stars who love platforms and applause: "You don't become an artist unless you've got something missing somewhere." Decades of fallen church celebrities have resulted in "stacked dead actors packed to the rafters."[6] The God-shaped hole that couldn't be filled by sex, drugs, and rock and roll, also couldn't be filled by fame, ministry accomplishments, or sermons to ever-growing crowds.

When Satan offered Jesus fame during his wilderness temptation, Jesus turned him down flat. Satan's offer to hand Jesus all the glory of the kingdoms of the world would be in modern terms likes, follows, and subscribers on an epic scale. Many would sell their souls for far less, but because Jesus was secure in the love of the Father.

6. Foo Fighters, "Stacked Actors," *There Is Nothing Left to Lose* (RCA / Roswell Records, 1999).

As the crowds continued to swell, Jesus's eyes remained locked on the *one* who's approval he sought. The entire Sermon on the Mount was about doing things that only the Father can see, living for an audience of *one*. All of us must stand on that same mountaintop with our own motives and make a decision. Disciple-making will never be the pathway to glory, and although Jesus's crowds came for miracles, Jesus came to make disciples.

If sprinting to the stage has the stronger pull, be aware (or beware): Disciple-making will always tug in the opposite direction—away from the crowds and into relationship. As the old saying goes, when the sun comes out, even the stars hide themselves. This is the direction the Twelve eventually went, as "they gazed steadfastly at the Sun of Righteousness, and in his effulgence they lost sight of the attendant stars."[7]

Teaching Pattern 3: Jesus Taught Them to Pursue the Marginalized

> As Jesus went on from there, he saw a man named Matthew sitting at the tax collector's booth. "Follow me," he told him, and Matthew got up and followed him. (Matt. 9:9–10)

His name was Levi, a name that once meant something. In Hebrew, *Levi* means "joined" or "attached," as in the tribe set apart for God—the priestly line. His parents had high hopes when they graced their baby with that name, dreaming he might serve in the temple, devoted to God, carrying on a sacred legacy. Holy. But, somewhere along the way, those dreams evaporated. Levi joined the ranks of Rome's tax collectors. Instead of bleeding sacrifices at the temple, he bled his own people. Instead of receiving sacrifices for Yahweh, he extorted taxes for the pagan caesar, who blasphemously claimed to be God. The name Levi, once tied to the hope of a sacred calling, now stirred disgust instead of devotion whenever it was mentioned in their circles. It had become a name detached from the promise it once held.

At his market stall in Capernaum, Matthew worked quill in hand, head

7. Bruce, *Training of the Twelve*, chap. 4.

down, heart numb. From the margins he watched as crowds parted for the miracles unfolding in the streets. He'd heard about the roof ripped open and the paralyzed man lowered down. It was reported that Jesus had said, "Your sins are forgiven." Not just healed—*forgiven*. Matthew was good at adding things up.

The Lamb of God—carrying the weight and authority to cleanse the soul.

Could it be true? Could this man really wipe a ledger of sins against God completely clean? For a tax collector, immersed in ledgers, records, and debts, the idea of a slate wiped bare wasn't just poetic; it was everything. If Jesus had the power to forgive sins . . . No, men like him didn't get second chances. Not in this world.

But "Jesus saw him."

Before Jesus left town on his tour, he walked right up to the tax booth, locked eyes with him, "Follow me." No lecture. No conditions. Just an invitation. Levi, the one who thought he was beyond saving, became Matthew, one of the Twelve. And one day he'd pen a gospel bearing his name, the name that was translated "gift of God," or, as we know it, *grace*.

When Jesus called Matthew, he wasn't just adding a warm body to the team as the seventh disciple to be chosen. Jesus was making a bold statement. Jesus pursued the last person on earth that a rabbi would pick to be a *talmid*. And he wasn't alone; after him came Mary Magdalen, possessed with seven demons. She became part of the posse too. The disciples watched heaven pursue what the world rejected. *And these are the people we need to disciple.*

As Jesus neared the end of his second year a pattern of ministering to the marginalized materialized; a hated Roman centurion, a forgotten widow, a despised sinful woman, hopeless demoniacs, pitiful blind men, and a shunned and ceremonially unclean woman with a bleeding condition:

- Healing the centurion's servant—Matthew 8:5–13; Luke 7:1–10
- Raising the widow's son at Nain—Luke 7:11–17
- Being anointed by a sinful woman—Luke 7:36–50
- Healing the demon-possessed men in the Gerasenes—Matthew 8:28–34; Mark 5:1–20; Luke 8:26–39

- Healing two blind men and a mute demoniac—Matthew 9:27–34
- Healing of Jairus's daughter and the woman with the issue of blood—Matthew 9:18–26; Mark 5:21–43; Luke 8:40–56

The disciples couldn't miss the lesson. Nor should we. Jesus made disciples among the marginalized. So well did the disciples learn this lesson that Paul recounts that the Twelve sent him to the gentiles with their blessing: "Only, they asked us to remember the poor, the very thing I was eager to do" (Gal. 2:10 ESV).

Today, the marginalized include those who are despised or forgotten: the poor, the elderly, orphaned, handicapped, immigrants, and the incarcerated. John Wesley learned that the gospel always runs fastest on the margins. When he "submitted to be more vile" and stepped out of the pulpits into the fields, prisons, and slums, the movement caught fire. On April 2, 1739, he wrote, "At four in the afternoon I submitted to be more vile, and proclaimed in the highways the glad tidings of salvation, speaking from a little eminence in a ground adjoining to the city, to about three thousand people."[8] That "being more vile" line was his own acknowledgment that to reach the poor coal miners and laborers, he had to break with the polite norms of Anglican ministry. Let others cling to propriety; disciple-makers take to the streets with David's words on their lips: "I will yet be more vile" (2 Sam. 6:22 KJV). That day, Wesley discovered what Jesus already knew: If you want to see a movement, you go to the margins. The world calls it "vile," but Jesus called it making disciples.

Teaching Pattern 4: Jesus Taught Them to Party

> While Jesus was having dinner at Levi's house, many tax collectors and sinners were eating with him and his disciples, for there were many who followed him. When the teachers of the law who were Pharisees saw him eating with the sinners and tax collectors, they asked his disciples: "Why does he eat with tax collectors and sinners?"

---

8. John Wesley, *The Journal of John Wesley*, ed. Percy Livingstone Parker (Christian Classics Ethereal Library), journal entry for April 2, 1739, https://www.ccel.org/ccel/wesley/journal.vi.iii.i.html.

On hearing this, Jesus said to them, "It is not the healthy who need a doctor, but the sick. I have not come to call the righteous, but sinners." (Mark 2:15–17)[9]

After calling Matthew, Jesus went to his house, sat at his table, and ate and drank with a pack of wild sinners. The only people who would be caught dead with Matthew were people whose reputations had died long ago. As the religious elite stood at the edge of the room, arms folded, asking, "Why does your teacher eat with *them*?" the kingdom was on full display. Jesus answered, "Where else would you find a doctor? With the sick." Make no mistake—Jesus was in full teaching mode here. He knew his disciples' ears had perked up to hear the explanation. For a Jew, who you ate with showed who you approved of—sharing a meal was the ultimate sign of acceptance. Jesus taught the Twelve that effective witness comes through *withness.*

If the kingdom looks like a feast for sinners, then it still pulls up a chair at tables the world avoids. And sometimes it arrives at 3:00 a.m. in the greasy diners of Honolulu. You know, the kind of places where the linoleum floor sticks to your shoes and the coffee tastes like it's been reheating since Tuesday. Tony Campolo had just finished speaking at an event in town. Unable to fall sleep in a hotel bed, he wandered into the diner—still open late. It was three o'clock in the morning. That's when they walked in—loud, laughing, rough around the edges—a group of prostitutes wrapping up their night. He overheard one of them—her name was Agnes—mention that tomorrow was her birthday. She wasn't fishing for attention, just saying it. "I've never had a birthday party," she added softly. Something about it lodged in Tony's heart, so after they left, he asked the cook behind the counter, Harry, if they could throw her a birthday party.

For a prostitute.

In a dingy diner.

Harry grinned. "Sure," he said. "I like it."

So, the next night, Tony came back early with decorations. They made a

9. Matthew 9:14–17; Mark 2:18–22; Luke 5:33–39.

cake. Word got out, and by 3:00 a.m. the place was packed with prostitutes. When Agnes walked in and saw the celebration—the balloons, the banner, the cake—it undid her. She stood there trembling. "For me?" she whispered. "Nobody's ever done anything like this for me." As they sang "Happy Birthday" to Agnes, tears rolled down her cheeks. When it came time to cut the cake, she asked—almost childlike—"Could we wait to cut it? I'd like to take it home. . . . I just want to look at it for a while longer." And she left the diner, walking out into the night, holding the cake in outstretched arms like it was a holy relic.

The diner was still. Tony said, "Let's pray."

"Hey," Harry said in an annoyed tone, "I didn't know you were a minister. What kind of church do you belong to, anyway?"

Tony smiled. "I belong to the kind of church that throws birthday parties for prostitutes at 3:00 a.m."

So did Jesus. So did the Twelve. While others keep their distance, the disciples watched Jesus throwing birthday parties for sinners, allowing grace to break into their lives through healings and deliverances.

You don't find Jesus talking about reaching people, you find him mixing and mingling with people! Jesus trained the Twelve to attend parties that would cause a party in heaven. After all, the kingdom of God isn't afraid of the dark. It knows exactly where to light the candles.

Teaching Pattern 5: Jesus Taught Them to Defy Legalism

Anyone who picks a tax collector or a prostitute to enter his *talmidim* isn't afraid to pick a fight with broken systems, especially when they stand between people and God. When in Jerusalem, Jesus made a point of intentionally "breaking" the Sabbath, allowing his disciples to pick grain on the Sabbath while they walked through a field (Matt. 12:1–8; Mark 2:23–28; Luke 6:1–5), or healing the man with the withered hand or the man at the pool of Bethesda (Matt. 12:9–14; Mark 3:1–6; Luke 6:6–11, John 5:1–5). He dismantled man-made restrictions and refused to be bound by rules that suffocated grace. He wasn't anti-Sabbath or even anti-tradition—he was just anti-legalism.

At the pool of Bethesda, a man had been lying crippled and helpless for thirty-eight years. Jesus healed him on the Sabbath, telling him with dramatic flair to pick up his mat and walk—breaking two man-made rules: walking *farther than allowed* and carrying *more than allowed* on the Sabbath. When questioned by the Pharisees, Jesus said, "My Father is always at his work to this very day, and I too am working" (John 5:17). Translation? *Am I working on the Sabbath? Yes. But only because Yahweh is also working.* Next time he visited Jerusalem, Jesus healed a blind man with spectacular Sabbath-breaking flair. First, he made mud (that's Jesus working) and told a man to go wash at the same pool (the man walking and working according to their traditions) and asked the Father to heal him (again, the Father working). A Sabbath-breaking party? That's next-level trolling.

When the people in each story were attacked, Jesus defended them. Disciple-makers may often find themselves needing to *shield new Christ followers from religious attacks.* I've discipled people only to watch religious leaders swoop in to nitpick them. My response? "Who said they had to be perfect?" Jesus took people on mission before they were ready. But we want people polished and proper before they're seen—lest they offend religious etiquette. Most of us are aware that the most effective evangelist is a new disciple.

When the Pharisees criticized the disciples for not fasting, Jesus stopped and explained that new wine bursts rigid old wineskins, but new wineskins are designed to give—stretching to expand. People who want everyone to fit into their rigid ideas from day one understand very little about the transformative work of the Holy Spirit. Disciple-makers must allow people to grow and adjust to the working of God in their lives—and that takes time. Jesus had much to say about religious people who don't lift a finger to make disciples but want right of first refusal to control them:

> "They tie up heavy, cumbersome loads and put them on other people's shoulders, but they themselves are not willing to lift a finger to move them." (Matt. 23:4)
>
> "Woe to you, teachers of the law and Pharisees, you hypocrites! You travel over land and sea to win a single convert, and when you have succeeded, you make them twice as much a child of hell as you are." (Matt. 23:15)

As C. S. Lewis so brilliantly put it, "Of all tyrannies a tyranny sincerely exercised for the good of its victims may be the most oppressive. It would be better to live under robber barons than under omnipotent moral busybodies."[10] Jesus stood in the gap and stood guard to protect his disciples from criticism, treating legalism like it was illegal.

Teaching Pattern 6: Jesus Taught Them to Gather So They Could Scatter

> He appointed twelve that they might be with him and that he might send them out. (Mark 3:14)

As things got intense, from a larger group of *mathetes*, Jesus selected five more to join his *talmidim* (Matt. 10:1–4; Mark 3:13–19; Luke 6:12–16). "He appointed twelve that they might be with him and *that he might send them out*" (3:14, emphasis mine).

That they might *be with* him (to train in year 2), and that he might *send* them (to do in year 3). The rhythm was simple: *gather, then scatter*. That's why Jesus named them apostles. The word *apostolos* translates to "sent-out one"—to us, a missionary. To them, an emissary. It was a Roman military term; Caesar sent messengers—"Sent-out ones"—to deliver the new edicts of the empire to establish the new order of the new ruler. Alain Caron adds, "Whenever someone wants to launch an invasion on a given territory or nation, the first thing he does is gather the team or troops he needs for the operation."[11]

A few things about these kingdom messengers were unique. The number twelve echoed the twelve tribes of Israel—both symbolic and strategic. As Schnabel puts it, "The number twelve speaks of the eschatological gathering of Israel"; in other words, he was rebuilding something ancient while launching something new.[12] Because the symbolic number twelve pointed back to the

10. C. S. Lewis, *God in the Dock: Essays on Theology and Ethics*, ed. Walter Hooper (Eerdmans, 1970), 292.
11. Alain Caron, *Apostolic Centers: Shifting the Church, Transforming the World* (Arsenal Press, 2013), chap. 2, Kindle.
12. Eckhard J. Schnabel, *Early Christian Mission Vol. 1: Jesus and the Twelve* (IVP Academic, 2004), 224.

sons of Jacob, the Twelve were all male; but because they heralded a new order, Jesus's mission also included women:

> Soon afterward he went on through cities and villages, proclaiming and bringing the good news of the kingdom of God. And the twelve were with him, and also some women who had been healed of evil spirits and infirmities: Mary, called Magdalene, from whom seven demons had gone out, and Joanna, the wife of Chuza, Herod's household manager, and Susanna, and many others, who provided for them out of their means. (Luke 8:1–3 ESV)

These women, once healed, followed him, traveled with him on mission, accepting the same call to disciple making as the *talmidim*. The unnamed "sinful woman" from Luke 7:36–50 was likely a prostitute in need of a new means of livelihood. In a culture that pushed prostitutes—and women in general—to the margins of society, Jesus pulled them to the center of his mission, inviting them into his community on mission. Instead of recipients of kingdom work; they became active participants—like the woman at the well, the first missionary of Jesus.

Paul took a page from the book of Jesus's ministry on female inclusion. In Romans 16, Paul greeted fellow workers in Rome—one-third of them women who played pivotal roles in the early church. Since Paul had never visited Rome at the time of writing, these women were likely ones he'd discipled on previous missionary journeys. Not tagalongs, but leaders and laborers, church planters, apostles, and prophets.

- Phoebe carried Paul's letter to the Romans and likely read it aloud to the church.
- Prisca (or Priscilla) taught Apollos, a powerful preacher, and corrected his theology.
- Junia was "outstanding among the apostles" (v. 7).

Like Lady Huntington during the Great Awakening or Lottie Moon among the Baptists, these women even funded the work of the gospel: "They provided for them out of their means" (Luke 8:3). Transformed by Jesus, they became disciple-makers in a kingdom that knows no hierarchy of worth. This was bigger than merely making disciples; by casting off cultural restraints Jesus modeled what the kingdom does.

What the Kingdom Does

Jesus did far more than what is recorded in this chapter. John wrote, "Now there are also many other things that Jesus did. Were every one of them to be written, I suppose that the world itself could not contain the books that would be written" (John 21:25 ESV). John obviously valued frugality with his ink and papyrus. But this chapter has focused on what Jesus taught his disciples about what the kingdom *does*—what they observed him doing throughout that second year as he moved primarily within the Teaching rhythm.

- Jesus taught them that leaders are made.
- Jesus taught them to focus on individuals.
- Jesus taught them to go after the marginalized.
- Jesus taught them to party.
- Jesus taught them to fight legalism.
- Jesus taught them to gather so they could scatter.

These lessons are not a one-time affair—disciples must repeatedly relearn them, as our Sons of Thunder tell us. Knowing the message of Jesus profits us little if we don't practice the ways of Jesus. The Twelve couldn't merely echo his message; they'd need to resemble the messenger. Jim Putman rightly points out that "we can't divorce the teachings of Jesus from the methods of Jesus and expect to get the results of Jesus."[13] Now that we've unpacked what the kingdom *did* in the second year, the next chapter turns to what the kingdom *taught*.

13. Jim Putman, "Is It Time for a New Restoration Movement? (Part 1)," *Christian Standard*, September 1 2023, https://christianstandard.com/2023/09/is-it-time-for-a-new-restoration-movement-part-1/.

CHAPTER 7

Principles of Teaching

Here I stand. I can do no other. So help me God. Amen.

—MARTIN LUTHER

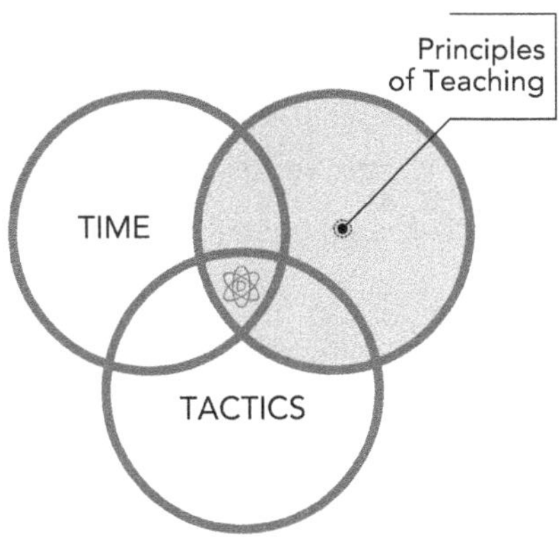

In 1804 Meriwether Lewis and William Clark set off into a vast wilderness, commissioned by President Jefferson to chart a passage through the vast and unmapped territory of the American West. They endured hardship, crossed mountains no one east of the Mississippi had seen, and blazed a trail to the Pacific. But their legacy wasn't only reaching the far edge of the continent—it was providing maps so that others could follow.

Many Christians are like explorers who've reached the destination. They've found life in Christ, but ask them how to lead someone else to that same place, and they're not sure where to start. They know the destination but can't tell anyone else how to get there or how to map the route.

That's what the Teaching rhythm was all about. In Jesus's second year of ministry, the objective was to make his followers "fishers of people." They knew how to fish but not how to cast a spiritual net around souls to draw others to Jesus. Disciple-making in the Teaching rhythm is primarily about introducing others to Jesus by communicating the good news of the King and bringing them into the kingdom. This chapter explores Jesus's teaching in that second year, so you can take that first step in disciple-making and help others find their way home.

The Gospel

The term *gospel* today isn't used much outside of church contexts, making it insider language, or jargon. Jargon is defined as specialized terminology associated with an insider group. It comes from the old English, godspel (god=good, spel=news). Over time it morphed into gospel, but the original Greek word *euangelion* had great significance in the ancient world. Chong Perkinson and Johnston elaborate on its original context:

> When most people hear the word "marathon," they think of the 26.2 mile race run in cities around the world. But before Marathon was a race, it was a battlefield—where, in 490 BC, a decisive victory turned the tide of the Greco-Persian War. Legend says a soldier named Pheidippides, ran from Marathon to Athens . . . with news of the win—then collapsed and breathed his last. The message he carried was the euangélion—good news of victory over the Persians.[1]

Jesus chose *euangelion* to describe the message of his coming. It was, first and foremost, good news—good news of a victory. Jesus launched the second

1. Tom Johnston and Mike Chong Perkinson, *The Organic Reformation: A New Hope for the Church in the West* (PraxisMedia, 2011), chap. 4, Kindle.

year of his ministry with an itinerant preaching tour focused on preaching the good news.

> I must proclaim the good news of the kingdom of God to the other towns also, because that is why I was sent. (Luke 4:43)

True to his promise, he hit the road.

> After this, Jesus traveled about from one town and village to another, proclaiming the good news of the kingdom of God. The Twelve were with him. (Luke 8:1)

But here's the twist: The gospel as we know it—the death and resurrection of Jesus—hadn't happened yet. So how could he preach it? He told his disciples, "I still have many things to say to you, but you cannot bear them now" (John 16:12 ESV).

Which raises the question—what *was* the good news Jesus was already proclaiming? Before the cross, how did his listeners understand it? What did good news mean to them?

Heaven Invading Earth

In Jesus's day, *good news* was political—the kind of announcement a herald would shout in the streets after a military victory: "A new king has won! Peace has been secured! A new era has begun!" The Romans used the term to announce Caesar's rise to power or a military conquest. It meant the world as you knew it was about to change. So, when Jesus came proclaiming the "good news of the kingdom of God," his audience didn't hear that as a private, internal, or merely spiritual message. They heard: *The king is here—and everything is about to change.* That's why Mark says Jesus began his ministry this way:

> "The time has come," he said. "The kingdom of God has come near. Repent and believe the good news!" (Mark 1:15)

To them, the gospel wasn't just about going to heaven when you die. Jesus's message was that heaven was breaking in now. It was about the return of the king; God's reign was arriving on earth to restore what was broken, set captives free, bring justice, mercy, healing, and hope.

But what exactly did it mean for the kingdom to arrive? In the previous chapter, we described what Jesus did to demonstrate the new kingdom. This chapter focuses on the Teaching principles that unpack what the good news of the kingdom was.

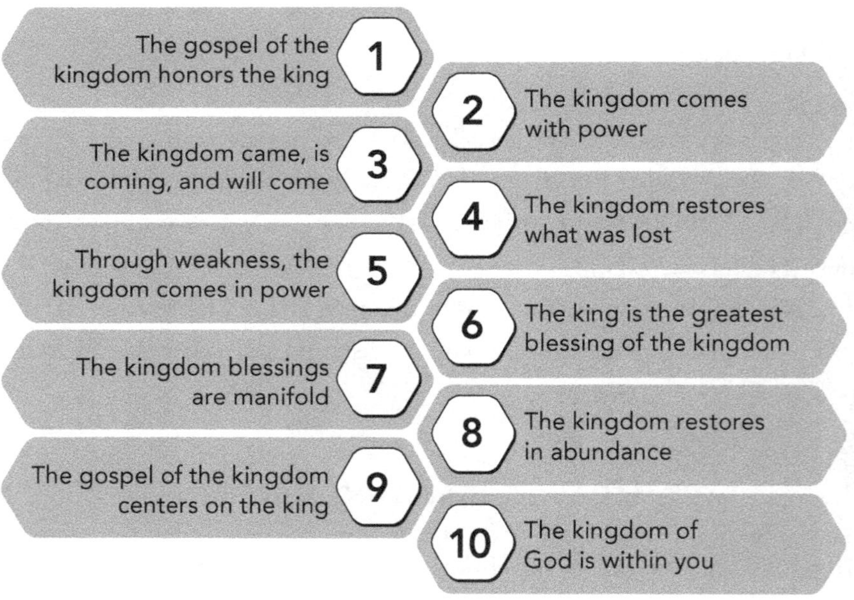

Teaching Principle 1: The Gospel of the Kingdom Honors the King

"'The time has come,' he said. 'The kingdom of God has come near. Repent and believe the good news!'" (Mark 1:15). Everywhere Jesus went during his second year, he talked about the *kingdom of God*—or, as Matthew preferred to call it, the kingdom of heaven. Jesus used the phrase *kingdom of God* or *kingdom of heaven* a combined 102 times across the Gospels—14 times in Mark, 31 times in Luke, and 55 times in Matthew (most often as kingdom of heaven).

So what exactly was the kingdom of God? Simple: the arrival of the king himself. The king had returned, stepping into enemy-occupied territory and liberating it from tyranny. It was Jesus turning up like John Wayne, saying, "Listen up. There's a new sheriff in town."

The Greek word for "kingdom" is *basileia* and refers to the jurisdiction of authority. As Trousdale and Sunshine summarize, "The kingdom is another way of talking about the Lordship of Christ. The most ancient confession of the Christian faith is 'Jesus is Lord,' meaning that he is Lord of all."[2] Jews under Roman authority understood what it meant for a territory to be under Caesar's rule—even if not everyone acknowledged his right to rule and submitted to it.[3] For Paul, confessing "Jesus is Lord" (Rom. 10:9) was salvation itself. It meant recognizing him as the rightful ruler of all things. D. Martyn Lloyd-Jones nailed it: The kingdom is the *rule of Christ in the hearts of men*. When Jesus said "The kingdom of God is at hand," it was less about a timeline and more an assertion of his authority over a fallen world. He was taking it back.

When people cry, "Thy kingdom come, thy will be done," it's like a national shout of "God save the King"—a longing for a righteous and just ruler. Admittedly, the news that the king had arrived was good news to some, bad news for others. Typically, we think of another kingdom invading as a hostile takeover, but if the people are oppressed and suffering under tyranny, a conquering king brings liberation. Jesus stated that he had "bound the strong man" who'd long oppressed them—what they witnessed was Jesus plundering his house. Satan could only watch helplessly as Jesus exercised his authority over "all manner of sickness and disease."

This is why Jesus's message began with "Repent!" It signaled a complete paradigm shift. The word *repentance* comes from two Greek words: the verb *maetanoein* ("to repent, change one's mind, feel remorse, be converted") and *epistrephein* ("to turn around"). Both speak of turning away *from*. But the verb *pisteuein* ("to believe") is used to refer to turning toward something. Jesus was

---

2. Jerry Trousdale and Glenn Sunshine, *The Kingdom Unleashed: How Jesus' 1st-Century Kingdom Values Are Transforming Thousands of Cultures and Awakening His Church* (DMM Library, 2018), chap. 2, Kindle.
3. Trousdale and Sunshine, *Kingdom Unleashed*, chap. 2.

asking the Jews to turn from their allegiance to their legalistic framework and return to God himself—by submitting to his reign. As Alan Hirsch says, "The word meta simply means beyond, above, or overarching. And the word noia (a derivative of the noun *nous*) refers to a way of thinking. Metanoia therefore involves paradigm shift to a new way of thinking—the recognition and rejection of various false frameworks for understanding the world. It is an enlightenment of sorts—waking up to a whole new world in which everything orients itself around Christ as Lord and King."[4]

Teaching Principle 2: The Kingdom Comes with Power

Unlike Rome, the kingdom of God didn't arrive by force, nor was it a theoretical teaching pulled from a textbook either. Jesus's ministry wasn't mere *talk* about the kingdom—he *was* the kingdom in motion. For the kingdom of God did not come with word only but with power (1 Cor. 4:20). That power came from a person—Jesus—who demonstrated his rule over sickness, death, and the elements. Schnabel observes, "Jesus not only talked about the royal presence of God but also demonstrated that presence in the miracles he performed."[5] They were *signs*—evidence of the authority he claimed and the message he preached. When he healed the paralytic lowered through the roof, first he declared, "Your sins are forgiven." To the shock of the religious leaders, he followed with a piercing challenge: "'But that you may know that the Son of Man has authority on earth to forgive sins'—he said to the paralytic—'I say to you, rise, pick up your bed, and go home'" (Mark 2:10–11 ESV).

Jesus's miracles weren't just acts of compassion; they were signs of his reign breaking into the world, reshaping it and making "sad things untrue."[6] As C. S. Lewis illustrated in *The Lion, the Witch and the Wardrobe*, the arrival of the

4. Alan Hirsch with Rob Kelly, *Metanoia: How God Radically Transforms People, Churches, and Organizations From the Inside Out* (100 Movements Publishing, 2023), chap. 1, Kindle.
5. Schnabel, *Early Christian Mission*, 222.
6. J. R. R. Tolkien, "The Field of Cormallen," chap. 4 in book VI The Return of the King (Houghton Mifflin, 1955).

king transforms everything, just as Aslan's presence turned winter into spring. Jesus's ministry was a living invitation to experience the kingdom here and now, where God's rule invades our reality. Declaring "Jesus is Lord" is a bold act of allegiance, a transfer from the domain of darkness into the kingdom of light (Col. 1:13). And when someone steps into that kingdom, they regain access to everything humanity lost in the fall. This is the essence of discipleship: surrendering to the king and stepping into the power of his kingdom.

Teaching Principle 3: The Kingdom Came, Is Coming, and Will Come

There are three ways that the kingdom is said to come:

Past: The kingdom *has come*—the King stepped into history and walked among us two thousand years ago. Christ is reigning now.

Present: The kingdom *is coming*—the kingdom is still expanding throughout the world, capturing hearts as men and women recognize and submit to his rule.

Future: The kingdom *will come*—the King will return to bring final justice, putting all rebellion that does not recognize his rule—including death and hell—under his feet.

The kingdom has come, is coming, and will come.

Hebrews places us in that intersection: "'You . . . [put] everything in subjection under his feet.' Now in putting everything in subjection to him, he left nothing outside his control. At present, we do not yet see everything in subjection to him" (Heb. 2:8 ESV)

Not yet.

Yet let's not miss this: Christ is already reigning. His resurrection didn't just promise future glory—it inaugurated his rule now. As Paul wrote, "He must reign until he has put all his enemies under his feet" (1 Cor. 15:25). Jesus is seated at the right hand of God, reigning now, even as the final battle plays out.

Every time Jesus healed or cast out a demon, it was a mere skirmish in an all-out cosmic war—one-sided as it is—Jesus taking more ground, conquering whatever powers oppressed humankind. The miracles merely pointed to who he was.

> "Do not believe me unless I do the works of my Father. But if I do them, even though you do not believe me, believe the works, that you may know and understand that the Father is in me, and I in the Father." (John 10:37–38)

This is why, when John the Baptist doubted and sent messengers from his prison cell to ask, "Are you the one who is to come, or should we expect someone else?" (Matt. 11:3), Jesus simply pointed to the evidence—the tangible manifestations of the kingdom's power. "Go back and report to John what you hear and see: The blind receive sight, the lame walk, those who have leprosy are cleansed, the deaf hear, the dead are raised, and the good news is proclaimed to the poor" (Matt. 11:4–5). His miracles were both declarations and demonstrations that a greater kingdom had come. When faith wavered in the cold damp of a prison cell, the wilderness prophet who had once thundered certainty simply needed a reminder: "Look at the signs, John. If these things are happening, then the King and his kingdom are here."

Admittedly, it's not always easy to see. Luke adds a phrase Jesus included in his message to John: "Blessed is anyone who does not stumble on account of me." Sometimes the kingdom doesn't come fast enough for our taste.

N. T. Wright elaborates on the tension:

> Revelation celebrates the sovereignty of Jesus from first page to last. But of course, neither Matthew nor Paul nor Revelation supposed for a minute that this meant that utopia had already arrived, that the vision of Isaiah 11 was already fully in place. Christians were being persecuted, facing violent opposition, celebrating the lordship of Jesus in a world where Caesar and his type of power still seemed to be solid and unshaken.[7]

7. N. T. Wright, *How God Became King: The Forgotten Story of the Gospels* (New York: HarperOne, 2012), chap. 8, Kindle edition.

And when Jesus sent the Twelve to announce the arrival of the kingdom, he also sent them with the power to prove it: "As you go, proclaim this message: 'The kingdom of heaven has come near.' Heal the sick, raise the dead, cleanse those who have leprosy, drive out demons" (Matt. 10:7–8). There is no denying that the message and the miracles were tied together, "because first Jesus 'did' and then he 'taught.'"[8] The miracles were a physical illustration of what the King brought spiritually: forgiveness, freedom, and fullness.

So to what degree is the kingdom of God still a part of the *good news* we are to bring others?

Teaching Principle 4: The Kingdom Restores What Was Lost

The good news about the king is what his kingdom brings—first, his loving rule. But before exploring what the kingdom restores, we must take stock of what was taken from us when our first parents defected from his kingdom. Although they gained the curse of self-rule, they lost far more. Yet when the king is restored to his rightful rule, we are restored, for he restores the blessings of his kingdom back to us.

At the dawn of creation, God planted a garden, a pocket-sized heaven on earth, called Eden, or Paradise. There God placed man at the very center of creation, with himself at the center of man's existence. He strolled regularly through Eden, taking walks with Adam and Eve, conversing with them, establishing a relationship built on trust, or faith. This was the kingdom of God, where God's presence brought our first parents purpose, peace, privilege, and many other things.

Yet when God briefly left them alone, their trust evaporated like morning dew as the serpent's words eclipsed God's. One whisper from the serpent and our first parents' trust shifted to what their own eyes saw, replacing God's word with their own judgment. Despite God's care and friendship, they lost their

---

8. Bob Burton, *The Spiritual DNA of a Church on Mission: Rediscovering the 1st Century Church for 21st Century Spiritual Awakening* (B&H Academic, 2020), Introduction, Kindle.

faith in him as a loving king, believing that the Serpent had their best interest in mind, not God. For their simple act of defiance, or self-rule, mankind was thrust outside God's kingdom, setting off a chain reaction that robbed all creation of experiencing the blessings of the kingdom.

What all Jews knew from the time that they were children in the synagogue was that the exchange cost us the kingdom blessings of access, innocence, peace, purpose, freedom, desire, and life itself.

Access: Adam and Eve were no longer able to walk with God in the cool of the day. Expelled from God's kingdom as rebels, they were thrust into an unforgiving wilderness. The two environments served as a constant contrast—the garden symbolic of the peace and beauty of God's reign against the cruel thorns and thistles accompanying self-rule.

Innocence: Their innocence had been shattered. The first sign of humanity's fall wasn't thunder or wrath but a quiet, gnawing shame: "They saw that they were naked." That simple realization betrayed something deeper: souls suddenly exposed, uncovered, and desperate to hide from the gaze of God. And yet, even in judgment, God moved in mercy. In a prophetic gesture of grace, he shed innocent blood to cover their guilt—fashioning garments from the hide of a slain animal. It was the first death they'd ever witnessed, the first glimpse of the cost that their rebellion demanded. Blood on the ground, a covering on their skin. To make them innocent again, Innocence himself would have to bleed so their shame could be covered. Atonement cost the death of innocence, but restoration would be more costly.

Peace: They lost their internal peace. The anxiety prompting the sewing together a makeshift covering of fig leaves proved insufficient to cover their sin, only increasing the anxiety. The never-ending nagging that we could be exposed shatters our relationship with ourselves, wrecking our relationships with God and others. Once, the sound of God's voice brought only joy, but now it brought only terror. Overnight, God went from a comforter to be sought to an enemy to be feared. Our first parents learned to hide from God, from each other, and from themselves. The anxiety of being discovered and exposed has plagued humankind ever since.

Purpose: Our purpose within the garden was well established: Walk with God, tend the garden, be fruitful, and multiply. With the loss of our unconscious reflecting glory back to our Creator came the loss of our purpose. Our souls, created to worship, were disoriented by the absence of an object of it. As Augustine confessed, "You have made us for yourself, O Lord, and our hearts are restless until they rest in you."[9] Thus, our hearts, prone to worship everything, will worship anything.

Desire: With the loss of purposeful fulfillment, the pursuit of our own pleasure replaces the pursuit of pleasing God. Like spiritual amnesia, we have lost the taste for what truly satisfies. Our problem isn't so much that we're driven by wrong desires but that the right desires—those placed in us by our Creator—have been constricted, if not strangled altogether. As C. S. Lewis writes, "It's not that our desires are too strong. It is that they are too weak."[10] Stronger desires to bless, love, and worship are felt like a faint pulse. Despite our "lives lived in quiet desperation" and unfulfilled longings, our souls catch glimpses of the ephemeral "something more" like a brief mirage that occasionally shimmers before vanishing.

Freedom: The illusion of freedom cost them their liberty. In Eden, the body served the soul. Now, their dead souls went along for the ride with whatever slavish desires the body dictated. Like an iPhone that is bricked, human souls no longer receive a signal from God, and therefore only the external hardware receives our attention. Our "freedom" to fulfill our will at whim leads to the bondage in a prison of our own making.

Life: Adam and Eve lost their right to eternal life. Every time their bodies replicated a cell, it was a lesser copy of itself, until their aging led to death. Death returned them to the clay from which they were formed, fulfilling the curse that God promised. Beings who don't fulfill their purpose on earth are not permitted to live there forever.

---

9. Augustine, *Confessions*, trans. Henry Chadwick (Oxford University Press, 1991), bk. 1, chap. 1.
10. C. S. Lewis, *The Weight of Glory and Other Addresses* (HarperOne, 2001), 26.

Now that we've taken stock of what was lost, we can appreciate what the kingdom restores: access, innocence, peace, purpose, desire, freedom, and eternal life.

Teaching Principle 5: Through Weakness, the Kingdom Comes in Power

Restoring our kingdom blessings wasn't cheap. As one puritan remarked, "It cost more to redeem us, than to make us."[11] The coming of the King was not enough. Despite his authority and power to free us, Aslan had to lay himself down on the stone table.

The greatest blessing of the kingdom will forever be *the King himself.* Eighteenth-century hymn writer Williams Pantycelyn wrote:

> He's greater than his blessings, he's greater than his grace,
> Far greater than his actions, whatever you may trace;
> I'll plead for faith, gifts, cleansing; for these I'll yearn quite sore,
> But on him only, always, I'll look and lean far more.[12]

There is no one like him. Unlike kings who conquer by dominance, Jesus surrendered himself in love for his sinful creation. He died our death, not his own, taking the punishment we deserved. In that divine reversal, Jesus suffered far more than crucifixion at the hands of men—he bore the eternal judgment of God for sin. On the cross, suspended between heaven and earth, Jesus took the crushing weight and full consequences of our damnation—so we never will. Out of pure love, and a desire to restore us to the kingdom, the Father poured out his wrath upon Jesus—exhausting it—so that there would never be another drop of wrath for me and you—ever.

His death removed our punishment, but his perfect life earned back the blessings of the kingdom. As Jesus inherited the curse of my sin, so I inherit

11. Thomas Watson, *A Body of Divinity* (London, 1692), 146.
12. Williams Pantycelyn, quoted in "A Brush with Death," Peter Jeffery, www.peterjeffery.org.uk/a-brush-with-death.

the blessings of his perfect obedience. Through weakness, the kingdom comes in power. As Revelation declares:

> "Now have come the salvation and the power
> and the kingdom of our God,
> and the authority of his Messiah.
> For the accuser of our brothers and sisters,
> who accuses them before our God day and night,
> has been hurled down.
> They triumphed over him
> by the blood of the Lamb
> and by the word of their testimony;
> they did not love their lives so much
> as to shrink from death." (Rev. 12:10–11)

That is an epic bit of heavenly smack talk right there. And it should be repeated whenever and wherever we can.

Teaching Principle 6: The King Is the Greatest Blessing of the Kingdom

Knowing that Jesus restored the Paradise lost, we now need to explore Paradise regained. Jesus repeatedly told *lost and found* parables: the lost sheep, the lost coin, and the lost son. More than our kingdom blessings, it was we who were lost, leading Jesus to seek and save us. He told two parables about the kingdom of heaven finding two people in two very different ways:

> "The kingdom of heaven is like treasure hidden in a field. When a man found it, he hid it again, and then in his joy went and sold all he had and bought that field.
>
> Again, the kingdom of heaven is like a merchant looking for fine pearls. When he found one of great value, he went away and sold everything he had and bought it." (Matt. 13:44–46)

In the first parable, a merchant feverishly scours the bazaars and marketplaces for that one purchase that will make him a fortune, fulfilling his wildest dreams. The first man was clearly *seeking* the pearl before he found it. The farmer, however, *accidentally* plows up buried treasure in someone else's field. One seeks, one does not—yet both find. The kingdom comes to each of us uniquely; some seek, some don't, but both react the same when they discover the immense value of the treasure: They sell everything to obtain the treasure at any cost, to the loss of everything else. This describes someone experiencing the awakening of their souls to their rightful king as they're ushered into the kingdom. They become willing to lose everything: possessions, pride, and their entire life as they know it. They stop arguing about Bigfoot or aliens—keenly aware of their sin and brokenness. Christ becomes the pearl of great price, the treasure that's been hidden. And for the first time in their lives, they realize that what they lose is nothing compared to what they gain in him. There is no phantom pot of gold at the end of the rainbow anymore; there is only God himself.

God is the central object of salvation; we are not. Jesus definitively stated that "this is eternal life, that they know you, the only true God" (John 17:3). To someone enraptured with the kingdom, salvation is not about the destination of heaven but a relationship with the King of heaven. Heaven is only heaven because Christ himself is there. When Jesus's disciples asked him, "Lord, show us the way to heaven," Jesus replied that he was the object, "I am the way, the truth, and the life." In other words, Jesus was saying, "I'm all of it." It is all wrapped up in Jesus himself, because having the King means having the entire kingdom—having it all.

With an eternal king, there are blessings eternal, yet the king himself remains the greatest treasure in the kingdom—the pearl of great price behind the pearly gates. All these blessings are merely the sparkling flash of his own radiance and glory. Therefore, when we talk about the good news, we must never separate the blessings of the kingdom from the King himself, or we miss the true glory of it.[13]

---

13. Pick up Pat Linnell's book *Grace Bomb* if you want to see how this works on the ground.

Teaching Principle 7: The Kingdom Blessings Are Manifold

The good news of the kingdom is like a multifaceted diamond—held up to the light, the more it glitters from every angle. Each facet reflects a different aspect of what the King has restored through his kingdom.

Many of us have heard Bill Bright's four spiritual laws:

1. God loves you and has a wonderful plan for your life.
2. Man is sinful and separated from God.
3. Jesus Christ is God's only provision for man's sin.
4. We must individually receive Jesus as Savior and Lord.[14]

These simple statements are a helpful summary of *one* facet of the diamond, but they cannot encapsulate the grandeur of the gospel any more than the ocean can be contained in a teacup. Exploring the multifaceted nature of the gospel of the kingdom will sharpen our agility as disciple-makers. Below are some additional examples of helpful ways that the good news of the kingdom has been proclaimed throughout history. Each can be used to share the gospel effectively in various situations, as the Spirit leads:

The gospel of the way home speaks of God's love and desire to bring us back home like the prodigal son. Trusting in Christ is the only way home. This is the gospel that Billy Graham preached.

The gospel of atonement proclaims that Jesus took our guilt and shame, nailing the law's demands to the cross. His atoning sacrifice justified

14. Bill Bright, *The Four Spiritual Laws* (Campus Crusade for Christ, 1952). Cru has since fleshed them out a bit to include the experience of a present relationship with God as opposed to a ticket to heaven: "[1] God loves you and offers a wonderful plan for your life. . . . [2] All of us sin and our sin has separated us from God. . . . [3] Jesus Christ is God's only provision for our sin. Through Him we can know and experience God's love and plan for our life. . . . [4] We must individually receive Jesus Christ as Savior and Lord; then we can know and experience God's love and plan for our lives"; "Would You Like to Know God Personally?," Cru, accessed April 22, 2025, www.cru.org/content/movementlife/ph/en/how-to-know-god/would-you-like-to-know-god-personally1.html.

us, giving us an innocent standing before God. This gospel is a gospel of forgiveness, as preached by Martin Luther and Charles Spurgeon.

The gospel of the new birth centers on the Spirit's work to awaken, indwell and re-create us. It was the heartbeat of the Great Awakening and the Methodist revivals of Whitefield and Wesley.

The previous list is far from exhaustive. It's just a glimpse as the jewel of salvation is turned, each facet catching the light. There are also these:

- The gospel of hope
- The gospel of justice
- The gospel of "God with us"
- The gospel of "God for us"

Each one shines brightly. But wait, there's more. Keep turning the diamond, and you'll see even more of the kingdom's radiance as his glory still catches different angles, as we'll explore below.

Teaching Principle 8: The Kingdom Restores in Abundance

Christ didn't just recover the lost blessings of the kingdom for us; he restored them a hundredfold. Adam and Eve knew God only as Creator, but we now know him as Redeemer. Our relationship with God has deepened from Creator-creation to Redeemer-redeemed. In Christ, the love Adam and Eve experienced as his creation is restored, but so much more. He adopted us as sons and daughters. We now experience the love the Father loved the Son with before the creation of the world:

> "I in them and you in me—so that they may be brought to complete unity. Then the world will know that you sent me and have loved them even as you have loved me." (John 17:23)

Adam and Eve never experienced the depths of this kind of love. Only kingdom blessings restored by the conquering King and his kingdom bring these types of blessings:

The gospel of kingdom access: The atoning death of Christ tore the temple curtain, flinging open the gates to God. Heaven's throne room is no longer off-limits. Jesus is now our high priest in heaven, having made a way for us to boldly *approach* the throne of grace to receive mercy and help in our time of need (Heb. 4:16). We don't need a priest, ritual, or spotless record to come close. Christ gave us access—not just so we would be tolerated but so we would be loved, just as he is. As Paul said, "Through whom we have gained *access* by faith into this grace in which we now stand . . ." (Rom. 5:2, emphasis mine).

The gospel of kingdom innocence: The blood of Jesus has washed us whiter than the snow. "God made him who had no sin to be sin for us, so that in him we might become the righteousness of God" (2 Cor. 5:21). We are no longer hiding in shame but walk in his presence as beloved children—washed, forgiven, cleansed, accepted, and unashamed.

The gospel of kingdom peace: Although we were once at war, fighting against the one who formed us, Jesus stepped in and made peace through his flesh. He became the peace offering between us and God. "Since we have been justified through faith, we have peace with God through our Lord Jesus Christ" (Rom. 5:1). Peace *with* God leads to the peace *of* God—our *shalom,* the blessing of life as the Creator intended.

The gospel of kingdom purpose: Having lost our peace with God, we searched vainly for a purpose. Before the fall, our purpose was to walk with God, tend the garden, "be fruitful and multiply." In Christ, our purpose is restored as image bearers who reflect his glory—we become fruitful and multiply through making disciples. How we do this is unique to every individual, "for we are God's workmanship, created in Christ Jesus to do good works, which God prepared in advance for us to do" (Eph. 2:10 ESV). The Greek word for "workmanship" is *poema, meaning* "handcrafted." God doesn't stop calling you when you experience salvation; salvation is the start of your calling.

The gospel of kingdom desire: Without purpose, a relentless pursuit to satiate our own pleasure replaces the taste for what truly satisfies. As the Spirit enters our souls, he reawakens our cravings for spiritual things, stirring a holy hunger. "Those who live in accordance with the Spirit have their minds set on what the Spirit desires" (Rom. 8:5). The Spirit rewires our desires, kindling a passion for the deeper joys of intimacy with God. Adding to the claim of the Westminster Confession, "The chief end of man is to glorify God and enjoy him forever,"[15] Piper adds that we glorify God best *by* enjoying him.[16]

The gospel of kingdom freedom: After replacing our desires, we discover that the Spirit brings freedom. The Spirit sets us free from our bondage to the will of the flesh, "that we should no longer be slaves to sin—because anyone who has died has been set free from sin" (Rom. 6:6–7). God miraculously joined your old life of sin to Christ as he was crucified, killing the old you that lived for self. Then you were supernaturally raised to newness of life by the power of the Holy Spirit. Removing your guilt is one thing; unlocking your freedom is another—and Christ did both. You don't have to *stay* stuck, bound to old habits or destructive patterns. Saving you was a greater miracle than sanctifying you. Which is harder? Raising someone to life from the dead, or freeing them from habits? If he accomplished the greater feat, he can accomplish the lesser one. The good news is more than the pardoning of your sin—it's the empowering of your freedom.

The gospel of kingdom life: The gospel isn't about making bad people good; it's about making dead people alive. "Just as sin reigned in death,

15. Westminster Shorter Catechism, Q.1. in The Westminster Confession of Faith (Free Presbyterian Publications, 1994), 289.
16. Piper puts it like this: "The chief end of man is to glorify God *by* enjoying him forever"; John Piper, "Our Grand Obligation," Desiring God, October 6, 1985, www.desiringgod.org/messages/our-grand-obligation.

so also grace might reign through righteousness to bring eternal life through Jesus Christ our Lord" (Rom. 5:21). This is the gospel Jesus preached when he declared, "I have come that they may have life, and have it to the full" (John 10:10). Eternal life doesn't start at death—it starts the moment you're united with Christ, and your soul is resurrected, fully alive in him.

Why am I laying these out for you in such detail? For the same reason I unpacked the rhythms in the last chapter. These were the principles that governed Jesus's practice, and understanding the blessings of the kingdom will light a fire in you to share them with others while making disciples.

Teaching Principle 9: The Gospel of the Kingdom Centers on the King

Our greatest danger isn't forgetting the gospel's many facets but *adding* to the gospel itself. That was the battle Paul fought fiercely with the Galatians. What looked like theological nitpicking to them was, to Paul, a matter of spiritual life or death.

The Galatians didn't reject Jesus—they just added one small requirement: circumcision. It seemed such a harmless tweak—like a spiritual upgrade. After all, more obedience couldn't be a bad thing, could it? It sounds almost laughable now—*circumcision* as the dealbreaker? But anything we add to the cross is equally absurd. In the Galatian churches of Lystra, Derbe, and Iconium, false teachers crept in whispering that circumcision *and* Jesus made you acceptable to God. Sure, circumcision had Old Testament roots, commanded by God as the sign of the covenant. But it was always a *sign* of faith, never the *source* of salvation.

Paul saw the distraction with circumcision for what it was: a total abandonment of grace. Because the moment you add anything to Christ, you stop trusting him entirely. That's why Paul didn't call it a variation but *another gospel*. And "a different gospel . . . is really no gospel at all" (Gal. 1:6–7). They managed to turn good news into bad. Paul knew the truth: The law was a death trap. Break one command and you're guilty of breaking all. But Jesus did what none of us could—he fulfilled the law, every line, every demand. He didn't come to abolish it but to accomplish it. And, by doing so, he opened the way to a gospel that rests entirely on trusting him alone. As Paul wrote, "The righteous will live by faith" (Gal. 3:11)—trusting Christ's fulfillment of the law, not striving to do it yourself.

Jerry Bridges summarizes it this way:

> How can we experience the righteousness of Christ as it was meant to apply to our daily lives? In Galatians 2:15–21, Paul provided much insight on this, beginning with this sentence: We know that a person is not justified by works of the law but through faith in Jesus Christ, so we . . . have believed in Christ Jesus, in order to be justified by faith in Christ and not by works of the law, because by works of the law no one will be justified (Galatians 2:16). In this single sentence Paul uses the word justified three times. The repetition emphasizes that we're justified not by our personal obedience to the law but by faith in Christ.[17]

Christ justified us by his death, which means that God looks at me just as if I'd never sinned. Bridges adds, "But here's another way of saying it: 'just as if I'd always obeyed.'"[18] He justified us by becoming our substitute for sin, as Keller summarizes: "As our substitute. He took the condemnation we deserve; he faced the trial that should be ours so that we do not have to face any more trials. So I simply need to ask God to accept me because of what the Lord Jesus has done."[19]

This wasn't just Paul's gospel; it was Jesus's too. A massive crowd pressed in, asking him, "What must we do to inherit eternal life?" (John 6:28). Jesus didn't give them a to-do list, but a name: "Believe in the one he has sent" (v. 29).

Just believe. Why is that so hard? To prove they were worthy, they wanted

---

17. Jerry Bridges and Bob Bevington, *The Bookends of the Christian Life* (Crossway, 2009), chap. 1, Kindle.
18. Bridges and Bevington, *Bookends*, chap. 1.
19. Timothy Keller, *The Freedom of Self-Forgetfulness: The Path to True Christian Joy* (10Publishing, 2013), chap. 3, Kindle.

something they could do or measure. We can never point to our salvation and say "*I* did this." We can only point to the cross and resurrection, saying, "He did this." That's why Paul pulled no punches with the Galatians. If you think even one religious act can make you right with God, you've missed the gospel by a mile.

And the circumcision crowd? They're still here with us. They didn't die out in the first century. You hear them every time someone says, "If you'd just ______, then God would accept you." Fill in the blank with anything, no matter what it is, and the one thing *it is* . . . is heresy. You've just modified a version of "Jesus-and theology":

Jesus *and* rule-keeping.

Jesus *and* church attendance.

Jesus *and* moral performance.

Adding anything to the cross means you're trusting in yourself. And if you trust in yourself—*even just a little*—you're still trying to be your own savior.

So far, all I've ever earned for myself is hell. But Jesus? He earned *everything* heaven offers. That's why when Jesus preached the gospel of the kingdom, he was ultimately proclaiming *himself.*

There is no gospel without Jesus. The gospel isn't grace-centered, faith-centered, or whatever-centered. It's *Jesus*-centered. Christocentric to the core. Flip open Revelation. In every heavenly scene where Christ is, crowns hit the ground, faces fall flat, and every voice cries out, "Worthy is the Lamb, who was slain" (Rev. 5:12).

Want grace-centered salvation? Perfect. But don't fixate on the stream. Go to the fountain. You don't get grace *apart from Jesus*. Those who center their lives on Christ will find themselves swimming in grace, grounded in the gospel, and anchored to the cross. But give it time, and your soul will be tempted to sneak something else onto the throne. Trust me. Whenever my Christianity becomes Peyton-centric—or anything-else-centric—we've got a problem. The scariest part? I often don't even *know* it. And that's the real danger.

That's why grace appeared as a person. Because focusing on him means I'm not focused on myself. I trust in Christ, and Christ alone. When grace gets disembodied from Jesus, it is reduced to just another cheapened theological concept—one that risks dragging us right back into Saul's pharisaical mindset before Damascus. Strangely, some people are more passionate about the doctrine of grace than they are about Christ himself, and ironically, some of the cruelest people I've encountered in church wave the banner of grace from a merciless pole. Arrogant, snarky, and superior to all who don't tick their boxes, they display much of theological formulas but little of Christ. Paul didn't say, "You've not so learned theology" or "The doctrine of grace has appeared that offers salvation to all people."[20] He said, "The grace of God has appeared . . ." and he meant Christ himself as grace incarnate. That's why I don't tell people to be gospel-centered, cross-centered, grace-centered, or anything-else-centered. I tell them to be *Christ-centered*. Alan Hirsch once said to me, "If you stay Christ-centered, you'll have all the others—and be a whole lot more enjoyable to be around."

This is essential in disciple-making. Because just like you're learning not to put yourself at the center of your own salvation, you can't put yourself at the center of someone else's. Making disciples isn't about you; it's about Jesus. Your job is to point people *past* you, not *to* you. Jesus once said that John the Baptist was the greatest of the prophets. Why? As Alistair Begg puts it, John

---

20. For the record, I love theology. I encourage people to read it. Heck, I even got a masters in theology. But if you know, you know. My hope is that people will not be distracted by it but allow all rivers to flow into the sea of Christ himself.

proclaimed the way, pointed the way, and then got out of the way.[21] Once when a group of Greeks approached Philip, they said, "Sir, we would like to see Jesus" (John 12:21). That's the disciple-maker's job—to make sure they do.

Teaching Principle 10: The Kingdom of God Is Within You

I realize that if you're reading this book, you're most likely a leader. You've heard the gospel, but let's start with a pulse check. If you're breathing, you still need the gospel. My mentor Peter Jeffery—Martyn Lloyd-Jones's protégé—regularly emphasized that "believers need the gospel." That's why the apostle Peter wrote to the early church, "It is right to refresh your memory . . . even though you know them and are firmly established in the truth" (2 Peter 1:12). In other words: "I know I've said this before—but you need to hear it again." Martin Luther was rumored to have said, "We need to hear the gospel every day, because we forget it every day." Sinners leak truth like a sieve.

Bob Thune, in *The Gospel-Centered Life*, gives a striking visual: When we first come to Christ, the cross feels massive, because our sin is great, and God's holiness even greater—so the gospel bridges the gap. But, over time, something shifts. As our behavior improves, we forget our desperate need. Our sin

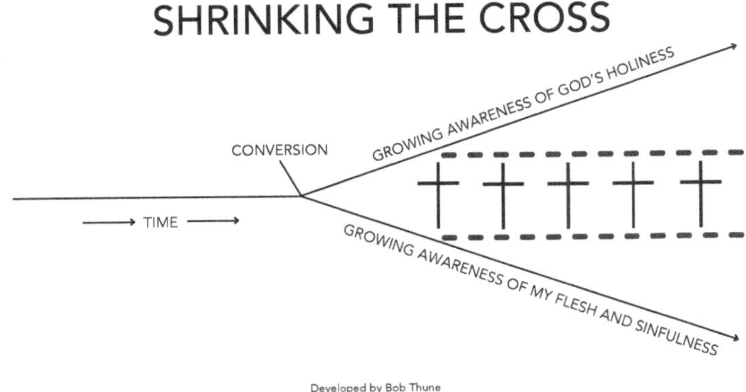

Developed by Bob Thune

21. This is from my memory of a sermon preached by Alistair on Christian radio. I'd have a devil of a time trying to find it, but I'm thankful for Alistair's wit.

seems more manageable, and as a result, God's holiness shrinks in our minds. Without realizing it, the cross shrinks in our minds.

And that's when trouble starts.

When we forget how sinful we are—and how holy God is—we settle for "little cross" Christianity. We start minimizing sin or hiding it altogether. Some of us become legalists, performing to cover the gap. Others get lax, brushing off sin as no big deal. Either way, it's losing sight of God's grace. As Tim Keller points out in *The Prodigal God*, the older brother—the religious one—resented grace, unable to stomach how freely it was given. Keller calls it "older brother syndrome"—and it's everywhere.

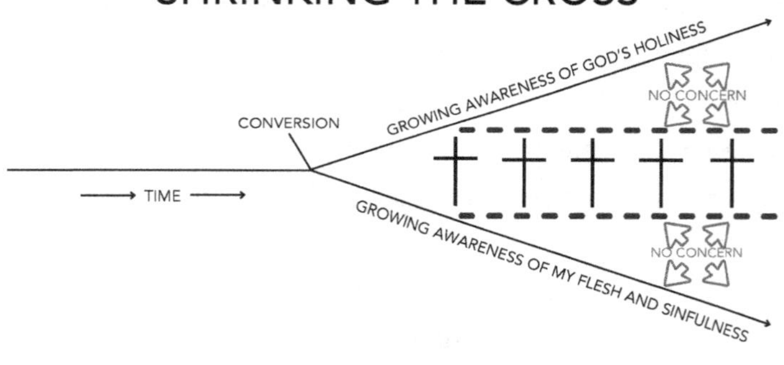

Developed by Bob Thune

Maybe you're wondering, *What's wrong with me? Why do I lose sight of the cross so easily?* Be encouraged: Even the apostles weren't immune. Peter himself lost sight of the cross too. In Galatians 2, Paul called him out: "When Cephas came to Antioch, I opposed him to his face. . . . He began to draw back and separate himself from the Gentiles . . . [fearing] the circumcision group. . . . Even Barnabas was led astray" (vv. 11–13). And Paul's indictment is telling: "They were not acting in line with the truth of the gospel" (v. 14).

Let that sink in: You can believe the gospel and live out of sync with it.

That's why Paul later urged, "in *view* of God's mercy, to offer your bodies as a living sacrifice" (Rom. 12:1, emphasis mine). The view matters. Lose sight of God's mercy—drift from the cross—and you'll live as if you don't need it. But you do. Every hour. Every breath.

As our view of God's holiness grows, so does our appreciation of the cross. That's "big cross Christianity"—and it comes from having a big view of Christ. Whenever the warning lights start going off in your Christianity, most likely a small view of Christ is the problem. A "big Christ Christianity" suffers little problems.

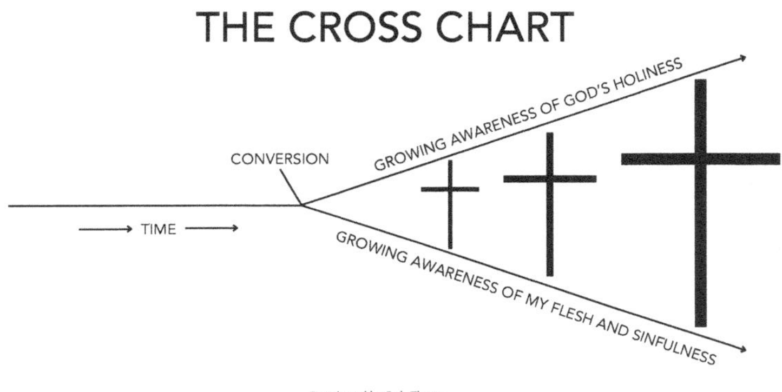

That's why disciple-making begins with your discipleship. You can't pass on what hasn't first taken hold in you. That's why I've spent this entire chapter outlining the gospel for you. Mike Chong Perkinson once said to me, "When the gospel works deeply within you, mission is an outcome, not an activity." When we know the gospel, really *know* it, the more naturally it flows through us into the lives of those we're discipling. Disciple-makers don't need seminary degrees—but they do need to know the gospel deep in their bones.

Grace

The English Puritans used to speak about the importance of gathering "fresh manna" daily. Our hearts need to be reminded regularly about the gospel. So how do we heed Paul's admonition to keep God's mercy "in full view"? The church has spoken of the *means of grace*—sacred rhythms that fix our eyes on Jesus.

Observe the early church in Acts 2:42–47:

> They devoted themselves to the apostles' teaching and to fellowship, to the breaking of bread and to prayer. . . . All the believers were together and had everything in common. . . . They broke bread in their homes and ate together with glad and sincere hearts, praising God and enjoying the favor of all the people.

This was their way of always keeping Christ in front of their eyes. And the result? "The Lord added to their number daily those who were being saved" (v. 47).

So what are the means of grace that we can partake of to keep Christ in full view and constantly remind ourselves of the good news of the kingdom?

Baptism

Baptism is one of the most powerful ways God delivers the blessings of his kingdom. It's a sacrament, or mystery, where the gospel is given to us in water and Word. As Paul reminded the Romans, "We were buried with Christ through baptism into death . . . that we too may live a new life" (Rom. 6:4). This is not something we do for God—it is something God has done for us. Baptism is how God marks us as his own, gives us the Spirit, and speaks his irrevocable "yes" over our lives. When we doubt, we return to the fount and lean back into our baptismal identity from Romans 6. As Luther taught, the Christian life is one of daily returning to our baptism—drowning the old self, and rising again in Christ. "A Christian life is nothing else than a daily baptism," he wrote, "once begun and ever to be continued."[22]

So if you're going to be a disciple-maker, remember that Jesus tells us to baptize disciples as part of making disciples. So if you haven't been baptized yet, what are you waiting for?

---

22. Martin Luther, *Large Catechism*, trans. F. Bente and W. H. T. Dau, "Part Fourth: Of Infant Baptism," in *Triglot Concordia: The Symbolical Books of the Ev. Lutheran Church* (Concordia Publishing House, 1921), Project Wittenberg, accessed September 20, 2025, https://www.projectwittenberg.org/pub/resources/text/wittenberg/luther/catechism/web/cat-13a.html.

Communion

The Lord's Supper pulls Christ into focus—not symbolically, but sacramentally. In the bread and wine, he gives us his body and blood again, just as he promised: "This is my body . . . this is my blood . . . for the forgiveness of sins" (Matt. 26:26–28). This meal is fresh grace you can taste—a visible, tangible gospel. We don't just remember Christ at the table—we receive him.

Luther nailed it (pun intended) when he said, "In the Sacrament you are to receive from the lips of Christ forgiveness of sin—it is a gift, not a work."[23] In other words, stop trying to earn what Christ is handing you for free. Paul told us to do this "as often as you eat this bread and drink this cup" (1 Cor. 11:26), because of our tendency to forget, like spiritual goldfish with a three-second memory when it comes to the gospel. Knowing us well, Jesus gave us this rhythm, a meal to receive Christ's sacrifice afresh.

These ordinary practices are anything but ordinary. They are windows that help us to regularly get a "full view" of the King and the grace of his kingdom.

Scripture

Finally, there is Scripture. What a vast treasure chest of blessings! If there is ever a place you can go to remind yourself of the good news, it's the Bible.

The Epistles teach us that in Christ, God's constant demeanor toward you is one of grace and peace. He desires to show you mercy and to restore *shalom*. His every intention for you is to draw you near to himself through his Son. Always. That's why in every epistle, no matter what the state of the church, Paul could open with the line "Grace and peace to you," not just a first-century "howdy" but an intentional reminder that no matter what state the gospel finds you in at any given time, you can bank on God's heart for you. Otherwise, why would Paul even waste his time writing to some of the churches as messed up as they were? Grace and peace. That's why.

---

23. Martin Luther, *Large Catechism*, "Part Fifth: Of the Sacrament of the Altar," trans. F. Bente and W. H. T. Dau, in *Triglot Concordia: The Symbolical Books of the Ev. Lutheran Church* (Concordia Publishing House, 1921), Project Wittenberg, accessed September 20, 2025 https://www.projectwittenberg.org/pub/resources/text/wittenberg/luther/catechism/web/cat-14.html.

- Grace and peace to you from God our Father and from the Lord Jesus Christ (Rom. 1:7).
- Grace and peace to you from God our Father and the Lord Jesus Christ (1 Cor. 1:3).
- Grace to you and peace from God our Father and the Lord Jesus Christ (2 Cor. 1:3).
- Grace to you and peace from God our Father and the Lord Jesus Christ (Gal. 1:3).
- Grace to you and peace from God our Father and the Lord Jesus Christ (Eph. 1:2).
- Grace to you and peace from God our Father and the Lord Jesus Christ (Phil. 1:2).
- Grace to you and peace from God our Father (Col. 1:2).
- Grace to you and peace (1 Thess. 1:1).
- Grace to you and peace from God our Father and the Lord Jesus Christ (2 Thess. 1:2).
- Grace, mercy, and peace from God the Father and Christ Jesus our Lord (1 Tim. 1:2).
- Grace, mercy, and peace from God the Father and Christ Jesus our Lord (2 Tim. 1:2).
- Grace and peace from God the Father and Christ Jesus our Savior (Titus 1:4).
- Grace to you and peace from God our Father and the Lord Jesus Christ (Philem. 1:3).
- May grace and peace be multiplied to you (1 Peter 1:2).
- May grace and peace be multiplied to you in the knowledge of God and of Jesus our Lord (2 Peter 1:2).
- Grace, mercy, and peace will be with us, from God the Father and from Jesus Christ the Father's Son, in truth and love (2 John 1:3).

Just let that sink in.

And so I leave you with the blessing of God that he always extends toward you in Christ: "Grace and peace."

CHAPTER 8

Practices for Teaching

The future has many names: The lazy call it the impossible. The fearful refer to it as the unknown. But the courageous embrace it by saying: "This is my challenge."

—VICTOR HUGO

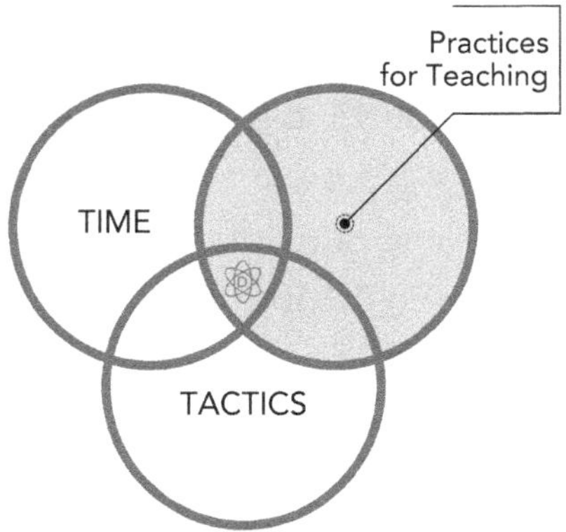

"I saw you while you were still under the fig tree."

Nathaniel froze. He hadn't told anyone about that moment.

It wasn't just that Jesus had *seen* him; it felt as though this stranger had looked into Nathaniel's soul. That fig tree, where Nathaniel had been hiding, was his quiet place of prayer and pondering. That's how Philip knew to find him in its shade, heart heavy with questions. On that day, he'd been wrestling with questions about himself and God, about how God blessed Jacob (later named Israel) despite his dishonesty.

The name "Israel" still clung to their national identity like a second skin. But the story beneath the name—lying for his birthright, deceiving his father—supplanted his brother. Nathaniel had grown up on those stories, but lately they haunted him. *If there was hope for Jacob, maybe there's hope for me?* Nathaniel felt far from guileless. Everyone wrestles with the span between who they are and who they want to be. Nathaniel knew he needed a Jacob-style head-on collision with God—but he wasn't just going to waltz into his campsite as he had with Jacob, was he?.

Right then Philip came running, breathless: "We've found the one Moses wrote about . . . Jesus of Nazareth!" Nazareth? Nathaniel's skepticism flared. "Can anything good come out of Nazareth?" A throwaway line, to shield himself from disappointment in another would-be messiah. A. B. Bruce speculates that "Nathanael's prejudice against Nazareth sprung not from pride, as in the case of the people of Judea who despised the Galileans in general, but from humility. He was a Galilean himself, and as much an object of Jewish contempt as were the Nazarenes."[1] Surely the Messiah was not going to come from anywhere near Nazareth. Philip was so insistent, though, his face so full of hope, that Nathaniel slowly got up and followed him back to a ring of young people circling a man around thirtyish. Jesus fixed on him with knowing eyes as he approached and said, "Here truly is an Israelite in whom there is no deceit" (John 1:47).

Those few words sliced through Nathaniel's doubt like a blade. No deceit. No guile. It wasn't a description. It was more of a declaration. But Jesus didn't just see who Nathaniel was; he saw who he *could be*. In a flash, he realized: This man spoke into his private wrestlings, looking past the Jacob he was and seeing the Israel he longed to be.

"How do you know me?"

Jesus answered, "I saw you while you were still under the fig tree before Philip called you."

---

1. A. B. Bruce, *The Training of the Twelve: How Jesus Christ Found and Taught the 12 Apostles; a Book of New Testament Biography* (1871; Pantianos Classics, 2018), chap. 1, Kindle.

Nathaniel's skepticism collapsed instantly. "Rabbi," he said, "you are the Son of God; you are the King of Israel."

He wasn't just reading a story now. He was living it. Jesus continued:

> "You believe because I told you I saw you under the fig tree? You will see greater things than that. . . . Very truly I tell you, you will see 'heaven open, and the angels of God ascending and descending on' the Son of Man." (John 1:50)

Jacob's ladder. The ladder between heaven and earth wasn't a place but a person. Heaven had just broken into earth and invaded Nathaniel's world.

Disciple-making at its core is less about having the right arguments and more about introducing people to a person—like Philip did. As we meet with people who are wrestling through their own private struggles, Jacob's ladder comes down in their life as God invades their world. People are as shocked as Nathaniel to discover that they are *known by God*, and want to know him in return.

In year 2, Jesus taught Nathaniel how to fish for souls—just as he'd plucked him like a ripe piece of fruit that day under the fig tree. As Jesus focused on the Teaching rhythm, he trained them intentionally through every conversation, one fig-tree encounter at a time.

Now it's your turn—do you believe heaven is still invading earth? For Nathaniel, heaven materialized when Philip brought him to Jesus. That's what the rhythm of Teaching looks like practically, and it's the focus of this chapter. This will not be a treatise on preaching but on how to teach someone about Jesus in the context of disciple-making.

He Is Still Calling Disciple-Makers

"Follow me, and I will make you fishers of people." With this simple sentence, Jesus invited ordinary people into an extraordinary mission. Above my writing desk, suspended on a wrought iron chain, is a facsimile of the contract from *The Hobbit*—the one thrust upon Bilbo Baggins by thirteen dwarves, and a wizard who believed in him long before he believed in himself. It's inked with sprawling clauses, folded streamers, and sealed with more wax than seems necessary for a journey, but I keep it there as a reminder: The call to make disciples often feels just like that contract—long, unclear, risky, and likely to make one late for dinner. If you're feeling that same reluctance, that's normal.

Bilbo wasn't ready either. No training, weapons, or grand speeches—just a reluctant heart and an underdeveloped gifting. Yet Gandalf saw something in him—an artistry for courage and resilience that even Bilbo didn't know he had. That's what disciple-making is like. You'll bumble, panic, and second-guess yourself the whole way. But if you go—faith nudging you past fear into the unknown—you may just find that God is weaving a world-saving story around your small, faithful "yes."

Bilbo and Gandalf converse at their adventure's end:

> Surely you don't disbelieve the prophecies, because you had a hand in bringing them about yourself? You don't really suppose, do you, that all your adventures and escapes were managed by mere luck, just for your sole benefit? You are a very fine person, Mr. Baggins, and I am very fond of you; but you are only quite a little fellow in a wide world after all![2]

Bilbo never imagined he could be useful in something so grand—and neither did Philip or Nathaniel. Yet that's the wonder of it: God sees in us what we can't yet see in ourselves, and calls us with a confidence that makes up for the lack in ours.

When John viewed the sweeping panoramic vision of our future eternity, he beheld every tongue, tribe, and nation gathered around Christ's throne, and—believe it or not—you were in the crowd. Look at you with your cameo! But even more thrilling? Some of those faces will be there because of you—because *you* made disciples.

---

2. J. R. R. Tolkien, *The Hobbit, or There and Back Again* (George Allen & Unwin, 1937; repr., Houghton Mifflin Harcourt, 2012), 305.

Divine Appointments on Desert Roads

Theoretical speculation about disciple-making will never fill the void action was meant to fill. It starts the way it did with Nathaniel: by daring to believe that God can work through us and taking the chance to invite someone to walk alongside you to get to know Jesus. While nobody can tell you how your relationships will start, how your conversations will go, or what the results will be, there are *principles* that lead to *practices* every disciple-maker should cultivate. This chapter will focus on the practices of the practices of the Teaching rhythm as you invite someone to take a closer look at Jesus. And nobody embodies that quite like Philip.

It wasn't the kind of place you'd expect a divine appointment. Just a dusty road, winding south from Jerusalem to Gaza, the kind of sunbaked stretch where travelers kept their heads down and their waterskins safe. You didn't come to this place unless you had to—and then you passed through it as quickly as possible. And yet that's exactly where the angel of the Lord directed Philip to go. Just go out and walk along the trade route in the middle of nowhere. No detailed briefing, no map marked with an X, just a simple instruction to go and a road that stretched into the horizon like a question mark.

Philip had just come from the revival fire in Samaria, where the Holy Spirit ripped through people like a wind, with diseases evaporating, demons fleeing, baptisms rippling like waves. Without complaining, he went to the wilderness trusting the Spirit's changing direction, blowing wherever it willed.

And then, through the shimmering heat of the road ahead, he saw a royal chariot. Inside sat a man of status and significance: a high-ranking Ethiopian official, the royal treasurer returning home from court business in Jerusalem. The scroll of Isaiah in hand, eyes scanning the ancient words, heart straining to understand. He needed teaching. And Philip realized that this was why he was here. This wasn't the Philip who grabbed Nathaniel under the fig tree—they just had the same name—but a similar encounter was about to unfold.

Not one of the original Twelve, Philip believed after the resurrection, starting at or around Pentecost. That made him a second-generation disciple. Like us, he didn't have a front row-seat to the calming of the storm, the multiplying of the loaves, or the other miracles. That's why he is the perfect case study for us. Like us, he was forced to rely on secondhand principles. Principles, unlike trendy methods or fickle fads, can be universally adapted to multiple situations. In Acts 8, Philip was out of his depth, finding himself blazing a trail nobody could map out for him, but he knew the principles (science) of disciple-making that led to the practices (art) we'll unpack in this chapter.

In Acts 8, Philip modeled a crash course in Disciple-Making 101—engaging all three rhythms: Time, Teaching, and Tactics.

- Tactics: He was sent on mission and went.
- Time: He sat alongside someone who was spiritually curious.
- Teaching: He opened the Scriptures and led him straight to Jesus.

PRACTICES FOR TEACHING

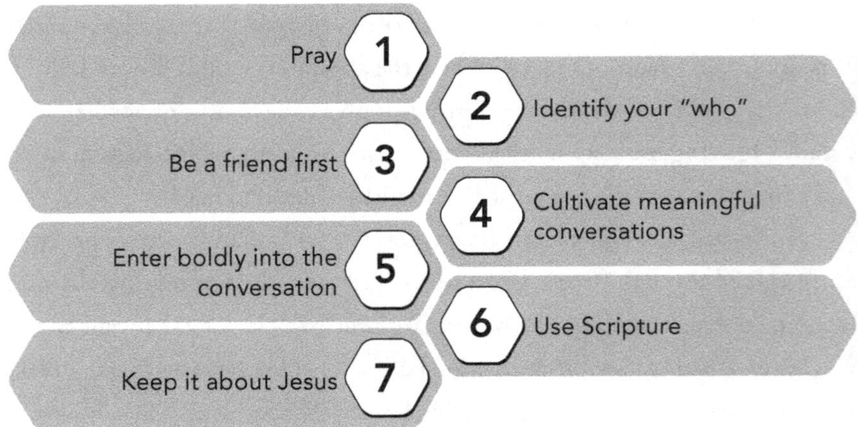

Teaching Practice 1: Pray

> Now an angel of the Lord said to Philip, "Go south to the road—the desert road—that goes down from Jerusalem to Gaza." So he started out . . . (Acts 8:26)

Before Philip made a move, he was in tune with heaven, listening for God's voice. Disciple-making begins in the secret place. Before the conversations, strategy, or practical steps, it begins with prayer. Philip didn't randomly bump into a seeker. God orchestrated the encounter and still operates on the same principle that A. W. Tozer outlines here:

> Twenty minutes on your knees in silence before God will sometimes teach you more than you can learn out of books and teach you more than you can ever learn in churches. And the Lord will give you your plans and lay them before you. If the boards of the churches would only learn to spend more time with God and less time debating, they could save all those midnight meetings where everybody leans back weary from discussing things. I tell you, you can cut down your time in debating and discussing if you spend more time waiting on God. He'll give you the Holy Ghost and He'll give you and teach you his plans.[3]

Make this a regular rhythm of your disciple-making: prayer, then action. Before you reach for a name or send a text, pray. Long before we arrive the Spirit is already at work arranging desert meetings, and whispering to those willing to listen. William Temple once said, "When I pray, coincidences happen. When I don't, they don't."[4] Remember Paul's reminder that "one sows, another waters, yet another reaps" and Jesus's first lesson to the Twelve: "I sent you to reap that for which you did not labor. Others have labored, and you have entered into their labor" (John 4:38 ESV). Only when you are in regular prayer do your eyes open to see "the harvest is plentiful" (Matt. 9:37), and in response God makes you the answer to your own prayer, by making you a worker: "Pray earnestly to the Lord of the harvest to send out laborers into his harvest" (Matt. 9:38 ESV). This was exactly how the Moravian mission movement was born:

> On August 27, 1727 . . . 24 men and 24 women agreed to spend an hour each day in scheduled prayer, covering all 24 hours in the day, seven days a week. The idea soon grew, and the practice of continual prayer went on

---

3. A. W. Tozer, *Total Commitment to Christ: What Is It? A Call to a Radical Faith* (Digital Fire, 2021), "Irrevocable Attachment," Kindle.
4. This quote has been popularly attributed to William Temple, though it is not found in his published works.

> non-stop for more than one hundred years. Out of this prayer meeting, the Moravians felt called to engage in foreign missions. This was the first major Protestant missionary movement not associated with colonization; it even predates what is usually considered the beginning of the modern mission movement with William Carey. Starting from a population of 300 in 1727, within 65 years they had sent 300 missionaries around the world, including to North and South America, Africa, Asia, the Caribbean, and the Arctic. They were the first to evangelize slaves; some even sold themselves into slavery to gain access to slave communities. The Moravians were also the first to send laymen into the mission field rather than just ordained ministers.[5]

Before sending them out, Jesus taught his would-be disciple-makers that everything began with prayer. Without the Moravians, there would be no John Wesley, no William Carey. The missionary movement in the West was birthed out of twenty-four people praying hundreds of years ago who took Jesus's instructions seriously instead of treating it like advice.

Teaching Practice 2: Identify Your "Who"

Together with your "two," your first assignment is to pray for God to identify your "who"—who you are going to teach to follow Jesus—the one whom Jesus is already drawing. And only experience will teach you what prayer sets in motion. When your knees hit the ground, coincidences appear on your life like divine fingerprints. Chariots roll up with scrolls open to Isaiah. As Bilbo the experienced wanderer counseled Frodo, "It's a dangerous business, Frodo, going out of your door. You step into the Road, and if you don't keep your feet, there is no knowing where you might be swept off to."[6]

And you never know who it's going to be. What you can be sure of is that your "who" is disconnected right now from the light source, which is Jesus. John

---

5. Jerry Trousdale and Glenn Sunshine, *The Kingdom Unleashed: How Jesus' 1st-Century Kingdom Values Are Transforming Thousands of Cultures and Awakening His Church* (DMM Library, 2018), chap. 3, Kindle.
6. J. R. R. Tolkien, *The Fellowship of the Ring* (Houghton Mifflin, 1954), 72.

wrote, "In him was life, and that life was the light of all mankind" (John 1:4). Jesus wants to enter their soul and light it up. Whoever you reach out to is made in his image and is wired for conducting that light—it's what their soul was made for. Step into the pursuit with confidence that God has been showing up in their lives, even before you get there. Be assured that the image of God in them may be a flicker, but it's still there. As C. S. Lewis notes, "Next to the Blessed Sacrament itself, your neighbor is the holiest object presented to your senses. . . . It is with the awe and the circumspection proper to them that we should conduct all our dealings with one another. . . . There are no ordinary people."[7]

They Need the Light

Therefore, we must reorient our thinking that our existing relationships and chance encounters are random, and recognize that a sovereign God produces the connections we often take for granted. Your potential "who" is most likely already walking in the light your life reveals. Once you bring them along on the journey with you and your "two," you will merely magnify that light.

Connect the Light from the Source

7. C. S. Lewis, *The Weight of Glory and Other Addresses* (HarperOne, 2001), 45–46.

Once you know your "who," the next prayers are for *when* and *how*.

- When will you step out?
- How will you begin the conversation?

We'll discuss how to approach these questions below, but the Discipology journal *Journey to Disciple-Making* is one option designed to help you and your two track each step of this journey: your prayers, people, and progress in making disciples. Like the Gospels that record the apostles' clumsy first steps, the journal is your own disciple-making chronicle; a record of how Jesus called another ordinary person, like you, to do extraordinary things.

Teaching Practice 3: Be a Friend First

> The Spirit told Philip, "Go to that chariot and stay near it." Then Philip ran up to the chariot. (Acts 8:29–30)

Philip didn't shout at the chariot from a distance or lob a gospel tract across the dunes. He climbed into the chariot and sat alongside the Ethiopian. Philip learned from the Spirit that disciple-making begins with *presence*—simply *being* with them. "The Spirit told Philip . . . stay near." The Spirit is telling us that as much as people need teaching, they need a companion—someone walking beside them, even if they're unsure where the road leads.

That's the good news about sharing the good news: You don't have to start by blundering into awkward spiritual conversations. Ralph Moore says if you can make a friend, you can make a disciple. When Jesus first asked the disciples what they were seeking, they didn't ask a spiritual question. "Rabbi, where are you staying?" Jesus simply said, "Come and see" (John 1:38). He shared a meal, slowed the pace, and let the relationship grow *before* revealing the mysteries of the kingdom. He didn't rush to a sales pitch.

People weren't projects to Jesus. His heart broke for people: "When he saw the crowds, he had compassion on them, because they were harassed and helpless, like sheep without a shepherd" (Matt. 9:36). He asked his future field workers to see the field as he did: "Open your eyes. The harvest is ripe." It's a dangerous prayer to ask God to show you what he sees, because you risk a broken heart. But if you open your eyes, you'll see

- friends who seem spiritually hungry,
- coworkers with questions,
- neighbors who are suffering, and
- seekers who have started praying.

Unlike mentorship, disciple-making refuses to compartmentalize: *Here's my spiritual time, and here's my social time.* Mentorship has a toggle switch between "religious talk" and "casual hangout." Ralph Moore says that "mentorship is a human shortcut when substituted for disciple-making. It is not nearly as personal or as effective as disciple-making."[8] But discipleship is where the rhythms of Time and Teaching *overlap*—life and faith seamlessly intertwined. For Jesus it was all one blended sacred and social rhythm: holy and human. Let your life speak the gospel whether you're breaking bread, swapping stories, watching the game, or opening Scripture.

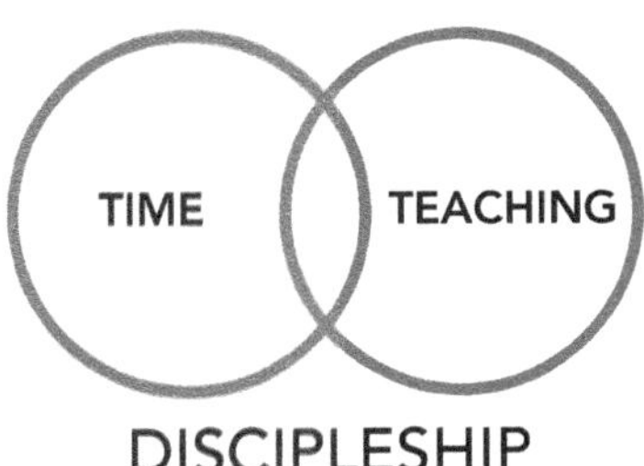

Friendship involves becoming a regular part of their lives—doing stuff together. Philip and the Ethiopian shared a ride across the middle of nowhere. Jesus discipled while walking roads, eating meals, paying taxes, crashing parties, and catching fish—especially eating meals. Ralph Moore made disciples in the garage rebuilding cars. I nerd out over hobbies with my disciples.

8. Ralph Moore, *Making Disciples: Developing Lifelong Followers of Jesus* (Baker Books, 2012), 44.

Most often, you just need to grab a bite with someone. In *A Meal with Jesus*, Tim Chester explores Jesus's strategy of mealtimes as mission in Luke's gospel:

- Luke 5: Jesus ate with tax collectors and sinners.
- Luke 7: He was anointed while dining at a Pharisee's home.
- Luke 9: He fed the five thousand.
- Luke 10: He visited the home of Mary and Martha.
- Luke 11: Another meal with Pharisees—and a strong rebuke.
- Luke 14: He taught about inviting the poor to our tables.
- Luke 19: He invited himself to Zacchaeus's house.
- Luke 22: He shared his final meal with the Twelve.
- Luke 24: He broke bread with two men from Emmaus and later with his disciples.

It's fair to say that Jesus ate his way through kingdom expansion. Now, I know what you're thinking: *When am I going to find time for this?* How many meals do you eat in a day? Two? Three? That's anywhere from fourteen to twenty-one scheduled meals to choose from. Now, what if just *one* of those a week were set aside to invite someone else? This sociological aspect of human nature sets the stage for great conversations.

And it's not always dinner—some folks aren't free in the evenings so you have to adjust your schedule. When I make disciples, I work around other people's schedules—sometimes meeting at 6:00 a.m. before their commute, or I turn up at their lunch break when invited. Remember, the best discipleship rhythm is the one you can *keep*. As in fitness, consistency beats intensity every time. So like Philip, find your own "vehicle" to journey alongside someone: sharing meals, attending social activities, joining clubs, or whatever else you're currently doing. Let the Holy Spirit open the doors. And when you're stuck—simply share a meal. That's what friends do.

Teaching Practice 4: Cultivate Meaningful Conversations

Do you understand what you're reading? (Acts 8:30)

Jogging alongside the royal chariot, Philip heard the Ethiopian official reading Isaiah aloud, but Philip didn't jump in with expository explanation. He asked good questions: "Do you understand what you're reading?" (Acts 8:30). Disciple-making isn't about talking *at* someone but talking *with* them.

It was a subtle invitation to talk about it: "Do you get it?"

The official's answer is telling: "How can I, unless someone explains it to me?" Most people, like the Ethiopian, are aching for deeper conversations—but they don't know who they can trust. Every day they swim in surface talk, endless scrolling, aching for someone to have meaningful conversations with. Philip artfully cast the question like a seasoned fly fisherman, gently teasing above the surface, and the Ethiopian took the bait, opening up wide.

Disciple-making is dependent upon good conversation, not having all the right words but being able to listen to the soul behind the sentences. Drew Hyun once told me that "I took two years of seminary courses on how to talk. I took nothing on how to listen." Admittedly, telling people how to talk to others is like telling someone how to dance. "Just move your body. Feel the music." Right. Super helpful when you're already paralyzed with awkwardness. Spending time with people, especially when you're not used to it, is like standing awkwardly at a high school dance. So for all the introverted disciple-makers out there—yes, I see you—here are few techniques to break the ice, get you off the wall, and find your rhythm.

First, it's not an accident that Jesus included dinner-table instructions when he sent his disciples. In Luke 10:8, Jesus said, "Eat what is put before you" (which Paul also quoted in 1 Corinthians 10:27—showing us again that he was always paying attention to Jesus's strategy). Jesus himself was a master conversationalist. That's why John's gospel is filled with conversations—because conversations equal conversions. Introverts don't have to be the life of the party; they just need to listen well—one of the hardest skills to master and the rarest skills in our society. When I say *listen*, let me be clear—it's listening to what interests *them*, not listening to ourselves going on about what we want to talk about. If you're an introvert, you've got this down. Introverts are generally better at asking good questions than extroverts—potentially making them more effective conversational disciple-makers.

Here's a crash course in the art of conversational disciple-making. Once you can listen, these are some additional microskills you'll need:

- Be curious. Let your care for the person drive your interest in the conversation.
- Ask them about themselves. Eventually, they'll go deep.
- Celebrate common ground, but welcome differing views. Resist the urge to correct anything and everything you don't agree with. Pick your battles.
- Summarize and mirror what they say to show you're really listening.
- Be present. Make eye contact. Remember details.

Finally, the most important tip regarding dancing is to *relax*—go with the flow. When I hang out with people over a pint or a coffee or while running errands, conversation unfolds naturally. Sometimes it's like an episode of *Friends*—everything's on the table. Other times, it's pure *Seinfeld*—a whole lot of talk about nothing. One minute we're swapping small talk, and the next, someone's pouring out their heart over a breakup, an addiction, or a childhood wound. That's when I tune in—not just to them, but to the Holy Spirit—waiting for that still, small voice (1 Kings 19:11–12 KJV), because that's when I need to enter boldly into the conversation.

Teaching Practice 5: Enter Boldly into the Conversation

> The eunuch asked Philip, "Tell me, please, who is the prophet talking about, himself or someone else?" Then Philip began with that very passage of Scripture and told him the good news about Jesus. (Acts 8:34–35)

When Philip saw the opportunity yawn open before him, he launched like Evel Knievel over Snake River Canyon. First, he waited for the Spirit to crack the door, then boldly stepped through and opened his mouth. If the linemen clear the lane, you run the ball. These moments are easy to miss if you're not paying attention—but Philip had long practiced proximity to God before practicing proximity to people. He recognized the Spirit's nudge when it came and didn't flinch. He embodied what Paul urged Timothy: "Be ready in season and out of season" (2 Tim. 4:2). Peter echoed it too: "Always be ready to give an answer to anyone who asks you for the reason for the hope within you" (1 Peter 3:15). You only write that when you know what it's like not to be ready—like Peter, afraid to testify in the courtyard, or too intimidated to stand up to the circumcision group.

If you ever get nervous talking about Jesus, you're not alone. Even the apostle Paul asked for prayer—*repeatedly*—for boldness: "Pray also for me, that whenever I speak, words may be given me so that I will fearlessly make known the mystery of the gospel" (Eph. 6:19). Paul may not have been the brash, confident preacher we have imagined. In fact, he might've been more reserved than we think.

The man who once breathed threats returned from Arabia trembling with a whisper rather than a roar. Paul, the once-proud Pharisee, repeatedly admitted fear, weakness, and total dependence on the Spirit. "I came to you with weakness, fear, and trembling; not with eloquent words lest the cross be emptied of its power" (1 Cor. 1:17). Because Paul felt the same pressure to stay quiet and play it safe, he asked for prayer that he wouldn't shrink back:

In Ephesians 6:19–20, he asked, "Pray also for me . . . that I may declare it fearlessly, as I should."

In Colossians 4:3–4, he pleaded, "Pray for us, too, that God may open a door for our message. . . . Pray that I may proclaim it clearly, as I should."

In 2 Thessalonians 3:1–2, he said, "Pray for us that the message of the Lord may spread rapidly and be honored. . . . And pray that we may be delivered from wicked and evil people."

In Romans 15:30–31, he wrote, "Join me in my struggle by praying to God for me . . . that I may be kept safe from the unbelievers in Judea and that the contribution I take to Jerusalem may be favorably received."

And it wasn't just Paul. Even the Twelve were daunted at times and gathered to pray for boldness, such as in Acts 4:29–31:

"Now, Lord, consider their threats and enable your servants to speak your word with great boldness. Stretch out your hand to heal and perform signs and wonders through the name of your holy servant Jesus."

After they prayed, the place where they were meeting was shaken. And they were all filled with the Holy Spirit and spoke the word of God boldly.

None of our heroes were above admitting their need of grace to overcome their fears. Don't form your fears, but take your prayers for boldness to the throne of grace. For when we are weak, he is strong.

Teaching Practice 6: Use Scripture

This is the passage of Scripture the eunuch was reading:

"He was led like a sheep to the slaughter,
    and as a lamb before its shearer is silent,
    so he did not open his mouth.
In his humiliation he was deprived of justice.
    Who can speak of his descendants?
    For his life was taken from the earth."

The eunuch asked Philip, "Tell me, please, who is the prophet talking about, himself or someone else?" Then *Philip began with that very passage of Scripture* and told him the good news about Jesus. (Acts 8:32–35, emphasis mine)

There's a reason Philip started with Scripture, because when you're helping someone discover Jesus, "the word of God is living and active, sharper than any two-edged sword, piercing to the division of soul and of spirit, of joints and of marrow, and discerning the thoughts and intentions of the heart" (Heb. 4:12). Last time I checked, I lacked the power to do any of that. But God himself declared, "My word will not return to me void, but will accomplish what I desire and achieve the purpose for which I sent it" (Isa. 55:11). The Word never misses or fails to hit its mark—even when it seems like nothing is happening—God is planting seeds, working supernaturally. Walking alongside someone through Scripture is one of the most powerful things a disciple-maker does. Our use of Scripture allows God to speak for himself.

How do we repeat Philip's experience without supernatural teleportation, royal chariots or scrolls of Isaiah? Simple—reach into your pocket. That rectangular distraction machine we call a phone might just be the most powerful disciple-making tool you own. And why not? Jesus always used whatever was already in the field—loaves, fish, fig trees, even a borrowed donkey. If he were sending you out today, he might paraphrase his commands to the Twelve, "Don't pack anything extra—just take your phone."

That's because the entire Bible is one click away. And most people aren't as closed off to Scripture as Christians presume. In fact, more than 85 percent say they want to understand the Bible better—but the two obstacles are these:

1. They don't have a lot of time.
2. When they try to read the Bible, they can't understand it.

They don't need a sermon, just someone who will come alongside them and explain Scripture to them.

That's where the Discipology plan on the Through the Word app comes in. The Discipology digital plan mirrors Philip's encounter in Acts 8, allowing you to walk alongside someone as they go through the gospel of John. Here's how it works; you and your two invite your who into the Discipology plan. Depending on the desired pace, you can move through John's gospel together a chapter a day (completing in just over three weeks), or a chapter a week (completing within six months). Within the app, you can leave audio or text feedback, keeping a discussion going, just like Philip and the Ethiopian. It's like riding along in a chariot, only now you're both holding phones instead of scrolls. You can explore the Discipology plan—relational, practical, and free—by visiting Discipology.com or scanning the QR code.

Teaching Practice 7: Keep It About Jesus

... and told him the good news about Jesus. (Acts 8:35)

Philip introduced the eunuch to a person. Disciple-making resists the temptation to sidestep too far into politics, philosophy, or theological debates. No matter what the eunuch's distractions, questions, or red herrings, Philip kept telling him about Jesus—just like Jesus kept the Samaritan woman focused on him. Seasoned disciple-makers can talk about anything—Bigfoot, aliens, even conspiracy theories—but they've learned the art of snapping back to Jesus, like a bungee cord pulling them to center. Every good faith conversation should circle back to him. In the seventies, hippies scrawled "Jesus Is the Answer" across public spaces. On one desert boulder, someone replied, "What's the question?" The truth is it doesn't matter. Jesus is the answer to the soul's deepest questions—even the ones we don't know how to ask.

When we introduce people to Jesus, we are not being slick high-pressure salesmen; disciple-making simply introduces them to a person, as Philip did with Nathaniel. Ray Simpson is helpful here: "Proselytism is about converting A to B, and it requires pressure. Evangelism is about bearing witness to Jesus and letting the Holy Spirit lead A."[9]

When we talk with people about God, we should listen for the barriers to following him. Jesus zeroed in on the rich young ruler's hidden obstacles—self-righteousness, idolatry, and greed—things the man couldn't name until Jesus exposed them. Today, people often mask their barriers behind smoke screens, but they're not the barriers.

Smoke screens are things like Bigfoot, aliens, conspiracy theories.

Barriers are things like selfishness, shame, and pride.

The smoke screens often pop up right as the Spirit is penetrating deeply. Objections aren't walls, they're windows—signs that truth is breaking

---

9. Ray Simpson and Brent Lyons-Lee, *St Aidan's Way of Mission: Celtic Insights for a Post-Christian World* (Bible Reading Fellowship, 2016), chap. 1, Kindle.

through. What sounds like resistance is often a flare fired from a sinking soul, trying to hold off the gospel as the waters are closing in.

The woman at the well pushed back like a seasoned skeptic—but only because Jesus pushed first, with truth that struck home. Throw a rock into a pack of dogs, and the dog that yelps is the one that got hit. Jesus didn't flinch. He listened, guiding the conversation gently back to himself:

Objection 1: "You're a Jew, I'm a Samaritan."
Response 1: "If you knew who was asking you for a drink, you'd ask him—and he'd give you living water."
Objection 2: "You have no bucket. Where can you get this water?"
Response 2: "Whoever drinks the water I give will never thirst again."
Objection 3: "Our ancestors worshiped on this mountain, but you Jews say Jerusalem is the place."
Response 3: "A time is coming when true worshipers will worship the Father in spirit and truth."

Jesus didn't crush her arguments—he disarmed them. Debates are like checkers—you jump your opponent, rack up points, and count who wins. But Jesus was playing chess, thinking moves ahead, not to win an argument but to win her heart.

His strategy? Listening well, answering wisely, and always circling back to the main thing: himself.

If objections throw you off, here are a few truths to anchor you:

- **God was working long before you showed up.** The Spirit had already begun the conversation; you're just joining it.
- **Objections mean you're getting close.** They're not pushing you away; they're testing to see if you'll stay.
- **You don't have to know everything.** It's okay to say "I don't know" or "Let me look that up." Jesus didn't answer every question directly either.

- **Stay kind. Stay calm. Stay human.** Don't turn it into a debate. Turn it into a dialogue. Remember, it's not about winning the argument; it's about winning a soul.
- **Keep bringing it back to Jesus.** No matter where the conversation goes, steer it to him. He is the answer they're really looking for—even if they don't know it yet.

Don't Procrastinate

Don't let this be just another book you read and forget on the shelf like that gym membership from 2020. Disciple-making isn't a theory—it's a call to action. Don't admire it. Don't debate it. *Do it.*

Once you know the gospel, there's really no wrong way to share it except not to. Still, people will always tell us we're doing it wrong because we do it differently than they do (or more commonly, don't). As Dwight Moody once said when someone criticized his approach to preaching the gospel: "It's clear you don't like my way of doing evangelism. You raise some good points. Frankly, I sometimes do not like my way of doing evangelism. But I like my way of doing it better than your way of *not* doing it."[10]

Fear stops more disciple-makers than failure ever could. We freeze—not because we're weak but because we hesitate. Why?

- Fear of the unknown
- Fear of inadequacy
- Fear of rejection

Legit fears—but 95 percent of what we fear never happens, and 85 percent of statistics are made up anyway. God is willing to walk you through whatever fears are holding you back. So let's address the three common fears that hold people back.

---

10. Dave Earley and David Wheeler, Evangelism Is . . . : How to Share Jesus with Passion and Confidence (B&H, 2010), 16.

- **Fear of the unknown?** *Just show up.* God never asked you to approve any plans—just to take the next step. You walk by faith, not by forecast. Would Bilbo have gone if he knew what awaited him at the start? Probably not. But would he have traded it after the journey ended? Not for the world.
- **Fear of inadequacy?** *You don't feel adequate? Good.* You're in whatever club Abraham, Moses, Gideon, David, Hezekiah, Isaiah, Jeremiah, Peter, and Paul were in. God doesn't call the qualified; he qualifies the called.
- **Fear of rejection?** *Expect it.* Jesus said that if they rejected him, they'd reject us too. I wish I could tell you that doesn't happen—but I can tell you that it's not you. The best disciple-makers and evangelists on the planet get rejected—because they're rejecting Jesus through you. Don't ever take it personally.

Procrastination is hell's favorite tactic. If Satan can't derail you, he'll just *delay* you. That's why Paul called fear a flaming dart: "Take up the shield of faith, with which you can extinguish all the flaming arrows of the evil one" (Eph. 6:16). The ancient archers kept the opposing armies at bay, their opponents too afraid to come within range of their arrows. Fear doesn't have to defeat you; it just has to stop you. God gave us the shield of faith so that we can advance without flinching. So decide. Raise your shield and simply take the next step . . . and the next . . . Just don't procrastinate.

My tendency to procrastinate nearly cost a young man his eternity. Let me explain. When I first started making disciples, I was a youth pastor—and my youth group was a train wreck. These kids had grown up in church and didn't want to be there. When I preached, they'd slump in their chairs like deflating balloons, mouths hanging open, eyes glazed over like zombies in a sermon-induced coma. Turns out, they were literally trying to drool on themselves as a game to pass the time and throw me off. Classic youth.

One Saturday morning, I was enjoying some downtime—cartoons on, coffee in hand—when I felt an unusual tug in my spirit: "Go to Nick's house." At first I brushed it off. I mean, the cartoon was good. But the tug became a shove. "*Go to Nick's. Now.*" It was clear. Urgent. And weird.

So I went.

Nick's dad answered the door. "Glad you're here," he said. "Gives me an excuse to drag his lazy butt out of bed." It was 10:30 a.m. He led me to Nick's room, where Nick was fully cocooned under his comforter. "Hey, Sleeping Beauty," his dad said. "Someone's here to see you."

Nick peeked out, squinting, and mumbled, "Hmm?"

"Yeah," I said. "This is gonna sound weird, but I felt like God told me to come here this morning. You okay?"

He sat up, wrapped in his large duvet like a giant gray caterpillar, still half asleep. "Mind if I sit?" I asked. He shrugged.

"I was wondering if I could read the Bible with you?"

Another shrug.

I cracked open 1 John 1:1—the same passage someone had used to disciple me back in the day. It wasn't the most polished method, but it had worked with me, and I'd seen it work with others.

So I cracked open 1 John 1:1. We read it together. I told him how Jesus wanted to be closer to him than he'd ever imagined, that he wanted a real friendship, the kind John described when he called himself *the disciple Jesus loved*—not because he was the favorite but because he actually believed it.

That's when I noticed it—a single tear running down Nick's cheek.

That was the moment. After fifteen years of sitting in church, one Spirit-led conversation cracked his heart wide open. All those years and nothing had broken through until one simple, awkward, Spirit-prompted moment of disciple-making interrupting my cartoons and his sleeping in.

Nick wasn't the same after that. He became a Jesus follower, a worship leader, a bold witness at school, and eventually a disciple-maker himself. Many of his classmates came to faith through his influence. What I didn't know that morning was just how critical the timing had been. The night before, his friends had scored drugs and planned to use them for the first time. The Holy Spirit had sent one cartoon-watching youth pastor to derail that plan—and it changed everything. That Saturday morning may have started with cartoons, but it ended with eternity breaking in.

Nick's story didn't end there. He led others to Christ, discipled his classmates, and eventually married a girl who had once admired his walk with Jesus from afar as an unbeliever. She followed Jesus too—because of him. Nick has since gone home to be with the Lord. But not before taking many others there with him. *It's never a good time to start . . . for us. But it's always a good time to start for others.* So when should you start? *Now.*

As Jesus said, "Open your eyes and look at the fields! They are ripe for harvest" (John 4:35).

Pray for workers. But don't be shocked when God's answer to that prayer is you.

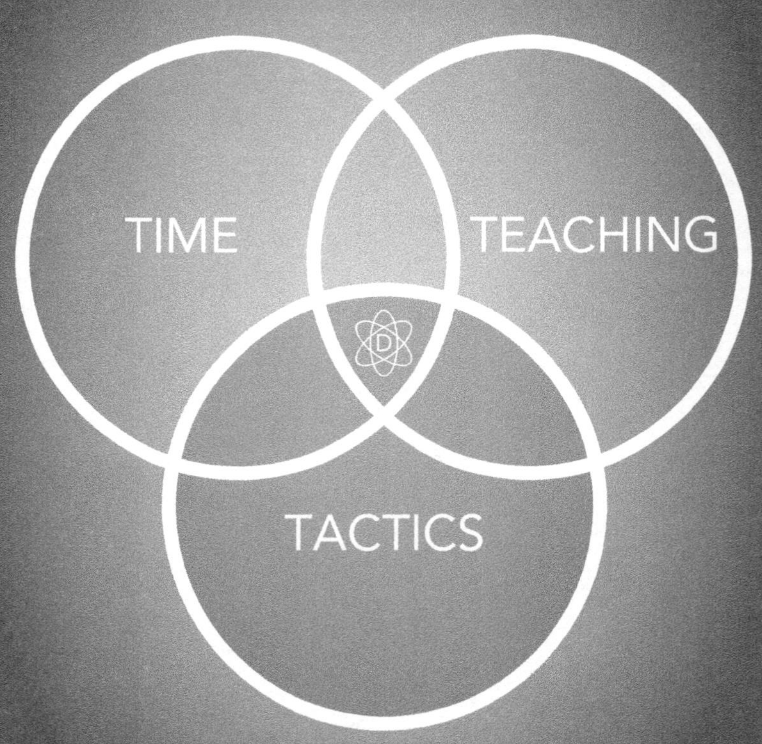
TIME
TEACHING
TACTICS
D

PART IV

TACTICS—WHERE DISCIPLES ARE SENT

Time and Teaching prepared the disciples, but to enter the Tactics rhythm, they had to be sent. Jesus pushed his followers out of the nest, turning knowledge into action, and action into impact. Jesus handed off his mission to imperfect people, trusting them to carry his kingdom forward. The work of disciple-making isn't complete until that last cog on the Discipology flywheel is spinning, and they're sent to make more.

CHAPTER 9

Patterns of Tactics

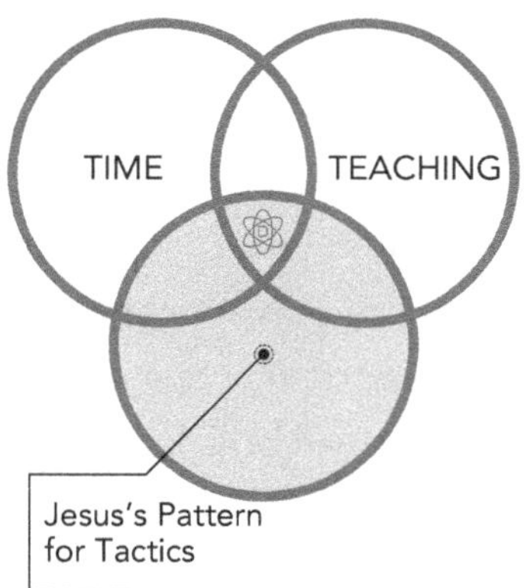

The dust of Galilean villages they'd just walked through still swirled in the air behind them, kicked up from the crowds who followed—crowds desperate for hope. And suddenly, Jesus seemed to be saying, "You've seen what I do—now it's your turn."

The disciples stood there wide-eyed and dumbstruck. Twelve teens staring at Jesus with the same stunned expression. Up until now, they'd shadowed him, watched miracles unfold, listened to teaching that made their heads spin, but this was different. Now *they* were the ones being sent. And if they'd heard Jesus correctly, not just to preach but to heal the sick and cast out demons.

Maybe Peter's jaw tightened as he scanned the horizon, wondering what kind of demons he'd face. Perhaps John stole a glance at his brother James, reading the same hesitation he felt in his own chest. Matthew, still getting used to being on *this* side of the kingdom, may have wondered what credible message could possibly come from the lips of a former tax collector.

And yet . . . none of them turned back.

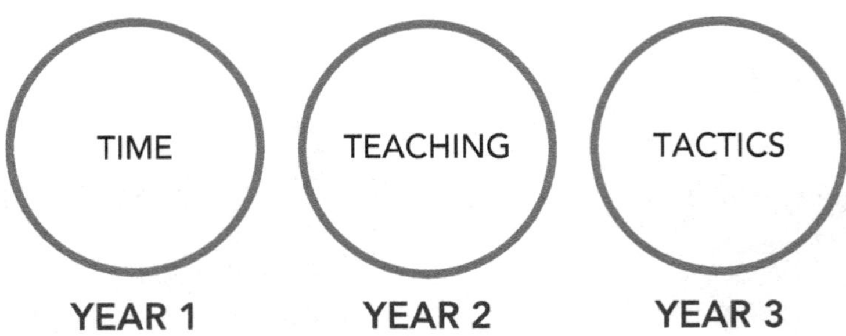

The Tactical Shift

As the third year dawned, Jesus flipped the tactical switch, handing off his mission to trembling hands. Like David of old, Jesus was a master strategist and tactician on the field, mobilizing his troops to advance the kingdom. Jesus dividing the twelve apostles into teams of two resembled Moses sending the twelve spies in pairs into the promised land. It was as if Jesus were strategizing his kingdom to retake the same ground.

However, as with Mordor, one does not simply walk into the Tactics rhythm—so Jesus drop-kicked the Twelve into it. Basic training was over. It was time to walk head-on into live fire. If experience is truly the best teacher, then we learn best by doing. Still, nobody ever feels ready.

MOBILIZATION

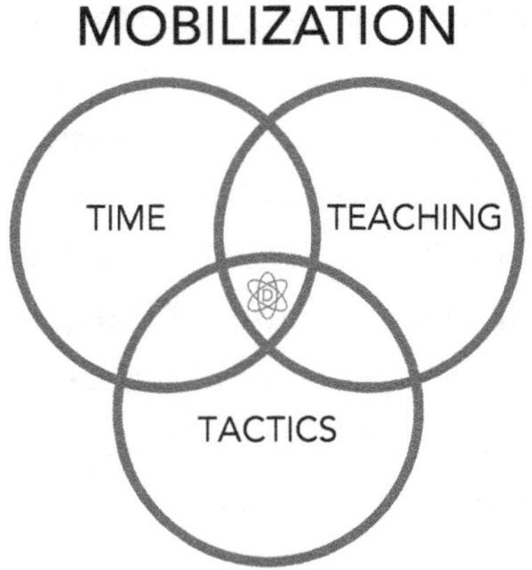

Jesus launched two missions that bookended the third year—one at the start of year 3 (sending the Twelve), and another at the end (sending the seventy-two). These two short-term missions were "preparatory" exercises, "a paradigm of permanent mission in the future," prototypes of the Great Commission.[1] He sent the Twelve throughout Galilee at the dawn of the year. At the year's dusk, he sent the seventy-two across Galilee, Judea, and Samaria, widening the boundaries of their targeted field. Only when they returned did Jesus shift gears, setting his face toward Jerusalem and his own death on the cross. Their training was complete. They were ready for his departure.

The sending of the Twelve—the first mission journey—was the first time the disciples got their hands dirty. In year 2, they'd simply been observing, but now in year 3, they were *doing*. Every single miracle the disciples had a personal hand in happened during the Tactics rhythm of the third year. They'd never preached before. Never done anything up to that point that they'd watched Jesus do the year before.

This brings us full circle—the chronological narrative revealing the following pattern:

Year 1–Time

Year 2–Teaching / Training

Year 3–Tactics

Once you see it, you can't unsee it.

But the third year has its own interesting pattern:

1. The first three to four months: Jesus sends out the Twelve (mission journey one)
2. The middle four to six months: Jesus continues to develop them through hands-on ministry
3. The final three to four months: Jesus sends out the seventy-two (mission journey two)

Josephus records the existence of 138 towns in Galilee alone at that time,

---

1. Eckhard Schnabel, *Early Christian Mission Vol. 1: Jesus and the Twelve* (IVP Academic, 2004), 293.

so each trip would have taken three to four months, leaving four to six months with Jesus between those two trips.[2] But what's most striking is what happened in the four to six months *between the two missions.* These are the tactics they engaged in during the intervening months between the two trips:

- The Twelve returned (Matt. 10:1–15; Mark 6:7–13; Luke 9:1–6).
- The Twelve fed five thousand (Matt. 14:13–21; Mark 6:30–44; Luke 9:10–17; John 6:1–14).
- Peter walked on water to come to Jesus (Matt. 14:22–33).
- The Twelve fed four thousand (Matt. 15:32–39; Mark 8:1–10).
- Peter, John, and James encountered Moses and Elijah and witnessed Jesus's transfiguration (Matt. 17:1–13; Mark 9:2–13; Luke 9:28–36; Matt. 17:24–27).
- The disciples were unable to cast a demon out of a boy (Matt. 17:14–21; Mark 9:14–29; Luke 9:37–43).
- The disciples asked whether they could call down fire from heaven on the Samaritans (Luke 9:51–56).

After the return of the seventy-two, there are further supernatural incidents where Jesus "sends them."

- The disciples miraculously find the donkey and her colt tied up for the triumphal entry (Matt. 21:1–7; Mark 11:1–7; Luke 19:29–35).
- The disciples miraculously find the upper room and reserve it (Matt. 26:17–19; Mark 11:1–7; Luke 22:7–13).

Because these incidents were intended to stretch and develop the disciples' faith, the events themselves weren't always the successes they look like on paper. Peter walked on water—briefly—before sinking. The disciples fed thousands with a handful of loaves, twice, yet still "had not understood about the loaves" (Mark 6:52). Nine disciples tried—and failed—to cast out a demon.

---

2. Eckhard J. Schnabel, *Early Christian Mission Vol. 1: Jesus and the Twelve* (IVP Academic, 2004), 308.

The Gospel writers repeatedly show the disciples stumbling forward, whether misreading the miracles, misunderstanding the mission, or misjudging Jesus himself. Despite our fear of failure, there is something so Christian about the sanctification of failing forward. And Jesus seemed to welcome it in the development of his disciples. John Maxwell says, "The difference between average people and achieving people is their perception of and response to failure."[3] Yet through every success or stumbling, it was all leading up to what Jesus was planning for them: "Very truly I tell you, whoever believes in me will do the works I have been doing—and they will do even greater things than these, because I am going to the Father." Had they never risked failure, the disciples wouldn't have missed doing *greater things*. In reality, they would have missed doing *anything*. In our Discipology training, one of our mantras is "The only true failure is the one who never tried." C. S. Lewis echoes, "Failures are finger posts on the road to achievement."[4]

Summary of the Third Year

For context, it's helpful to get the big picture of the third year. For reference, the following list cites everything that happened in year 3 leading up to the triumphal entry:

CHRONOLOGY OF JESUS'S THIRD YEAR

Jesus asks the disciples to pray for more workers *(Matthew 9:37–38, Luke 10:2)* Jesus calls the disciples to pray for more laborers to be sent into God's harvest.

Jesus sends out the twelve apostles *(Matthew 10:1–42, Mark 6:6–13, Luke 9:1–6)* Jesus commissions the Twelve with authority to heal and proclaim the kingdom.

3. John C. Maxwell, *Failing Forward: Turning Mistakes into Stepping Stones for Success* (Thomas Nelson, 2000), 16.
4. Arthur H. Bell and Dayle M. Smith, *Winning with Trust in Business* (Thomson South-Western, 2007), 102.

3

Jesus speaks about John the Baptist after his death *(Matthew 14:1–12, Mark 6:14–29, Luke 9:7–9)* Jesus reflects on John's role as a prophet and affirms his significance.

4

Jesus has the disciples feed the 5,000 *(Matthew 14:13–21, Mark 6:30–44, Luke 9:10–17, John 6:1–15)* Jesus multiplies loaves and fish to feed a massive crowd near Bethsaida.

5

Jesus and Peter walk on water *(Matthew 14:22–33, Mark 6:45–52, John 6:16–21)* Jesus walks across the Sea of Galilee; Peter briefly joins him before **sinking in doubt.**

6

Jesus heals the sick in Gennesaret *(Mark 6:53–56)* Wherever Jesus goes, people bring the sick to him, and he heals them all.

7

Jesus heals the Syrophoenician woman's daughter *(Matthew 15:21–28, Mark 7:24–30)* Jesus commends the faith of a Gentile woman near Tyre and heals her daughter.

8

Jesus heals a deaf and mute man *(Mark 7:31–37)* Jesus travels to the Decapolis and opens a man's ears and loosens his tongue with a word and a touch.

9

The disciples feed the 4,000 *(Matthew 15:32–39, Mark 8:1–10, Matthew 16:5–12, Mark 8:14–21)* Jesus again multiplies food, teaching the disciples about God's provision. This time, it's near the Decapolis.

10

Jesus heals a blind man at Bethsaida *(Mark 8:22–26)* Jesus restores sight through a two-stage healing, leading the man to clarity.

11

Peter declares Jesus as the Messiah *(Matthew 16:13–20, Mark 8:27–30, Luke 9:18–27)* Peter boldly confesses that Jesus is the Christ, near Caesarea-Philippi.

12

The Transfiguration *(Matthew 17:1–13, Mark 9:2–13, Luke 9:28–36)* Jesus is revealed in dazzling glory alongside Moses and Elijah, possibly at Mount Hermon.

13

Jesus heals a demon-possessed boy that the disciples could not help *(Matthew 17:14–21, Mark 9:14–29, Luke 9:37–43)* Jesus rebukes an unclean spirit and teaches the disciples about faith.

14

The disciples travel with Jesus to Jerusalem *(John 7:2–10)* Jesus journeys quietly to the festival amid rising opposition.

15

John and James ask to call down fire on the Samaritans *(Mark 3:17, Luke 9:57–56)* Jesus rebukes the disciples' desire for judgment after rejection in Samaria.

16

Jesus sends the 72 *(Luke 9:51–62, Luke 10:1–24)* Jesus resolutely heads toward Jerusalem and sends messengers to prepare the way.

17

Jesus visits Martha and Mary *(Luke 10:38–42)* Jesus teaches Martha and Mary the importance of listening over busyness in Bethany.

18

Jesus heals a woman on the Sabbath *(Luke 13:10–17)* Jesus sets a woman free from eighteen years of disability, challenging Sabbath legalism.

19

Jesus dines at a Pharisee's house *(Luke 14:1–24)* Jesus heals a man at the meal and tells parables about humility and God's banquet.

20

Jesus raises Lazarus from the dead *(John 11:1–44)* Jesus calls Lazarus out of the tomb near Bethany, revealing his power over death.

21

Jesus heals ten lepers *(Luke 17:11–19)* Ten are cleansed, but only one returns to thank Jesus for healing. This happens near the border of Galilee and Samaria.

22

Jesus welcomes the children *(Matthew 19:13–15, Mark 10:13–16, Luke 18:15–17)* Jesus blesses children, affirming their place in God's kingdom.

23

Jesus heals blind Bartimaeus *(Matthew 20:29–34, Mark 10:46–52, Luke 18:35–43)* Jesus restores Bartimaeus's sight in Jericho, in response to his persistent faith.

24

Jesus calls Zacchaeus down from the tree and eats with him *(Luke 19:1–10)* Jesus invites himself into Zacchaeus's home in Jericho, declaring that salvation has come.

Jesus enters Jerusalem triumphantly *(Matthew 21:1–11, Mark 11:1–11, Luke 19:28–44, John 12:12–19)* Jesus rides into Jerusalem as crowds proclaim him king with palm branches.

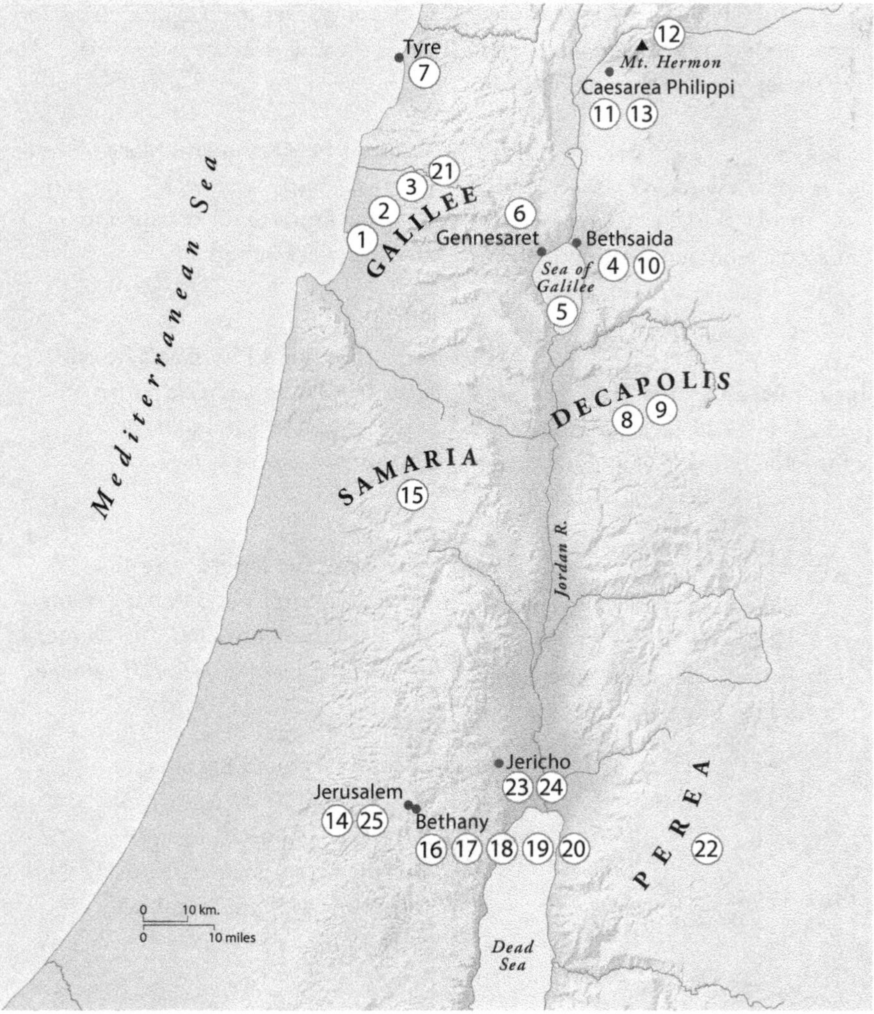

Although Jesus did much during his third year, including the pivotal events of Holy Week, this chapter will focus on Jesus's tactical patterns. From these, we can gather the principles and practices that will guide our own disciple-making in the next few chapters. In this chapter, we'll zoom in on how the disciples were activated by Jesus when they:

- Participated on mission
- Participated in performing tasks
- Participated in supernatural ministry
- Participated in a transformative event

By examining these key activation milestones during that third year, we'll draw out the patterns for disciple-making that Jesus modeled to activate his disciples in the Tactics rhythm.

PATTERNS OF TACTICS

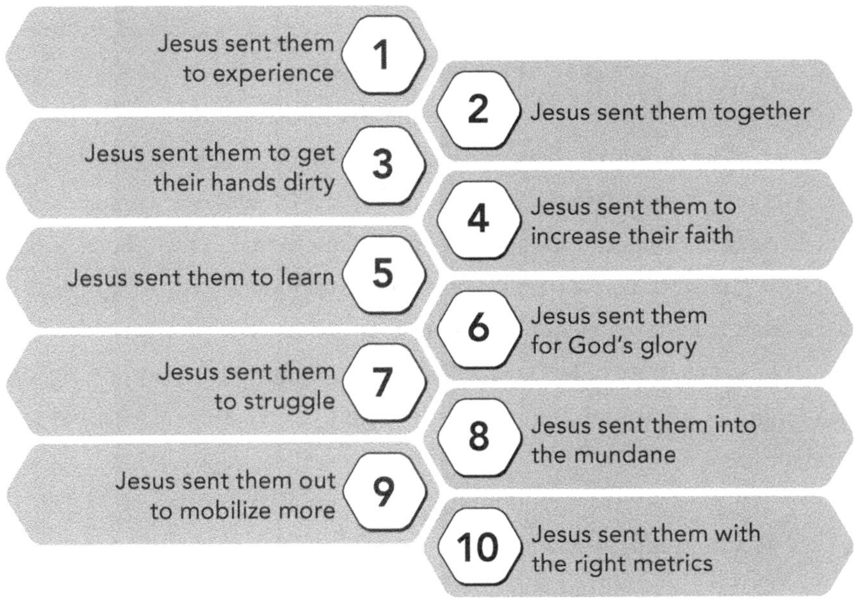

Tactics Pattern 1: Jesus Sent Them to Experience

Jesus Sends Out the Twelve (Matt. 10:1–42; Mark 6:6–13; Luke 9:1–6)

> Jesus called his twelve disciples to him and gave them authority to drive out impure spirits and to heal every disease and sickness. (Matt. 10:1)

Jesus sending the Twelve teaches us that disciple-maker training isn't complete until our disciples are deployed themselves. All parents know that your babies can't lead if they never leave. And God ordained that "a man will *leave* his mother and father and be united to his wife" (Matt. 19:5, emphasis mine). A refusal to *go out* is the refusal to grow up—the insistence to remain a child.

Jesus sent them for two reasons: (1) the need of the disciples to be developed and (2) the need of the masses outweighed Jesus's capacity to fill it. Right before sending his disciples, Jesus eyed the heaving masses, moved with compassion for the helpless and harassed multitudes. If only we could see what Jesus saw in that moment. Jesus wanted his disciples to see the crowds through his eyes, so he addressed them, "Open your eyes. The harvest is plentiful, but the laborers are few. Ask the Lord of the harvest to send out workers." They likely nodded along, clueless about his intentions to make them the answer to their own prayers. A few days later—their naive "amens" still hanging in the air—Jesus issued their marching orders.

Those marching orders, or the "briefing" for their first months-long mission journey, are found in Matthew 10 (and Luke 9), and they unfold lean and mean:

- Responsibilities (Matt. 10:7–8): Proclaiming the kingdom, healing the sick, casting out demons
- Reliance (Matt. 10:9–10): Depending upon God for necessities
- Results (Matt. 10:11–15): Accepting or rejecting the message
- Response (Matt. 10:16): Responding to danger

Instead of including a packing list, Jesus instructed them to travel light but trust heavy. No money belts, no bags, or contingency plans needed—just the bare essentials. Why? To produce an intense reliance upon the Holy Spirit.

It's important to understand that these instructions were unique to this one-off training exercise. Though we aren't bound by the rigid restrictions placed on the Twelve, the cadence of Jesus's commands still provides a blueprint for the universal principles of disciple-making. Schnabel asserts that the briefing lays the groundwork for a broader, enduring missional lifestyle.[5] Otherwise, the gospel writers most likely wouldn't have included them(Luke even records them twice—one for each journey). Knowing that kingdom expansion didn't hinge on the Twelve alone, the apostles left breadcrumbs for us to find our way.

Paul certainly followed the path laid out by Jesus here, clinging to it like a lifeline after the disastrous results of his first missionary journey to Galatia.[6] Adopting the instructions for his second missionary journey, Paul likely absorbed them from Barnabas, whom Clement of Alexandria asserted was one of the seventy-two.[7] Paul directly refers to Jesus's instructions (Luke 10:7) when laying out his own ministry philosophy in 1 Corinthians 9:14: "In the same way, the Lord has commanded that those who preach the gospel should receive their living from the gospel." Through these instructions, Paul extracted the timeless principle *The provision comes with the commission.*[8]

Like a man chewing the meat, and spitting out the bones, Paul absorbed the Spirit-dependent core of Jesus's instructions, while setting aside what was specific to the Twelve and seventy-two. He could separate the principles the particulars. For example, Paul didn't limit himself from taking provisions but traveled with scrolls and requested supplies: "When you come, bring the cloak

5. Schnabel, *Early Christian Mission*, 305.
6. I spend significant time in my book *Church Plantology* tracing much of what Paul adopted from Jesus' ministry and embedded into his own practice among the gentiles across his second and third missionary journeys.
7. Eusebius, "The Disciples of Our Savior," in *Church History* (ca. 324), Bible Hub, accessed August 20, 2025, https://biblehub.com/library/pamphilius/church_history/chapter_xii_the_disciples_of_our.htm. Outside of Clement and church tradition, this is unverifiable.
8. Alain Caron, *Apostolic Centers: Shifting the Church, Transforming the World* (Arsenal Press, 2013), chap. 2, Kindle.

that I left with Carpus at Troas, also the books, and above all the parchments" (2 Tim. 4:13). He even brought a personal physician—Luke. That's not a lack of faith—it's wisdom when you've been repeatedly flogged, stoned, or shipwrecked. As Luther put it, "God calls in two ways, either by means or without means."[9]

Jesus wasn't training the Twelve to think that planning or being prepared like a Boy Scout was inherently unspiritual. Nor was he mandating minimalism. Being vulnerable served a purpose, however: stripping away their safety nets to embed a reflex of dependence on the Holy Spirit under pressure. Had they taken all they'd needed, they may never have looked up. Those limitations would be lifted later, but they'd never forget the lessons learned on those two journeys. Like Mr. Miyagi training Daniel LaRusso in *The Karate Kid* to sand the floor, paint the fence, and "wax on, wax off"—demeaning menial chores that felt like pointless busywork. But Miyagi was hardwiring muscle memory, drilling those foundational movements until they became second nature.

To that end, in 1974, Ralph Winter, director of the US Center for World Missions, addressed the Lausanne Congress for World Evangelization about the rediscovery of these first-century principles:

> In some places where few churches had ever been planted, some intrepid Southern Baptist missionaries began to pioneer a radical new strategy based on Jesus' own ministry model. Instead of using traditional missionary practices, they used Jesus' disciple-making instructions in Luke 10 and Matthew 10. They took Jesus' teachings literally when he said that disciple-makers would endure hardships and make big sacrifices. They decided to trust that Jesus' model of ministry was just as relevant today as it was for the Twelve and the seventy-two.[10]

Two thousand years after Jesus uttered these instructions, missionary organizations rediscovered mobilization and "unstuck" world missions again.

---

9. Martin Luther, Lectures on Galatians Chapters 1–4, vol. 26 of Luther's Works: The American Edition, ed. Jaroslav Pelikan (Concordia, 1963), 13–78.
10. Jerry Trousdale and Glenn Sunshine, *The Kingdom Unleashed: How Jesus' 1st-Century Kingdom Values Are Transforming Thousands of Cultures and Awakening His Church* (DMM Library, 2018), chap. 1, Kindle.

And things shifted. Consider the following statistics about how the kingdom has expanded since the rediscovery of Jesus's principles of sending:

> There were nine million Christians in Africa in 1900; by 2000, there were 335 million (37 times as many) with most of the growth occurring since the 1960s.
>
> In Latin America in 1900, there were 50,000 Protestants; today, there are more than 64 million (1,280 times as many), again with most of the growth occurring since the 1960s. A significant majority of these Protestants identify themselves as Charismatic or Pentecostal Evangelicals. The number of Christians in Asia grew from 101 million to 351 million between 1970 and 2010.
>
> In China, it has been estimated that 10,000 people per day become Christ followers, and even by conservative estimates, Christianity has grown 4,300 percent in 50 years. By 2030, China will have more Christians living in it than any other nation on earth. There are 3.7 times as many Protestants in Africa as in North America—and the gap grows dramatically every year.
>
> This has happened just in recent decades. In 1980, sixty-five percent of the world's missionaries were sent out from the Global North; by 2020, that situation will be reversed, as sixty-three percent will be coming from the Global South.[11]

Tactics Pattern 2: Jesus Sent Them Together

The Twelve Apostles Named (Matt. 10:2–4; Mark 3:16–19; Luke 6:13–16; Acts 1:13)

> First, Simon (who is called Peter) and his brother Andrew; James son of Zebedee, and his brother John; Philip and Bartholomew; Thomas and Matthew the tax collector; James son of Alphaeus, and Thaddaeus; Simon the Zealot and Judas Iscariot, who betrayed him. (Matt. 10:2–4)

11. Trousdale and Sunshine, *Kingdom Unleashed*, chap. 1.

There are no MVPs or star players in the kingdom of God—that's why Jesus didn't send individuals but scattered them in pairs, two by two.

> First, Simon (who is called Peter) *and* his brother Andrew; James son of Zebedee, *and* his brother John; Philip *and* Bartholomew; Thomas *and* Matthew the tax collector; James son of Alphaeus, *and* Thaddaeus; Simon the Zealot *and* Judas Iscariot, who betrayed him.

That lineup is not just a listing of names but a pairing of pairs—six tandem teams. The word *and* listed between the names of the apostles is Matthew's way of identifying the pairs, coupling the twos into their missional buddy system. Batman and Robin, Mulder and Scully, Spike Spiegel and Jet Black—dynamic duos are just better. Every Sherlock needs a Watson. Frodo needed Sam. Even Han didn't fly solo. That rhythm continued after the resurrection too, although this time Simon the Zealot got a more decent partner.[12] In Acts 1:13, when the apostles are regathered in the upper room, we find them still listed in pairs:

> Peter, John, James *and* Andrew; Philip *and* Thomas, Bartholomew *and* Matthew; James son of Alphaeus *and* Simon the Zealot, *and* Judas son of James. (emphasis mine)

Paul followed it too. Leaving the Ephesus hub at the close of Paul's third missionary journey, they were deployed in pairs (Acts 20:4):

- Pair 1: "Sopater son of Pyrrhus from Berea"
- Pair 2: "Aristarchus and Secundus from Thessalonica"
- Pair 3: "Gaius from Derbe, Timothy also"
- Pair 4: "Tychicus and Trophimus from the province of Asia"

Lonnie Frisbee, a powerful voice during the Jesus movement of the 1960s and '70s, gave a practical reason for young men to pair up while evangelizing:

---

12. Judas Iscariot would have been a tough partner for anyone.

temptation. "Still, we did have our weaknesses. We would usually go out into the community in pairs. If, however, people in our household went out alone, sometimes they would take drugs. It was a really strong weakness. We finally got to the place where we would never go out alone."[13] Jesus paired them in wisdom, for this and other reasons.

For this reason, you're pairing with your two. *The Journey to Disciple-Making: A Discipology Journal* was designed so that each of you can reflect on your training and compare notes in those wobbly first steps of disciple-making.

Tactics Pattern 3: Jesus Sent Them to Get Their Hands Dirty

Feeding of the Five Thousand (Matt. 14:13–21; Mark 6:30–44; Luke 9:10–17; John 6:1–15)

> Then he gave them to the disciples, and the disciples gave them to the people. (Matt. 14:19)

Coming back from their first mission trip, the Twelve sat around the evening campfire waiting for dinner—swapping stories in bursts of wonder, interrupting each other, laughing, re-enacting moments when heaven broke in through them. But the celebration was cut short. The news circling around the campfire hit like a gut-punch: John the Baptist was dead. Beheaded.

Something shifted in Jesus, as if a dark shadow had fallen over him. Quietly, with a far-off look, Jesus gathered them and led them away, seeking solitude. "Let's go to a quiet place and get some rest," he said, but it was more than weariness in his voice. His face drawn, his shoulders visibly sagging, and his steps slow, Jesus moved out as they stood stunned in place. Maybe it was because John wasn't just the forerunner, he was also family—Jesus's cousin. Nobody knew what to say, and Jesus didn't explain—he just walked.

---

13. Lonnie Frisbee with Roger Sachs, *The Jesus Revolution*, 2nd ed. (Freedom Publications, 2017), "The Living Room," Kindle.

But the crowds found them anyway. Just like they always did. And, as usual, an immediate sea of need rushed to envelop Jesus. By now the sun had dipped low on the hills of Bethsaida, casting long shadows across the crowd—and thousands pressed in, restless. Hungry. The disciples, already exhausted, glanced at one another in panic as Jesus turned to them with a calm that only made it worse. "You give them something to eat." The words hit like a slap.

Feed them? With what?

Nobody wanted to look foolish, but the silence grew heavier.

Finally, Philip stepped forward, blurting out the obvious: "It would take more than half a year's wages to buy enough bread . . ." Everyone nodded, murmuring approval, relieved it wasn't them who had to say it. Just then, Andrew came forward with a boy, young, wide-eyed, clutching five small loaves and two dried fish. A pathetic showing, really. But Jesus took the boy's lunch in his hands, blessed it, broke it and handed it back one piece at a time to each disciple. "Tell the people to sit down," he said, like it was time to eat.

It still didn't make sense. What were they supposed to do with half a loaf and thousands of people? But as their fingers tore off the first chunk, something unexplainable happened. There was enough to break off another. And another. Somehow the bread didn't run out—there was always more than enough. Same with the fish. As the disciples stepped into the crowd, the miracle spread from their hands like fire, and a hush of holy awe settled over them. That was the moment they realized that the miracle wasn't happening in Jesus's hands. The miracle was happening in theirs. Jesus was just looking on, with an intensity in his eyes.

Jesus could have nodded his head and blinked his eyes like a genie, yet he didn't hoard the miracles or micromanage the ministry. Fully engaged in the Tactics rhythm, Jesus entrusted them and handed them the reins. He delegated real responsibility—not busywork. He was finally letting them do the *cool stuff*—the kind of things they'd never have had the confidence to dared try on their own.

Go back in time—to the very first thing you ever did for God. Not the big, public moments but the small ones that loomed large at the time. I remember being asked to vacuum the sanctuary after a midweek Bible study—just a vacuum and a dirty carpet. But in my soul? Fireworks! I was buzzing with the thought: *I'm vacuuming the floor . . . for Jesus!* The fact that someone trusted me with anything felt like grace. I knew at that moment that if I could do anything for God—anything at all—then I'd serve Jesus until the day I die.

Jesus dignified the small but also upped the ante because disciples don't grow by sitting in the stands but as you put the ball in their hands and whisper, "Run." True, they might fumble the ball, but they might also score a touchdown. Unless we pass the ball, we'll never know—and neither will they. The only way to ensure your disciples never fail is to never let them try. If our disciples are to become disciple-makers, there comes a time when we are in their way. We need to loosen our grip on ministry and risk letting them fail—just like somebody risked with us. The ventures we think are too holy to delegate or too sacred to share are the very things that will activate others.

Tactics Pattern 4: Jesus Sent Them to Increase Their Faith

Jesus Walks on Water (Matt. 14:22–33; Mark 6:45–52; John 6:16–21)

> "Lord, if it's you," Peter replied, "tell me to come to you on the water." (Matt. 14:28)

After feeding the five thousand, Jesus sent out his disciples—into the dark waters. While they pushed off from the shore and strained at their oars against the wind, he climbed the mountain alone to pray. As a storm rose on the Sea of Galilee, the familiar became threatening. These seasoned fishermen were used to the water, but tonight they were stuck in the middle of the sea, worn out, beaten by the waves, and going nowhere fast.

Then, through the rain and spray, a figure approached walking on the water as if it were dry land. They blinked the rainwater away from their eye sockets, trying to make sense of what their impaired vision was registering.

Panic spiked as someone screamed something about a ghost, but one voice cut through the chaos—Peter's. Ever the one to act before he thought, he shouted, "Lord, if it's really you, tell me to come to you on the water."

Jesus's familiar voice responded, "Come."

That single word became Peter's launching pad into the miraculous. Climbing over the edge, he stepped out onto what should have sunk him. And for a few glorious moments, he walked wet into the stormy sea with trembling faith. As rain pelted him, and the wind gales howled, his eyes dropped from Jesus to the waves. That's when Peter's old familiar fear crept in. He felt himself sinking. Desperation erupted. "Lord, save me!" Immediately, Jesus grabbed his arm. Peter felt a firm grip and heard a question above the howling wind: "You of little faith, why did you doubt?"

"Little faith." It was less a rebuke and more a challenge for Peter to overcome his fear the next time round. And there would always be a next time for Peter. He was far from a failure, but he still needed to grow in his faith. It's like learning to bowl; you sit down between frames thinking, *Okay, next time less curve, more aim . . . maybe don't launch it into the next lane.* You're replaying what went wrong, psyching yourself up for another go. That's what blundering in disciple-making in ministry feels like—preparation for the next time. And, trust me, I've got a collection in the Ministry Blunders Hall of Fame that I should probably see a therapist about.

The only real failure in this passage wasn't Peter's sinking but the failure of the eleven others to trust Jesus's call. Peter had "little faith," but they had none. For that split second when Peter flung his body over the railing, he let go of all he knew about the sea as a fisherman. The rest just clung to the sides, white-knuckled and shivering as the wind howled. Yet to them, faith still whispered, *Come.* Peter alone answered the call. He would keep leading out in faith, like when he preached at Pentecost and baptized Cornelius, a gentile.

This incident wasn't a pass or fail but preparation for when Jesus would leave them to stand on their own. A. B. Bruce notes, "The storm on the lake . . . was for the twelve an important lesson in faith, helping to prepare them for the future which awaited them. The temporary absence of their Master was a preparation for his perpetual absence."[14] That third year, Jesus was constantly pushing them, challenging them. When we challenge our disciples to stretch beyond their natural abilities, we make way for the supernatural, and they rise to the occasion. As Tom Johnston observes, "We must understand that growth development, and learning can only take place in the presence of challenge."[15] Their challenge might range from placing their hand on someone to pray for healing to merely praying out loud for the first time. Either way, those we disciple must be challenged to stand on their own—while we're still there—if we ever hope to see them stand after we're gone.

Tactics Pattern 5: Jesus Sent Them to Learn

Feeding of the Four Thousand (Matt. 15:32–39; Mark 8:1–10)

"How many loaves do you have?" Jesus asked. (Matt. 15:34)

Different crowd. Different setting. Same lesson. But now Jesus was watching to see whether they'd caught the lesson from the first rodeo. The setting: People followed them for three days straight. They were hungry and far from home. This time, it wasn't five loaves and two fish—it was seven loaves and a few small fish. The disciples knew the drill. Like the first time, somehow as they broke off the bread in their hands to distribute to others, the big piece didn't seem to get any smaller. So far, familiar territory.

Before long, everyone was fed to satisfaction, with seven basketfuls of leftovers. It was clear—Jesus was reinforcing the previous lesson when they'd fed the five thousand, checking whether the disciples would actually *learn* it this time.

After picking up the leftover bread in baskets, they left by boat and landed across the sea in the town of Magadan. After a run-in with the Pharisees, they got back into the boat, their mood somber. Everyone rowed quietly as they

---

14. A. B. Bruce, *The Training of the Twelve: How Jesus Christ Found and Taught the 12 Apostles; a Book of New Testament Biography* (1871; Pantianos Classics, 2018), chap. 9, Kindle.
15. Tom Johnston, *The Way of the Master: The Leader Development Methodology of Jesus* (pub. by author, 2021), 239.

headed back, resentful that they'd crossed the Sea of Galilee yet again—this time for nothing. To make matters worse, nobody had packed any of the left-overs of the miraculous bread, and after all this rowing, they were famished.

Jesus finally broke the silence. "Beware the leaven of the Pharisees." They whispered among themselves, "Is it because we forgot the bread?" Reading between the lines, Jesus responded to their confusion, "Why are you talking about bread? Don't you remember the five thousand? The four thousand? How many baskets you picked up afterward?" They sheepishly answered with numbers. Jesus was flummoxed: "How is it you still don't understand?" They gave the right numbers; they just didn't do the math. Jesus was trying to teach them something both times, but they'd missed it completely.

Mark recounts that after the feeding of the five thousand, Jesus "climbed into the boat with them, and the wind died down. They were completely amazed, for they had not understood about the loaves; their hearts were hardened" (Mark 6:51–52). What was the lesson of the loaves, the one they'd missed the first time? They'd seen bread multiply in their hands, yet they still defaulted to panic in moments of need. Now the feeding of the four thousand was their second round meant to teach them, Jesus circling back to test the knowledge of the Twelve. Repetition is a hallmark of master disciple-making. Even after the resurrection, he spent forty days reinforcing the very things they'd already seen and heard, because he knew: The human heart learns slowly, and clarity comes in waves.[16]

Sometimes reinforcing vital principles with our disciples seems to take more time than we possess. We expect instant transformation, but Jesus modeled repetition, going at the pace of the learner. If we rush past the pace of the Rabbi, we stop forming disciples and start forging Pharisees—people who adopt practices but bypass the principles. They outwardly conform to rules and standards without experiencing true inner transformation. And the world's already got enough of those . . .

Slow down, and teach your disciples so that they can learn what God is

---

16. Mark 16:9–11; John 20:11–18; Matt. 28:9–10; Mark 16:12–13; Luke 24:13–35; Luke 24:34; 1 Cor. 15:5; John 20:19–23; Luke 24:36–49; John 20:24–29; John 21:1–23; Matt. 28:16–20; 1 Cor. 15:6; 1 Cor. 15:7; Luke 24:50–53; Acts 1:3–12.

trying to teach them. You can learn more about how to *lead like Jesus* by checking out Discipology.com.

Tactics Pattern 6: Jesus Sent Them for God's Glory

The Transfiguration (Matt. 17:1–13; Mark 9:2–13; Luke 9:28–36)

> And as the men were parting from him, Peter said to Jesus, "Master, it is good that we are here. Let us make three tents, one for you and one for Moses and one for Elijah"—not knowing what he said. (Luke 9:33 ESV)

The next milestone in the disciples' supernatural journey happened not in the valleys below but on the peak of a mountain—possibly Mount Hermon. While tradition has long favored Mount Tabor, geography suggests otherwise. Just before this moment, Jesus and his disciples were in Caesarea Philippi, nestled at the base of Hermon, the tallest peak in the region. Mount Tabor, though picturesque, rises only 1,800 feet and at that time was home to a Roman garrison, hardly the setting for a sacred encounter. Hermon, on the other hand, towers over 9,000 feet, a true "high mountain," as Matthew described it.

But Jesus didn't bring Peter, James, and John to Hermon for the panoramic view. He brought them to glimpse the edge of heaven. There, on that mountain, the veil was pulled back as Christ's glory exploded into light. Moses and Elijah appeared in blazing splendor, and the Father's voice broke storm clouds like thunder: "This is my Son, whom I love . . . listen to him." The heavens opened for a brief, blazing moment—and there was context. The day before, a tense question had hung in the air like lightning poised to crack: "Who do you say I am?" Jesus asked. The disciples shifted nervously, eyes darting, but Peter—trembling, yet bold—answered, "You are the Christ, the Son of the living God" (Matt. 16:13–20; Mark 8:27–30; Luke 9:18–21). That confession shifted something. All three Synoptic Gospels place the transfiguration immediately after Peter's confession, like heaven's confirmation seal, stamped on earth's declaration. Jesus had said, "The gates of death will not overcome my church" (Matt. 16:18, my paraphrase). Now, standing with him were Moses and Elijah, two ancient prophets long dead, yet alive. Eternity had broken into time—sending a divine signal: *Death has no dominion here.*

As Jesus's glory burned brighter than the sun, the disciples dropped to the ground, overwhelmed—undone. Peter, for once in his life, fumbled for words. "And as the men were parting from him," Peter offered to build tents, anything to prolong the glory of the moment. But this wasn't a moment to keep. It was a glimpse of glory to prep them for a king who would suffer, die, and rise, and reign. They'd been let in on a secret, one needed to share. They'd stolen a glimpse of Jesus as he really was—the ancient of days—a preview of what John saw in Revelation. The veil had momentarily slipped, and Jesus's glory eclipsed even their greatest heroes—Moses and Elijah—and that glory would need to be shared. That's why they couldn't stay.

Every disciple needs a mountaintop moment, an experience of glory that wrecks them in the best way. But we can't let them camp out there. Part of disciple-making is guiding people into his presence—and then leading them back down the mountain on mission. The goal of year 3 was activation, so bringing that glory *back down* to the valley—from glory to grit—was the tactical lesson. Piper concludes, "Missions exist because there are still places where worship does not."[17] Others who don't see his glory, must. Therefore, we must balance the experiences of the mountaintop with the need of the valley by keeping our head in the clouds and our hands in the dirt.

Tactics Pattern 7: Jesus Sent Them to Struggle

Healing a Demon-Possessed Boy (Matt. 17:14–21; Mark 9:14–29; Luke 9:37–43)

> And when he had entered the house, his disciples asked him privately, "Why could we not cast it out?" (Mark 9:28 ESV)

17. John Piper, *Let the Nations Be Glad! The Supremacy of God in Missions*, 2nd ed. (Baker Academic, 2003), 17.

While Jesus stood ablaze in divine glory on the mountaintop, the scene at the foot of the mountain couldn't have been more different. Down below, the remaining nine disciples were locked in a struggle with a desperate father. He had dragged his tormented, demon-possessed son to them, begging for help. With all their might they tried desperately to free the boy. Commands were shouted. Hands were laid. But nothing worked . . . and the boy just kept convulsing, eyes rolled back, foaming at the mouth.

By the time Jesus descended the mountain, amid the crowd of arguing religious leaders and murmuring people, the father, weary and red-eyed with grief, stepped forward with a damning summary: "I asked your disciples to drive out the spirit—but they couldn't."

Oof. That sucker punch hit the nine disciples like a humiliating hit to the gut.

"You unbelieving generation," Jesus replied. "How long shall I stay with you?" Then, without theatrics, Jesus rebuked the unclean spirit, and the boy's rigid frame crumpled—free at last.

That night, huddled around the campfire, away from the crowds, the disciples were deflated, eyes cast down, heads low with shame and voices lower. One mustered the courage to ask the burning question, "Why couldn't we cast it out?"

They were supposed to be ready. They had done this before. But this time, something was different—and it exposed the fault lines in their feebleness.

"This kind," Jesus said, "only comes out by prayer . . . and fasting."

This kind. *So there were kinds?* This told them that they didn't even know what they didn't know . . .

Believe it or not, this may have been one of the most powerful moments so far. It was an embarrassing moment for the disciples—but one they desperately needed. Jesus sanctified the struggle. And this is the disciple-maker's dilemma: Our disciples don't do things like we do. They don't always succeed. Like parents watching their child struggle to walk—stumbling, falling, and getting back up—stepping in to help too much can actually delay their development. As Miles Stanford states, "Many believers are simply frantic over the fact of failure in their lives, and they will go to all lengths in trying to hide it, ignore it, or rationalize about it. And all the time they are resisting the main instrument in the Father's hand for conforming us to the image of his Son!"[18] *Failure* should be cut from our vocabulary; the word we're looking for is *struggle*—and it's the only way to grow in making disciples.

Tactics Pattern 8: Jesus Sent Them into the Mundane

Jesus Pays the Temple Tax with a Miraculous Coin (Matt. 17:24–27)

> "Take the first fish you catch; open its mouth and you will find a four-drachma coin. Take it and give it to them for my tax and yours." (Matt. 17:27)

It started with a simple question: "Does your teacher pay the temple tax?" Peter, perhaps speaking a little too quickly, answered, "Yes." But when he got back to where Jesus was, he was already waiting with a question of his own.

"What do you think, Simon? From whom do the kings of the earth collect taxes—from their children, or from others?"

Peter answered, "From others."

"Then the children are exempt," Jesus said. "But so that we don't cause offense . . . go throw out a line. The first fish you catch will have a coin in its mouth. Use it to pay the tax for both of us." Classic rabbi stuff. Instead of just handing him two coins, Jesus sent Peter on a mission.

And just like that, Peter found himself walking toward the water again, not to try walking on water this time—or have his faith tested by storms—but to pay a bill. This wasn't one of those headline miracles. This miracle wasn't flashy, nor did it shake the heavens, but it didn't need to because in the kingdom of God, the mundane is never just mundane. The lesson: Jesus wanted Peter to bring God into any and every situation.

Most of the other disciples were likely too young to be taxed. Matthew, the ex-tax collector, may have already paid his dues for life before walking off

18. Miles J. Stanford, *The Green Letters: Principles of Spiritual Growth* (Zondervan, 1981), 82.

the job. But for Peter, this moment mattered. Jesus was showing him that the supernatural doesn't hover above real life—it permeates it. He didn't separate the sacred from the mundane but wove them together. When the silver coin gleamed in his hand, it wasn't just provision, but a reminder that no detail is too small for God's attention. The same God who multiplied the loaves, helped him walk on water, and healed the broken through his hands, was just as present in the payment of his taxes. R. C. Sproul outlines the struggle for many learning this lesson, "So many of us are practical atheists. We may be theoretical theists, but our lives betray a practical kind of atheism . . ."[19] Practical atheists compartmentalize spirituality—keeping God in the church box, or left behind when rising from their knees to rush into a day. But what if God is closer than we thought, wanting to move among the mundanity of our hours?

The idea of "thin places" comes from ancient Celtic Christianity and refers to times when the boundary separating heaven and earth feels especially thin, almost transparent. In these moments the veil between the physical and spiritual evaporates just enough to sense the presence of God. Having lived in Wales for twelve years, I can attest: Some spaces carry his presence more tangibly. There is a theology of place in the Bible, but this isn't about geography. The Celts bathed those places in prayer, and as former animists (believing spirits inhabited the natural world), reflexively blended Christ into the mundane. Taking a cue from the sacraments, they wanted his Spirit to saturate the everyday things of life. The result seems to have left divine fingerprints in Wales, the Land of Revivals—where the Spirit of God continued to pour himself out for hundreds of years. Perhaps our experience of God in the mundane would become more regular if we invited him into those spaces, asking God to make cameos in mundanity.

Jesus engaged Peter in a vital tactic of disciple-making: Teach your disciples how to handle the real-world stuff, like trusting God to provide for mundane details like taxes, bills, and daily needs. "Give us this day our daily bread . . ." There it is again—the lesson of the loaves—because sometimes the lessons about God breaking in to everyday life show up as a silver coin in a fish's mouth.

---

19. R. C. Sproul, *What Is Faith?* (Thomas Nelson, 2000), 16.

Tactics Pattern 9: Jesus Sent Out to Mobilize More

The Sending of the Seventy-Two (Luke 10:1–24)

> After this the Lord appointed seventy-two others and sent them two by two ahead of him to every town and place where he was about to go. (Luke 10:1)

The second wave of missionary disciple-makers at the end of the third year, were not seventy-two random volunteers.[20] The phrase "seventy-two others" strongly implies they were *in addition* to the Twelve.[21] Many of them were likely the fruit of the Twelve's earlier mission—new recruits gathered from villages and towns throughout Galilee, brought back to Jesus, and discipled by the apostles themselves. Somewhere in the intervening six months between the two missions, they'd become apprentices. The number seventy-two likely wasn't accidental either. Genesis 10 lists seventy-two nations in the Table of Nations.[22] It's possible Jesus was signaling something deeper: that this was a preview of a mission that would go beyond Israel. A glimpse of the global gospel. A prophetic echo of the Great Commission before it was ever spoken.

Jesus didn't need another three years to train these workers because the flywheel was spinning. What he needed was disciples who could disciple others. If Jesus divided them equally, each of the Twelve could have been responsible for six apprentices. Their immersive training would have happened in the four-to-six-month space between the two journeys, but Jesus was sending them like he had the Twelve. Unlike the first mission—where Jesus sent them to follow up behind him—he was sending them ahead of him. Luke tells us plainly, "The Lord . . . sent them two by two ahead of him to every town and place where he was about to go" (Luke 10:1). And this time the scale was bigger. Seventy-two missionaries. Thirty-six pairs. Jesus expanded the mission field beyond familiar Galilee, and into Judea, Samaria, and culturally mixed

20. Schnabel, *Early Christian Mission*, 319.
21. Schnabel, *Early Christian Mission*, 321.
22. Schnabel, *Early Christian Mission*, 321.

regions with significant gentile populations. The Twelve would learn that they were nothing special, that God would work through others ordinary people just like them. The seventy-two would learn the same lessons the Twelve had: To trust God. To rely on the Holy Spirit. To expect God to turn up. And when they returned, they would be just as excited.

Tactics Pattern 10: Jesus Sent Them with the Right Metrics

The Return of the Seventy-Two (Luke 10:17)

> The seventy-two returned with joy and said, "Lord, even the demons submit to us in your name."

When the seventy-two returned from their mission, just like the Twelve, they were electrified—eyes wide, voices raised, hearts still pounding from what they'd just experienced. "Lord!" they exclaimed. "Even the demons submit to us in your name!" The power of God thrilled through their own hands—the power of his words reverberated through their own voices.

Jesus responded with a striking declaration: "I saw Satan fall like lightning from heaven." It was a cosmic mic drop intended to lift their gaze even higher. "Don't rejoice that the spirits submit to you," he said, "but rejoice that your names are written in heaven."

Jesus recalibrated the disciples' metric of success to *knowing and being known by God*. Authority is powerful, but identity is deeper. This brings us right back around to the Discipology flywheel. No matter what our accomplishments, what we are *becoming* is more important than what we are *doing*. Time over Tactics. Jesus was helping them avoid an identity grounded in what they were *doing* and brought them back to *being*. Jesus was saying, "You think demons cast out of people is impressive? Satan himself has been cast out of heaven, but your names are engraved there for all eternity! That's something to get excited about!"

And every disciple they ever made would get their names engraved there too.

Disciple-making requires the right metrics for measuring success. Spoiler alert: Disciple-making, like *Soylent Green,* is about people—and that includes you.[23] God cares far more for you than anything you can ever do for him.

The Master's Tactics

There's no sign over the doorway to the Tactics rhythm reading, "Abandon all hope, ye who enter here." As C. S. Lewis was rumored to say, "You can't go back and change the beginning, but you can start where you are and change the ending." That's disciple-making—starting right where you are.

Remember, the word *disciple* simply means "learner" or "student." You'll always be learning, and so will your disciples. Flip through the Gospels and you'll see Jesus shaking his head, calling his students "slow to believe" (Luke 24:25). Turns out, it isn't just you. Jesus didn't wait until his disciples were polished, and your disciples won't be either. Now that we've examined Jesus's patterns in the third year, the real question is, Are you willing to send them out not when they *feel* ready but when the time is *right*? That posture takes courage and enough humility to risk failure. It also takes the attitude of Bono: "Yes, I sometimes fail, but at least I'm willing to experiment."[24]

---

23. *Soylent Green* is a vintage Charlton Heston science fiction movie. My dad and Heston were friends, and my brother's godfather played the attendant who euthanized people. This was an easter egg for my brother. IYKYK.
24. "U2 Frontman Speaks Out: Top 20 Bono Quotes," Escape to Reality, last modified May 10, 2010, https://escapetoreality.org/2010/05/10/u2-frontman-speaks-out-top-20-bono-quotes/.

CHAPTER 10

Principles of Tactics

The church is the only institution that exists primarily for the benefit of those who are not its members.

—WILLIAM TEMPLE

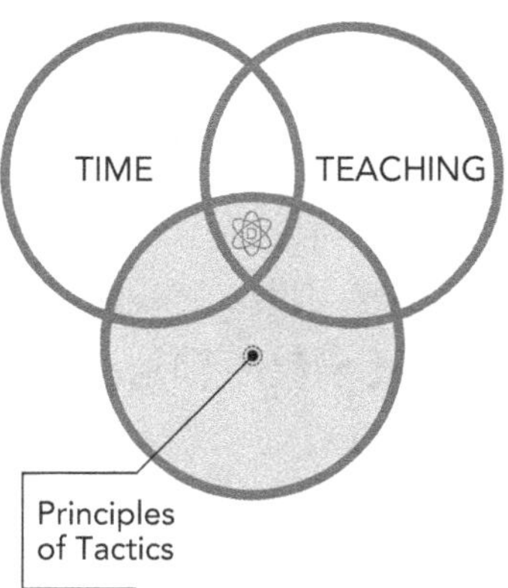

The Marvel Cinematic Universe meticulously crafted the Infinity Saga narrative over eleven years, weaving together stories from films such as *Iron Man*, *Captain America*, and *Thor*, building toward the cinematic crescendo of *Avengers: Endgame*. This film grossed nearly $3 billion worldwide, becoming the highest-grossing film of all time upon its release. From the beginning, Marvel knew where it was going, and when it came time for *Endgame*, the investment paid off.

Before Jesus ever uttered the words "Follow me," he had already planned his endgame—the Great Commission, when he'd turn to his disciples and say, "Go into all the world." In the previous chapter, we traced the patterns of the Tactics rhythm. But what were the principles behind them? This chapter connects the dots between his patterns and the strategy that carried the disciples on a trajectory from a quiet seaside village to the ends of the earth. My hope is that this chapter stirs a deeper respect for Jesus's tactical brilliance as we learn the principles of the Tactics rhythm.

Tactics Principle 1: The Great Commission Is the Template for Disciple-Making

Sending the Twelve on their short-term mission throughout Galilee was a fire drill for the Great Commission—the real fire came at Pentecost. During Jesus's final year, he walked them through the Tactics rhythm to train them for the Great Commission itself—the mandate of perpetual disciple-making:

> Then Jesus came to them and said, "All authority in heaven and on earth has been given to me. Therefore, go and make disciples of all nations, baptizing them in the name of the Father and of the Son and of the Holy Spirit, and teaching them to obey everything I have commanded you. And surely, I am with you always, to the very end of the age." (Matt. 28:18–21)

Many people read the Great Commission without ever deconstructing its core elements. The primary charge is clear: *make disciples.*

But how?

We've discussed how Time and Teaching play a part, but what specific *Tactics* lead to disciples being made? The answer is contained within the Great Commission—the means embedded in the mandate. They would make disciples by doing five specific things:

- Mission—"Go"
- Evangelism—"Baptizing"
- Teaching—"Teaching"
- Discipleship—"To obey"
- Abiding—"I will be with you"

The Great Commission provides a cohesive framework of disciple-making, helping us navigate the how behind the what. If we do these five things, disciples will be made and the kingdom will expand "until the end of the age."

1. **Going** prioritizes people outside of the kingdom.
2. **Baptizing** evangelizes people into the kingdom.
3. **Teaching** grounds people in the ways of the kingdom.
4. **Obeying** transforms people's lives through the kingdom.
5. **Abiding** keeps us operating in the power and presence of the kingdom.

These five practices were like Jesus's infinity stones, each one accomplishing something different in the disciple-making process. In this chapter we'll unpack what each of them does, but spoiler alert: None of them bend reality or alter time. Jesus trained the disciples in all five, one at a time. Every miracle, teaching, and practice reinforced a tactic to prep them for the Great Commission.

The three years with Jesus was their training.

The Great Commission was their final exam.

The book of Acts was their grade.

Therefore, Acts should reflect the Twelve engaging in the five Tactics of disciple-making in the Great Commission:

Did they *go*?

Did they *baptize*?

Did they *teach*?

Did they see transformed, *obedient* lives?

Did they *abide* in and rely on the power and presence of the Holy Spirit?

And, as a result, were disciples made?

Luke's account in Acts 2:42–47 checks "all of the above" on the Scantron. The passage below reveals that all five practices of the Great Commission were present in the early church (note the italics):

> They devoted themselves to the apostles' *teaching* and to fellowship, to the breaking of bread and to prayer. Everyone was filled with awe at the many *wonders and signs* performed by the *apostles*. All the believers were *together* and had everything in common. They sold property and possessions to *give* to anyone who had need. Every day they continued to meet together *in the temple courts*. They *broke bread* in their homes and ate together with glad and sincere hearts, *praising God* and enjoying the favor of all the people. And the Lord added to their number daily those who were being saved. (Acts 2:42–47, emphasis mine)

This description in Acts is often referred to as the "golden age" of the church. But what was the butter that made it better? Simple. The five practices are all listed as present and accounted for, lived out on the ground by the disciples they'd made in Jerusalem. What people often miss is that Acts 2:42–47 doesn't focus on the activity of the Twelve but what *their disciples* were doing. Jesus hadn't merely trained his disciples, he'd trained his *disciple-makers*. Now that the apostles were activated on mission, they activated others using the same five practices Jesus had trained them in.

The result? "The *Lord added to their number daily* those who were being saved" (Acts 2:47).

Matthew 28:20–21 was the cause.

Acts 2:42–47 was the effect.

Now that the Tactics rhythm was engaged, the flywheel turned—and all five cylinders of the Great Commission fired to activate disciple-making. Without these *Tactics* the engine of mobilization would have remained dormant, like pistons waiting for a spark.

GREAT COMMISSION	ACTS 2
Going	"Every day they continued to meet together in the temple courts. They broke bread in their homes." (v. 46)
Baptizing	"Those who accepted his message were baptized." (v. 47)
Teaching	"They devoted themselves to the apostles' teaching." (v. 42)
Obeying	"to fellowship, to the breaking of bread. . . . All the believers were together and had everything in common. They sold property and possessions to give to anyone who had need." (vv. 42, 44–45)
Walking in the Spirit	". . . and to prayer. Everyone was filled with awe at the many wonders and signs performed by the apostles." (vv. 42–43)

The church desperately needs a return to all five of these practices in the Tactics rhythm for us to see advancements like the early church witnessed. When reformers like Martin Luther hit the church scene, they intended the Reformation to look back, not to the Middle Ages but to the early church. Their motto was *semper reformanda*—"Always reforming." That was a reformation of theology; we need a reformation of praxis. Only a recovery of these first-century practices will bring us first-century results.

Tactics Principle 2: Jesus Modeled the Five Practices of Disciple-Making

If the Twelve graduated their training with honors, it is only because they had an outstanding teacher. Because Jesus was a master trainer, we can assume a few points:

Jesus would never send the Twelve to practice things he hadn't modeled.

Jesus would never send the Twelve to practice things he hadn't trained them to do.

No rabbi worth his salt would issue instructions he didn't model personally. Therefore, if we examine the Gospels closesly, we should see the five practices of making disciples outlined in the Great Commission all throughout Jesus's ministry. In other words, *Did Jesus personally model and train the Twelve in the five practices that he embedded in the Great Commission?*

"Go"

Did Jesus go? Without question. Jesus didn't wait for the lost to come to him—he went to them as a missionary. Not only did he leave his hometown of Nazareth to begin his public ministry in the mission field of Galilee, Judea, and Samaria, but he crossed the greatest divide of all: Heaven to earth. Jesus gets the award for most distance traveled! Incarnating himself into our world as a missionary he became "the prototype missionary."[1] His second year of ministry was marked by constant movement—town to town, village to village—strategically modeling the rhythm of mission later entrusted to his disciples. Not only did his disciples travel on mission everywhere he went, but he also sent them out on missions of their own—twice.

"Baptizing Them in the Name of the Father, the Son, and the Holy Spirit"

Did Jesus baptize? Yes and no. John tells us,

> After this, Jesus and his disciples went out into the Judean countryside, where he spent some time with them, and baptized. (John 3:22)

He adds later that "Jesus himself was not baptizing, but his disciples were"

---

1. Eckhard J. Schnabel, *Early Christian Mission Vol. 1: Jesus and the Twelve* (IVP Academic, 2004), 702.

(John 4:2). Jesus preached but delegated the baptismal responsibility to the Twelve, making it an important part of his ministry:

Once again, Paul, modeled himself after Jesus, minimizing his own role in baptism to empower others: "I thank God that I did not baptize any of you except Crispus and Gaius, so no one can say that you were baptized in my name. (Yes, I also baptized the household of Stephanas; beyond that, I don't remember if I baptized anyone else.) For Christ did not send me to baptize, but to preach the gospel—not with wisdom and eloquence, lest the cross of Christ be emptied of its power" (1 Cor. 1:14–17). This was not an oversight, but an intentional strategy to enlist others to join in. It is quite probable, in this case, that Jesus may have avoided personally baptizing people in case it undercut anyone who wasn't baptized by him—but he made time for his disciples to do it.

"Teaching Them"

Did Jesus teach? Constantly. He said, "One is your Teacher, the Christ" (Matt. 23:10 NKJV). From the moment he opened his mouth in Galilee, teaching was central to his ministry. He taught on mountains, in synagogues, from fishing boats, at dinner tables, and on the road. As a rabbi Jesus taught by immersion—making every moment a lesson. He frequently took the Twelve aside to debrief—unpacking the meaning behind the parables, and miracles. No pulpit hog, Jesus sent them to preach his message in his stead during their mission journeys.

"To Obey Everything That I've Commanded You"

Did Jesus model obedience? He kept the ceremonial and moral law perfectly, honored God in every action, and embraced a life of full dependence upon his Father. Hebrews tells us he "learned obedience through what he suffered" (Heb. 5:8). But Jesus also taught the disciples to obey, modeling obedience for them. The disciples saw firsthand how he submitted to the Father's will daily, walking the road of obedience ahead of them, so they'd know what transformation looked like. He knew that one day others would look to their lives to define it.

"And Surely I Am with You Always, to the Very End of the Age"

This was Jesus's encouragement that the same power and presence of the Holy Spirit that was with him would continue with them. Jesus himself continually modeled a dependence on the Spirit's power and presence. From the moment of his baptism, he was anointed without measure (John 3:34), and every word he spoke, every miracle he performed, flowed from that anointing. In fact, the very title Messiah means "anointed one." In the Old Testament, kings and priests were anointed with oil, but Jesus was anointed by the Spirit himself. To that end, he instructed the disciples to wait for the Spirit's anointing in Acts 1:8 to empower them in the Great Commission.

Many Christians don't realize that Jesus didn't rely on his divine nature to accomplish the mission. Instead, he limited himself as a man and relied fully upon the power of God. To make the point, consider the following verses:

> "For I have not spoken on my own authority, but the Father who sent me has himself given me a commandment—what to say and what to speak. And I know that his commandment is eternal life. What I say, therefore, I say as the Father has told me." (John 12:49–50)

> "Do you not believe that I am in the Father and the Father is in me? The words that I say to you I do not speak on my own authority, but the Father who dwells in me does his works." (John 14:10)

> So Jesus answered them, "My teaching is not mine, but his who sent me." (John 7:16)

> "When you have lifted up the Son of Man, then you will know that I am he, and that I do nothing on my own authority, but speak just as the Father taught me." (John 8:28)

> "Truly, truly, I say to you, the Son can do nothing of his own accord,

but only what he sees the Father doing. For whatever the Father does, that the Son does likewise." (John 5:19)

"I can do nothing on my own. As I hear, I judge, and my judgment is just, because I seek not my own will but the will of him who sent me." (John 5:30)

Jesus answered them, "I told you, and you do not believe. The works that I do in my Father's name bear witness about me." (John 10:25)

The Twelve witnessed firsthand what Spirit-empowered ministry looked like, which was foundational to their understanding as the Spirit filled them to do the "greater works" that Jesus promised.

The five practices weren't slipped in at the end, like Steve Job's famous "one more thing"—the way he'd unveil an iPhone at the end of a keynote. Their presence in Jesus's tactical strategy proves that the Great Commission didn't come out of left field. Nor did it contain instructions he conjured out of thin air; it was a continuation. Jesus intentionally sent them out to do the same things he did. "As the Father sent me, I am sending you" (John 20:21). When the apostles heard the Great Commission, they heard Jesus saying, *Go be me in the world now. Keep making disciples by doing the five things I was doing in the world before I was taken out of it—this is what you've been training for.* Bob Burton puts it this way: "The first-century church only did what they saw Jesus doing."[2]

Tactics Principle 3: Jesus Empowers the Church for the Five Tactics

This is exactly how Paul understood the five disciple-making activities in relation to the church's mission. Paul didn't invent the framework but understood

2. Bob Burton, *The Spiritual DNA of a Church on Mission: Rediscovering the 1st Century Church for 21st Century Spiritual Awakening* (B&H Academic, 2020), Introduction, Kindle.

that the church mobilized in the five practices of disciple-making; it filled the Jesus-shaped vacuum left in the world:

> And God placed all things under his feet and appointed him to be head over everything for the church, which is his body, the fullness of him who *fills everything in every way.* (Eph. 1:22–23, emphasis mine)

According to Paul, Jesus fills all things *through the church.* Pay attention: The church is God's plan A—there is no plan B, which is why we can't afford to get this wrong. Paul was trying to tell the Ephesians that they had not only inherited the same mission as the Apostles, they had also received the same *empowering.*

Paul described the handoff of these five activities from Jesus to the church so clearly:

> But to *each one of us* grace has been given as Christ apportioned it. This is why it says:
>
> "When he ascended on high,
> he took many captives
> and gave gifts to his people."
>
> (What does "he ascended" mean except that he also descended to the lower, earthly regions? He who descended is the very one who ascended higher than all the heavens, in order to fill the whole universe.) So Christ *himself gave the apostles, the prophets, the evangelists, the pastors and teachers,* to equip his people for works of service, so that the body of Christ may be built up until we all reach unity in the faith and in the knowledge of the Son of God and become mature, attaining to the whole measure of the fullness of Christ. (Eph. 4:7–13, emphasis mine)

The apostles had the Great Commission; what they lacked was the power to accomplish it. Thankfully, Jesus didn't take all his gifts with him when he ascended. "You will receive power when the Holy Spirit comes on you; and you will be my witnesses" (Acts 1:8). Before Christ ascended, he instructed the disciples to wait for the power needed to accomplish the Great Commission. In Ephesians 4, however, Paul shifts the focus from practices to the APEST empowering gifts—apostles, prophets, evangelists, shepherds, and teachers—linking these roles to fulfilling Christ's ultimate goal: filling the world with himself. As Paul writes, "He who descended is the very one who ascended higher than all the heavens, in order to fill the whole universe" (Eph. 4:10).

But how will the King accomplish this? The next verse provides the answer: "So Christ himself gave the apostles, the prophets . . ." (v. 11). Why? "To equip the saints to do the work of the ministry" (v. 12). And what is that ministry, Paul? It's five practices, five empowerings—all aimed at one goal: filling the world with Jesus through disciple-making.

Paul paints the picture of Jesus as a victorious king returning from battle, giving out the spoils of his kingdom expansion—the empowering of apostolic boldness, prophetic insight, evangelistic urgency, shepherding care, and teaching clarity. In other words, the five gifts were given like the infinity stones to empower the gauntlet of the five practices.

GREAT COMMISSION (MATT. 28)	APEST (EPH. 4)
Go	Apostle
Baptizing	Evangelist
Teaching	Teacher
To obey	Shepherd
I will be with you	Prophet

Paul switched from activities to the people who reveal that aspect of Jesus more than others. He listed apostles, prophets, evangelists, shepherds, and teachers. Let's be honest—those five terms have picked up some excess baggage—so much so that many have ditched these terms altogether or selectively use only the terms they believe are still in operation. One of my previous books, *The Unstoppable Church*, gives an apologetic for these often misunderstood gifts still being relevant and necessary for the mission of the church. For years, misunderstanding of these gifts distorted them to represent hierarchical titles or offices rather than as descriptions of collaborative gifts empowering all believers. To attempt to salvage the concept by reclassifying and redefining them, Alan Hirsch and Michael Frost coined a new acronym out of Ephesians 4: APEST.

A - **A**postle
P - **P**rophet
E - **E**vangelist
S - **S**hepherd
T - **T**eacher

This empowering is not limited to leaders but rather is given to all disciples: "But to *each one of us* grace was given according to the measure of Christ's gift" (Eph. 4:7 NKJV, emphasis mine). He doesn't only empower the few—he gave them to all. Peter echoed this at Pentecost, speaking of the empowering of the Spirit for all believers, men and women, young and old: "For the promise is for you and for your children and for all who are far off, everyone whom the Lord our God calls to himself" (Acts 2:39 ESV). When it comes to empowering us for the Great Commission, the Holy Spirit is no respecter of persons.

In *The Lion, the Witch and the Wardrobe,* Aslan doesn't send the Pevensie kids into battle empty-handed. Instead, he gives each of them a unique gift, tailor-made for the role they would play in the coming war to restore Narnia. Peter receives a sword and shield. He resembles the apostolic leader, tasked with leading the charge into new territory. Susan is given a bow and a magical horn; she's an evangelist, calling for help and striking from afar to bring others in. Lucy is handed a healing cordial and dagger; she's a shepherd bringing restoration and care to the wounded on the battlefield. Even Father Christmas shows up as a kind of prophetic figure, delivering gifts that reveal each child's destiny before he or she fully understands it. And what about the teacher? That's the wisdom they all gain along the way—the grounding in truth, often mirrored in characters like Professor Kirke or Aslan himself, who explains the deeper magic behind it all. Most importantly, nobody is the king. The

Pevensies are mere princes and princesses; Aslan reigns alone in the hierarchy. They are a team, who together possess the essential gifts to represent Aslan. Every gift is different—each one vital, yet none is effective without the others. The battle for the kingdom is won not by one weapon but by every gift being used as it was intended. Those who've equated these gifts with position, power, or authority have done themselves, and the church, a great disservice.

Although these gifts are available to everyone, we each reflect Jesus through them in unique ways. These are not hierarchical titles or positions but descriptions of how we reveal aspects of Jesus. Paul highlights this in 1 Corinthians 12:20–30 with rhetorical questions: "Are all apostles? Are all prophets? Are all teachers?" This shows that each of us carries a unique "flavor" of Jesus, a distinct way we reveal him to others.

Acts 1:8 ties this empowerment to revealing Jesus: "You will receive power when the Holy Spirit comes upon you, and you will be my witnesses" (Acts 1:8, emphasis added). Notice it says "witnesses," not "evangelists." Witnesses testify about Jesus in diverse ways, as the Spirit empowers us in unique combinations. Each of us naturally reveals Jesus in one of the five APEST ways more than the others. However, as we grow and learn from others, we can develop the other four aspects to reflect Jesus more fully.

How each of those five empowering gifts reveal Jesus to others varies:

The apostolic gift of Jesus: People are prioritized on mission—the "Go" part.

The prophetic gift of Jesus: People experience God—the "I will be with you always" part.

The evangelistic gift of Jesus: People are romanced by his death and resurrection—the "baptizing" part.

The shepherding gift of Jesus: People receive transformation—the "obey all I've commanded you" part.

The teaching gift of Jesus: People grow in the wisdom of God through the Word of God—the "teaching" part.

By the time Paul wrote the letter to the Ephesians, he was a seasoned missionary veteran with three missionary journeys under his belt. He had personally witnessed Christ's kingdom ripping across the Mediterranean and filling communities with the five activities of the King. This wasn't theory to Paul. Whenever you operate in one of these giftings, you bring the presence of Christ to a community in a unique way. That's why the Great Commission doesn't give us the option to pick our favorite and ignore the others.

To be clear, we are all called to engage in the five practices of disciple-making. But we may not have the same gifting in all five areas. This is why Paul told Timothy, "Do the work of an evangelist" (2 Tim. 4:4). It wasn't Timothy's primary APEST gifting, but that didn't mean it wasn't his responsibility. The Great Commission isn't a buffet where you can skip the broccoli; it's a set menu. As Nathan Brewer said, "Since Christ is our ultimate role model, we should desire to emulate him in all five of these aspects, both on an individual level and on a corporate church body level. On a personal level, every believer can develop and mature in these five areas that fully represent Christ."[3] Paul witnessed churches operating in all five gifts, embodying Christ in their community and fulfilling his goal to "fill all things" (Eph. 4:10 NKJV)—one community at a time.

Tactics Principle 4: Jesus Embodied All Five Empowering Gifts

In the same way that Jesus mastered and embodied all five practices of the Tactics rhythm, he also embodied all five of their respective empowering gifts: Apostle. Prophet. Evangelist. Shepherd. Teacher. He moved like a missionary, walked in the power and presence of the Spirit, preached like an evangelist, shepherded people into life transformation, and taught with authority. The New Testament is not shy about identifying Jesus with all five empowering gifts across the APEST spectrum.

3. Nathan Brewer, *The Pulse of Christ (Revised and Expanded): A Fivefold Training Manual* (100 Movements Publishing, 2022), chap. 1, Kindle.

Apostle

Jesus was the Sent One (*apostolos*). He was "the apostle and forerunner of our faith" (Heb. 3:1).

Prophet

He was the prophet Moses promised according to Peter in Acts 3:22: "Moses said, 'The Lord your God will raise up for you a prophet like me from among your own people; you must listen to everything he tells you.'"

Evangelist

Jesus came evangelizing. "For this reason I have come—to proclaim the good news of the kingdom" (Mark 1:38).

Shepherd

Jesus laid down his life for the sheep, saying, "I am the Good Shepherd," and Peter would later call him "the Shepherd and Overseer of our souls" (1 Peter 2:25).

Teacher

"You have one Teacher," (Matt. 23:8) Jesus said, meaning himself, gladly welcoming the title "rabbi," or teacher.

Not only that, but Jesus also summarized his own mission in APEST terms when he unrolled the scroll of Isaiah in Nazareth. It was prophesied that the Messiah would engage in these five activities:

> The Spirit of the Lord is upon me,
> because he has anointed me
> to bring *good news* [evangelist] to the poor.
> He has *sent me* [apostle] to proclaim release to the captives
> and *recovery of sight* [prophet] to the blind,
> to let the *oppressed* go free [shepherd],
> to *proclaim* [teacher] the year of the Lord's favor. (Isa. 61:1; Luke 4:18, emphasis mine)

If these practices were the core of Jesus's ministry, shouldn't they be the core practices of his church? For far too long the mission of the church has been disconnected from Jesus's mission. Christ ascended to heaven so that his church could continue his mission on earth. But here's the trick: When we operate in these five practices, heaven comes down to earth. The kingdom comes and the king is embodied within a community. Those five activities bring the atmosphere of the kingdom so that people experience him, even before they believe in him.

APEST and the Great Commission

APEST	PRINCIPLE	GREAT COMMISSION
Apostolic	Missionary, sent out one	"Go"
Prophetic	Power and presence of God	"I am with you always"
Evangelistic	Gospel saturation	"baptizing them"
Shepherding	Transformational soul care	"to obey everything I've commanded you"
Teaching	Scriptural understanding	"teaching them"

Let's throw down the rug that really ties the room together. Examining the APEST empowering, the Great Commission, and their outworking in Acts, we see the Tactics rhythm woven through them all like a single thread. And like the Stormtrooper banging his head on the doorway in the control room in *Star Wars: Episode IV—A New Hope*, once you see it, you can't ever unsee it.

The Great Commission in Action

APEST	GREAT COMMISSION	ACTS 2	PRINCIPLES
Apostle	"Go"	"They met in temple courts and house to house" (v. 45)	Innovating on mission by living sent
Prophet	"I am with you always"	"Awe came upon every soul" (v. 43)	Experiencing the power and presence of the Holy Spirit

Evangelist	"baptizing them"	"And the Lord added to their number daily" (v. 47)	Romancing people with the grace of God
Shepherd	"to obey"	"They devoted themselves to fellowship" (v. 42)	Investing in people's souls for life transformation
Teacher	"teaching them"	"Devoted to the apostles' teaching" (v. 42)	Rooting disciples in truth through the Word of God

By now you've probably noticed that if a church leans on only one of these practices, it gives an incomplete picture of who Jesus is—one-fifth at best—presenting a community with one aspect of kingdom of God, rather than the complete picture. For example, if your church focuses only on teaching, learning is the main event, and the church is called a campus. If it leans only on evangelism, gatherings resemble stadium crusades where altar calls take center stage. When prophecy dominates, it can veer into excess, like Corinth, where nobody bothered with a seat belt. To fully reveal him, they must all work together. As John wrote, "He who says he abides in Him ought himself also to walk just as He walked" (1 John 2:6 NKJV)." How did Jesus walk? In all five empowering gifts. Therefore, when the church walks in all five, the following happens:

Apostolic gift—keeps the church walking on mission
Prophetic gift—keeps the church walking in the Spirit
Evangelistic gift—keeps the church walking in grace
Shepherding gift—keeps the church walking in transformational community
Teaching gift—keeps the church walking in the Word

This is where Paul arrives after speaking about the APEST: "From him the whole body, joined and held together by every supporting ligament, grows and builds itself up in love, *as each part does its work*" (Eph. 4:16). This balance and collaboration of all five empowered practices is essential if the body is to look anything like Jesus.

Tactics Principle 5: Jesus Modeled the Empowering Gifts in the Gospels

Using the handle of APEST, we can examine the Gospels to see how Jesus modeled all five infinity stones before handing the gauntlet to the Twelve. For space and time, we will analyze only his first year:

MEETING THE FIRST DISCIPLES

- Dinner with John and James **(Shepherd)**
- Going to Bethsaida to recruit Philip and Nathaniel **(Apostle)**

WEDDING OF CANA

- Spending time with the six disciples **(Shepherd)**
- Changing the water into wine **(Prophet)**

GOING TO JERUSALEM

- Modeling obedience by observing the Passover **(Shepherd)**
- Cleansing the temple **(Prophet)**
- Speaking with Nicodemus **(Evangelist)**

THE RETURN JOURNEY HOME THROUGH SAMARIA

- Choosing the route through Samaria **(Apostle)**
- Sitting on the well to converse with the Samaritan woman **(Shepherd)**
- Speaking prophetically into her life **(Prophet)**
- Correcting her about worship **(Teacher)**
- Proclaiming himself to be the Messiah **(Evangelistic)**
- Instructing the disciples about mission **(Teacher)**

CAPERNAUM

- Settling down into the village **(Apostolic)**
- Deepening his friendship with the six **(Shepherd)**

- His circuit tour around Northern Galilee on the Sabbath
- Teaching **(Teacher)**
- Proclaiming himself to be the Messiah in Nazareth **(Evangelist)**

Score: shepherd 5, apostle 3, prophet 3, evangelist 3, teacher 3

YEAR 1	APOSTLE	PROPHET	EVANGELIST	SHEPHERD	TEACHER
NUMBER	3	3	3	5	3

Not surprisingly, the first year, focusing on the Time rhythm, receives a higher shepherding score on the APEST scale. Time is the shepherding jam. "Teaching them to obey" is another phrase for life transformation. Character formation happens best via transformational community—the very thing Jesus provided in that first year. It's the months of travel that can't be quantified in the list of events, but if it they could, the shepherding score would be off the scale. In year 2, Jesus operated in the evangelist, teacher, and prophet functions more as he engaged in the Teaching rhythm. Which leaves year 3, the year of the Tactics rhythm, when he functioned primarily as the catalytic mobilizer.

To see the other years, visit Discipology.com.

Tactics Principle 6: Jesus Intended His Church to Spread Out in Five Directions

But what if churches only expanded the kingdom through one of the five gifts? We'd fill the world with *part* of Jesus—but never all of him. We'd never see the kinds of fully formed disciples described in Acts 2. Many of us have found ourselves in a particular camp that favors one of the five gifts over the others—prophets over teachers, or teachers over prophets. Our fragmented approach is captured well by the old poem "The Blind and the Elephant," known in its Western form as "The Wise Men of Indostan."

It was six men of Indostan,
To learning much inclined,
Who went to see the Elephant
(Though all of them were blind),
That each by observation
Might satisfy his mind.[4]

In the famous poem, one man feels the elephant's leg and insists it's a tree. Another grabs the trunk and mistakes it for a snake. Each touches something real—but none sees the whole. The same thing happens in the body of Christ. We're fragmented. Our tribes gather around our preferred expression of Jesus, each gravitating toward a specific APEST gifting.

Word-based churches attract teachers.

Pentecostal/charismatic denominations attract prophetic people.

Mega Churches and church growth networks attract evangelistic people.

Missional and house church movements attract people with shepherd's hearts.

And church planting movements, and missionary organizations attract apostolic people.

The graph below expresses how we sometimes segment into our respective corners, rather than coming into the middle.

APEST in Historic Movements

APEST	SPECIALTY	MOVEMENT
Apostolic	Multiplication	Multiplication/church planting movement
Prophetic	Experience and supernatural	Charismatic movement
Evangelistic	Outreach	Evangelical/church growth movement
Shepherding	Community	Missional movement/house churches
Teaching	Theology and exegesis	Fundamentalism/Reformed movement

4. John Godfrey Saxe, *The Poems of John Godfrey Saxe* (Boston, 1868), 259–61.

All serve a vital function. Apostolic leaders drive multiplication, fueling church-planting movements. Prophets hunger for divine encounter, often rallying around the charismatic stream. Evangelists mobilize for outreach, shaping the evangelical and church growth movements. Shepherds prioritize community, breathing life into house churches and missional communities. Teachers dig deep into doctrine, often anchoring the reformed and fundamentalist movements.

But too often those who excel in one gift criticize those who lead with another. The prophet sees the teacher as too tethered to books. The evangelist views the shepherd as too insular. A. W. Tozer recalls the damage done by fundamentalism, when teaching was seen as the vital gift to the exclusion of the others:

> Fundamentalism, as it spread throughout the various denominations and non-denominational groups, fell victim to its own virtues. The Word died in the hands of its friends. Verbal inspiration, for instance (a doctrine which I have always held and do now hold), soon became afflicted with rigor mortis. The voice of the prophet was silenced and the scribe captured the minds of the faithful. . . . It assumes, for instance, that if we have the word for a thing we have the thing itself. If it is in the Bible, it is in us. If we have the doctrine, we have the experience.[5]

When a teacher exposits on the spiritual gift passages in Corinthians, the prophetic person asks, "Okay, are you ready to do any of that stuff now?" The flip side is also true: When the prophetic person starts going toward excess, the teacher grounds them back into balance.

True kingdom expansion doesn't flow through any one of the gifts alone, although they can catalyze it forward in one direction. For example, the church growth movement, largely led by evangelists, scaled the church up in size via conversions. However, it takes all five working in unity to mobilize outward

---

5. A. W. Tozer, *Keys to the Deeper Life* (Pioneer Library, 2014), "No Revival Without Reformation," Kindle.

in all five directions. If the five activities of the Great Commission inform us how to go about it, then no single part of the Body can fulfill the Great Commission alone. One tribe might be great at the teaching part; another at the presence and power of God part. Only *together* can we reveal the full measure of Christ to the world. As Brian Sanders writes, "When Christians work together in sincere worship and genuine community to accomplish a part of the mission of God, they function as the church."[6] In short, one-fifth of Jesus's gifts to the church will never accomplish all that Jesus wants.

So how do you know if your church is functioning in all five of these gifts to make disciples?

You measure it. That's why we've created the Disciple-Making Assessment Tool. It's a team resource to help you evaluate how your church is doing in each of the five areas of disciple-making. And yes—it's totally free.

When those five gifts come together, the body starts to look like Jesus again, and the world sees more than merely Jesus's arm or leg.

This is why Paul called the church a body. Think about how your body works together. Now look down at your hand. Most of us have five fingers, unless we're clumsy woodworkers, blundering butchers, or uncoordinated door slammers. Although each finger is different, none of them is threatening on its own. But ball them into a fist and you've just created a powerful weapon. Each finger represents one of these gifts: The index finger points to heaven (like the prophet), the middle finger brings the gospel of offense (evangelist), the ring finger speaks of relationships (shepherd), while etiquette teaches the pinky to extend outward while drinking tea, like the teacher concerned with finer points of theology. But the thumb? The thumb is the unifier. Apostolic people hold the others together, uniting them on mission as a formidable force for kingdom impact. To do all of that, we need one another. That's why we need to recapture the vision of churches that look more like Jesus, that use all five empowering gifts from Ephesians 4 to accomplish the five tactics of making disciples.

---

6. Brian Sanders, *Microchurches: A Smaller Way* (UG Media, 2019), Introduction, Kindle.

Because when the body of Christ is mobilized, it doesn't just move out in one direction—it moves outward in all five. At least that's what it did in Acts. Consider the APEST empowering that fueled the early church as they fulfilled the Great Commission. Luke harnesses APEST metrics to describe the expansion of the kingdom in Acts.

APEST Metrics in the Early Church

JERUSALEM	
"You will receive power when the Holy Spirit comes on you. . ." Acts 1:8	Prophetic
"All of them were filled with the Holy Spirit. . ." Acts 2:4	Prophetic
"About 3,000 souls were added to them." Acts 2:41	Evangelistic
"They devoted themselves to the apostles' teaching." Acts 2:42	Teaching
"Meeting in houses and temple courts." Acts 2:42	Apostolic
"The Lord added to the church daily those who were being saved." Acts 2:47	Evangelistic
"The number of the men came to be about 5,000." Acts 4:4	Evangelistic
"They were all filled with the Holy Spirit and spoke the word of God boldly." Acts 4:31	Prophetic, Evangelistic
"The apostles performed many signs and wonders among the people." Acts 5:12	Apostolic, Prophetic
"Believers were increasingly added to the Lord." Acts 5:14	Evangelistic
"The number of disciples was multiplying." Acts 6:1	Shepherding
"The number of the disciples multiplied greatly in Jerusalem." Acts 6:7	Shepherding
"But the word of the Lord grew and multiplied." Acts 12:24	Evangelistic, Teaching
JUDEA, GALILEE, SAMARIA	
"Those who were scattered went everywhere preaching the word." Acts 8:4	Apostolic, Evangelistic
"Both men and women were baptized." Acts 8:12	Evangelistic
"Simon himself also believed; and when he was baptized. . ." Acts 8:13	Evangelistic
"The Spirit told Philip, 'Go to that chariot and stay near it.'" Acts 8:29	Prophetic

The Ethiopian eunuch was baptized. Acts 8:38	Apostolic
Saul (Paul) was baptized. Acts 9:18	Apostolic, Evangelistic
"The churches . . . were multiplied."	Apostolic
JOPPA	
"Many believed on the Lord." Acts 9:42	Evangelistic
CAESAREA	
Cornelius and his household were baptized. Acts 10:48	Evangelistic
ANTIOCH (SYRIA)	
"A great number believed and turned to the Lord." Acts 11:21	Evangelistic
"A great many people were added to the Lord." Acts 11:24	Evangelistic
"During this time some prophets came down from Jerusalem to Antioch. One of them, named Agabus, stood up and through the Spirit predicted that a severe famine would spread over the entire Roman world." Acts 11:27–28	Prophetic
"But the word of God continued to spread and flourish." Acts 12:24	Evangelistic, Teaching
"When Barnabas and Saul had finished their mission, they returned from Jerusalem . . ." Acts 12:25	Apostolic
"In the church at Antioch there were prophets and teachers: Barnabas, Simeon called Niger, Lucius of Cyrene, Manaen and Saul." Acts 13:1	Prophetic, Teaching
"The Holy Spirit said, 'Set apart for me Barnabas and Saul . . .'" Acts 13:2	Prophetic
"The word of the Lord spread through the whole region." Acts 13:49	Evangelistic, Teaching
"The word of the Lord was being spread throughout the region." Acts 13:49	Evangelistic, Teaching
ICONIUM, LYSTRA, DERBE (GALATIAN TOWNS)	
"A great multitude of both Jews and Greeks believed." Acts 14:1	Evangelistic, Apostolic
"They returned to Lystra, Iconium and Antioch, strengthening the disciples and encouraging them to remain true to the faith and made many disciples." Acts 14:21–22	Shepherding, Teaching
"Paul and Barnabas appointed elders for them in each church and, with prayer and fasting, committed them to the Lord." Acts 14:23	Teaching

JERUSALEM COUNCIL	
"The apostles and elders met to consider this question . . . Then the apostles and elders, with the whole church, decided to choose some of their own men and send them to Antioch." Acts 15:6, 22	Apostolic, Prophetic, Evangelistic, Shepherding, Teaching
ANTIOCH	
"Paul and Barnabas remained in Antioch, where they and many others taught and preached the word of the Lord." Acts 15:35	Evangelistic, Teaching
GALATIA	
"The churches . . . increased in number daily." Acts 16:5	Apostolic
"The Spirit of Jesus would not allow them to . . ." Acts 16:6–7	Prophetic
PHILIPPI	
Lydia and her household were baptized. Acts 16:15	Evangelistic
The jailer and his household were baptized. Acts 16:33	Evangelistic
THESSALONICA	
"A great multitude of devout Greeks believed." Acts 17:4	Evangelistic
BEREA	
"Many of them believed." Acts 17:12	Evangelistic
ATHENS	
"Some men joined him and believed." Acts 17:34	Apostolic, Evangelistic
CORINTH	
"Many of the Corinthians, hearing, believed, and were baptized." Acts 18:8	Evangelistic
"So Paul stayed in Corinth for a year and a half, teaching them the word of God." Acts 18:11	Teaching
"Some Jews who went around driving out evil spirits tried to invoke the name of the Lord Jesus over those who were demon-possessed." Acts 19:13	Prophetic
EPHESUS	
Twelve men "were baptized in the name of the Lord." Acts 19:5	Evangelistic
"So the word of the Lord spread widely and grew in power." Acts 19:20	Evangelistic, Teaching

"Keep watch over yourselves and all the flock of which the Holy Spirit has made you overseers. Be shepherds of the church of God." Acts 20:28	Shepherding
"I know that after I leave, savage wolves will come in among you and will not spare the flock. Even from your own number men will arise and distort the truth in order to draw away disciples after them." Acts 20:29–30	Prophetic
CAESAREA	
"He had four unmarried daughters who prophesied. . . . Coming over to us, he took Paul's belt, tied his own hands and feet with it and said, 'The Holy Spirit says, "In this way the Jewish leaders in Jerusalem will bind the owner of this belt and will hand him over to the Gentiles.'" Acts 21:9, 11	Prophetic

In Acts, the APEST makes repeated cameos as both qualitative and quantitative metrics. Luke records them as the key transition points in Acts: "The word of God spread," "They were all filled with the Spirit," "The number of disciples increased," "Those who were baptized numbered five thousand," "The number of churches multiplied." Let's put them through our framework again:

APEST	QUANTITATIVE AND QUALITATIVE METRICS
Apostle (Quantitative)	"The number of churches multiplied." (Acts 9:37)
Prophet (Qualitative)	"They were all filled with the Spirit." (Acts 2:4)
Evangelist (Quantitative)	"Those who were baptized were 5,000." (Acts 4:4)
Shepherd (Qualitative)	"They broke bread in their homes and ate together with glad and sincere hearts." (Acts 2:46)
Teacher (Quantitative)	"The Word of God spread." (Acts 6:7)

Are any of these metrics more important than any other? Or are they all part of how the Great Commission plays out when it's *acted* out?

We talk a lot about mobilization, but Acts shows us what it looks like on the ground when the tactics cog of the mobilization flywheel kicks into gear. This is how you describe a disciple-making movement. Apostles break new ground so others can follow. Prophets speak what others are afraid to say.

Evangelists bring the comforts and demands of the gospel. Shepherds create community space for healing and transformation. Teachers unpack the truth until it clicks. None of these are optional. Each piston in the APEST cylinder is essential. Take one out, and the engine misfires. But when all five ignite, the church mobilizes as it was meant to.

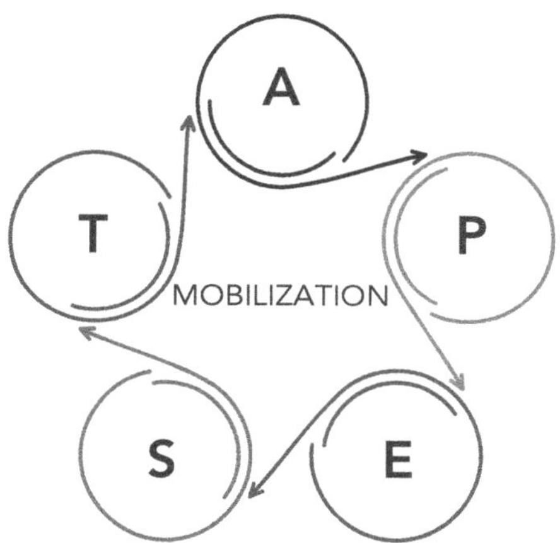

Tactics Principle 7: Jesus's Kingdom Lets Everybody Play

Jesus also can't fill the world with himself if the APEST is only for leaders. In the 1980s, the Trix rabbit used to steal cereal from children, until at the end of the episode, the kids grabbed it back with a slogan. "Silly rabbit, APEST is for kids." Until the church rescues the APEST from leaders, no mobilization movement of everyday disciples happens.

In the wake of his ascension, Jesus left an APEST-shaped hole in the world—and asked his church to fill it. Not with celebrity pastors but with *disciples* who do what he did. To be clear, his hopes weren't pinned on the Twelve, but on the second, third, and fourth generations of disciples made by them. Strangely, the different giftings of APEST have been trendy over the years. The evangelist leader was at the forefront of the church growth movement. The apostolic leader championed multiplication. But that's the problem. It was about them, the leader. The focus on multiplication was great, but it celebrated the *apostolic* piece of mobilization above all else. But what about the other four areas?

Put your finger on the pulse. Put a mood ring on a young person and talk to them about church planting. You'll see they're bored. But if you talk to young people about *embodying Christ in their community* through the APEST, they'll come running. Now shift the talking points to the following, and keep an eye on that mood ring:

Prioritizing people on mission (Apostolic)
Experiencing God (Prophetic)
Romancing them with grace (Evangelistic)
Providing soul care (Shepherding)
Bringing wisdom through the Word (Teacher)

When you talk about these five things, that mood ring turns red. Their heartbeat speeds up. They start talking in excited tones. Young people don't give a rip about church planting right now—it's not trendy—but they're extremely interested in embodying Christ in their community. That's the real heartbeat behind Ephesians 4: grassroots-level, everyday believers operating in their gifts, filling neighborhoods, cafés, campuses, and city blocks with the tangible power and presence of Jesus. Everyone can do that because, in the kingdom, everybody plays.

Peter nailed this at Pentecost. When the crowd shouted, "Go home Peter, you're drunk!" Peter responded,

> "These people are not drunk, as you suppose. It's only nine in the morning! No, this is what was spoken by the prophet Joel:
>
> 'In the last days, God says,
> I will pour out my Spirit on all people.
> Your sons and daughters will prophesy,
> your young men will see visions,
> your old men will dream dreams.
> Even on my servants, both men and women,
> I will pour out my Spirit in those days,
> and they will prophesy.'" (Acts 2:15–18)

Peter's decision to quote Joel in his Pentecost sermon might seem like an odd choice at first glance. Joel is an obscure minor prophet best known for a locust plague. But in Joel's prophecy God promised to pour out his Spirit on *all people*—activating spiritual gifts regardless of age, sex, or social status. It was a pivotal moment. Peter knew the kingdom wouldn't advance if people remained spectators. So he zeroed in on the Spirit's arrival as divine activation—power to mobilize *everyone*. Looking the crowd in the eye, he boldly declared, "This promise is for you." What resulted is what we've focused on from Acts 2:42–47, when the believers were activated in the five core activities of the Great Commission.

But more importantly, it didn't stop there—it carried on to the fourth generation. When persecution scattered the church a few years later, ordinary Spirit-empowered believers brought the gospel north to Antioch:

> Now those who had been scattered by the persecution that broke out when Stephen was killed traveled as far as Phoenicia, Cyprus and Antioch, spreading the word only among Jews. Some of them, however, men from Cyprus and Cyrene, went to Antioch and began to speak to Greeks also, telling them the good news about the Lord Jesus. The Lord's hand was with them, and a great number of people believed and turned to the Lord. (Acts 11:19–21)

It wasn't intentional; it was like Bob Ross's "happy accidents." Nobody wanted to plant a church. There were no apostles, or big names—just well-discipled everyday believers. Mobilization caused multiplication. When Barnabas arrived to investigate, he found a movement. Antioch became the springboard to the ends of the earth. Luke is telling us that the kingdom expanded through ordinary everyday believers. The lesson of Acts is that mobilization isn't reserved for a select few. It's for the student, the barista, the nurse, or firefighter. If you're in Christ, you've been handed a piece of his ministry—wired with an expertise in one aspect of his ministry and hardwired to grow in the other four. That is your calling. So, the question isn't whether you've been called. The question is *Which part of Jesus's ministry has he wired into you?* And how will you partner with another person, wired differently than you (your "two"), to reveal who Jesus is to the world?

What Paul Learned from Jesus

If you've read Paul's letters or traced his trailblaze across the map of the Mediterranean at the back of your Bible, you know one thing for sure: The man had a plan. He didn't run aimlessly. He wasn't shadowboxing: "I do not fight like a boxer beating the air," he said (1 Cor. 9:26). Paul had a strategy—he knew exactly what he was doing and why. His trajectory owed itself to a strategy he'd taken from someone else's system.

And where did he learn it?

Paul patterned his ministry after the borrowed blueprints of the one he followed. At some point on Paul's second missionary journey, he realized that, like Jesus, his time was short. Putting himself in the center of everything he was trying to accomplish just wasn't cutting it—especially after being locked up so much of his journey. Paul shifted his modus operandi from trying to do everything himself and pouring himself into the lives of others who would multiply the mission after he was gone. Sound like anyone else featuring prominently in this book? I'll give you a hint: First name begins with a *J*. Last name, if you can call it that, begins with a *C*.

Paul's third missionary journey ripped a page right out of Jesus's playbook. He planted Ephesus to become a mobilization hub. Paul's third missionary journey played out like Jesus's third year. Instead of constantly moving, Paul stayed put—intentionally reproducing himself in others and deploying them throughout the province of Asia. As a result, Epaphroditus planted churches in Colossae, Laodicea, and Hierapolis (Col. 4:12–13). Tychicus helped advance the gospel throughout Asia Minor (2 Tim. 4:12; 1 Cor. 16:19). From that one city, the gospel rippled outward. Seven churches were planted across Asia Minor—Colossae, Laodicea, Smyrna, Pergamum, Sardis, Thyatira, and Philadelphia. You know them as the seven churches of Asia, addressed in Revelation chapters 2 and 3. And the same will happen today. Hear me . . . and if not, hear Dr. Luke: If you want to start a movement within your community, focus on the five empowered practices of disciple making—everything flows out from that. Otherwise, Jesus wouldn't have told his disciples to focus on those five things in his parting words.

The Infinity Gauntlet

Christ promised his ongoing presence *through* the church mobilized in his ministry, on his mission. Christ is *with* us, expanding the kingdom *through* us, energizing his gifts *in* us.

Did we really imagine that the creator of the universe who designed the migratory instincts of monarch butterflies and tuned the sonar of sea traversing whales wouldn't have an incredible strategic design to fill the universe with himself?

Paul mined the ministry of Jesus like a treasure map. As a rabbi, he probed the eye-witnesses. As a partner in mission, he gleaned from Barnabas. And, over time, he revered Jesus not just as Lord but also as the *Master strategist.* Paul's failure with the Galatians taught him that Jesus's three-year-strategy warranted a second look. By the time he returned to Galatia on his second missionary journey, he brought a better strategy—teams, training, and structure—learned from Jesus. Soon after, the gospel spread like wildfire.

Later, Saint Patrick, Saint Aidan, and the Celtic missionaries would achieve similar success, adapting first-century tactics apostolic teams.[7] Many of us begin ministry copying what we've seen—whether or not it works. But sooner or later, if you want to make disciples like Jesus, you'll face the same crossroads Paul did, when he made the necessary shift.

I don't mean that to sound harsh—just honest. It was my journey too. At twenty-two, I became the lead pastor of a growing megachurch in Huntington Beach, Southern California. Within two years, my preaching grew the church to an impressive number. I seemed destined to be a pulpiteer. When I moved

7. George G. Hunter III, *The Celtic Way of Evangelism, 10th Anniversary Edition: How Christianity Can Reach the West . . . Again*, revised and updated (Abingdon Press, 2011), chap. 1, Kindle.

overseas to Wales, I became the evangelist at Sandfields, the historic church of Dr. Martyn Lloyd-Jones, where revival once swept through.[8] I trained under his protégé, Peter Jeffery, but even as my platform grew, something felt off. I could exposit Acts but could barely do anything in the stories. And my preaching gift didn't make a dent in the surrounding community of post-industrial South Wales, where only 1.3 percent of the population attended church. After 9/11, my American missionary support vanished. I soon found myself on the factory floors to pay the bills. It was there, getting my hands dirty with factory work that I learned the necessity of getting my hands dirty with disciple-making.

Soon, people began to come to faith in the factory. I was like Tony Stark, in a dungeon, forging an Iron Man suit from spare parts, crafting my own escape. It was my remaking. The Great Commission became my arc reactor, the power source implanted in my chest that kept me going. Discipling. Shepherding. Multiplying leaders. Walking in the Spirit. Relaxing into community. One by one, the gifts started waking up in me. Not all at once, and not perfectly. But something irreversibly shifted. And each one of them was like dropping one of the Infinity Stones into a gauntlet. It didn't negate my need for teams but reinforced it as each gift awakened in me, showing me I was weaker in some than others.

Back to Paul.

Imagine him standing on the edge of history, fully aware of what Jesus had entrusted to him—not just a message but also the mobilization of the gentiles. Paul had fully embraced all five of the gifts. Was he an apostle? He said so in every letter. Was he a prophet? I think writing a chunk of the New Testament qualifies him as such. Was he an evangelist? Don't waste my time. Was he a shepherd? His epistles reveal a tenderness—metaphors like giving birth, nurturing like a mother, and being a "father in Christ" pull at the heart strings. Was he a teacher? The epistle to the Romans is the Shakespeare of Christian theology, unequaled to this day. Was he weaker in some than others? Absolutely. That's why teams were his jam.

---

8. Bethan Lloyd-Jones, *Memories of Sandfields* (1983; Banner of Truth, 2008); Iain H. Murray, *Martyn Lloyd-Jones: The First Forty Years 1899–1939* (Banner of Truth Trust, 1982).

When Paul stepped into the fullness of those five gifts, it was like Iron Man slipping on the Infinity Gauntlet. Suddenly he had a power that was beyond himself, a power that could alter the future. He knew *this could change everything.* The movement wouldn't end with him. The church wouldn't die in Jerusalem or Rome. This was bigger than him. It was eternal. And the good news is that, like the Avengers, we're not asked to do it alone but alongside others with different superpowers. We each bring something different to the fight.

And now it's your turn.

The gauntlet is yours—if you've got the stones.

Snap. And the kingdom advances.

CHAPTER 11

Practices for Tactics

Travel in perpetual pilgrimage as guests of the world.

—SAINT COLUMBANUS

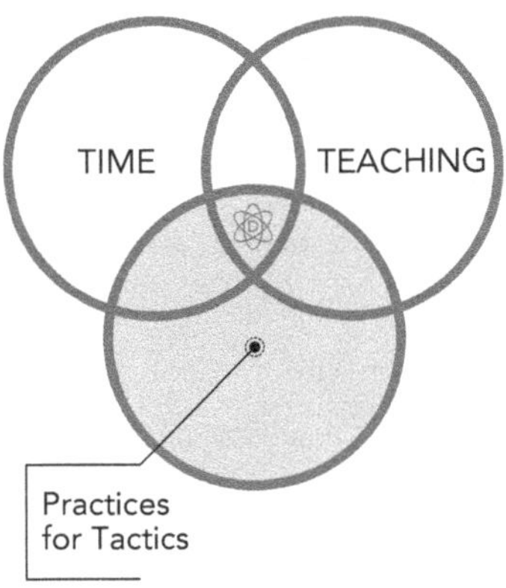

John found James before the sun crested the hills. He'd been running, but his heart was still pounding from the encounter with Jesus. He barely had words, but he didn't need a sermon. Just an urgent whisper: "We've found him." James dropped his nets, not because he understood everything, but because he trusted the voice of his brother. John's first reflex was to bring his brother.

It was also Andrew's first reflex: "*The first thing Andrew did* was to find his brother Simon and tell him, 'We have found the Messiah' (that is, the Christ). And he brought him to Jesus" (John 1:41–42, emphasis mine).

And Andrew's not alone. The woman at the well left her jar forgotten in the dust as she ran toward the village to tell others, casting aside the shame that had long silenced her: "Come, see a man who told me everything I ever did. Could this be the Messiah?" (John 4:28–30). The townspeople followed, drawn like moths to the burning flame kindled anew within her.

For each of these people, bringing people to Jesus was natural. They didn't need to be sent—they just went. Therefore, it shouldn't surprise us if those we're discipling bring others along on the journey to meet Jesus.

- John brought James to Jesus.
- Andrew brought Peter to Jesus.
- Philip brought Nathaniel to Jesus.

As you are making disciples people will inevitably ask, "Can my friend/sibling/spouse come too?" That's when mobilization starts to lead to multiplication. Relax. Breathe. This is normal. No sooner do disciples take Jesus in than they are ready to spread him out to others. All disciples are *sent*, but many just *went*. Think of disciple-making like breathing—there's an inhalation and an exhalation, a gathering and scattering.

Breathing is a reflex, under the control of the parasympathetic nervous system, the part we are unconscious of. Your brain works nonstop to unconsciously do the most important activity for sustaining your fragile life. Breathing in. Breathing out. Gathering in new air. Expelling the air from our lungs to create negative thoracic pressure, triggering another inhalation reflex. It's a cycle. We breathe approximately sixteen times a minute, completely oblivious to the miracle effortlessly taking place through us. Should it stop, we won't last long. Neither will a movement, which is why Jesus trained his followers to do both reflexively. Like a newborn baby inhaling oxygenated air, pulling it into itself from the atmosphere, so many in John's gospel began to gather others to Jesus the second they took their first breath.

Learning to Breathe

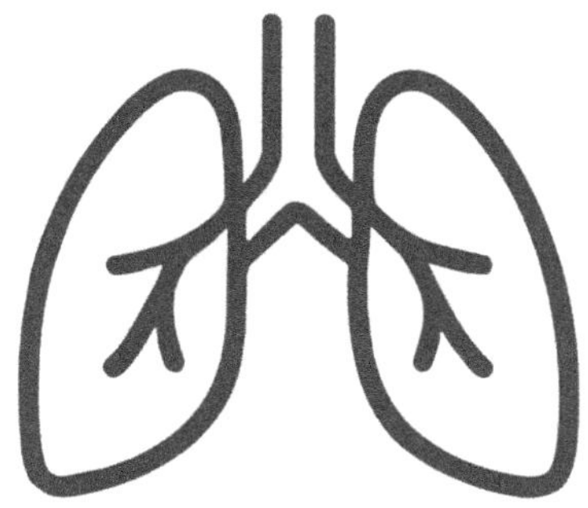

Gathering   Scattering

The movements of gathering and scattering should be as rhythmic to Christians as breathing. Think of gathering and scattering as the lungs of the church. Gathering is the inhale—embodying Christ's presence together. Scattering is the exhale—multiplying that presence into the world. Both are necessary. Without either of them, the body suffocates. *To cease to breathe is to cease to live.* Charles Spurgeon was once asked to pick between two important spiritual disciplines. He quipped back, "Which would you rather do—breathe in, or breathe out?"[1] It is the same with the church—both are necessary for life. If the body of Christ doesn't—inhale and exhale—gather and scatter—we won't last long.

Yet the church has, in many ways, forgotten how to breathe. It's why we're on life support.

We've gathered well, but we've held our breath. We've scattered—occasionally—but it usually amounts to starting another worship service rather than embarking on mission. What many are calling microchurch is simply remembering how to exhale—scattering in public space with focused mission. And, as with Andrew or the woman at the well, it happens through personal connections. You can't market into existence what only mobilization can achieve.

---

1. Charles Spurgeon, quoted in Jonathan Hayashi, "20 Charles Spurgeon Quotes That Changed My Life," Evangelica Sola, accessed July 26, 2025, https://jonathanhayashi.com/20-charles-spurgeon-quotes-that-changed-my-life.

Jesus knew this. It's why he designed mobilization like a "Welsh Secret": something you only tell one person at a time. Jesus knew that the most effective marketing campaigns don't just aim for visibility but word of mouth. As Howard Schultz, CEO of Starbucks, titled one of the chapters in his book "The Best Way to Build a Brand Is One Person at a Time."[2] He's not wrong. Before the internet, the unexpected success of Billy Bigmouth Bass at the turn of the century proves it. Before the internet was a thing—everybody had one—this quirky, singing fish. It became a household sensation not because of massive advertising budgets but because people couldn't stop talking about it. As Jonah Berger, author of *Contagious*, notes, "Word of mouth is the primary factor behind 20 percent to 50 percent of all purchasing decisions."[3] There's nothing new under the sun—especially when it comes to human behavior. When you find a good thing, like Big Mouth Billy Bass, you want to share it with others. This chapter will explore the connection between mobilization and its effect—multiplication.

This was the picture of what the Holy Spirit did at Pentecost, when each individual had a tongue of fire above their head. The wind was blowing, and that fire was now going to spread, one person at a time, unleashing an all-consuming fire that wouldn't stop until it touched everything in its path, turning the world upside down. They couldn't stay huddled up in the upper room anymore, because when Christ is in your midst, it's so good that your disciple-making gathering becomes like a campfire that everyone wants to bring others to.

Gathering Around the Campfire

What is it about the atmosphere of a campfire? The inviting aroma of woodsmoke, the orange glow pushing back the darkness, the community—all drawing people closer to be seen, known, and welcomed. You huddle close for warmth.

---

2. Howard Schultz, *Pour Your Heart into It: How Starbucks Built a Company One Cup at a Time* (Hyperion, 1997), chap. 18.
3. Jonah Berger, *Contagious: Why Things Catch On* (Simon & Schuster, 2013), Introduction, Kindle.

CAMPFIRE ATMOSPHERE

Go back in time with me a few thousand years, and into the mind of the apostle John. Sitting under the stars, firelight flickers across faces still dusty from the road. It's the third year with Jesus. You've already been on your first mission trip with the other eleven disciples. You're bone tired from another day of ministering with Jesus. Across the flames sits Jesus—debriefing the day with you all. Your blistered feet ache from the journey, but you're still laughing with everyone. Then he looks at each person, his gaze going to you, resting for a second, then moving to the others. And you know in that moment, *He's assessing our readiness, what we've learned. He's already sent us out, and we gathered more people to him.* And you can already sense that he'll be sending you out again.

Increasingly—in these holy huddles—the warmth of his presence wraps around you like firelight, and you feel a deep ache: *Others should know him this way.* You feel the weight of a sacred guilt—that you've tasted joy others haven't. And you know you can't keep it to yourself. You must scatter to gather others in. Decades later, you'll pen some of the final words of Scripture in a letter that will be called 1 John. With that same ache in your heart, you invite others to huddle in closer around the campfire with Jesus:

> That which was from the beginning, which we have heard, which we have seen with our eyes, which we looked upon and have touched with our hands . . . we proclaim also to you, *so that you too may have fellowship with us*; and indeed our fellowship is with the Father and with his Son Jesus Christ. I write this so that your joy would be full. (1 John 1:1–4, emphasis mine)

"We heard him." "We saw him." "We touched him." Full joy. You make the invitation—"Come, draw near, feel the heat of the firelight, and know the presence that changed everything."

Tactics Practice 1: Gathering and Scattering

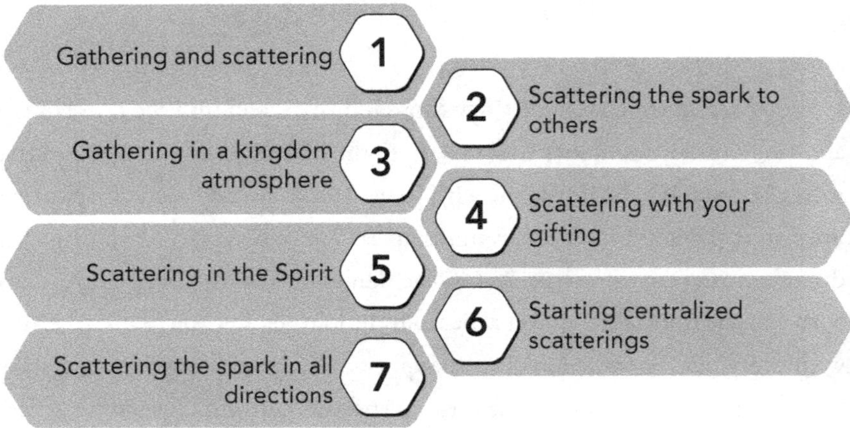

Gathering and scattering was natural to Jesus. Around those campfires, he was drawing the apostles in close. But he also created the desire for them to deploy the spark far and wide to start new campfires to light up the darkness. It's what happens when you gather in a way that makes them want to GO. "He appointed twelve that *they might be with him* and that he might *send them out* to preach" (Mark 3:14, emphasis mine).

Gathering: "That they might *be with him*."
Scattering: "That he might *send them out*."

The early church had gatherings big and small—seeing the usefulness of both. Unlike large churches that snub their noses at smaller churches—or smaller gatherings who judge larger—they embraced both in Jerusalem—centralized and decentralized gatherings.

> Every day they continued to meet together in the temple courts. They broke bread in their homes and ate together with glad and sincere hearts. (Acts 2:46)

> Day after day, in the temple courts and from house to house, they never stopped teaching and proclaiming the good news that Jesus is the Messiah. (Acts 5:42)

Can you see the pattern?

There were centralized gatherings that met in temple courts: public spaces, visible to the community, gathering with crowds. But there were also decentralized gatherings that met from house to house, in private spaces, and provided relational, family-style community.

What if your church could learn to do this too? Gathering and scattering isn't a new thing—it's a New Testament thing. It's trendy to call it microchurch. But it's not a new model of church; it was a *practice* of the New Testament church.

At first, *gathering and scattering* sounds a lot like *centralizing and decentralizing*. But while they overlap, they're not identical—and they often work together in strategic rhythm, like inhalation and exhalation. Neither is more useful than the other. They both accomplish different things, and Jesus's disciples did both. Consider the difference below.

> **Centralized Gatherings:**
>
> On Sundays, we centralize. The Sunday service is the most centralized gathering in most churches—just as it was in the early church. Its focus aligns with the Teaching rhythm, aimed at evangelizing the crowds and serving as the entry point on the disciple-making flywheel.
>
> **Decentralized Gatherings:**
>
> But when that larger gathering breaks into smaller groups—life groups, home studies, men's or women's fellowships—it decentralizes. These smaller rhythms do what the big services can't: foster discipleship.

They thrive at the intersection of the Time and Teaching rhythms, where relationships grow deep and life transformation happens. While Sundays represent the Teaching rhythm, midweek groups move disciples into the Time rhythm.

But what about disciple-making? For that you need a decentralized *scattering*.

When the disciple-makers described in this book decide to meet independently and make disciples outside of the decentralized gathering (life group)—they've decentralized from the group—scattering on mission. In fact, whenever disciples gather two or more, Jesus said he's in their midst. Jesus validated decentralized gatherings and scatterings.

Imagine your life group meets every Tuesday night (a decentralized gathering). To make disciples, each person pairs off with a disciple-making partner—his or her two—as described in this book. Now you've created a decentralized scattering. Together they train for ten minutes a day in the Discipology plan on the Through the Word app.

You can choose to go any speed you like, but the Discipology plan has fifty-two steps. You can take it for fifty-two days or cover one a week for a year. Whatever path you take, for the next fifty-two steps, everyone's on mission. Each pair meets weekly outside of the midweek gatherings (let's say your home groups are Tuesday nights). During this time you step missionally into the rhythms of someone who doesn't yet know Jesus—the "who" taking your decentralized gathering three "or more" according to Jesus. And he'll be right there. The Discipology plan launches them straight into a guided journey through John's gospel that they invite their disciple to walk through with them.

But the two disciple-makers don't abandon their life group (or decentralized gathering) during those fifty-two days or weeks. The life group still gathers as usual, praying together, encouraging one another, and sharing stories from the front lines.[4] All we've done is add the Tactics rhythm over top

4. There is even a small-group study that small groups, life groups, or youth groups can go through during this time to reinforce what they're learning. These and other tools are provided as donor-supported materials at Discipology.com.

of what your church was already doing. And now *everyone* is activated—and deployed.

Can you imagine what that would do to your church?

It would do a few things:

1. It would mobilize your existing disciples.
2. It would lead to a wave of new believers coming to faith in Christ.
3. It would multiply your *discipleship* groups (mobilization leads to multiplication).
4. It would multiply your *disciple-making* groups (microchurches).

The flywheel is turning now. You've activated people in *Time, Teaching,* and *Tactics*. If you're a pastor, what you've always longed for is finally within reach. You've mobilized an army of Spirit-filled believers to saturate your community—something no program or business model could ever manufacture–only Spirit dependent people. This was the mobilization Jesus embedded in the DNA of the early church. And now it's in yours.

TYPE	EXAMPLES	CAMPFIRE
Centralized gathering	Sunday mornings	A bonfire
Decentralized gathering	Small groups, discipleship groups, or midweek life groups	Smaller campfires
Decentralized scattering	Two-by-two pairs deployed for disciple-making	Lit kindling
Centralized scattering	Two-by-two pairs gather with a growing group of nonbelievers (microchurch)	A newly started campfire

Tactics Practice 2: Scattering the Spark to Others

Every time you attend a decentralized gathering—like a life group or women's study—it's like sitting around a campfire. You feel the warmth, bask in the glow, and share in the easy camaraderie. Allow me to paint the scene: You're soaking in the atmosphere, stars blinking overhead, woodsmoke curling into the night air. You're eating and laughing, your skin absorbing the heat of the flames. Other than the glow of your fire and sparks dancing up through the smoke and into the pines, nothing stirs in the surrounding darkness. The crackle of fire and the hiss of sparks rising through the pines breaks the silence. You think to yourself that life just doesn't get any better than this.

Then headlights cut through the night.

A car rolls into the empty site next to yours. A weary family climbs out, fumbling with their gear in the darkness, shivering with cold. You hear tent poles clatter, the shuffling of tired feet, and the bickering of people running on empty. They're about to enter a dark tent, joyless and chilled, while you sit here with a roaring fire, warm food, and enough room to share. You glance at your fire and then at the stack of spare logs. Without a word, you pull a log from your pit and carry it over. With a few logs under your arm, you kneel and place the ember in their fire ring. A gift of warmth. Of light. Of presence.

That's the first step—you left the gathering of your campfire momentarily. You scattered to get someone else. It's what John did for James. It's what Andrew did for Peter. What Philip did for Nathaniel. What the Samaritan woman did when she ran back to her village. It's taking lit kindling to others. Where it will eventually lead varies: It could be bringing them to the campfire (centralized gathering) or, in some cases, bringing the campfire to them (centralized scattering). That shouldn't be step two but perhaps step fifty-three.

The early church had a name for discipling outsiders before they were ever brought to the church gathering—it was called *the discipline of the catechumenate.* Think of it as a training ground for seekers. If you wandered into a church gathering in the second century, you'd be invited to hang back, listen, learn, and walk with believers. Justin Martyr described how catechumens were instructed in the gospel before baptism and only then admitted to the Eucharist.[5] Hippolytus got even more specific—three years of training, with lives carefully examined, before baptism.[6] Cyril of Jerusalem wrote entire

5. Justin Martyr, *First Apology*, 61–65.
6. Hippolytus of Rome, *Apostolic Tradition*, 15–20.

lecture series just for catechumens, and Augustine penned *On the Catechizing of the Uninstructed* for pastors tasked with walking seekers step-by-step into faith. In other words, the movement exploded because they discipled the not-yet-believers into the kingdom *before* they ever set foot at the Lord's Table.

I've read the Bible for a long time and still can't find the place where Jesus invited people to the temple or synagogue. He took the fire to them. This is what the Discipology plan was designed to do. I've literally taken the past thirty-five years of how I was discipled, and how I've made disciples, and placed it within a digital design. Look, if I had fifty-two days to walk beside you, I would, but the Discipology plan is the next best thing. I'll see you in there, where you'll be given fifty-two micro steps to making disciples. Go on, grab your two, and get in there!

Tactical Practice 3: Gathering in a Kingdom Atmosphere

TYPE	RHYTHMS	OUTCOME	PURPOSE
Centralized gathering	Teaching	Information	Evangelism and entry to the flywheel
Decentralized gathering	Teaching and Tactics	Transformation	Discipleship
Decentralized scattering	Time, Teaching, and Tactics	Activation	Disciple-making
Centralized scattering	Time, Teaching, and Tactics	Multiplication	Mobilization movements

The kingdom of God is much like the campfire; it brings the atmosphere, the warmth, the light, the aroma of Christ himself to a dark place. The Celtic missionaries were masters at bringing the kingdom where it was not:

> In 635, Aidan and his twelve "apostles" journeyed south and crossed over into Northumbria, crossing from one race, one religion and one language to another. He gave the rest of his life to incarnate Christ among foreign peoples—the pagan Anglo-Saxons and the remnants of the Celtic Britons

> who had survived the invaders and who spoke what we now call Welsh. Aidan came, like the two previous missioners, with a message, but unlike them he also modelled the message. He did this in two ways: first, by living a way of life that reflected gospel values, and second, by creating little "colonies of heaven" that modelled something of the kingdom of God on earth.[7]

When we decentralize to make disciples, we're not just bringing "church" to people, we're bringing an aspect of Christ himself, creating "colonies of heaven"—the atmosphere of the kingdom of God on earth. And this atmosphere is kindled by, you guessed it, the five activities of the Great Commission—*going*, *baptizing*, *teaching*, *obeying*, and *abiding*. Every time you do one of those things, it's like you're carrying lit kindling from our campfire into the dark.

And the fire itself? That's Christ's presence. Every time we decentralize on mission (going) he comes with us—*is in our midst*—to bring the aroma of life (baptizing), the light (teaching), the camaraderie (obeying), and the heat (abiding in his presence).

THE ACTIVITIES THAT CREATE KINGDOM ATMOSPHERE

Bringing one log can start the fire, but add more logs, and suddenly the flames leap higher, casting more light, more warmth, more life. People experience more of Christ—his truth, his grace, his presence. As the fire grows,

7. Ray Simpson and Brent Lyons-Lee, *St. Aidan's Way of Mission: Celtic Insights for a Post-Christian World* (Bible Reading Fellowship, 2016), chap. 1, Kindle.

the darkness retreats and the atmosphere of the kingdom begins to take hold. The breakdown below looks at the campfire through the lens of the Great Commission—teaching, abiding, baptizing, obeying:

> The log of teaching provides the *light* of the Word of God.
> The log of abiding provides the *warmth* of the prophetic power and presence of the Spirit.
> The log of baptizing provides an inviting *aroma* of grace and a way to start over.
> The log of obeying provides *community* where life transformation takes place.

And when we scatter on mission—taking any kindling of this with us—that's the *apostolic spark* that spreads communities far and wide.

GOD'S PRESENCE IGNITES A FLAME

Think back to Acts 2:42–48 again. When the tongues of fire lit on top of the apostles' heads, they started a bonfire—bright and blazing for all to see. But more importantly, when that wind blew, the fire spread. Consider how all these logs were lighting the campfire in Jerusalem. This time, using APEST language to describe the same logs:

The Teaching Log: Light

> They devoted themselves to the apostles' teaching. (Acts 2:42)

People come in and gather with us and experience the wisdom of Christ through gaining knowledge of God's word. This log provides illumination.

The Prophetic Log: Warmth

> Everyone was filled with awe at the many wonders and signs performed by the apostles. (Acts 2:43)

When this log is present in our gatherings, people can experience what my Welsh forefathers prayed for before every meeting: the felt presence of God. They lived through revival and knew the power and presence of God. Perhaps the gifts are used, or prayer and prophesy have a place, and as Paul said, "But if an unbeliever or an inquirer comes in while everyone is prophesying, they are convicted of sin and are brought under judgment by all, as the secrets of their hearts are laid bare. So they will fall down and worship God, exclaiming, 'God is really among you!'" (1 Cor. 14:24–25).

The Evangelistic Log: Aroma

> The Lord added daily to those being saved. (Acts 2:48)

People can smell the burning woodsmoke of the gospel, and like Paul points out, the smell of burning wood can mean something good to some—a cozy autumn evening—and disastrous ruin to others. The aroma of a campfire is inviting and encourages others to join our circle.

The Shepherding Log: Community

> Fellowship . . . breaking of bread . . . They had all things in common . . . (Acts 2:42–48)

One of life's simplest pleasures is community around a campfire. The presence of God transforms us together, and he promised, "Where two or more gather, there I will be in the midst of you" (see Matt. 18:20).

THE ACTIVITIES OF THE KINGDOM THAT CREATE THE ATMOSPHERE OF THE KING

The Apostolic Spark

> Every day they continued to meet together in the temple courts. They broke bread in their homes and ate together with glad and sincere hearts. (Acts 2:46)

When people are prioritized on mission and we go to them where they are, in the rhythm of gathering and scattering, we ignite the apostolic spark of sending.

THIS WILL ALWAYS CREATE A SPARK THAT SPREADS

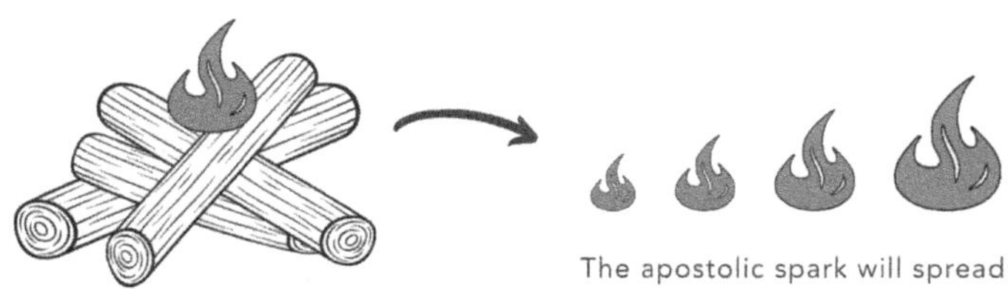
The apostolic spark will spread

Here is how they align with the APEST gifting from Ephesians 4. If all are present, both our gathering and scattering will communicate the fullness of Christ's kingdom. This is what it practically means to embody Christ within your community.

- Go—apostolic spark: Prioritizing people on mission
- Abide—prophetic log: Experiencing the power and presence of God

- Baptize—evangelistic log: Extending grace through second chances
- Obey—shepherd log: Investing time in others for life transformation
- Teach—teacher log: Communicating the wisdom of God through the Word of God

And when you've got all of that, it should spread faster than Big Mouth Billy Bass. And it will happen naturally (or rather supernaturally). As Charles Spurgeon observed,

> The Christian church was designed from the start to be aggressive. It was not intended to remain stationary at any period, but to advance onward until its boundaries became commensurate with those of the world. It was to spread from Jerusalem to Judea, from Judea to Samaria, and from Samaria until the uttermost parts of the earth. It was not intended to radiate from one central point only; but to form numerous centers from which its influence might spread to the surrounding parts. . . . The plan upon which the apostles proceeded . . . was to plant churches in all the great cities and centers or influence in the known world.[8]

Tactical Practice 4: Scattering with Your Gifting

In *The Lord of the Rings: The Return of the King*, Gondor calls for aid. On a lonely peak a single beacon bursts into flame—one small light against the vast dark. But from that first fire, a chain reaction ignites across the mountains. Hill after hill, tower after tower, each beacon catches the blaze, flaring to life until the darkness itself seems to retreat from the blaze. That's what happens in disciple-making. You start a fire small enough to warm a few hearts, but the Discipology flywheel lights a thousand lights blazing across the hills. Just ask Ralph Moore and John Wesley.

---

8. Charles H. Spurgeon, "The Church—Conservative and Aggressive," May 19, 1861, in *Metropolitan Tabernacle Pulpit*, vol. 7, Spurgeon Center, www.spurgeon.org/resource-library/sermons/the-church-conservative-and-aggressive.

Wesley took some convincing at first: "I could scarce reconcile myself to this strange way of preaching in the fields, of which he [Whitefield] set me an example on Sunday; having been all my life till very lately so tenacious of every point relating to decency and order, that I should have thought the saving of souls almost a sin if it had not been done in a church."[9] Thankfully, he reread the Gospels, noting that Jesus and the Twelve were almost always outside—and, once convinced, he went on to mobilize the masses. But he didn't believe preaching to crowds was enough. His movement was based on mobilization: believers empowered to scatter—not through programs but through *Spirit-filled people.* Most ministries today are vision-driven, structured around five-year plans, vision-driven models, and boardroom strategies. But New Testament ministry is *gift-driven.* It equips believers to discover, develop, and deploy their gifts outward into the community. But ministry isn't like straight lines on a white board; it's messy, filled with Spirit-led detours and unpredictable people. So instead of lines, I draw circles.

Picture your gathering's influence as a circle, with each dot representing someone's gift or passion. Maybe someone's gift is compassion, or helps. It may not be overtly evangelistic, but all spiritual gifts radiate Jesus to a broken

9. John Wesley, *The Journal of John Wesley*, entry dated April 2, 1739, ed. Percy Livingstone Parker (Moody Press, 1951), 46.

world, and the circle expands. New people come to faith, bringing new gifts. And new gifts shift into an additional direction of mission. Thus, the cycle repeats, bringing new people, new gifts, and new mission. For example, in one of our European networks, the mayor asked us to help unwed teen moms. Two chefs on our team stepped in to teach healthy cooking in a decentralized gathering. Yet another ran sixteen-player *Halo* tournaments for college students. People came to faith through each.

DISCOVERING THE GIFTS OF OTHERS

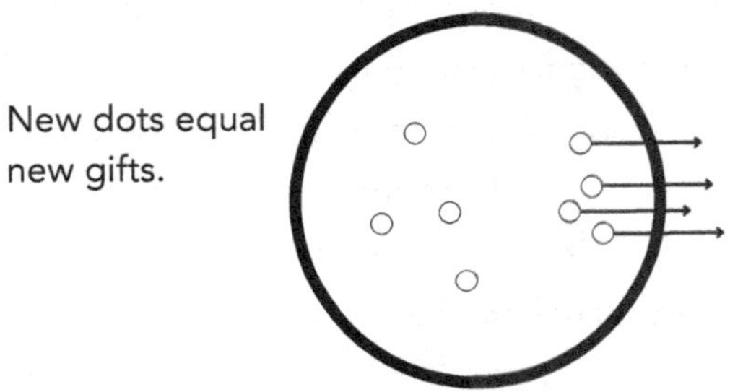

The Holy Spirit had a design when handing out brains, heart, courage, and home like the Wizard of Oz. David Bowie once stated, "I hate my voice . . . I'd give my right arm . . . well maybe somebody else's arm if I could find somebody else to sing my music for me—but singing goes with the territory of song writing."[10] Imagine if Bowie, the man who spawned three major music genres, hadn't used his singing gift—just because he couldn't stand the sound of his own voice. Learn from Bowie—what you may think is useless and "not good enough" could be used powerfully to bless somebody else. If we don't push people to use their gifts but focus only on the one gift of the speaker, our churches will resemble Dallas Willard's critique: "The church is like a football game: twenty-two people on the field, badly in need of rest, and forty thousand in the stands, badly in need of exercise."[11]

---

10. David Bowie, "David Bowie - 'Heathen' Album EPK, 2002," July 21, 2025, https://www.youtube.com/watch?v=ugSW8T4FDY0.
11. Jan Johnson, *Renovation of the Heart in Daily Practice: Experiments in Spiritual Transformation* (NavPress, 2006), 107.

DEVELOPING THE GIFTS OF OTHERS

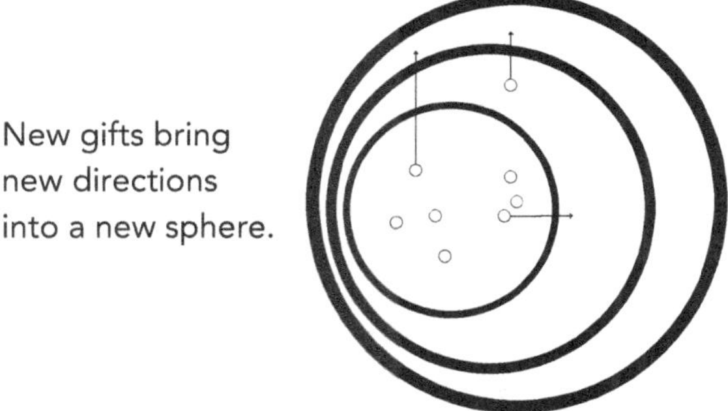

When the mobilization flywheel is spinning, this is how mobilization creates multiplication:

New people bring new gifts.
New gifts open new directions.
New directions lead to more people.
Then your group gets too big.

And once people are awakened in their gifts, good luck holding them back. They'll be like the woman at the well—unable to stay silent. Even when Jesus told the healed not to spread the word, they shared it anyway like a Welsh secret.

Tactical Practice 5: Scattering in the Spirit

If you truly activate your people, it's a chaotic and inconvenient strategy, according to Colin Marshall, "It will mean we will have to relinquish control of our programs for, as the gospel is preached, Christ will gather his people into all kinds of fellowships that may or may not fit into our neat structures."[12] In other words, it should come with a label: "Warning: combustible materials. Fire may spread."

12. Colin Marshall and Tony Payne, *The Trellis and the Vine* (Matthias Media, 2024), chap. 2, Kindle.

Engineers design wind turbines and determine their placement—they don't create the wind but learn to harness it by understanding its predictable patterns. Similarly, activated believers are like wind tunnels, with the Spirit rushing through them, and your church can harness that power as these groups scatter.

Now, imagine your discipleship group committing to this rhythm annually, until it becomes as natural as traditions like No-Shave November or Dry January. Here are a few "wind rally points" you can establish on your church calendar to channel this energy effectively.

- **Disciple-Making December:** Fifty-two days set aside leading up to Christmas to intentionally train disciple makers and make new disciples. According to Lifeway Research, 56 percent of unchurched people say they'd likely attend church if invited by someone they know during the Christmas season.[13] Imagine if your church was mobilized to go get them?
- **Sent Season:** Imagine if *Lent* season was followed by *sent* season—when the whole church embraces life on mission after Pentecost.
- **Disciple-making March Madness:** A full-court press for the kingdom, a focused march into new territory for the kingdom because the church wants to win.

The pastor could kick it off with a sermon series on disciple-making. Every discipleship group can distribute copies of *The Disciple-Maker's Journey: A Discipology Journal* to track their progress. Every time they scatter, they gather back to that same life group, now alive with stories and new believers. But don't be surprised that one gathering of two or more grows into something larger when their disciples can't stop bringing others to meet him too. Many of us remember being new to the faith, full of zeal, brimming with ideas to reach people. But instead of being hoisted onto shoulders and paraded around the

---

13. Lifeway Research, "Less Than Half of Americans Attend Church at Christmas," *Americans Views* (blog), December 3, 2024.

room, we were met with "Yeah . . . we don't really do that here. But hey, VBS needs more helpers." We had pulled a log from the campfire, ready to carry it into the darkness—only to have someone douse the flames. They may not have used a fire extinguisher, but the message was clear: *We don't like people playing with fire around here. It might spread quickly.*

Tactical Practice 6: Starting Centralized Scatterings

When more people get invited to gather around the campfire to experience Christ, it *should* be encouraged. Releasing people in their gifts will start more fires, scattering the apostolic sparks outward. But when more people start joining you, your two, and your who, it becomes a centralized scattering. The definition of a centralized scattering is a group that gathers for mission rather than discipleship. Some call it microchurch. In Britain, a movement I was familiar with practiced Jesus's gathering-and-scattering strategy. When their scatterings became gatherings, and multiplied, they called them "crazy 8s." The simple system worked like this: When a group reached twenty, they split into two—one group of twelve, the other of eight. Along the way, disciple-makers were being trained two by two.

DEPLOYING THE GIFTS OF OTHERS

When mission is facing out in new directions, people lead in their gifts rather than being driven out by force.

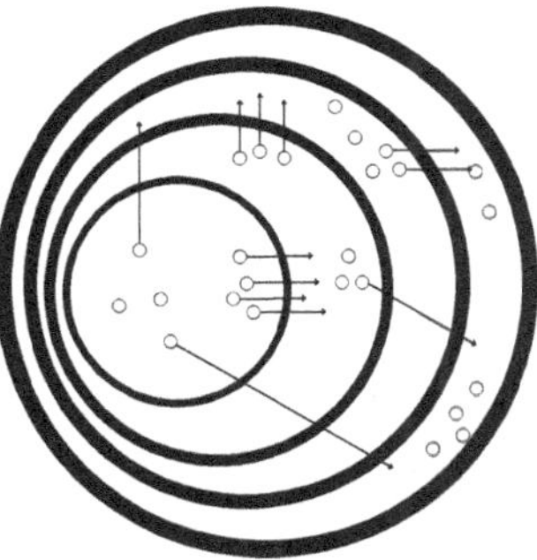

The more experienced leader took the smaller group of eight—because it was harder. The newer leader took the group of twelve, with momentum behind them. Both continued as scattered gatherings, building relationships until disciple-making numbered the group at twenty again. When that happened, it was time to break off and repeat the process. Their centralized gatherings were on Sundays, but those centralized scatterings on mission were how they multiplied.

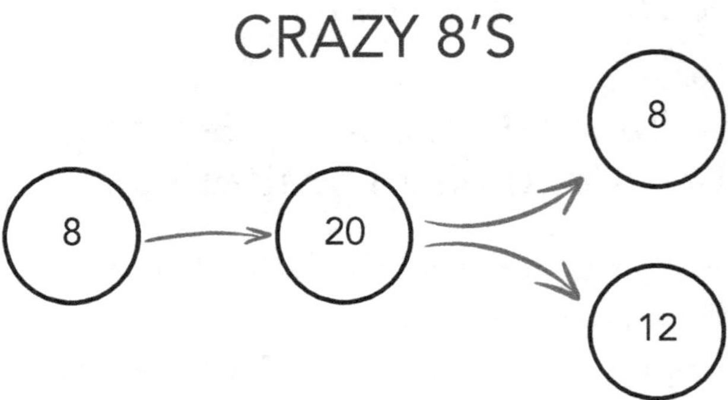

When I met them, they had already scattered into a network of over a thousand and counting. It's the essence of microchurch—not some hip, next-gen thing, but the ancient *practice* of the church throughout the ages. Let me repeat that:

> It's not a *model* meant for *some* churches. It's a *method* meant for *all* churches.

This is why it's problematic to juxtapose a centralized gathering on Sundays with a centralized scattering (or microchurch) as if they're at odds. They're no more at odds than inhalation is with exhalation. As a committed Anglican minister, Wesley made sure that the "meetings of the Wesleyan societies were carefully scheduled so as not to conflict with any of the services of the Church of England." And "We are loyal Anglicans and not in competition or opposition to the Church of England."[14] That means that your Sunday Services are not the problem. It's not what happens *inside* the church that is the

14. D. Michael Henderson, *John Wesley's Class Meeting: A Model for Making Disciples* (Rafiki Books, 2016), chap. 3, Kindle.

issue, it's what doesn't happen *outside*. You do not need to be anything other than a decentralized exhalation of your centralized scattering.

Tactical Practice 7: Scattering the Spark in All Directions

Jesus added further instructions to the Great Commission before he was taken up: "You will be my witnesses in Jerusalem, and in all Judea and Samaria, and to the ends of the earth" (Acts 1:8). Jesus didn't just rattle off random places. His mandate was to expand outward in concentric circles from the epicenter of Jerusalem—to Judea, Samaria, and finally to the ends of the earth.

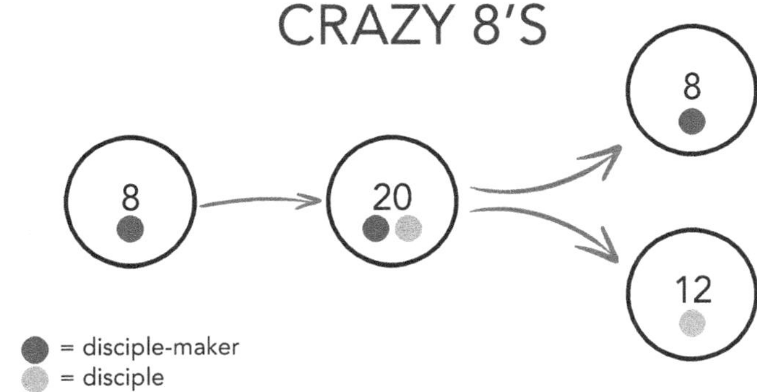

This is exactly how the narrative of the book of Acts unfolded. Pentecost set *Jerusalem* ablaze in chapters 2 through 5. Then, in chapters 6 through 9, Saul's persecution moved people outward to *Judea* and eventually *Samaria*, spreading Christ's witness like a wildfire. Finally, starting in Acts 10, Peter, Paul, and Barnabas make moves to the *ends of the earth* by reaching the gentiles. The rest is history.

Like the apostles, we also have our own concentric circles as we consider scattering, complete with an epicenter and a backstop:

- Jerusalem is your neighborhood.
- Judea is your town or city.
- Samaria is the marginalized.
- The ends of the earth are still the ends of the earth.

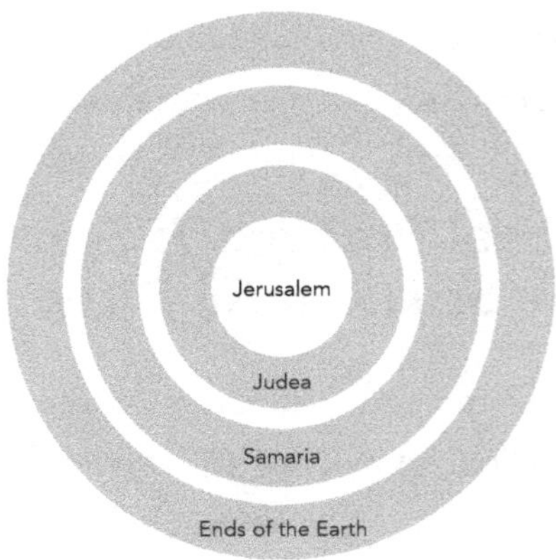

It's always easier to scatter in our home turf of Jerusalem, where the streets are familiar, the culture is second nature, the relationships are already built, people know our story, speak our language, and share our rhythms of life. Scattering here doesn't require crossing cultural boundaries or learning new customs but being intentional with the people we already see every day. Our neighbors, coworkers, classmates, and friends—like Cheers, it's where everybody knows your name. It's where we're most comfortable and, therefore, the easiest place to begin living on mission.

SCATTERING IN JERUSALEM

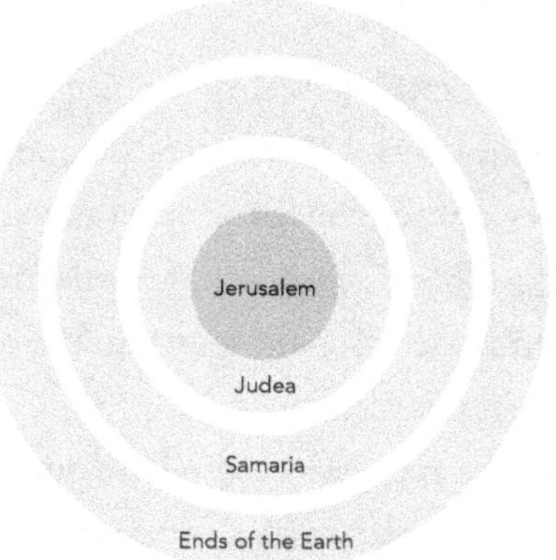

Scattering in Judea is about moving beyond your circle of comfort and reaching into different segments of your city. It requires more boldness and intentionality than reaching your immediate friends and people you interact with on a regular basis. It means intentionally going out of your way in your city so that it "would grieve if you picked up and left?"[15]

SCATTERING IN JUDEA

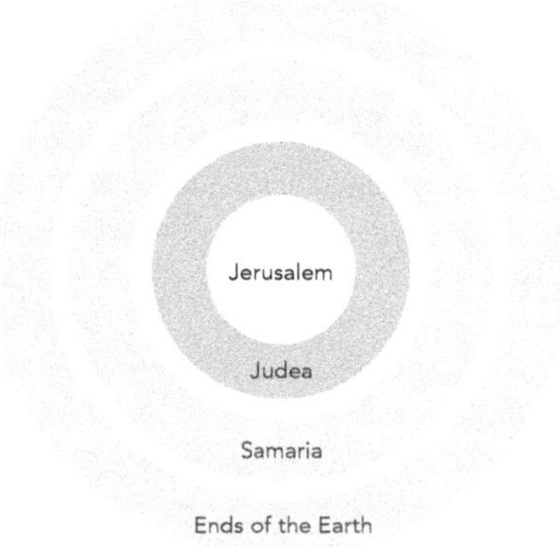

Marginalized groups are a moving target—the majority in one city might be a marginalized minority in another. A person can be in a secure position during one part of their life and later marginalized by becoming homeless or mentally ill. As Joseph Mattera observes, this attention to people outside our groups is part of the apostolic impetus: "Since apostles of Christ represent the Lord himself, by nature they have to be trans-national, trans-cultural, and multi-generational and have a desire for kingdom advancement, not just the enlargement of their ministry."[16] Howard Snyder adds, "The goal of disciple-making is to form a community that looks and acts like Jesus; that shows forth the character of Christ and the power of the Spirit in its social context. The church does this by being a reconciled and reconciling community. It does this most effectively when it visibly embodies reconciliation between rich and poor, men and women, and people of different racial and ethnic identities."[17] Imagine if the church were known to be the one place on earth where you would find this.

15. Darrin Patrick and Matt Carter, *For the City: Proclaiming and Living Out the Gospel* (Zondervan, 2011), chap. 1, Kindle.
16. Joseph Mattera, *An Anthology of Essays on Apostolic Leadership* (pub. by author, 2014), Introduction, Kindle.
17. Howard A. Snyder with Joel Scandrett, *Salvation Means Creation Healed: The Ecology of Sin and Grace; Overcoming the Divorce Between Earth and Heaven* (Cascade Books, 2011), chap. 9, Kindle.

SCATTERING IN SAMARIA

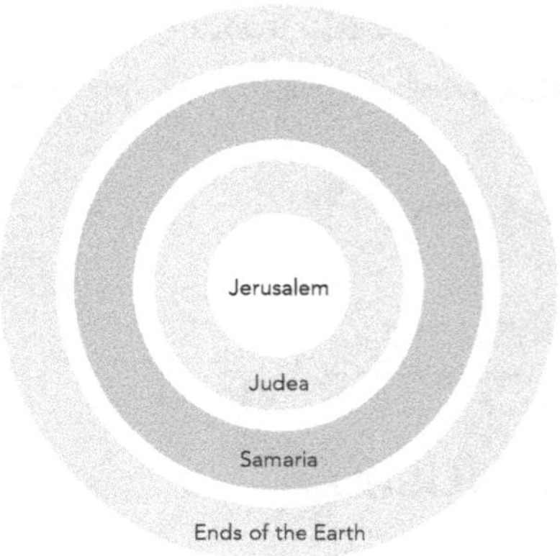

Ends of the earth? You're already there. In relation to Jerusalem, you're overseas. That's why it's important to "live sent" from where we are. Mission is a mindset, and you can live deployed where you are at this moment. But know this: The center of Christianity has shifted during my lifetime, as if the globe has shifted on its axis. According to Gene Wilson, "82 percent of Christians lived in the global West and North, and missionaries from those Christianized regions went out to unreached people groups in the East and south. Now, in the twenty-first century, two-thirds of the world's Christians live in the global south (Latin America, Africa, and Asia), and by 2050 that number is expected to grow to 77 percent."[18] So which culture's version should we take to the ends of the earth? No one's. Robert Linthicum states, "The primary work of the

SCATTERING TO THE ENDS OF THE EARTH

Jerusalem
Judea
Samaria
Ends of the Earth

18. Gene Wilson, *Emerging Gospel Movements: The Role of Catalysts* (Wipf & Stock, 2021), chap. 1, Kindle.

church is to proclaim to the world's systems a new vision of the world—a world with all its systems living in a shalom community and thus creating together, through the grace of God, the 'kingdom of our Lord and his Christ.'"[19]

Based on the same five activities we discussed above, you can focus on reaching one circle with one particular emphasis. For example, you might start with your neighborhood, reaching your street.

Spreading Fire

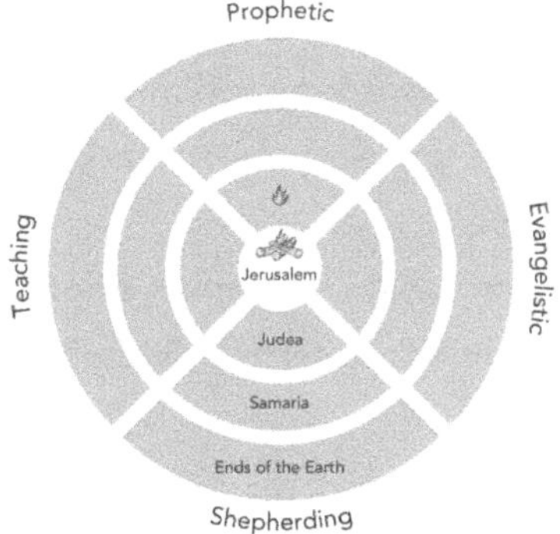

You may also scatter into your Judea in an evangelistic way or your Samaria in a shepherding way. The apostolic gift doesn't have a quadrant simply because every time you scatter, you're acting apostolically. There are twenty combinations of ways to scatter, but the important thing is to simply do one. Over time, those you send will start to fill out the grid like a missional bingo.

When it comes to starting new campfires in places like Jerusalem, Judea, Samaria, and beyond, no one group can possibly cover all twenty different combinations of mission and gifting. You were never meant to carry this alone. Disciple-making is deeply personal, but it was never meant to be private. It's something we do *together*—fanning each other's flames, encouraging one another when the embers burn low, and celebrating as the light spreads across the hills.

19. Robert Linthicum, *Transforming Power: Biblical Strategies for Making a Difference in Your Community* (IVP, 2003), 127.

Here are a few combinations of how to multiply in the four sectors with the five different activities of disciple-making.

Combo Moves

- You start a weekly dinner for your neighbors to connect. That's shepherding in your Jerusalem.
- You start a signing ministry in your Sunday service for the deaf so that they can hear the gospel. That's evangelizing in your Samaria—reaching a marginalized group.
- You offer free life-skills workshops (budgeting, parenting) infused with biblical principles in the public library—that's apostolically reaching your Judea.
- You help train overseas pastors through Zoom classes or short-term trips—that's teaching to the ends of the earth.

By now you've seen it. The spark that starts when you gather in his name. The fire that spreads when you scatter with intention. The rhythm of disciple-making that Jesus modeled—gathering close, then sending out. And this chapter is just a taster.

This book gives you the *why*, *what*, and *how* of disciple-making. But to really learn the how, you'll need to be sent—to get activated. There is no other way around activation but to go through. The theory is essential—but it's the practice that transforms.

What you've read in this chapter is just the beginning, merely the tip of the iceberg of our training at Discipology.com to catalyze others and to mobilize movement. There you'll find practical tools, step-by-step training, and a community of disciple-makers like you. If you'd like to dive deeper than this book, join us at Discipology.com. We look forward to joining you on your journey into disciple-making.

To find out more, scan the QR code.

It's not what we know but what we do with what we know that changes the world.

Conclusion

In *The Farthest Shore*, Ursula Le Guin gives us a vision of the true nature of what it means to disciple a young leader. By the time young Prince Arren meets Ged, the Arch-mage of Earthsea—the most powerful wizard in the known world—he's an old man. He's been sent to gather Ged for a journey across the sea to save the world. Tales abound about Ged's exploits. Bards sing songs about his skill. Poems are written about his legendary feats of wisdom. And yet, he fails to impress the young prince, who is scandalized by just how ordinary Ged is after sharing a boat voyage with him for a few nights.

Ged—Archmage, windwalker, once reckless with power—chooses not to summon a wind to move his boat but rows quietly, and rhythmically with blistered hands and a gentle demeanor. Prince Arren wonders if Ged still has any power and doubts his choice of companion.

Ged has the power, but he intentionally chooses the path of presence.

He doesn't command storms or summon dragons for show anymore. He sleeps on the ground. He walks dusty roads and speaks only when needed. Prince Arren spends much of the journey wondering when the power will show up—when Ged will finally prove himself. He embraces the mundane, not because he's any less powerful than he was but because he no longer has anything to prove. But the real lesson isn't in what Ged can *do*. It's in who Ged *is*.

Le Guin offers a moment so quiet, most readers miss its power:

"He knew now that it is the presence of the Arch-mage that speaks, not his voice or his staff or his power."[1]

---

1. Ursula K. Le Guin, *The Farthest Shore* (Atheneum, 1972), chap. 9.

Ged knew that the leadership journey wasn't about conjuring the wind or stopping thieves from mugging them, but about forming a soul. Therefore, Ged's greatness was restraint. And rather than trying to be impressive, he was trying to make someone else strong. And that's the essence of disciple-making. We don't change the world by dazzling people, but by letting others in the boat with us. There, we row alongside them, and let our presence form them more than our performance.

For the true disciple-making lesson that Ged has yet to teach Prince Arren is this: A great leader must not jump in and lead all the time. They must *step back*. They must *not be the hero*. They must resist the urge to dazzle or dominate and instead make space for others to rise. Ged mutes himself in the story purposefully, so that the young prince, soon to be king, can learn to the do the same for others around him. Ged knows that Arren can only be a great king if he uses his calling to raise up others to reach their full potential.

Ged rows not because he's weak, but because he's strong enough *not to need the spotlight*. He allows them to be attacked and defeated by robbers so that Arren can learn that when he's king, nobody will be there to save him. He must learn to fight for others.

That image has stayed with me. Not just because it touches me as an aging leader, but because it captures the deep truth of disciple-making. Rowing faithfully and intentionally in a small boat, like Ralph or Ruby Moore—real disciple-makers who teach others to navigate. That's how Jesus made disciples. And it's how we must finish the journey he began.

Disciple-making is intentionally slow and relational, and, yes, sometimes it blisters your hands. But if the Son of God chose to walk dusty roads instead of flying over them, it was to form them into disciple-makers who would go on to "do greater works." In the story, Ged and Arren journey to confront a sweeping darkness that spells certain defeat for Ged, yet he knows his time is nearing an end—and it is the time for ordinary men and women. Ged makes the journey—not for himself, but for Arren.

If we would lead with the same sacrifice, the same Spirit, we would see another movement burst into life. For we face the challenge of the darkness sweeping across the West and must walk with the next generation into the darkness if we ever hope to defeat it. It may be too late for Generation X to save the world, but perhaps Gen Z, representing the final letter of the alphabet, represents the great reset. The question is, will Gen X hand it off to them? They say that if older men want legacy, younger men want destiny—and disciple-making provides both. It's my hope and prayer that the next generation will prove that ministry can be redesigned on what Jesus, the apostles, and Paul modeled to the first-century church. His Discipology strategy is waiting to mobilize the next generation to reach their generation, just like it did in the first century when he intentionally focused on the young to turn the world upside down.

The temporary shift of the pandemic left many leaders disoriented. After all, they had spent decades being trained to think big—*bigger crowds, bigger services, bigger impact*. Now they didn't know what they wanted. But COVID didn't give us what we wanted—it gave us what we *needed*: a reset that exposed our lack of mobilization. Scholars will look back and record that COVID was the start of the mobilization movement.

Since then, leaders have been asking some of the right questions but drawing unhelpful conclusions. After all, I get the same emails as most leaders. Everyday my inbox is filled with the same gurus you see—trying to sell me the same silver bullet systems—all aimed at leaders, as if we were the answer. But we aren't the answer. We never were. Gandalf wasn't the answer any more than Morpheus was. Willimon and Hauerwas put it this way:

> When we are baptized, we . . . become part of a journey that began long before we got here and shall continue long after we are gone. Too often, we have conceived of salvation—what God does to us in Jesus—as a purely personal decision, or a matter of finally getting our heads straight on basic beliefs, or of having some inner feelings of righteousness about ourselves and God, or of having our social attitudes readjusted . . . we argue that salvation is not so much a new beginning but rather a beginning in the middle, so to speak. Faith begins, not in discovery, but in remembrance. The story began without us, as a story of the peculiar way God is redeeming the world, a story that invites us to come forth and be saved by sharing in the work of

> a new people whom God has created in Israel and Jesus. Such movement saves us by (1) placing us within an adventure that is nothing less than God's purpose for the whole world, and (2) communally training us to fashion our lives in accordance with what is true rather than what is false.[2]

Jesus, like Ged, has the power to lift his pinky finger and "magic" everything the way he wants it. But that's not how he wants it. He wants us to become disciples who can make disciples. This was his strategy, and it's still his plan. And when the world needed a mobilized church, many of us realized we had no map. But we realized we not only needed better maps, we needed pioneers willing to blaze a trail.

That's what I hope this book has given you—a better map. One drawn not in boardrooms but in the dust of Galilee. A map that traces the actual steps Jesus took to make disciples—where he went, what he did, who he invested in, and how he formed them to become like him. My prayer is that it's helped you locate yourself as a pioneer in the journey—and chart a path forward for others too. That you will leave a pattern for others to follow . . . while still knowing just how much to hold back, so that they can rise up.

If we'll let go of the ring, as Ralph Moore put it, we can release our grip on the future, knowing that the task ahead of us is never as great as the power behind us.

---

2. Stanley Hauerwas and William H. Willimon, *Resident Aliens: Life in the Christian Colony*, expanded 25th anniversary ed. (Abingdon Press, 2014), chap. 3, Kindle.

Acknowledgments

Dedicated to my mother—our mothers are the first disciplers we ever know.

Looking back, I know I can never repay the debt owed to those who poured into me. They had no monetary incentive for doing so. There was nothing special in me that they should take the time, but they changed my life. This book is an extension of what they modeled to me. If we open that door a crack, it needs to swing wide, back to the Master disciple-maker himself.

Along the way, there have been people who have specialized in one rhythm.

Time

- Peter Warren—Thank you for modeling what it meant to pray, and for giving of your time.
- Pete "Maverick" Mitchell—Thanks for wasting time with me every week on the podcast. I think we're occasionally useful to people.

Teaching

- D. Martyn Lloyd-Jones—Where would I be without the Doctor when I was cutting my teeth on exposition?
- Charles H. Spurgeon—You taught me to be myself and that a sense of humor is a terrible thing to waste.
- Peter Jeffery—The greatest preacher I ever heard. My mentor. Thank you for modeling the anointing of the Holy Spirit when you stood in the pulpit.

Tactics

- Dan Berg—People still can't believe it when I tell them the stories of how you activated me. It is largely because of you that I am who I am today—as a leader, as a man.
- Eric Fulmer—Not only did you share Jesus with me, but you gave me my first taste of mission. I was just days old in the Lord, and you commissioned me to reach my fellow students; I never forgot it.

  You both practiced all three rhythms in my life—I can never thank you enough for that.

The Through the Word Team

- Ryan McCarter—Thank you for championing this project and believing in it.
- Kris Langham—Your encouragement on this project kept me going. Plus, I liked the pictures you drew.
- To the rest of the team—Thanks for allowing me margin to build this project.

The NewBreed Team

- Ryan McCarter—Didn't you already make a cameo?
- Brooks "the Hammer" Hamon—Where do I even start? How many images and graphs did you make for this? Over 150?
- Beau Moffatt—Thanks for giving me the bad-friend pass when chained up in the book dungeon.
- Chestly Lunday—Thanks for being my cellmate in the book dungeon and passing me notes through the cracks in the wall.
- Kurt Blake—Thanks for holding the rope for me while I crawled down this hole.
- Andrea Jones—Oh, Ima save yours for last!

The Inklings

Marcus Jones, Mike Chong Perkinson, John Alwood, Noah Short, Andy Froiland, Pete Lhamon, Kris Langham, Chestly Lunday, Andrea Jones, Joshua Brown.

The Exponential Team

To the entire team, but specifically

- Dave Ferguson—For writing the foreword and partnering with me on this project.
- Jason Stewart—For honoring this book with admission into the Exponential Series.
- Terri Saliba—For always rooting for us from the sidelines.
- Bill Couchenour—For continuing to catalyze leaders across America to see mobilization and multiplication.
- Larry Walkemeyer—For just being you, Larry (and anyone who knows you knows what I mean).

The Zondervan Team

- Ryan Pazdur, publisher—I brag about you and your desire to publish books that will change things.
- Kyle Rohane, acquisitions editor—Where would I be without an editor like you, brother? Wait . . . don't answer that.
- Serena DeKryger, marketing director—The adventure is just beginning!

The Free Methodists

To my tribe, my family, my home—This book is for you. You embody all five of these qualities so well. As Bono said, "You don't know, you don't get it do you? You don't know just how beautiful you are." Get on those boots!

Special thanks to

- Steve Laube—My agent and bold champion of everything I've ever written. It's amazing what God can whip up out of wisdom, coffee, heat, and a sack of dust.
- Todd Wilson—For your friendship, partnership, and mentorship, and for putting me on your wallet card.
- Mike Chong Perkinson—My soul friend and mentor in all things rabbinic; you even taught me the Hebraic meaning of Spock's hand sign and the dangers of playing with superglue.

- Dr. Tom Johnston—Other half of the Praxis network and my backup rabbi.
- Trey Jones, the smarter of the Jones brothers—for our talks, your encouragement, and genuine celebration of every win; my best friend and fellow inheritor of that Y chromosome.
- Liberty Jones—You are a leader, and I pray that you discover how much of a gift God has put in you to influence others.
- Eden Jones—You are the nicest person I have ever met; when I think of Christlike character, I often think of you.

Finally, my wife, Andrea Jones. Never have I ever learned so much about the transformational nature of community as I have in this marriage. Few will know how you sacrificed so that this book could be written. As people thank me, I will always think in the back of my mind, "Thank my wife." Thank you for releasing me for the better part of a year to write this. But, more importantly, thank you for living in all three rhythms with me over these past thirty years or so.

To all of those whom I've left out, which I will always regret, I echo the philosopher, Mediocretes, who said, "Eh . . . good enough."

APPENDIX

Summary of Patterns, Principles, and Practices for Time, Teaching, and Tactics

Patterns of Jesus

TIME

1. Jesus Was a Follower First
2. Jesus's Disciple-Making Used Existing Relationships
3. Jesus's Disciple-Making Happened on the Way
4. Jesus's Conversations Equaled Conversions
5. Jesus Exposed Them to Mission Early
6. Jesus's Disciple-Making Happened in Community
7. Jesus Invested More with Few
8. Jesus Slowed Himself Down to Make Disciples

TEACHING

1. Jesus Taught Them Leaders Are Made
2. Jesus Taught Them to Focus on Individuals
3. Jesus Taught Them to Pursue the Marginalized
4. Jesus Taught Them to Party
5. Jesus Taught Them to Defy Legalism
6. Jesus Taught Them to Gather So They Could Scatter

TACTICS

1. Jesus Sent Them to Experience
2. Jesus Sent Them Together
3. Jesus Sent Them to Get Their Hands Dirty
4. Jesus Sent Them to Increase Their Faith
5. Jesus Sent Them to Learn
6. Jesus Sent Them for God's Glory
7. Jesus Sent Them to Struggle
8. Jesus Sent Them into the Mundane
9. Jesus Sent Them Out to Mobilize More
10. Jesus Sent Them with the Right Metrics

Principles

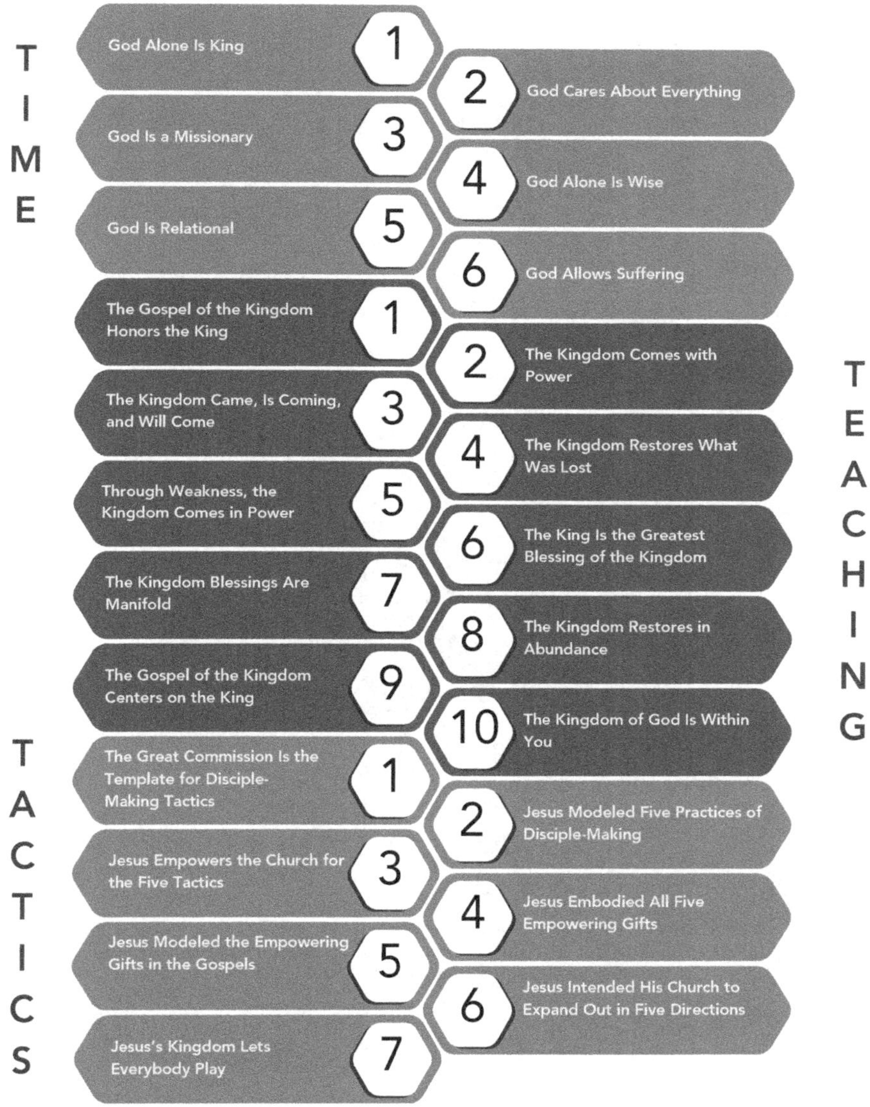

TIME

1 God Alone Is King
2 God Cares About Everything
3 God Is a Missionary
4 God Alone Is Wise
5 God Is Relational
6 God Allows Suffering

TEACHING

1 The Gospel of the Kingdom Honors the King
2 The Kingdom Comes with Power
3 The Kingdom Came, Is Coming, and Will Come
4 The Kingdom Restores What Was Lost
5 Through Weakness, the Kingdom Comes in Power
6 The King Is the Greatest Blessing of the Kingdom
7 The Kingdom Blessings Are Manifold
8 The Kingdom Restores in Abundance
9 The Gospel of the Kingdom Centers on the King
10 The Kingdom of God Is Within You

TACTICS

1 The Great Commission Is the Template for Disciple-Making Tactics
2 Jesus Modeled Five Practices of Disciple-Making
3 Jesus Empowers the Church for the Five Tactics
4 Jesus Embodied All Five Empowering Gifts
5 Jesus Modeled the Empowering Gifts in the Gospels
6 Jesus Intended His Church to Expand Out in Five Directions
7 Jesus's Kingdom Lets Everybody Play

Practices

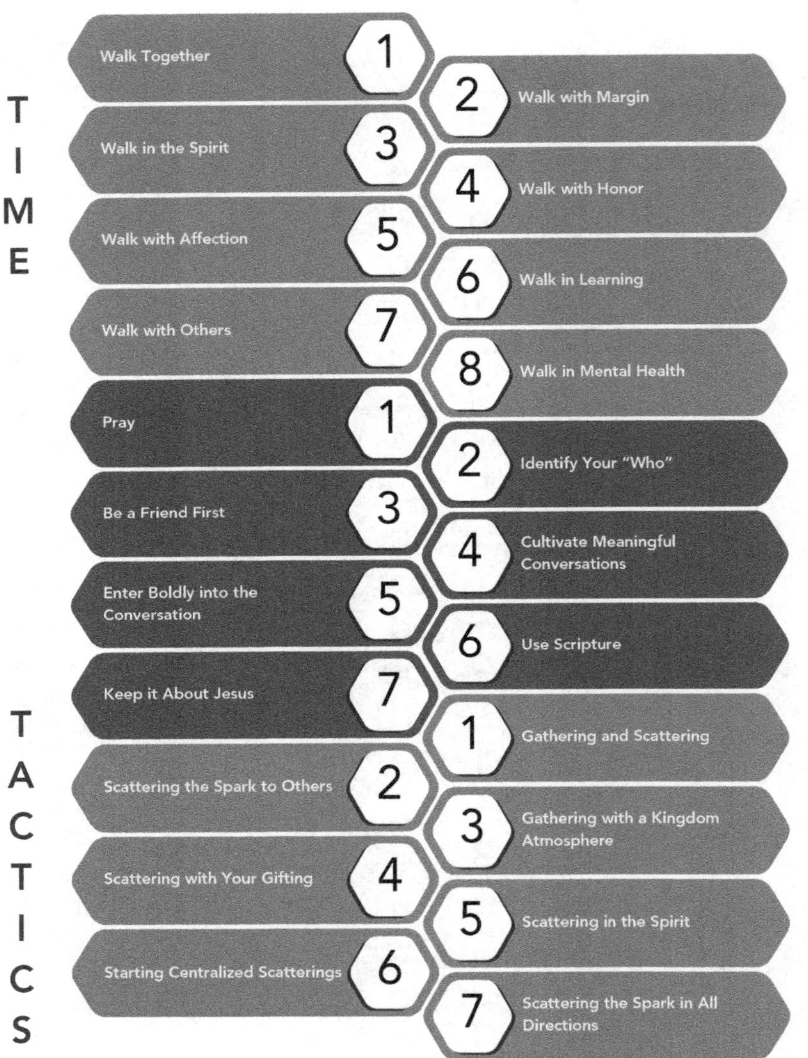
TIME
1 Walk Together
2 Walk with Margin
3 Walk in the Spirit
4 Walk with Honor
5 Walk with Affection
6 Walk in Learning
7 Walk with Others
8 Walk in Mental Health
TEACHING
1 Pray
2 Identify Your "Who"
3 Be a Friend First
4 Cultivate Meaningful Conversations
5 Enter Boldly into the Conversation
6 Use Scripture
7 Keep it About Jesus
TACTICS
1 Gathering and Scattering
2 Scattering the Spark to Others
3 Gathering with a Kingdom Atmosphere
4 Scattering with Your Gifting
5 Scattering in the Spirit
6 Starting Centralized Scatterings
7 Scattering the Spark in All Directions

Time Rhythm

PATTERNS
1 Jesus Was a Follower First
2 Jesus's Disciple-Making Used Existing Relationships
3 Jesus's Disciple-Making Happened on the Way
4 Jesus's Conversations Equaled Conversions
5 Jesus Exposed Them to Mission Early
6 Jesus's Disciple-Making Happened in Community
7 Jesus Invested More with Few
8 Jesus Slowed Himself Down to Make Disciples
PRINCIPLES
1 God Alone Is King
2 God Cares About Everything
3 God Is a Missionary
4 God Alone Is Wise
5 God Is Relational
6 God Allows Suffering
PRACTICES
1 Walk Together
2 Walk with Margin
3 Walk in the Spirit
4 Walk with Honor
5 Walk with Affection
6 Walk in Learning
7 Walk with Others
8 Walk in Mental Health

Teaching Rhythm

PATTERNS

1. Jesus Taught Them Leaders Are Made
2. Jesus Taught Them to Focus on Individuals
3. Jesus Taught Them to Pursue the Marginalized
4. Jesus Taught Them to Party
5. Jesus Taught Them to Defy Legalism
6. Jesus Taught Them to Gather So They Could Scatter

PRINCIPLES

1. The Gospel of the Kingdom Honors the King
2. The Kingdom Comes with Power
3. The Kingdom Came, Is Coming, and Will Come
4. The Kingdom Restores What Was Lost
5. Through Weakness, the Kingdom Comes in Power
6. The King Is the Greatest Blessing of the Kingdom
7. The Kingdom Blessings Are Manifold
8. The Kingdom Restores in Abundance
9. The Gospel of the Kingdom Centers on the King
10. The Kingdom of God is Within You

PRACTICES

1. Pray
2. Identify Your "Who"
3. Be a Friend First
4. Cultivate Meaningful Conversations
5. Enter Boldly into the Conversation
6. Use Scripture
7. Keep It About Jesus

Tactics Rhythm

PATTERNS

1 Jesus Sent Them to Experience
2 Jesus Sent Them Together
3 Jesus Sent Them to Get Their Hands Dirty
4 Jesus Sent Them to Increase Their Faith
5 Jesus Sent Them to Learn
6 Jesus Sent Them for God's Glory
7 Jesus Sent Them to Struggle
8 Jesus Sent Them into the Mundane
9 Jesus Sent Them Out to Mobilize More
10 Jesus Sent Them with the Right Metrics

PRINCIPLES

1 The Great Commission Is the Template for Disciple-Making Tactics
2 Jesus Modeled Five Practices of Disciple-Making
3 Jesus Empowers the Church for the Five Tactics
4 Jesus Embodied All Five Empowering Gifts
5 Jesus Modeled the Empowering Gifts in the Gospels
6 Jesus Intended His Church to Expand Out in Five Directions
7 Jesus's Kingdom Lets Everybody Play

PRACTICES

1 Gathering and Scattering
2 Scattering the Spark to Others
3 Gathering with a Kingdom Atmosphere
4 Scattering with Your Gifting
5 Scattering in the Spirit
6 Starting Centralized Scatterings
7 Scattering the Spark in All Directions

Bibliography

Archer, Gleason L. *Encyclopedia of Bible Difficulties*. Grand Rapids: Zondervan, 1982.

Augustine. *Confessions*. Translated by Henry Chadwick. Oxford: Oxford University Press, 1991.

Baker, Warren, and Eugene Carpenter, eds. *The Complete Word Study Dictionary: Old Testament*. Chattanooga: AMG Publishers, 2003.

Barker, Joel A. *Paradigms: The Business of Discovering the Future*. Harper Business, 1993.

Barna Group. "Growing Together: A Three-Part Guide for following Jesus and Bringing Friends on the Journey." Barna Group, 2022.

Barna Group. "New Research on the State of Discipleship." *Barna Group*. Accessed April 28, 2025. https://www.barna.com/research/new-research-on-the-state-of-discipleship/.

Barna Group. "Two in Five Christians Are Not Engaged in Discipleship." *Barna Group*. Accessed April 28, 2025. https://www.barna.com/research/christians-discipleship-community/.

Beale, G. K. and Mitchell Kim. *God Dwells Among Us: A Biblical Theology of the Temple*. IVP Academic, 2021.

Berger, Jonah. *Contagious: Why Things Catch On*. New York: Simon & Schuster, 2013.

Blair, Leonardo. "Pastor with 9,000-Member Congregation Says Churches Should Stop Focusing on Numbers." *The Christian Post*. September 24, 2013. https://www.christianpost.com/news/pastor-with-9000-member-congregation-says-churches-should-stop-focusing-on-numbers.html?page=3.

Brewer, Nathan. *The Pulse of Christ (Revised and Expanded): A Fivefold Training Manual*. 100 Movements Publishing, 2022. Kindle edition.

Bridges, Jerry, and Bob Bevington. *The Bookends of the Christian Life*. Crossway, 2009. Kindle edition.

Bright, Bill. *The Four Spiritual Laws*. San Bernardino, CA: Campus Crusade for Christ, 1952.

Bruce, A. B. *The Training of the Twelve: How Jesus Christ Found and Taught the 12 Apostles; A Book of New Testament Biography*. Pantianos Classics, 2018. Kindle edition.

Burton, Bob. *The Spiritual DNA of a Church on Mission: Rediscovering the 1st Century Church for 21st Century Spiritual Awakening*. B&H Academic, 2020. Kindle edition.

Campbell, Regi. *Mentor Like Jesus: His Radical Approach to Building the Church*. RM Press, 2016. Kindle edition.

Caron, Alain. *Apostolic Centers: Shifting the Church, Transforming the World*. Arsenal Press, 2013. Kindle edition.

Center for Creative Leadership. "The 70-20-10 Rule for Leadership Development." *CCL*, April 24, 2025. https://www.ccl.org/articles/leading-effectively-articles/70-20-10-rule/.

Chan, Francis with Mark Beuving. *Multiply: Disciples Making Disciples*. David C Cook, 2012.

Coleman, Robert E. *The Master Plan of Evangelism*. Revell, 1993.

Comer, John Mark. *Practicing the Way: Be with Jesus. Become like Him. Do as He Did*. WaterBrook, 2024. Kindle edition.

Cooke, Tony. "Encouraging Lessons from John Wesley." TonyCooke.org. https://www.tonycooke.org/.

Cooper, Michael T. *Ephesiology: A Study of the Ephesian Movement*. William Carey Publishing, 2020. Kindle edition.

Cordeiro, Wayne. "Rebuilding Character." *Life Journal Daily with Pastor Wayne*. New Hope West. Accessed April 16, 2025. https://newhopewest.com/life-journal-daily-with-pastor-wayne/rebuilding-character/.

Cru. *Would You Like to Know God Personally?* Accessed April 22, 2025. https://www.cru.org/content/movementlife/ph/en/how-to-know-god/would-you-like-to-know-god-personally1.html.

Cruickshank, Jessie. *Ordinary Discipleship: How God Wires Us for the Adventure of Transformation*. Colorado Springs, CO: NavPress, 2023.

Dawkins, Richard. Interview by Jordan B. Peterson. *The Jordan B. Peterson Podcast*, episode 318. October 17, 2023. YouTube video, 1:33:59. https://www.youtube.com/watch?v=U0u3-2CGOMQ.

Degreed. *How the Workforce Learns: 2020 Survey Report*. https://degreed.com/resources/research/how-the-workforce-learns.

Devenish, David. *Fathering Leaders, Motivating Mission: Restoring the Role of the Apostle in Today's Church*. Authentic, 2011. Kindle edition.

DeYoung, Kevin. "The Gates of Hell." Ligonier Ministries. November 19, 2011. https://learn.ligonier.org/devotionals/gates-of-hell.

Dunbar, Robin. *How Many Friends Does One Person Need?: Dunbar's Number and Other Evolutionary Quirks*. London: Faber & Faber, 2010.

Dyer, Wayne W. *The Power of Intention: Learning to Co-Create Your World Your Way*. Carlsbad, CA: Hay House, 2004.

Earley, Dave, and David Wheeler. *Evangelism Is . . .: How to Share Jesus with Passion and Confidence*. Nashville: B&H Publishing Group, 2010.

Edwards, Jonathan. "The Excellency of Christ." In *The Works of Jonathan Edwards*. Vol. 1. Edinburgh: Banner of Truth Trust, 1974.

Emetuche, Damian. "Church Planting: Biblical, Theological, and Missiological Considerations." Global Missiology. January 2012. https://www.globalmissiology.org.

Eusebius. *Ecclesiastical history*. Vol. 1. Patrologia Graeca, vol. 20, col. 177.

Exponential. "Ralph Moore." *Exponential*. Accessed April 9, 2025. https://exponential.org/person/ralph-moore-2/.

Fairchild, Mark R. *Christian Origins in Ephesus and Asia Minor*. 2nd ed. Peabody, MA: Hendrickson Publishers, 2017.

Ferguson, Dave and Jon Ferguson. *BLESS: 5 Everyday Ways to Love Your Neighbor and Change the World*. Salem Books, 2021.

Ferguson, Dave, and Warren Bird. *Hero Maker: Five Essential Practices for Leaders to Multiply Leaders*. Grand Rapids: Zondervan, 2018.

Frisbee, Lonnie, with Roger Sachs. *Not By Might Nor By Power: The Jesus Revolution*. Freedom Publications, 2019. Revised edition. Kindle edition.

Frost, Michael, and Alan Hirsch. *The Faith of Leap: Embracing a Theology of Risk, Adventure & Courage*. Revised edition. 100 Movements Publishing, 2025. Kindle edition.

Garrison, David. *Church Planting Movements: How God Is Redeeming a Lost World*. Midlothian, VA: WIGTake Resources, 2004. https://www.scribd.com/document/78434678/Garrison-Church-Planting-Movements.

Halter, Hugh. *Happy Hour: Etiquette and Advice on Holy Merriment*. Franklin, TN: 100 Movements Publishing, 2023.

Halter, Hugh. *Righteous Brood: Making the Mission of God a Family Story*. Life as Mission Series. 100 Movements Publishing, 2023. Kindle edition.

Halter, Hugh, and Matt Smay. *AND: The Gathered and Scattered Church.* Zondervan, 2010. Kindle edition.

Hankey, Dai. *Offensive: Cross-Driven Mission*. Ignite, 2008.

Harvard Business Review. "Why Employees Who Teach Others Are More Productive." March 2021. https://hbr.org/2021/03/why-employees-who-teach-others-are-more-productive.

Hauerwas, Stanley, and William H. Willimon. *Resident Aliens: Life in the Christian Colony* Expanded 25th Anniversary Edition. Abingdon Press, 2014. Kindle edition.

Henderson, D. Michael. *John Wesley's Class Meeting: A Model for Making Disciples.* Rafiki Books, 2016. Kindle edition.

Hiestand, Gerald L., and Todd Wilson. *Tending Soul, Mind, and Body: The Art and Science of Spiritual Formation.* IVP Academic, 2019.

Hirsch, Alan. *Disciplism: Reimagining Evangelism Through the Lens of Discipleship.* 100 Movements Publishing, 2024. Kindle edition.

Hirsch, Alan. *The Forgotten Ways: Reactivating the Missional Church.* Grand Rapids: Brazos Press, 2006.

Hirsch, Alan, and Rob Kelly. *Metanoia: How God Radically Transforms People, Churches, and Organizations from the Inside Out.* 100 Movements Publishing, 2023. Kindle edition.

Horton, John J. *Employer Expectations, Peer Effects and Productivity: Evidence from a Series of Field Experiments.* arXiv preprint, August 2010. https://doi.org/10.48550/arXiv.1008.2437.

Hunter, George G., III. *The Celtic Way of Evangelism, Tenth Anniversary Edition: How Christianity Can Reach the West . . . Again*. Abingdon Press, 2011. Kindle edition.

Im, Daniel. *No Silver Bullets: Five Small Shifts That Will Transform Your Ministry.* B&H Books, 2017. Kindle edition.

Iorg, Jeff. *Seasons of a Leader's Life: Learning, Leading, and Leaving a Legacy.* B&H Books, 2013.

Jeffrey, Peter. *Christian Handbook: A Straightforward Guide to the Bible, Church history and Christian Doctrine.* Evangelical Press, 1988.

Johnston, Tom. *The Way of the Master: The Leader Development Methodology of Jesus.* Independently published, 2021.

Johnston, Tom, and Mike Chong Perkinson. *The Kingdom Quest: Preparing to Church Plant in the Post-Christian West.* PraxisMedia, 2019. Kindle edition.

Johnston, Tom, and Mike Chong Perkinson. *The Organic Reformation: A New Hope for the Church in the West.* PraxisMedia, 2011. Kindle edition.

Jones, John Morgan, and William Morgan. *The Calvinistic Methodist Fathers of Wales: Volume I.* Banner of Truth, 2010.

Jones, Peyton. *Church Plantology: The Art and Science of Planting Churches.* Exponential Series. Zondervan, 2021. Kindle edition.

Jones, Peyton. *Reaching the Unreached: Becoming Raiders of the Lost Art.* Grand Rapids: Zondervan, 2017.

Kamei, Kenju, and John Ashworth. "Peer Learning in Teams and Work Performance: Evidence from a Randomized Field Experiment." *Journal of Economic Behavior & Organization* 207 (2023): 413–32. https://doi.org/10.1016/j.jebo.2023.01.015.

Kee, Samuel. *Soul Tattoo: A Life and Spirit Bearing the Marks of God.* David C Cook, 2014. Kindle edition.

Keller, Timothy. *The Freedom of Self-Forgetfulness: The Path to True Christian Joy.* 10Publishing, 2013. Kindle edition.

Kim, Jay Y. *Analog Church: Why We Need Real People, Places, and Things in the Digital Age.* Downers Grove, IL: IVP, 2020. Kindle.

Lane, Timothy S., and Paul David Tripp. *Relationships: A Mess Worth Making.* New Growth Press, 2006. Kindle edition.

Lewis, C. S. *A Grief Observed.* HarperOne, 2009. Kindle edition.

Lewis, C. S. *The Four Loves.* New York: Harcourt Brace, 1960.

Lewis, C. S. *Letters of C. S. Lewis.* HarperOne, 2017. Kindle edition.

Lewis, C. S. *Mere Christianity.* New York: HarperOne, 2001.

Lifeway Research. *2025 Becoming Five Multiplication Study: Research Report.* Prepared for Exponential. Orlando: Exponential, 2025.

Lifeway Research. "Less Than Half of Americans Attend Church at Christmas." *Americans Views,* December 3, 2024.

LinkedIn Learning. Workplace Learning Report 2025: The Rise of Career Champions. https://learning.linkedin.com/resources/workplace-learning-report.

Linthicum, Robert. *Transforming Power: Biblical Strategies for Making a Difference in Your Community.* Downers Grove, IL: InterVarsity Press, 2003.

Luther, Martin. *Large Catechism.* Translated by F. Bente and W. H. T. Dau. In *Triglot Concordia: The Symbolical Books of the Ev. Lutheran Church.* St. Louis: Concordia Publishing House, 1921. Project Wittenberg. Accessed

September 20, 2025. https://www.projectwittenberg.org/pub/resources/text/wittenberg/luther/catechism/web/cat-13a.html.

Luther, Martin. *Lectures on Galatians Chapters 1–4*. Vol. 26 of *Luther's Works: The American Edition*. Edited by Jaroslav Pelikan. St. Louis: Concordia, 1963 (1535).

Lloyd-Jones, Bethan. *Memories of Sandfields*. Edinburgh: Banner of Truth Trust, 2008.

Lloyd-Jones, D. Martyn. *The Kingdom of God*. Wheaton, IL: Crossway Books, 2010.

Lloyd-Jones, D. Martyn. *Preaching and Preachers*. Grand Rapids, MI: Zondervan, 1971.

Maddox, Randy L. *Responsible Grace: John Wesley's Practical Theology*. Kingswood Books, 1994.

Marshall, Colin, and Tony Payne. *The Trellis and the Vine*. Matthias Media, 2024. Kindle edition.

Martin, Nicole Massie. *Nailing It: Why Successful Leadership Demands Suffering and Surrender*. Downers Grove, IL: InterVarsity Press, 2025.

Mattera, Joseph. *An Anthology of Essays on Apostolic Leadership*. 2015. Kindle edition.

McCall, Taylor, and Hugh Halter. *Brave Cities: The Archaeology, Artistry, and Architecture of Kingdom Ecosystems*. 100 Movements Publishing, 2024. Kindle edition.

Mental Health America. *The State of Mental Health in America*. Accessed September 20, 2025. https://mhanational.org/the-state-of-mental-health-in-america/.

Moore, Ralph. *Making Disciples: Developing Lifelong Followers of Jesus*. Grand Rapids, MI: Baker Books, 2012.

Murray, Iain H. *D. Martyn Lloyd-Jones: The First Forty Years 1899–1939*. Edinburgh: Banner of Truth Trust, 1982.

Myers, Joseph R. *The Search to Belong: Rethinking Intimacy, Community, and Small Groups*. Grand Rapids, MI: Zondervan, 2003.

Packer, J. I. *A Quest for Godliness: The Puritan Vision of the Christian Life*. Wheaton, IL: Crossway Books, 1990.

Pantycelyn, Williams. Quoted in "A Brush with Death." *Peter Jeffery*, accessed June 24, 2025. https://www.peterjeffery.org.uk/a-brush-with-death/.

Patrick, Darrin, and Matt Carter. *For the City: Proclaiming and Living Out the Gospel*. Zondervan, 2011. Kindle edition.

Perkinson, Mike Chong, and Tom Johnston. *The Organic Reformation: A New Hope for the Church in the West*. Reno, NV: PraxisMedia, 2009.

Piper, John. *Let the Nations Be Glad!: The Supremacy of God in Missions*, 2nd ed. Grand Rapids, MI: Baker Academic, 2003.

Piper, John. "Our Grand Obligation." Desiring God. October 6, 1985. https://www.desiringgod.org/messages/our-grand-obligation.

Planck, Max. *Scientific Autobiography and Other Papers*. New York: Philosophical Library, 1950.

"Prevalence, Severity, and Unmet Need for Treatment of Mental Disorders." World Health Organization World Mental Health Surveys. *Journal of the American Medical Association*. June 2004.

Prinz, Emanuel. *What Actually Starts Movements: Partnering with God for Kingdom Multiplication*. Kansas City, MO: 100 Movements Publishing, 2025.

Putman, Jim. "Is It Time for a New Restoration Movement? (Part 1)." *Christian Standard*. September 2023. https://christianstandard.com/2023/09/is-it-time-for-a-new-restoration-movement-part-1/.

Raymont, Henry. "Steinbecks' Letters Will Be a Book." *The New York Times*, June 2, 1969.

Reeves, Michael. *Delighting in the Trinity: An Introduction to the Christian Faith*. IVP Academic, 2012. Kindle edition.

Rushik, JR. *The Disciple Makerspace: A Relational Rhythm for Planting Churches Without Compromising the Beauty, Simplicity, and Power of the Biblical Church*. Independently published, 2013.

Russell, Walt. *Sustainable Church: Growing Ministry Around the Sheep, Not Just the Shepherds*. Quoir, 2016.

Sanders, Brian. *The 6 Seasons of Calling: Discovering Your Purpose in Each Stage of Life*. Moody Publishers, 2022.

Sanders, Brian. *Microchurches: A Smaller Way*. UG Media, 2019. Kindle edition.

Sanders, Brian. *Underground Church: A Living Example of the Church in Its Most Potent Form*. Zondervan, 2018.

Schnabel, Eckhard. *Early Christian Mission Volume 1: Jesus and the Twelve*. Downers Grove, IL: InterVarsity Press, 2004.

Schnabel, Eckhard J. *Jesus in Jerusalem: The Last Days*. Grand Rapids: Eerdmans, 2018.

Shearer, Kris. "Are We Our Real Selves?" *The Daily Record*. November 11, 2010. https://www.the-daily-record.com/story/news/2010/11/11/are-we-our-real-selves/19639355007/.

Shelley, Percy Bysshe. "Ozymandias." Poetry Foundation. Accessed September 20, 2025. https://www.poetryfoundation.org/poems/46565/ozymandias.

Silliman, Daniel. "Pastors Wonder About Church Members Who Never Came Back Post-Pandemic." *Christianity Today*. September 26, 2023. https://www.christianitytoday.com/2023/09/covid-study-church-attendance-change-pews-people/.

Simpson, Ray. *A Pilgrim Way: New Celtic Monasticism for Everyday People*. Kevin Mayhew, 2005.

Simpson, Ray, and Brent Lyons-Lee. *St Aidan's Way of Mission: Celtic Insights for a Post-Christian World*. Bible Reading Fellowship, 2016. Kindle edition.

Skinner, Betty Lee. *Daws: A Man Who Trusted God*. Colorado Springs, CO: NavPress, 1974.

Smith, Steve, with Ying Kai. *T4T: A Discipleship Re-Revolution*. WIGTake Resources, LLC, 2011. Kindle edition.

Spurgeon, Charles H. *Lectures to My Students*. Grand Rapids: Zondervan, 1954.

Stewart, James A. *Invasion of Wales by the Spirit Through Evan Roberts*. Revival Literature, 2004.

Sunde, David. *Homegrown Disciples: Parenting Rhythms for Drawing Your Kids into Life with God*. NavPress, 2025.

Sunde, David. *Small-Batch Disciplemaking: A Rhythm for Training the Few to Reach the Many*. Colorado Springs, CO: NavPress, 2024.

Teter, John. *The Power of the 72*. Downers Grove, IL: InterVarsity Press.

Thompson, Wright. *Pappyland: A Story of Family, Fine Bourbon, and the Things That Last*. New York: Penguin Press, 2020.

Tolkien, J. R. R. *The Fellowship of the Ring*. Boston: Houghton Mifflin, 1954.

Tolkien, J. R. R. *The Hobbit, or There and Back Again*. London: George Allen & Unwin, 1937. Reprint, Boston: Houghton Mifflin Harcourt, 2012.

Tozer, A. W. *Keys to the Deeper Life*. Pioneer Library, 2014. Kindle edition.

Tozer, A. W. *The Knowledge of the Holy*. New York: Harper & Brothers, 1961.

Tozer, A. W. *Total Commitment to Christ: What Is It? A Call to a Radical Faith*. Digital Fire, 2021. Kindle edition.

Trioano, Gabriel. "40 Statistics You Should Know About Online Communities." Social Plus. Accessed April 9, 2025. https://www.social.plus/blog/40-statistics-you-should-know-about-online-communities.

Trousdale, Jerry, and Glenn Sunshine. *The Kingdom Unleashed: How Jesus' 1st-Century Kingdom Values Are Transforming Thousands of Cultures and Awakening His Church*. DMM Library, 2018. Kindle edition.

U2. "Sometimes You Can't Make It on Your Own." *How to Dismantle an Atomic Bomb.* Interscope Records, 2004. Compact disc.

Vander Laan, Ray. *In the Dust of the Rabbi Discovery Guide: Learning to Live as Jesus Lived.* That the World May Know Series. HarperChristian Resources, 2015. Kindle edition.

von Balthasar, Hans Urs. *The Grain of Wheat: A Spiritual Journey.* San Francisco: Ignatius Press, 1991.

Wagner, C. Peter. *Changing Church: How God Is Leading his Church Into the Future.* Baker Publishing Group, 2004. Kindle edition.

Warren, Tish Harrison. *Liturgy of the Ordinary: Sacred Practices in Everyday Life.* InterVarsity Press, 2019.

Wesley, John. *The Journal of John Wesley.* Edited by Percy Livingstone Parker. London: Christian Classics Ethereal Library. https://www.ccel.org/ccel/wesley/journal.vi.iii.i.html.

Wesley, John. Letter to Alexander Mather, August 6, 1777. In *The Letters of John Wesley, 1777.* Wesley Center Online. Accessed September 20, 2025. https://wesley.nnu.edu/john-wesley/the-letters-of-john-wesley/wesleys-letters-1777/.

Wesley, John. *The Letters of the Rev. John Wesley.* Vol. 8. Edited by John Telford. London: Epworth Press, 1931.

Wesley, John. *"On Laying the Foundation of the New Chapel, Near the City Road, London."* Sermon 132. *John Wesley Sermons.* ResourceUMC. Preached April 21, 1777. Accessed September 20, 2025. https://www.resourceumc.org/en/content/sermon-132-on-laying-the-foundation-of-the-new-chapel-near-the-city-road-london.

Wesley, John. *Primitive Physick: Or, An Easy and Natural Method of Curing Most Diseases.* 14th ed. Bristol, 1770.

Westminster Shorter Catechism, Q.1. In *The Westminster Confession of Faith.* Glasgow: Free Presbyterian Publications, 1994, 289.

Wieland, Rob. "2020 Was the Best Year Ever for Dungeons & Dragons." *Forbes.* May 19, 2021. https://www.forbes.com/sites/robwieland/2021/05/19/2020-was-the-best-year-ever-for-dungeons—dragons/.

Willard, Dallas. *The Scandal of the Kingdom: How the Parables of Jesus Revolutionize Life with God.* Grand Rapids, MI: Zondervan, 2024.

Wilson, Gene. *Emerging Gospel Movements: The Role of Catalysts.* Wipf & Stock, 2022. Kindle edition.

Wilson, Todd. *More: Find Your Personal Calling and Live Life to the Fullest Measure.* Zondervan, 2016.

Wright, N. T. *How God Became King: The Forgotten Story of the Gospels.* New York: HarperOne, 2012. Kindle edition.

Yuan, Eric S. "A Message to Our Users." *Zoom Blog.* April 22, 2020. https://blog.zoom.us/a-message-to-our-users/.

EX EXPONENTIAL RESOURCES
MULTIPLIER
HOW HEALTHY LEADERS CREATE LASTING IMPACT
DAVE FERGUSON